Lecture Notes in Artificial Intelligence 11375

Subseries of Lecture Notes in Computer Science

More information about this series at http://www.springer.com/series/1244

Danny Weyns · Viviana Mascardi ·
Alessandro Ricci (Eds.)

Engineering Multi-Agent Systems

6th International Workshop, EMAS 2018
Stockholm, Sweden, July 14–15, 2018
Revised Selected Papers

 Springer

Editors
Danny Weyns ⓘ
Department of Computer Science
KU Leuven
Leuven, Belgium

Alessandro Ricci ⓘ
Department of Computer Science
and Engineering
University of Bologna
Cesena, Forli/Cesana, Italy

Viviana Mascardi ⓘ
Department of Computer Science,
Bioengineering, Robotics and Systems
Engineering
Università degli Studi di Genova
Genoa, Italy

ISSN 0302-9743   ISSN 1611-3349 (electronic)
Lecture Notes in Artificial Intelligence
ISBN 978-3-030-25692-0   ISBN 978-3-030-25693-7 (eBook)
https://doi.org/10.1007/978-3-030-25693-7

LNCS Sublibrary: SL7 – Artificial Intelligence

This Springer imprint is published by the registered company Springer Nature Switzerland AG
The registered company address is: Gewerbestrasse 11, 6330 Cham, Switzerland

Preface

The workshop on Engineering Multi-Agent Systems (EMAS) has a threefold goal: (i) To enhance our knowledge and expertise in MAS engineering to move forward the state-of-the-art; (ii) define new directions for MAS engineering, relying on results and recommendations stemming from a diverse range of research areas; and (iii) investigate how practitioners can use or adapt established processes and methodologies for the engineering of large-scale and open MAS.

The EMAS workshop has been held as part of AAMAS since 2013, and was previously affiliated with AAMAS through the AOSE, ProMAS and DALT workshops since their inception. This 6th edition of the EMAS workshop, which was co-located for the first time with IJCAI/ECAI and ICML alongside AAMAS, took place in Stockholm, Sweden, during July 14–15, 2018. On average, around 40 people attended the different sessions of the workshop.

EMAS 2018 received 32 submissions by authors from all over the world. After a thorough review process, 21 papers were accepted for presentation at the workshop. After the workshop, authors of selected papers were invited to submit revised and extended versions of their workshop paper. This resulted in 17 chapters that are clustered around the following themes: Programming Agents and MAS, Agent-Oriented Software Engineering, Formal Analysis Techniques, Rational Agents, Modeling and Simulation, and Frameworks and Application Domains. In addition, this volume includes a state-of-the-art chapter that reflects on the role and potential of MAS engineering in a number of key facets that characterize modern software engineering practice. We have provided a brief overview of the sections:

State of the Art

Chapter 1: "Engineering Multi-Agent Systems Anno 2025" by Viviana Mascardi and Danny Weyns opens the volume by reflecting on the role and potential of MAS engineering on a number of key facets that characterize modern soft-ware engineering practice. In particular, the chapter looks at agile development, Cloud and edge computing, distributed ledgers and blockchain, Cyber-Physical Systems and Internet of Things, and green computing, highlighting opportunities for EMAS engineering, but also the challenges these facets raise.

Programming Agents and MAS

Chapter 2: "Pitfalls of Jason Concurrency" by Álvaro Fernández Díaz, Clara Benac Earle and Lars-Åke Fredlund examines to what extent the Jason programming language helps programmers in coping with difficulties caused by intra-agent concurrency, e.g., race conditions due to multiple agent intentions. The chapter analyzes a number of strategies to mitigate concurrency problems present either in the original Jason language, or in later language extensions.

Chapter 3: Alessandro Ricci, Rafael H. Bordini, Jomi F. Hübner and Rem Collier present "AgentSpeak(ER): Enhanced Encapsulation in Agent Plans." AgentSpeak(ER) extends the AgentSpeak(L) language to support encapsulation and allow for improving Belief-Desire-Intentions (BDI) agent programming, in addition to other relevant aspects, such as program modularity, readability, failure handling, reactivity and goal-based reasoning.

Agent-Oriented Software Engineering

Chapter 4: In their chapter "Improving the Usability of a MAS DSML," which received the EMAS 2018 best paper award, Tomás Miranda, Moharram Challenger, Baris Tekin Tezel, Omer Faruk Alaca, Ankica Barišić, Vasco Amaral, Miguel Goulão and Geylani Kardas point out the need for evaluating the usability of domain-specific modeling languages (DSMLs) for MAS to leverage their adoption in practice. The authors evaluate a concrete MAS DSML, and based on the insights obtained, developed a new improved version of the language.

Chapter 5: Artur Freitas, Rafael H. Bordini and Renata Vieira present their proposal for "Designing Multi-Agent Systems from Ontology Models." This work aims at facilitating MAS engineering through ontology models that support code generation. The approach is aligned with the JaCaMo framework, and supported by a tool that generates the core code of a MAS application; the underlying ontology allows for reasoning about the MAS models under development.

Chapter 6: Massimo Cossentino, Luca Sabatucci and Valeria Seidita discuss the "Engineering Self-adaptive Systems: From Experiences with MUSA to a General Design Process," and deal with complex-self adaptive systems operating in changing and uncertain environments. Through a retrospective analysis on the use of the MUSA middleware (Middleware for User-Driven Service Adaptation), the authors identify the characteristics of a design approach for these kinds of systems.

Chapter 7: The paper "Stellar: A Programming Model for Developing Protocol-Compliant Agents" by Akın Günay and Amit Chopra presents the Stellar programming model that aims at simplifying the development of protocol compliant agents. A major benefit of Stellar is its independence from imperative control flow structures, which gives substantial flexibility to developers when implementing agents, compared to approaches that rely on this structure for compliance.

Formal Analysis and Techniques

Chapter 8: The paper "Slicing Agent Programs for More Efficient Verification" by Michael Winikoff, Louise A. Dennis and Michael Fisher focuses on efficient model checking of agent programs using an improved method of program slicing. The proposed approach analyzes a program prior to verifying it to simplify the program by removing parts that are invariant to the verification results.

Chapter 9: Łukasz Białek, Barbara Dunin-Kęplicz and Andrzej Szałas introduce "Belief Shadowing," a lightweight and tractable approach for belief interference, that aims at adapting beliefs to new circumstances, such as belief change or revision. The idea is to perform a transient swap of beliefs, when part of one belief base is to be shadowed by another belief base representing new observations and/or beliefs of superior agents/teams. In this case no changes to belief bases are needed, substantially improving system performance.

Chapter 10: Timotheus Kampik, Juan Carlos Nieves and Helena Lindgren move a step towards "Empathic Autonomous Agents." The authors explore the notion of an empathic autonomous agent that proactively searches for conflicts with other agents, combining a utility- and rule-based approach for resolving conflicts. The authors propose an initial theoretical outline with an architecture for emphatic agents. Several challenges remain open, e.g., handling complex environments.

Chapter 11: The chapter "Dynamic Global Behaviour of Online Routing Games" by László Zsolt Varga focuses on how to measure and ensure global behavior of large-scale, open decentralized MAS. The paper shows how the inter-temporal expectations of selfish planning agents influence the quality of the global behavior of the MAS in a realistic urban traffic scenario. A critical challenge is to design the environment to drive agents toward an optimum or equilibrium.

Modeling and Simulations

Chapter 12: Igor Conrado Alves de Lima, Luis Gustavo Nardin and Jaime Simão Sichman present "Gavel: A Sanctioning Enforcement Framework." Gavel enables agents to decide the most suitable sanctioning method, with the aim of improving agency governance. The framework is evaluated through a simulation of the Public Goods Game Model with the CArtAgO simulation framework.

Chapter 13: In the chapter "Adding Organizational Reasoning to Agent-Based Simulations in GAMA," John Bruntse Larsen introduces organizational reasoning in agent simulation platforms (e.g., GAMA) to model complex social systems. The approach combines bottom-up design of BDI models with top-down organizational reasoning. The author formalizes the operational semantics of organizational reasoning and illustrates its application with a healthcare example.

Chapter 14: Tasio Méndez, J. Fernando Sánchez-Rada, Carlos A. Iglesias and Paul Cummings propose an agent-based model for "Analyzing Radicalism Spread Using Agent-Based Social Simulation." The model, that consists of a Network Model and an Agent Model, aims at improving the understanding of the influence of social links on the spread of radicalism. The Network Model updates the agent relationships based on proximity and homophily; it simulates information diffusion and updates the agents' beliefs. The model is implemented in Python.

Frameworks and Application Domains

Chapter 15: In the chapter "Engineering World-Wide Multi-Agent Systems with Hypermedia," Andrei Ciortea, Olivier Boissier and Alessandro Ricci propose an approach to engineer large-scale, evolvable MAS using hypermedia. In line with the notion of agent environments, agents are situated in a distributed hypermedia environment. Agents use hypermedia to discover and interact with other entities in the MAS. This allows the MAS to evolve at runtime and to be seamlessly distributed across the Web. A demonstrator is used to evaluate the approach.

Chapter 16: "Designing a Cognitive Agent Connector for Complex Environments: A Case Study with StarCraft" by Vincent Koeman, Harm Griffioen, Danny Plenge and Koen Hindriks describes the design of a connector that supports interfacing cognitive agents in rich environments. The approach is applied to the real-time strategy game StarCraft with the aim of establishing a design method for developing connectors for these kinds of environments. StarCraft is particularly suitable as a testbed as it requires sophisticated strategies for coordinating hundreds of units that need to handle short-term as well as long-term goals.

Chapter 17: In the chapter "Decision Process in Human-Agent Interaction: Extending Jason Reasoning Cycle," Antonio Chella, Francesco Lanza and Valeria Seidita discuss how to support agents' decision making processes using their internal state. The authors propose an extension of the Jason reasoning cycle to deal with the implementation level of the decision process and to include elements derived from the internal state. This work is intended to contribute to the challenges of knowledge representation and creation of plans at runtime.

Chapter 18: Arthur Casals, Amal El Fallah-Seghrouchni, Orso Negroni and Anthoni Othmani present how "Exposing Agents as Web Services in JADE." The chapter shows how intelligent agents using a BDI architecture can be exposed as web services and integrated with existing Cloud services. The approach is studied in the context of an agent-based personal assistant. The aim is to better understand: (i) What is the current state of production-ready MAS, and (ii) how hard it is for a software developer to understand and implement MAS-based solutions.

We would like to thank all authors for their contributions, the members of the Program Committee and the additional reviewers for their excellent review work, the members of the Steering Committee for the valuable suggestions and support, the IJCAI/ECAI and AAMAS organizers for hosting and supporting EMAS 2019, and last but not least Springer, in particular Alfred Hofmann and Anna Kramer, for providing us with the opportunity to publish this volume.

April 2019

Danny Weyns
Viviana Mascardi
Alessandro Ricci

Organization

Workshop Organizers

Danny Weyns   KU Leuven, Belgium, Linnaeus University, Sweden
Viviana Mascardi   University of Genova, Italy
Alessandro Ricci   University of Bologna, Italy

Programme Committee

Matteo Baldoni	University of Torino, Italy
Luciano Baresi	Politecnico di Milano, Italy
Cristina Baroglio	University of Torino, Italy
Olivier Boissier	Mines Saint-Etienne, Institut Henri Fayol, France
Rafael H. Bordini	PUC do Rio Grande do Sul, Brazil
Daniela Briola	University of Milan-Bicocca, Italy
Fabiano Dalpiaz	Utrecht University, The Netherlands
Louise Dennis	University of Liverpool, UK
Lavindra de Silva	University of Cambridge, UK
Jürgen Dix	Clausthal University of Technology, Germany
Amal El Fallah-Seghrouchni	Sorbonne Université, France
Adriana Giret	Universitat Politècnica de València, Spain
Jorge Gomez-Sanz	Universidad Complutense de Madrid, Spain
James Harland	RMIT University, Australia
Vincent Hilaire	UTBM, IRTES-SET, France
Koen Hindriks	Delft University of Technology, The Netherlands
Benjamin Hirsch	EBTIC, Khalifa University, UAE
Tom Holvoet	Katholieke Universiteit Leuven, Belgium
Jomi Fred Hubner	Federal University of Santa Catarina, Brazil
Malte S. Kließ	Delft University of Technology, The Netherlands
Nadin Kokciyan	King's College London, UK
Joao Leite	Universidade NOVA de Lisboa, Portugal
Yves Lespérance	York University, Canada
Brian Logan	University of Nottingham, UK
Philippe Mathieu	University of Lille I, France
John-Jules Meyer	Utrecht University, The Netherlands
Fabien Michel	LIRMM, Université de Montpellier, France
Frederic Migeon	IRIT, France
Jörg P. Müller	Clausthal University of Technology, Germany
Ingrid Nunes	Universidade Federal do Rio Grande do Sul, Brazil
Enrico Pontelli	New Mexico State University, USA
Valeria Seidita	Università degli Studi di Palermo, Italy
Viviane Torres da Silva	IBM Research, Brazil

Guillermo R. Simari	Universidad del Sur in Bahia Blanca, Argentina
Tran Cao Son	New Mexico State University, USA
Jørgen Villadsen	Technical University of Denmark, Denmark
Gerhard Weiss	Maastricht University, The Netherlands
Michael Winikoff	University of Otago, New Zealand
Neil Yorke-Smith	Delft University of Technology, The Netherlands
Rym Zalila-Wenkstern	University of Texas at Dallas, USA

Additional Reviewers

Bita Banihashemi	York University, Canada
Arthur Casals	EPUSP, Brazil
Angelo Ferrando	University of Liverpool, UK
Eleonora Giunchiglia	University of Oxford, UK
Vincent Jaco Koeman	Delft University of Technology, The Netherlands

Steering Committee

Matteo Baldoni	University of Torino, Italy
Rafael H. Bordini	PUC do Rio Grande do Sul, Brazil
Mehdi M. Dastani	Utrecht University, The Netherlands
Jürgen Dix	Clausthal University of Technology, Germany
Amal El Fallah-Seghrouchni	Sorbonne Université, France
Brian Logan	University of Nottingham, UK
Jörg P. Müller	Clausthal University of Technology, Germany
Ingrid Nunes	Universidade Federal do Rio Grande do Sul, Brazil
Alessandro Ricci	University of Bologna, Italy
M. Birna van Riemsdijk	Delft University of Technology, The Netherlands
Danny Weyns	KU Leuven, Belgium, Linnaeus University, Sweden
Michael Winikoff	University of Otago, New Zealand
Rym Zalila-Wenkstern	University of Texas at Dallas, USA

Contents

State of the Art

Engineering Multi-agent Systems
Anno 2025

Viviana Mascardi[1(✉)] and Danny Weyns[2,3]

[1] University of Genova, Genova, Italy
`viviana.mascardi@unige.it`
[2] KU Leuven, Kulak, Kortrijk, Belgium
`danny.weyns@kuleuven.be`
[3] Linnaeus University, Växjö, Sweden

Abstract. Modern software-intensive systems are increasingly blending cyber, physical, and social elements, demanding higher degrees of autonomy and adaptability than ever before. In combination with the ever growing integration and scale of systems, and the inherent uncertainties modern systems face, the principles from MAS engineering remain particularly attractive for engineering systems in a wide variety of domains today. In this chapter, we reflect on the role and potential of MAS engineering on a selection of key facets that characterize modern software engineering practice. We focus at facets that we believe are important in relation to MAS engineering. Concretely, we look at agile development, Cloud and edge computing, distributed ledgers and blockchain, Cyber-Physical Systems and Internet-of-Things, and finally green computing. For each of these facets we highlight opportunities to EMAS engineering, but also the challenges these facets raise. We conclude with highlighting a number of ethical issues that the engineers of modern software-intensive systems and thus also MAS will face in the years to come.

Keywords: Multi-agent systems · Software engineering

1 Introduction

The engineering of software agents and Multi-Agent Systems (MAS) took off in the mid 1990s and raised the attention of many researchers from both Artificial Intelligence (AI) and Software Engineering [35,58,62,76]. AI has been described as the study of agents that receive percepts from the environment, perform actions there, are able of reasoning about their environment, perceptions and actions, of learning from interactions with the environment, and of interacting and coordinating [53]. This metaphor makes agents appealing to a wide audience interested in classical and distributed AI. On the other hand, the notion of software agents as autonomous components that encapsulate their own behaviour and jointly can solve complex problems has been a rich source of inspiration for software engineers with an interest in decentralized systems.

© Springer Nature Switzerland AG 2019
D. Weyns et al. (Eds.): EMAS 2018 Workshops, LNAI 11375, pp. 3–16, 2019.
https://doi.org/10.1007/978-3-030-25693-7_1

In the early days of MAS research, agents were mainly treated as autonomous software elements with particular architectures. MAS on the other hand were composed of such agents that communicate with one another to realize complex, distributed functions. The emphasis has been on key properties of agents such as autonomy, social ability, reactivity, pro-activeness [77]. A later complementary approach considered a MAS as a system of agents that is embedded in an agent environment, which provides a first-class abstraction for coordination [46,48,49,51,65,73,74]. Over time, the focus of research on the engineering of MAS went through a variety of stages, putting emphasis on different aspects, such as communication, coordination and cooperation [40,59], engineering methodologies [34,79], design patterns [22,36,55] and software architecture [56,68,69,72], declarative specifications [33], and programming languages [8,9].

With the advent of novel paradigms such as autonomic computing [26,38], self-adaptation [24,50,70], pervasive computing [54], and context awareness [25], software-intensive systems evolved towards a blend of cyber, physical, and social elements [32,52], demanding higher degrees of autonomy and adaptability than ever before [47,75]. Given the ever increasing integration and scale of systems, and the inherent uncertainties modern systems face, the metaphor of agent and MAS still matches these systems, hence principles from MAS engineering remain particularly attractive for engineering systems in a wide variety of domains today.

In this chapter, we reflect on the role and the potential of MAS in a selection of key facets that characterize modern software engineering practice and that we believe are important in relation to MAS engineering. Concretely, we look at agile development, Cloud and edge computing, distributed ledgers and blockchain, Cyber-Physical Systems (CPS) and Internet of Things (IoT), and green computing. For each of these topics we highlight opportunities to the EMAS community, but also the challenges they raise. Finally, we wrap-up and highlight a number of ethical issues that software engineering in general and MAS engineering in particular will increasingly face in the years to come.

2   Agile Software Development

The "Manifesto for Agile Software Development" [6] that was released in 2001, stressed a set of principles that shift value in software engineering: (i) from processes and tools to individuals and interactions, (ii) from comprehensive documentation to working software, (iii) from contract negotiation to customer collaboration, and (iv) from following a plan to responding to change. These principles provide the basis for the state of the practice in software engineering today.

With the introduction of agile approaches in practice, a number of traditional methodologies for engineering multi-agent systems have been "extended" to fit with some of the principles of agility, see for example [17,30], while some new methods were proposed as well, see for example [19,39]. However, little evidence has been provided for the added value of these methods in practice, and over time the interest in the topic gradually decreased.

Nevertheless, the principles that underlie agile software development are nowadays widely applied in practice. This raises the question of what agile software development means for the engineering of MAS. As has been argued multiple times in the past, the most effective way for MAS engineering to add value to software engineering practice is by integration rather than replacing existing practice, see for example [45, 71]. We provide two inspiring ideas in this direction.

One attractive idea would be to study and develop MAS-based tools for supporting agile engineering; i.e., agents that support the implementation of agile engineering methods of any kind of software applications, including MAS themselves. In particular, agents can offer viable solutions for supporting flexible interactions and collaboration among team members that go beyond rigid negotiation protocols. Agents can help finding a suitable balance between reactivity (the need of timely response to change) and rationality (the need of following a plan). While many agile development tools exist, incorporating agents may enhance these tools by (for example): facilitating flexible interactions among the team members, see e.g., [63], suggesting optimized schedules for teams working at different geographical locations, and balancing the development plan and supporting the planning of deviations from it, providing support for what-if analysis of the most critical scenarios to be tested, see e.g., [13]. Such additional features may contribute to increased productivity of software developers.

Another interesting idea could be the realization of *AaaS: "Agents as a Service."* A recent communication published on Forbes[1] points out that, after the waves of Software, Platform, and Infrastructure as a Service, the next wave is exploiting AI as a service. Big players such as Amazon, Google, Microsoft, and IBM are already offering such services, and startups like Dataiku, BigML, and others are entering the business. The current focus is mainly on "Machine Learning as a service," which is just an initial step in the full exploitation of AI. With *AaaS*, we envision the provisioning of services to help specifying, designing, implementing, verifying and validating software using agents and MAS, which are not necessarily based on machine learning. Examples would be services to engineer trust models, rule-based reasoning, sophisticated coordination and cooperation strategies, and support for normative systems.

Realizing "MAS-based tools for supporting agile engineering" and "agents as a service" opens a wide spectrum for future research. This includes studying the concrete usage scenarios for such tools and services, understanding the basic principles required to realize the tools and services, implementing them, and last but not least, empirically validating them. Whatever path followed, such research must go hand in hand with state of the practice in software engineering.

3   Cloud and Edge Computing

Cloud computing refers to infrastructure that provides on-demand computer system resources, in particular computing power and data storage, without the

---

[1] https://www.forbes.com/sites/janakirammsv/2018/02/22/the-rise-of-artificial-intelligence-as-a-service-in-the-public-cloud.

need for active management by users. Cloud computing aims at achieving coherence and economies of scale. People often refer to Cloud as data centers that are available to many users over the Internet. The term "cloud computing" was originally introduced by A. Regaldo at Compaq in the mid 1990s [20] and became popular when Amazon released its Elastic Compute Cloud in 2006 [1].

Clouds can be privately owned by a single organization or public to many organizations, or a combination of both (hybrid cloud). The main enabling technology for cloud computing is virtualization, which separates physical computing resources into "virtual" resources, each of which can be easily used and managed to perform computing tasks.

Conceptually, a Cloud is a centralized provider of resources, challenging the very idea of using MAS, which assumes the need for decentralization. However, while Cloud computing had clearly demonstrated its utility, its conceptual centralized architecture has been challenged by several trends. Among these are growing difficulties in accessing information in large Cloud infrastructures that deal with huge amounts of data, resulting in a lack of quality of the obtained content [57]. Another development that challenges the Cloud as a conceptually centralized resource is the raise of the Internet of Things, with potentially huge numbers of devices that have only limited resources [7].

These trends have recently led to the notion of Edge (or Fog) computing [7]. Edge computing is based on an architecture of edge devices that carry out a substantial amount of computation and storage, while keeping the communication locally and interacting with a backbone Cloud only if necessary. According to Cisco [18], Internet traffic is moving towards the edge: "*edge networking continues to gain more intelligence and capacity to support evolving network demands and superior network experiences.*" Edge computing realizes closer proximity to end-users and wider geographical distribution. This evolution makes Edge computing a natural fit with the paradigm of MAS. In particular, pushing intelligence to the edge of the network at distributed devices that sense the environment, produce huge amounts of data, autonomously decide which data are relevant and which may be discarded, and coordinate based on some criterion (geographical proximity, type of sensed events, format of produced data, etc.) are clearly characteristics of agents and MAS. Nevertheless, little research has been devoted to the adoption of MAS for edge computing (one example is [60]). However, there are plenty of opportunities in this area.

One interesting idea could be to employ a hierarchical MAS architecture. At the bottom level, software agents are associated with edge devices forming an "edge MAS." These simple "micro agents" equipped with sensors and actuators may be capable of filtering out data based on some criteria, process the data they manage based on instructions received from "coordinator agents" at a higher level in the hierarchy, and perform local actions as needed. Coordinator agents would coordinate a set of micro agents and guide them in their tasks to achieve the required functional goals of the system as well as the quality goals such as: minimize redundancy of data transmission, optimize the power consumption of edge devices, and minimize the exposure of sensitive data to comply with privacy policies. The set of micro agents managed by coordinator agents may be selected dynamically, as edge devices may be mobile or they may be switched on and off, and so would be their associated micro agents. To that end, the coordinator agents need to negotiate in order to coordinate the management tasks of the micro agents. Furthermore, coordinator agents could be managed themselves by "back-end agents" that are situated at the next level of the hierarchy. Back-end agents are provided with high-level goals that they break down into tasks that are allocated to coordinator agents. The back-end agents interact with users through the Cloud to have their goals achieved and return results.

Realizing such MAS hierarchy will be a challenging endeavor. It requires an architecture that combines vertical coordination (at each layer decomposing and delegating complex tasks to the next layer of agents, taking into account the resources available at each layer) as well as horizontal coordination (dynamic coordination and distribution of responsibilities among agents at each layer). Particular challenges here include the alignment of coordination within and across layers, the management of potentially huge amounts of data, dealing with strict resource constraints, and dynamics in the operating conditions that are difficult or impossible to predict before deployment and hence can only be resolved during operation.

4   Distributed Ledgers and Blockchain

Distributed ledgers can be described as "asset databases that can be shared across a network of multiple sites, geographies or institutions. All participants within a network can have their own identical copy of the ledger. Any changes to the ledger are reflected in all copies in orders of minutes, or in some cases even seconds." [2] Distributed ledgers require several underlying technologies, which differ in the way transactions are validated and stored. A common technology is a blockchain [61]. A blockchain is a growing list of records, called blocks. Each block contains a cryptographic hash of the previous block, a timestamp, and transaction data (generally represented as a Merkle tree). Distributed ledgers may be permissioned or permissionless regarding if anyone or only approved people can run a node to validate transactions. Ledgers also vary in the consensus algorithm, e.g., using proof of work, proof of stake, and voting systems.

A core aspect of distributed ledgers is that there is no central administrator or centralized data storage. Hence, distributed ledgers share the intrinsic property of decentralization with MAS. Some of the potential key benefits of distributed ledgers for MAS are support for: (i) automation of establishing agreement among entities that in principle do not trust each other, and (ii) inherent support for security, which is a critical but poorly studied concern in MAS engineering. A recent review of 14 studies that consider blockchain technology in MAS highlight application scenarios, motivations, assumptions, strengths and limitations, and challenges for future research in this area [16].

---

[2] https://assets.publishing.service.gov.uk/government/uploads/system/uploads/attachment_data/file/492972/gs-16-1-distributed-ledger-technology.pdf.

One particular interesting idea for integrating distributed ledger technology with MAS is combining them with so called "smart contracts." A smart contract defines a protocol that allows to facilitate, verify, or enforce the negotiation of a contract among stakeholders, in a digital way. These transactions are tractable and irreversible without requiring involvement of third parties. Integrating distributed ledgers with smart contracts and MAS paves the way to new interesting scenarios. An example is automating the governance of groups of geographically distributed people that are represented by software agents acting on their behalf. Such an approach could dramatically reduce the cost for reaching an agreement, while formally enforcing relationships between people, institutions, and their assets, using standardized transaction rules.

Exploiting the opportunities that distributed ledger technology and smart contracts may offer for MAS requires several challenges to be resolved. Among these are current limitations in the scalability of blockchain technology, the need to ensure the correctness of smart contracts in particular with respect to security requirements, and the need to ensure the required level of privacy and anonymity of users. While these are challenges that go beyond the integration with MAS, they are crucial for the adoption of the technology integrated with MAS.

5   Cyber-Physical Systems and Internet-of-Things

E. Lee described Cyber-physical systems (CPS) as *"integrations of computation and physical processes. Embedded computers and networks monitor and control the physical processes, usually with feedback loops where physical processes affect computations and vice versa"* [41]. Compared to traditional embedded systems, i.e. hardware-intensive systems with well-defined interfaces and boundaries delivering specific services to their end-users under often stringent reliability and safety requirements, CPS are more interconnected and more dependent on software for their operation. Recently, the notion of "smart" CPS has been coined [15], emphasizing that such CPS are enhanced with additional software that enables these systems to make autonomously (or semi-autonomously) decisions that traditionally have been made by humans. An example domain is road traffic management that integrates interaction between roadside sensors, local controllers, networked vehicles and in-car advisory systems to manage traffic. Other examples are smart power grids in which software-rich metering and appliance switching, and distribution management software, directly affect the physical process of delivering electricity.

A closely related area is the Internet of Things (IoT) [3,4] that extends Internet connectivity into physical devices and everyday objects. These devices and objects can communicate locally with each other and with users via gateways over the Internet to collect monitored data and perform control actions. An example is building management for managing heating, ventilation, air conditioning, access control, and lighting. Another example is smart products used in agriculture where software-rich processes make decisions based on for example grain processes and weather forecasts, while interacting with the controllers of autonomous machines in the fields.

Despite the natural fit between large-scale CPS and IoT on the one hand and MAS on the other hand, only a few researchers have proposed agent-oriented solutions for modelling, simulating, and analyzing CPS, examples are [42,64,66, 67,78]. However, there is a huge potential for the MAS community to contribute to the engineering of CPS and IoT. The large body of work on agent interaction protocols, coordination mechanisms, trust models, holonic models, and agent-based modeling and simulation, can be exploited to help tackling the challenges of engineering of CPS and IoT.

One concrete idea for the engineering of CPS and IoT is supporting the cooperation across entities within and across systems, which is needed to enable the constituting elements of such systems to work together effectively (for example, the cooperation between self-driving cars or unmanned aerial vehicles). Since such cooperation is tied to the context and situation, the formation of cooperative teams requires a dynamic solution that opportunistically reshapes the teams during operation addressing the situations at hand. Such on-the-fly formation of teams requires teams to become first-class citizens in the design and operation of CPS and IoT. The body of work on team formation provides a starting point to tackle these challenges but realizing an effective solution raises many issues. As highlighted by the US National Science Foundation[3] realizing practical solutions to CPS and IoT poses the following challenges:

- Which architecture better suits the intertwining of physical and software components, and their interaction?
- How to deal with distributed decision making and coordination?
- How to simulate, test and verify CPS?
- How to trust autonomous systems that learn from their experience?
- Which methodology can better cope with these issues?

Another prominent issue that has been raised is the privacy and security of users related to the devices used in CPS and IoT and their intention of pervasive presence. Any MAS solution that wants to be effective in practice will need to deal with these issues.

6   Green Computing

Green computing aims at reducing environmental impact that results from operating the computing artefacts [12,21]. In particular, green computing aims at maximizing energy efficiency throughout the lifetime of products and recyclability of defunct products and factory waste. Green computing is important for all classes of computing systems, ranging from hand-held systems and embedded system to large-scale data centers. Since modern computing systems blend people, software, and hardware, any green computing initiative must cover all of these areas. However, a solution cannot ignore user satisfaction, return on investment, and regulatory compliance.

---

[3] https://www.nsf.gov/publications/pub_summ.jsp?ods_key=nsf19553.

Agents and MAS have a huge potential to contribute to green computing. We highlight one particular area: optimized management and distribution of electric power. The idea of exploiting agents and MAS for saving energy dates back to 2000 [23], and the topic has been addressed over the years in connection to several domains, including CPS [80], micro-grids [27], and smart grids [43]. A recent survey discusses how MAS have been applied in energy optimization problems [31].

An interesting idea to enhance electric power distribution could be through novel bio-inspired optimization techniques. Swarms of agents might look for available sources of renewable energy and might leave traces leading to those that still have power to sell. Alternatively, sources of energy may emit computational fields that inform interested parties of available energy. Some of the sources of energy may be know in advance, others may appear or disappear at will. However, in most cases the available sources of energy will vary over time. Hence, the search for available energy needs to be carried out at run time, in a highly dynamic environment. Such search may be guided by different criteria, including neighborhood (e.g., environment-safe power plants first), and balance between the "quality" of energy w.r.t. environmental footprint and the cost to transport the energy from source to consumer.

Realizing such MAS enabled green energy provisioning platform comes with numerous challenges; the results achieved by the MAS community in designing swarm-based MAS platforms, supporting the ability to express policies and trust, providing mechanisms to balance individual versus global goals, and mechanisms to enforce global policies, may help in tackling them. Besides technical challenges, regulatory issues must be also considered: the software solution needs to be aligned with the underlying laws of electricity as well as the economics of supply and demand.

7   Conclusions

In this chapter, we have reflected on the role and potential of MAS engineering in a number of key facets that characterize modern software engineering practice. We have in particular focused on the facets that challenge the very principles of MAS, such as Cloud computing and distributed ledgers that challenge the inherent decentralized nature of MAS. For each facet, we highlighted the motivation and emerging developments, and we exemplified initial efforts in the context of MAS engineering. Then we proposed novel ideas that could drive research in MAS engineering for each of the facets, and we highlighted some of the challenges.

We conclude this chapter with a final facet, that is orthogonal to all the other facets we presented and will be crucial for the future of software engineering and thus also MAS engineering: ethics. The advance of systems becoming increasingly intelligent ("smarter") and taking decisions on behalf of humans raises various ethical issues. Recent efforts such as [44] and [5] explored ethics in different stages of the software engineering lifecycle. Ethics and intelligent machines has emerged as a main concern for both scientists, politicians, and users in general. The Asilomar AI Principles[4] put forward ethical guidelines, both in the short and in the long term. These guidelines invite the MAS engineers to rigorously deal with various ethical aspects. We highlight three principles. For example, the sixth principle states: "Safety: intelligent systems should be safe and secure throughout their operational lifetime, and verifiably so where applicable and feasible." Aligning with this principle will require MAS engineers to employ verification techniques (at development time and at runtime) suitable for autonomous, open, dynamic, distributed systems. While many efforts have been done in this direction, see for example [2,10,11,14,28,29,37], verifying MAS is still an open issue. The seventh principle states: "Failure Transparency: If an intelligent system causes harm, it should be possible to ascertain why." Aligning with this principle requires the system to have well defined capabilities and responsibilities that allow to inspect and explain their behavior to different stakeholders. The tenth principle states "Value Alignment: Highly autonomous intelligent systems should be designed so that their goals and behaviors can be assured to align with human values throughout their operation." Dealing with this principle calls for an explicit representation of goals and behaviours of autonomous systems. While some of these ethical principles are closer to common practice in MAS engineering, others are not and will require a cultural shift in the way we perform research and build solutions for users in practice.

We hope that our reflections on key facets in the engineering of software-incentive systems and the opportunities and challenges these facets raise for MAS engineering will be a source of inspiration for researchers to further progress our field in the coming years and transfer the output of our research to practice.

References

1. Amazon elastic compute cloud (2006). https://docs.aws.amazon.com/ec2/index.html
2. Ancona, D., Briola, D., El Fallah Seghrouchni, A., Mascardi, V., Taillibert, P.: Efficient verification of MASs with projections. In: Dalpiaz, F., Dix, J., van Riemsdijk, M.B. (eds.) EMAS 2014. LNCS (LNAI), vol. 8758, pp. 246–270. Springer, Cham (2014). https://doi.org/10.1007/978-3-319-14484-9_13
3. Ashton, K.: That 'internet of things' thing. RFID J. **22**, 97–114 (2009)
4. Atzori, L., Iera, A., Morabito, G.: The internet of things: a survey. Comput. Netw. **54**(15), 2787–2805 (2010)
5. Aydemir, F.B., Dalpiaz, F.: A roadmap for ethics-aware software engineering. In: Proceedings of the International Workshop on Software Fairness, FairWare 2018, pp. 15–21. ACM (2018)
6. Beck, K., et al.: Manifesto for agile software development (2001). http://agilemanifesto.org/
7. Bonomi, F., Milito, R., Zhu, J., Addepalli, S.: Fog computing and its role in the internet of things. In: Proceedings of the First Edition of the MCC Workshop on Mobile Cloud Computing, MCC 2012, pp. 13–16. ACM (2012)

---

[4] https://futureoflife.org/ai-principles/.

8. Bordini, R.H., et al.: A survey of programming languages and platforms for multi-agent systems. Informatica (Slovenia) **30**(1), 33–44 (2006)
9. El Fallah Seghrouchni, A., Dix, J., Dastani, M., Bordini, R.H. (eds.): Multi-Agent Programming. Springer, Boston (2009). https://doi.org/10.1007/978-0-387-89299-3
10. Bordini, R.H., Dennis, L.A., Farwer, B., Fisher, M.: Automated verification of multi-agent programs. In: ASE, pp. 69–78. IEEE Computer Society (2008)
11. Bordini, R.H., Fisher, M., Visser, W., Wooldridge, M.: Verifiable multi-agent programs. In: Dastani, M.M., Dix, J., El Fallah-Seghrouchni, A. (eds.) ProMAS 2003. LNCS (LNAI), vol. 3067, pp. 72–89. Springer, Heidelberg (2004). https://doi.org/10.1007/978-3-540-25936-7_4
12. Bozzelli, P., Gu, Q., Lago, P.: A systematic literature review on green software metrics. VU Amsterdam Technical report (2013)
13. Briola, D., Mascardi, V.: Can my test case run on your test plant? A logic-based compliance check and its evaluation on real data. In: Costantini, S., Franconi, E., Van Woensel, W., Kontchakov, R., Sadri, F., Roman, D. (eds.) RuleML+RR 2017. LNCS, vol. 10364, pp. 53–69. Springer, Cham (2017). https://doi.org/10.1007/978-3-319-61252-2_5
14. Briola, D., Mascardi, V., Ancona, D.: Distributed runtime verification of JADE multiagent systems. In: Camacho, D., Braubach, L., Venticinque, S., Badica, C. (eds.) Intelligent Distributed Computing VIII. SCI, vol. 570, pp. 81–91. Springer, Cham (2015). https://doi.org/10.1007/978-3-319-10422-5_10
15. Bures, T., et al.: Software engineering for smart cyber-physical systems - towards a research agenda: report on the first international workshop on software engineering for smart CPS. SIGSOFT Softw. Eng. Notes **40**(6), 28–32 (2015)
16. Calvaresi, D., Dubovitskaya, A., Calbimonte, J.P., Taveter, K., Schumacher, M.: Multi-agent systems and blockchain: results from a systematic literature review. In: Demazeau, Y., An, B., Bajo, J., Fernández-Caballero, A. (eds.) PAAMS 2018. LNCS (LNAI), vol. 10978, pp. 110–126. Springer, Cham (2018). https://doi.org/10.1007/978-3-319-94580-4_9
17. Chella, A., Cossentino, M., Sabatucci, L., Seidita, V.: Agile PASSI: an agile process for designing agents. Comput. Syst. Sci. Eng. **21**(2), 133–144 (2006)
18. Cisco visual networking index: forecast and trends, 2017–2022 white paper (2019). https://www.cisco.com/c/en/us/solutions/collateral/service-provider/visual-networking-index-vni/white-paper-c11-741490.html
19. Clynch, N., Collier, R.: SADAAM: software agent development-an agile methodology. In: Proceedings of the Workshop of Languages, Methodologies, and Development Tools For Multi-agent Systems (LADS 2007) (2007)
20. Compaq. Internet solutions division strategy for cloud computing. CTS Presentation (1997)
21. Curry, E., Guyon, B., Sheridan, C., Donnellan, B.: Developing a sustainable IT capability: lessons from Intel's journey. MIS Q. Exec. **11**(2), 61–74 (2009)
22. Dastani, M., Testerink, B.: Design patterns for multi-agent programming. Int. J. Agent-Oriented Softw. Eng. **5**(2/3), 167–202 (2016)
23. Davidsson, P., Boman, M.: Saving energy and providing value added services in intelligent buildings: a MAS approach. In: Kotz, D., Mattern, F. (eds.) ASA/MA -2000. LNCS, vol. 1882, pp. 166–177. Springer, Heidelberg (2000). https://doi.org/10.1007/978-3-540-45347-5_14

24. de Lemos, R., et al.: Software engineering for self-adaptive systems: research challenges in the provision of assurances. In: de Lemos, R., Garlan, D., Ghezzi, C., Giese, H. (eds.) Software Engineering for Self-Adaptive Systems III. Assurances. LNCS, vol. 9640, pp. 3–30. Springer, Cham (2017). https://doi.org/10.1007/978-3-319-74183-3_1

25. Dey, A.K.: Understanding and using context. Pers. Ubiquitous Comput. **5**(1), 4–7 (2001)

26. Dobson, S., et al.: A survey of autonomic communications. ACM Trans. Auton. Adapt. Syst. **1**(2), 223–259 (2006)

27. Eddy, Y.F., Gooi, H.B., Chen, S.X.: Multi-agent system for distributed management of microgrids. IEEE Trans. Power Syst. **30**(1), 24–34 (2015)

28. Ferrando, A., Dennis, L.A., Ancona, D., Fisher, M., Mascardi, V.: Verifying and validating autonomous systems: towards an integrated approach. In: Colombo, C., Leucker, M. (eds.) RV 2018. LNCS, vol. 11237, pp. 263–281. Springer, Cham (2018). https://doi.org/10.1007/978-3-030-03769-7_15

29. Fisher, M., Wooldridge, M.: On the formal specification and verification of multi-agent systems. Int. J. Coop. Inf. Syst. **6**(01), 37–65 (1997)

30. Gómez-Rodríguez, A.M., González-Moreno, J.C.: Comparing agile processes for agent oriented software engineering. In: Ali Babar, M., Vierimaa, M., Oivo, M. (eds.) PROFES 2010. LNCS, vol. 6156, pp. 206–219. Springer, Heidelberg (2010). https://doi.org/10.1007/978-3-642-13792-1_17

31. González-Briones, A., De La Prieta, F., Mohamad, M., Omatu, S., Corchado, J.: Multi-agent systems applications in energy optimization problems: a state-of-the-art review. Energies **11**(8), 1928 (2018)

32. Henson, C., Anantharam, P., Sheth, A.: Physical-cyber-social computing: an early 21st century approach. IEEE Intell. Syst. **28**(01), 78–82 (2013)

33. Hindriks, K.V., de Boer, F.S., van der Hoek, W., Meyer, J.-J.C.: Agent programming with declarative goals. In: Castelfranchi, C., Lespérance, Y. (eds.) ATAL 2000. LNCS (LNAI), vol. 1986, pp. 228–243. Springer, Heidelberg (2001). https://doi.org/10.1007/3-540-44631-1_16

34. Iglesias, C.A., Garijo, M., González, J.C.: A survey of agent-oriented methodologies. In: Müller, J.P., Rao, A.S., Singh, M.P. (eds.) ATAL 1998. LNCS, vol. 1555, pp. 317–330. Springer, Heidelberg (1999). https://doi.org/10.1007/3-540-49057-4_21

35. Jennings, N.R., Sycara, K.P., Wooldridge, M.: A roadmap of agent research and development. Auton. Agent. Multi-Agent Syst. **1**(1), 7–38 (1998)

36. Juziuk, J., Weyns, D., Holvoet, T.: Design patterns for multi-agent systems: a systematic literature review. In: Shehory, O., Sturm, A. (eds.) Agent-Oriented Software Engineering, pp. 79–99. Springer, Heidelberg (2014). https://doi.org/10.1007/978-3-642-54432-3_5

37. Kacprzak, M., Lomuscio, A., Penczek, W.: Verification of multiagent systems via unbounded model checking. In: AAMAS, pp. 638–645. IEEE Computer Society (2004)

38. Kephart, J.O., Chess, D.M.: The vision of autonomic computing. IEEE Comput. **36**(1), 41–50 (2003)

39. Kirby Jr., J.: Model-driven agile development of reactive multi-agent systems. In: COMPSAC (2), pp. 297–302. IEEE Computer Society (2006)

40. Kraus, S.: Negotiation and cooperation in multi-agent environments. Artif. Intell. **94**(1), 79–97 (1997). Economic Principles of Multi-Agent Systems

41. Lee, E.A.: Cyber physical systems: design challenges. In: ISORC, pp. 363–369. IEEE Computer Society (2008)

42. Leitão, P., Colombo, A.W., Karnouskos, S.: Industrial automation based on cyber-physical systems technologies: prototype implementations and challenges. Comput. Ind. **81**, 11–25 (2016)
43. Li, J., Wei, H., Xia, X.: The multi-agent model and method for energy-saving generation dispatching system. In: 2010 International Conference on Power System Technology, pp. 1–8, October 2010
44. Lurie, Y., Mark, S.: Professional ethics of software engineers: an ethical framework. Sci. Eng. Ethics **22**(2), 417–434 (2016)
45. Lützenberger, M., Küster, T., Masuch, N., Fähndrich, J.: Multi-agent system in practice: When research meets reality. In: Proceedings of the 2016 International Conference on Autonomous Agents & Multiagent Systems, AAMAS 2016, pp. 796–805. International Foundation for Autonomous Agents and Multiagent Systems (2016)
46. Mamei, M., Zambonelli, F.: Programming pervasive and mobile computing applications: the TOTA approach. ACM Trans. Softw. Eng. Methodol. **18**(4), 15:1–15:56 (2009)
47. Muccini, H., Sharaf, M., Weyns, D.: Self-adaptation for cyber-physical systems: a systematic literature review. In: Proceedings of the 11th International Symposium on Software Engineering for Adaptive and Self-Managing Systems, SEAMS 2016, pp. 75–81. ACM (2016)
48. Omicini, A., Ricci, A., Viroli, M.: Artifacts in the A&A meta-model for multi-agent systems. Autonomous Agents and Multi-Agent Systems **17**(3), 432–456 (2008)
49. Omicini, A., Ricci, A., Viroli, M., Castelfranchi, C., Tummolini, L.: Coordination artifacts: environment-based coordination for intelligent agents. In: AAMAS, pp. 286–293. IEEE Computer Society (2004)
50. Oreizy, P., et al.: An architecture-based approach to self-adaptive software. IEEE Intell. Syst. Appl. **14**(3), 54–62 (1999)
51. Parunak, H.V.D., Weyns, D.: Guest editors' introduction, special issue on environments for multi-agent systems. Auton. Agent. Multi-Agent Syst. **14**(1), 1–4 (2007)
52. Rajkumar, R., Lee, I., Sha, L., Stankovic, J.A.: Cyber-physical systems: the next computing revolution. In: Sapatnekar, S.S. (ed.) Proceedings of the 47th Design Automation Conference, DAC 2010, Anaheim, California, USA, 13–18 July 2010, pp. 731–736. ACM (2010)
53. Russell, S.J., Norvig, P.: Artificial Intelligence – A Modern Approach, 3rd edn. Pearson Education, London (2010)
54. Satyanarayanan, M.: Pervasive computing: vision and challenges. IEEE Pers. Commun. **8**(4), 10–17 (2001)
55. Schelfthout, K., Coninx, T., Helleboogh, A., Holvoet, T., Steegmans, E., Weyns, D.: Agent implementation patterns. In: Workshop on Agent-Oriented Methodologies, 17th Annual ACM Conference on Object-Oriented Programming, Systems, Languages, and Applications (OOPSLA02) (2002)
56. Shehory, O., Sturm, A.: Multi-agent systems: a software architecture viewpoint. In: Shehory, O., Sturm, A. (eds.) Agent-Oriented Software Engineering: Reflections on Architectures. Methodologies, Languages, and Frameworks, pp. 57–78. Springer, Berlin Heidelberg (2014). https://doi.org/10.1007/978-3-642-54432-3_4
57. Shi, W., Cao, J., Zhang, Q., Li, Y., Xu, L.: Edge computing: vision and challenges. IEEE Internet Things J. **3**(5), 637–646 (2016)
58. Shoham, Y.: Agent-oriented programming. Artif. Intell. **60**(1), 51–92 (1993)

59. Singh, M.P.: Agent communication languages: rethinking the principles. Computer **31**(12), 40–47 (1998)
60. Suganuma, T., Oide, T., Kitagami, S., Sugawara, K., Shiratori, N.: Multiagent-based flexible edge computing architecture for IoT. IEEE Network **32**(1), 16–23 (2018)
61. Swan, M.: Blockchain: Blueprint for a New Economy. O'Reilly Media Inc., Sebastopol (2015)
62. Sycara, K.P., Pannu, A., Williamson, M., Zeng, D., Decker, K.: Distributed intelligent agents. IEEE Expert **11**(6), 36–46 (1996)
63. Tambe, M.: Towards flexible teamwork. J. Artif. Intell. Res. **7**, 83–124 (1997)
64. Ulieru, M.: Design for resilience of networked critical infrastructures. In: 2007 Inaugural IEEE-IES Digital EcoSystems and Technologies Conference, pp. 540–545. IEEE (2007)
65. Van Dyke Parunak, H.: "Go to the ant": engineering principles from natural multi-agent systems. Ann. Oper. Res. **75**, 69–101 (1997)
66. Wang, L., Haghighi, A.: Combined strength of holons, agents and function blocks in cyber-physical systems. J. Manuf. Syst. **40**, 25–34 (2016). SI: Challenges in Smart Manufacturing
67. Wang, S., Wan, J., Zhang, D., Li, D., Zhang, C.: Towards smart factory for industry 4.0: a self-organized multi-agent system with big data based feedback and coordination. Comput. Netw. **101**, 158–168 (2016)
68. Weyns, D.: An architecture-centric approach for software engineering with situated multiagent systems. Ph.D., Katholieke Universiteit Leuven, Belgium (2006)
69. Weyns, D.: Architecture-Based Design of Multi-Agent Systems. Springer, Heidelberg (2010). https://doi.org/10.1007/978-3-642-01064-4
70. Weyns, D.: Software engineering of self-adaptive systems. Handbook of Software Engineering, pp. 399–443. Springer, Cham (2019). https://doi.org/10.1007/978-3-030-00262-6_11
71. Weyns, D., Helleboogh, A., Holvoet, T.: How to get multi-agent systems accepted in industry? IJAOSE **3**(4), 383–390 (2009)
72. Weyns, D., Holvoet, T.: Architectural design of a situated multiagent system for controlling automatic guided vehicles. J. Agent-Oriented Softw. Eng. **2**(1), 90–128 (2008)
73. Weyns, D., Michel, F.: Agent environments for multi-agent systems – a research roadmap. In: Weyns, D., Michel, F. (eds.) E4MAS 2014. LNCS (LNAI), vol. 9068, pp. 3–21. Springer, Cham (2015). https://doi.org/10.1007/978-3-319-23850-0_1
74. Weyns, D., Omicini, A., Odell, J.: Environment as a first class abstraction in multiagent systems. Auton. Agent. Multi-Agent Syst. **14**(1), 5–30 (2007)
75. Weyns, D., Ramachandran, G.S., Singh, R.K.: Self-managing internet of things. In: Tjoa, A.M., Bellatreche, L., Biffl, S., van Leeuwen, J., Wiedermann, J. (eds.) SOFSEM 2018. LNCS, vol. 10706, pp. 67–84. Springer, Cham (2018). https://doi.org/10.1007/978-3-319-73117-9_5
76. Wooldridge, M., Jennings, N.R.: Agent theories, architectures, and languages: a survey. In: Wooldridge, M.J., Jennings, N.R. (eds.) ATAL 1994. LNCS, vol. 890, pp. 1–39. Springer, Heidelberg (1995). https://doi.org/10.1007/3-540-58855-8_1
77. Wooldridge, M., Jennings, N.R.: Intelligent agents: theory and practice. Knowl. Eng. Rev. **10**(2), 115–152 (1995)
78. Zalila-Wenkstern, R., Steel, T., Leask, G.: A self-organizing architecture for traffic management. In: Weyns, D., Malek, S., de Lemos, R., Andersson, J. (eds.) SOAR 2009. LNCS, vol. 6090, pp. 230–250. Springer, Heidelberg (2010). https://doi.org/10.1007/978-3-642-14412-7_11

79. Zambonelli, F., Jennings, N.R., Wooldridge, M.J.: Developing multiagent systems: the Gaia methodology. ACM Trans. Softw. Eng. Methodol. **12**(3), 317–370 (2003)
80. Zhao, P., Simões, M.G., Suryanarayanan, S.: A conceptual scheme for cyber-physical systems based energy management in building structures. In: 2010 9th IEEE/IAS International Conference on Industry Applications - INDUSCON 2010, pp. 1–6, November 2010

Programming Agents and MAS

Pitfalls of Jason Concurrency

Álvaro Fernández Díaz, Clara Benac Earle, and Lars-Åke Fredlund[✉]

Grupo Babel, DLSIIS, ETSIINF, Universidad Politécnica de Madrid, Madrid, Spain
alvarofdezdiaz@gmail.com,{cbenac,lfredlund}@fi.upm.es

Abstract. Jason is a well-known programming language for multiagent systems where fine-grained concurrency primitives allow a highly-concurrent efficient execution. However, typical concurrency errors such as race conditions are hard to avoid. In this chapter, we analyze a number of such potential pitfalls of the Jason concurrency model, and, describe both how such risks can be mitigated in Jason itself, as well as discussing the alternatives implemented in eJason, an experimental extension of Jason with support for distribution and fault tolerance. In some cases, we propose changes in the standard Jason semantics.

Keywords: Jason programming · Concurrency

1 Introduction

Jason [1] is a well-known programming language for multiagent systems (MASs) with a well established formal semantics based on Agent Speak [6].

Programming multiagent systems is not an easy task, as it involves coordinating the concurrent execution of a set of independent agents (akin to processes in mainstream concurrent programming), each of which may also be composed of a set of independently executing intentions (in mainstream programming often named threads). In Jason agents communicate through message passing, affording a high-level of control, whereas intra-agent communication between intentions is realised through asserting and retracting beliefs in the shared belief base.

In previous work we have introduced eJason [3,4], an extension to Jason where new features have been added to cope with distribution and fault-tolerance in MAS. As a first step to extend Jason with these features, we analyze in this chapter to what respect the concurrency model of Jason enables programmers to develop concurrent multiagent systems without running into the usual pitfalls of concurrency, i.e., difficult to handle race conditions. Clearly the fine-grained concurrency primitives present in Jason, where the belief database is shared among all concurrent interactions, promise highly-concurrent efficient execution, but at the same time the programmer should be provided with convenient high-level language constructs for controlling the amount inter-agent concurrency.

Intra-agent concurrency has been an issue of study for some time, in particular regarding how to resolve conflicts among goals when agents pursue multiple goals. In [7] conflicts are handled in the goal level by representing conflicting

© Springer Nature Switzerland AG 2019
D. Weyns et al. (Eds.): EMAS 2018 Workshops, LNAI 11375, pp. 19–33, 2019.
https://doi.org/10.1007/978-3-030-25693-7_2

goals. A difficulty with this approach is that all plans for a conflicting goal are considered conflicting, i.e., non-conflicting alternative plans that can achieve the same goal are not considered. This issue is addressed in [8] which examines different strategies for resolving conflicts, such as dropping intentions, or modifying intentions with regards to the selection of plans for solving goals. Automatic detection of conflicts is the approach followed by [9], where means for reasoning about the goal interactions are incorporated into the commercial BDI agent development platform JACK, and evaluated empirically.

In this chapter we take Jason as the programming platform of study and discuss its semantics and implementation with regards to some concurrency problems that may arise.

The rest of the chapter is structured as four sections, each describing a potential difficulty with a Jason concurrency mechanism, discuss how the difficulties can be mitigated in Jason itself, and alternative solutions implemented in eJason. In Sect. 2 we discuss mechanisms to control the amount of concurrency among a set of interaction, whereas Sect. 3 examines the possibility that the context of a plan may be false when the plan body starts executing. Next, in Sects. 4 and 5 we consider the mechanisms for handling failing achievement and test goals respectively, and alternatives to such early failures, i.e., goal suspension. Section 6 discusses how the changes implemented in eJason impacts the reasoning cycle of agents, whereas Sect. 7 draws conclusions.

2   Mechanisms for Synchronizing Access to Shared Beliefs

A Jason agent can possess several foci of attention, corresponding to the different intentions of the agent. These intentions compete for the attention of the agent, and the decision on which intention to execute, in each iteration of the reasoning cycle, is determined by the intention selection function of the agent. The execution order of the different intentions is not always irrelevant. The plans in the different intentions access and update the information stored in the belief base. Therefore, the modification of the set of beliefs, derived from the execution of an intention, may affect the outcome (or even prevent the execution) of other executable intentions. The programmer must then consider these data dependencies between the different intentions, and, when necessary, control the synchronisation of the execution of such intentions.

2.1   Nondeterministic Execution Implies Nondeterministic Belief Bases

To illustrate the difficulties that may be caused by sharing beliefs among a set of interactions, consider the Jason agent in Fig. 1, which counts the number of files that were loaded.

Consider an agent with only this plan in its plan base and with initial goals $g_1 = {}$!load(file1) and $g_2 = {}$!load(file2). The intentions corresponding to these goals are composed by one instance of the plan above, i.e., $I_1 = [p_1]$ for g_1

```
+!load(File) <-
    load(File);              // a
    ?files_loaded(Num);      // b
    -+files_loaded(Num+1).   // c
```

Fig. 1. Jason plan for the file counter

and $I_2 = [p_2]$ for g_2 with plan bodies $\{a_1; b_1; c_1\}$ and $\{a_2; b_2; c_2\}$, respectively, where a_1 represents the formula a applied to g_1, and so on.

Tracing the execution of the agent code, using the standard intention selection function, may show that the counter is not always properly updated, as sometimes it only records the loading of one file, while, in fact, two files have been loaded. A simple exploration of all possible execution traces, represented by the different possible interleavings of the actions in the plan bodies, exposes the root causes of the problem. These interleavings are depicted in Fig. 2. This figure shows a graph where each node, labelled $I_1 I_2 Ctr$, represents a different configuration of the mental state of the agent such that $I_i \in \{a_i, b_i, c_i\} \cup X$ for $i \in \{1, 2\}$ corresponds to the action to be executed if the intention I_i gets selected by the intention selection function (the symbol X is used as a placeholder if the corresponding intention has been fully executed) and Ctr is the value of the counter (i.e., a belief `file_loaded(Ctr)`). For instance, the node $b_1 X 1$ corresponds to a mental state such that the selection of the intention I_1 implies the execution of the formula b_1, the intention I_2 has been fully executed and the belief base contains a belief `files_loaded(1)`. Note then that the node $X X 2$ corresponds to the outcome desired (i.e., the counter is properly updated), while the node $X X 1$, shadowed in the graph, corresponds to an undesirable one (i.e., when the counter only records the loading of a single file, instead of two). The different edges in the graph represent the transition between mental states, and their label corresponds to the formula executed during that transition. For instance, the outgoing edge a_1 (resp. a_2) from the node $a_1 a_2 0$ to the node $b_1 a_2 0$ (resp. $a_1 b_2 0$) represents the transition triggered by the execution of the formula $a_1 = $ `load(file1)` (resp. $a_2 = $ `load(file2)`). The analysis of the execution traces shows that the undesired outcome occurs when the actions b_1 and b_2 (i.e., the actions where the value of the counter is read) have been executed without the execution of neither c_1 nor c_2 (i.e., the actions that update the counter) in-between (i.e., all traces containing the state $c_1 c_2 0$). The reason is that, in these cases, one of the intentions is handling outdated information regarding the counter and, therefore, the result is incorrect.

2.2   Jason Solutions

In a sense, the problem is a standard one in concurrent programming, i.e., how to prohibit "bad" program executions where the concurrent execution of different threads (or intentions in Jason) incorrectly interfere with each other due to concurrent access to a shared program state (in Jason, the belief base). The

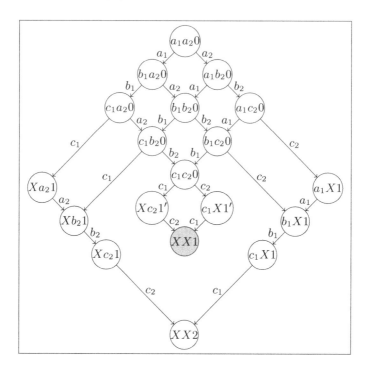

Fig. 2. Possible interleavings for the counter update example.

Java programming language, for instance, has synchronized objects to prevent concurrent access, and a number of more advanced mechanisms for controlling concurrent access available in the `java.util.concurrent` library.

Atomic Plans. The Java implementation of Jason enables the labelling of plans as a way of including meta-level information that alters the reasoning cycle of the agent. The label *atomic* is one of such labels. A plan labelled as atomic, also referred to as *atomic plan*, is such that, once this plan is selected for execution during an iteration of the reasoning cycle, all subsequent iterations will also select this intention until the atomic plan is fully executed. More informally, the atomic label represents a way of temporarily disabling the multiplicity of foci of attention, keeping the attention of the agent in the intention until the atomic plan is executed.

In order to avoid the data dependency explained in the previous section, an atomic plan can be used. For instance, by replacing the plan in Fig. 1 with the two (semantically dependent) plans provided in Fig. 3.

The revised plans guarantee that the formulas b and c are always executed consecutively, removing the execution traces that led to the wrong result. This solution can be used not only for belief updates, but also more generally to

```
+!load(File) <-
    load(File);               //a
    !update_counter.

@up[atomic]
+!update_counter <-
    ?files_loaded(Num);       //b
    -+files_loaded(Num+1). //c
```

Fig. 3. File counter with an atomic plan

implement behaviours that require the agent to maintain its focus of attention on the same intention for several iterations of the reasoning cycle.

Note that such a solution may require the introduction of additional plans in order to delimit the scope for the atomic execution.

2.3   eJason Solution: Critical Sections

The eJason language proposed the definition of critical sections to reduce the amount of concurrency among interactions. Syntactically a critical section is enclosed within braces, i.e., "{{" and "}}". When an agent executes a formula within a critical section, there can be no concurrent change in the focus of attention as long as the critical section has not been exited. Using critical sections as the synchronisation mechanism, the counter agent may be written as shown in Fig. 4.

```
+!load(File) <-
    load(File);
    {{?files_loaded(Num);
    -+files_loaded(Num+1)}}.
```

Fig. 4. File counter with eJason critical sections

This plan provides the same functionality as the combination of the two plans in Fig. 3, i.e., Jason atomic plans and eJason critical sections are equivalent. In the case of atomic plans, the parametrisation (via labelling) of the intention selection function requires the programmer to consider the different intentions that may conflict, and establish a priority order for their execution. In contrast, using critical sections, the programmer only identifies the program regions which should be executed without interference from other intentions of the agent.

Labelling Conflicting Plans. Recently Jason has been extended with a new interesting feature [10], where plans may be declared as *conflicting* with other plans, with the intention that conflicting plans may not be concurrently executed, whereas non-conflicting plans can be. In the example above, we can specify that the up plan conflicts with itself, by using the *conflict identifier* self. Then, the [atomic] declaration can be removed. Thus, in a sense, the possibility to explicitly label plans as conflicting refines the notion of atomic plans.

The ASTRA Approach. Another approach to controlling concurrency in languages based on AgentSpeak is demonstrated by the ASTRA [2] language. There critical sections are associated with an identifier (similar to the Java synchronized blocks), such that for any identifier, at any time there is at most one intention executing a critical section labelled by that identifier. Clearly, similarly to the approach with labelling conflicting plans, this proposal also permits an increased amount of concurrency (compared with using an universally shared critical section) among a set of concurrent interactions.

2.4   What Is the Right Solution?

Providing programming languages with effective tools for managing finely grained concurrency is currently a very active research area, largely driven by the increased commercial availability of multi-core processors. However, there is, in our opinion, no clear consensus on what the right programming model and the right concurrency primitives are, and it is not surprising that the same situation holds for programming languages related to AgentSpeak.

Considering the eJason solution, for instance, it, in our opinion, represents a step forward in that it defines formally, in the eJason semantics, the behaviour of the new construct. On the other hand, to program highly concurrent agents by sharing a single critical section is likely to prove too inefficient in practise.

Borrowing inspiration from Java again, apart from the critical sections, whether labelled to permit more concurrency or not, we find the locks and conditions provided by the java.util.concurrent.locks library, which permits the programming of more flexible locking policies compared with basic critical sections. One interesting adaptation of that library is represented by the work on shared resources [5], where concurrent executions are guarded by concurrency preconditions, such that the execution of a resource blocks until its concurrency precondition (which are general predicates on the resource state) becomes true. As an item of future work, it would be interesting to implement this approach in eJason, essentially labelling critical section with general predicates over the agent state restricting access. Of course, in such an approach, care has to be taken in order to ensure efficient execution.

3   Executing Selected Event Plans in Matching Contexts

Consider a simplified multi-agent system with a classical client-server architecture. The client agents should write information into different files. In order to avoid conflicts generated by simultaneous write attempts to the same file by different agents, the access to the file is managed by a server agent. A client agent

```
+!write(FName, Text) : true <-
    .send(server, achieve, lock(FName));
    .wait("+granted(FName)");
    write(Text, FName);
    .send(server, achieve, unlock(FName)).
```

Fig. 5. Jason code for the client agents

sends a message to the server agent to request the exclusive rights to access a file before it can write into the file. When the exclusive access to the file is no longer necessary, the client agent sends a message to the server agent to unlock the resource.

An implementation in Jason of the a client is depicted in Fig. 5. Before a client agent writes some text, `Text`, into a file, `FName`, it must first send an achieve message to the server requesting the lock over the file (i.e., delegating a goal of the shape `!lock(FName)` to the server). Then, it waits for the notification about the acquisition of exclusive access to the file. This notification is represented by a belief update event `+granted(FName)`. After the reception of this notification, the client agent writes the text into the file and requests the server to unlock the file (again, delegating this task as an achievement goal).

The Jason code for the server agent is shown in Fig. 6. The plan, referred to as `PSrv1`, handling the achievement goal to lock some file, `FName`, delegated from some client, `Client`, requires such a file to exist and not to be blocked by another agent. If these conditions hold, the first plan can be applied, which amounts to adding a mental note, `+blocked(Client, FName)`, recording that `Client` has exclusive access to the file `FName`. Then, it notifies the client by sending a tell message with the belief `granted(FName)`. The plan handling the achievement goal to unlock a file, referred to as `PSrv2`, checks whether the file exists and whether it is locked by the same agent that attempts to unlock it. The recipe provided by this plan implies erasing the aforementioned mental note that records the exclusive access granted to the agent `Client` over the file `FName` and, finally, notifying this client agent about the successful unlocking of the file.

```
+!lock(FName)[source(Client)] :     //PSrv1
   file(FName) & not blocked(_,FName)<-
       +blocked(Client,FName);
       .print("Agent ",Client," locks ",FName);
       .send(Client, tell, granted(FName)).

+!unlock(FName)[source(Client)] :  //PSrv2
   file(FName) & blocked(Client,FName) <-
       -blocked(Client,FName);
       .print("Agent ",Client," unlocks ",FName);
       .send(Client, tell, unlocked(FName)).
```

Fig. 6. Jason code for the file server agent

Unfortunately, according to the semantics of Jason, a possible execution of the above server, in the presence of another unrelated intention (I), is the following:

1. Two clients ($c1$ and $c2$) attempt to lock the same file, and send lock requests to the server.
2. The server receives both lock requests, and selects the event corresponding to the request from ($c1$), selects the plan corresponding to the case where the server is not blocked, and instantiates an intention corresponding to that plan.
3. However, instead of executing the intention corresponding to the new event, the unrelated intention I is chosen instead.
4. Next, the event corresponding to the lock event by $c2$ is chosen, and the corresponding new intention is executed, thus locking the resource.
5. Finally, the intention corresponding to the lock request by $c1$ is executed, but *in a state where the plan context is no longer valid*, as the server is now blocked (by beginning serving request $c2$).

The problem here stems from the fact that the evaluation of a plan context and the execution of its plan body are decoupled. The Jason semantics allow several iterations to take place between the one in which the plan context is evaluated and deemed applicable; and the iteration in which the plan is chosen for execution.

In our opinion this is a severe problem, making it quite hard to write reliable event handling code.

3.1   Jason Implementation Solution: Always Select Event Intentions

In the current Jason implementation this problem is addressed in the default intention selection function, by always placing the intention updated in the reasoning cycle first in the "intention queue", and using a round-robin intention scheduling strategy [1]. Note that a programmer can still replace this default intention selection function with another one which, albeit faithful to the semantics, suffers from the above problem.

3.2   eJason Solution: Consecutive Evaluation and Execution of a Plan

The original solution implemented in eJason was to examine the agent plan chosen to handle a particular event, and with a satisfied context. If this plan begins with a critical section, the corresponding intention is always executed first. Otherwise the evaluation of the context and the execution of the intention is, potentially, decoupled.

3.3 A Better Solution: Modifying the Jason Semantics

In retrospect the eJason implementation is not particularly satisfying. Having to specify a critical section for potentially every agent plan is a classical instance of unwanted boilerplate code. On the other hand the current Jason implementation solution is far from perfect too, as it, as far as we can understand, always gives priority to event handling over executing other intentions. Instead, in our opinion, it would be beneficial to modify the Jason semantics to remove the doubt whether a Jason implementation may ever decouple the execution of the plan context from beginning to execute the plan body. Permitting an interleaved execution of these basic plan steps complicates the task of a Jason programmer, with little gain.

Thus we argue for a Jason semantics change which: (i) strongly couples the execution of the plan context with the evaluation of the first part of the plan body, and (ii) does not give priority to handling events compared to executing intentions. We plan to publish the resulting semantics in a forthcoming publication.

4 Ensuring that Achievement Goals Are Not Dropped

In the example in Fig. 6, whenever a server agent gets the lock over a file, the requests from different client agents to lock the same file are disregarded, i.e., simply dropped, by the server agent, since the context of the relevant plan PSrv1 cannot be satisfied.

This is another illustration of the difficulties posed by concurrent, or nondeterministic execution. That is, if we cannot precisely control the order and timing in which beliefs are asserted, or retracted, we may fail to predict situations (system states) where a goal may incorrectly be dropped because its context is not satisfiable. In other words, we risk creating *fragile* programs which normally work well but, in rarely encountered scenarios, fail. For programming such concurrent systems we believe it would be advantageous to have goal matching mechanisms that are less sensitive to the way the belief base changes over time.

As a second example, illustrating the difficulties in programming plans that are robust to all different situations where they may be tried, consider the agent below:

```
at(office). // Initial belief

!go(home). // Initial goals
!read(book).

+!read(Item): at(home) <-
  read(Item).

+!go(home): at(office) <-
  drive(home).
```

This agent is initially at the office and possesses, simultaneously, the desires of going home and reading a book. There are two possible outcomes for the execution of this agent. In both of them, the agent goes home (as the plan to accomplish such desire is always applicable in the initial state). However, the agent does not always satisfy its desire of reading a book, since the plan for doing so may be evaluated too soon (in the office), and thus dropped.

A programmer intending the agent to achieve both goals has to ensure that the goals are selected in the desired order. This requires considering all the possible interleavings and implementing some suitable synchronisation mechanism. The complexity of this synchronisation increases exponentially with respect to the number of goals to synchronise.

4.1   Jason Solution: Explicitly Requeue Achievement Goals

The simplest solution to avoid dropping all the achievement goals that cannot be immediately handled due to the lack of applicable plans implies recording them within the mental state in order to pursue them in the future. This solution can be achieved, e.g., adding a new plan, PSrv3, whose context matches whenever the file is already blocked by a different client agent. Following this plan, the server agent records the requests that cannot be immediately served by, e.g., returning the achievement goal addition event to the set of events:

```
+!lock(FName)[source(Client)] :     //PSrv3
   file(FName) &  blocked(_,FName)<-
   !lock(FName)[source(Client)]. // requeue
```

This solution, and similar ones, require the programmer to introduce a number of "fail-back" plans whose context is satisfied whenever the contexts of other (preferred) plans are not. This can obscure the code, and moreover, is dangerously fragile as it is easy to overlook situations where plans may fail due to non-satisfied contexts.

Besides, note that by just enqueueing again the selected achievement goal addition event, the mental state of the agent is reinstated after a complete iteration of the reasoning cycle, hence consuming computational resources without changing the aforementioned mental state. Moreover, given the non-determinism of the selection functions, this event may be selected in consecutive iterations of the reasoning cycle, possibly enqueueing it in all such iterations (this behaviour is guaranteed if the belief base of the agent has not been updated, e.g., by other intentions, in-between), degrading the performance of the agent.

4.2   eJason Solution: Requeuing Not Applicable Achievement Goals

The alternative approach proposed in this chapter implies not generating a failure event for achievement goal addition events (i.e., events of the shape $\{+!g, \iota\}$). Instead, when one of these events is selected and there are no relevant or applicable plans for it, the event is returned to the set of events of the agent (i.e., requeued). This way, the programmer does not need to be concerned about the timing of the selection of these events as they can be selected again later. For instance, the agent in the simple example above would always go home and read a book (i.e., avoiding possible race conditions), hence resulting in a single possible outcome for the agent program.

Note that it could be the case that the intention of the programmer were to provide a means for the agent to abandon its desire of reading a book when not at home. In our opinion, such behaviour should not rely on the randomness of the intention selection function. Instead, the constructs already provided by the language, like the internal action *.drop_intention*, should be used. The following example shows how this construct can be used in this case:

```
at(office). // Initial belief

!go(home). // Initial goals
!read(book).

+!read(Item): at(home) <-
  read(Item).

+!read(Item): not at(home)<-
  .drop_intention(read(Item)).

+!go(home): at(office) <-
  drive(home).
```

Note that this alternative semantics is also available in the Jason implementation, by enabling a special configuration parameter, requeue, at startup. However, our proposal is to declare this alternative semantics *the standard Jason semantics*, as is the case in eJason.

5   Suspending Test Goals

Similar to the situation with achievement goals, whenever a programmer introduces a test goal, $?g$, into the body of a plan, p, the programmer must consider the possibility that such a test goal may fail (along with the whole plan). This failure occurs if the test, g, cannot be satisfied when the corresponding test goal addition event, $\{+?g, \iota\}$, is selected by the event selection function of the agent. Many Jason programs, we believe, could be written more clearly if test goals which cannot be satisfied are "suspended" until they become valid.

5.1   eJason Solution: Providing a New Suspending Test Operator

In eJason we have introduced a new operator "??" for expressing that we want a test goal to suspend until it is satisfiable. The semantics of a goal $??g$ is similar to the semantics of a $?g$ test goal. The difference lies in the treatment that the corresponding goal addition event, respectively $\{+??g, \iota\}$ and $\{+?g, \iota\}$, receives from the eJason interpreter. When the test g cannot be satisfied using the information in the belief base of the agent, for some test goal $\{+??g, \iota\}$, this event is returned to the set of events of the agent (note the similarity to the proposed semantics for achievement goal addition events). Therefore, this event will be selected again at a later iteration of the reasoning cycle.

To illustrate the behaviour of the operator let us code an agent that delegates some tasks $t1$ and $t2$ to other agents *alice* and *bob*, respectively, and then gathers the result of executing the tasks:

```
gather_results(Res1,Res2) :-
  result(t1, Res1) & result(t2, Res2).

+!task3(Result) <-
  .send(alice, achieve, t1);
  .send(bob, achieve, t2);
  ??gather_results(Res1,Res2);
  operation(Res1,Res2,Result).
```

Note that the new operator "??" is used to introduce a mechanism to suspend the execution of an intention until some conditions are met. This mechanism provides a functionality similar to that of the internal action `.wait(Event)`. However, while `.wait` relies on the occurrence of a single event or a logical expression (e.g., querying the belief base), as condition for the reactivation of an intention, the operator "??" establishes a goal g that must be matched in order to reactivate the intention.

The new operator can help simplify code, as shown in Fig. 7, where the behaviour of the client agent introduced in Fig. 5 no longer requires the inclusion of two separate, though semantically dependent, plans.

```
+!write(FName, Text) :true <-
  .send(server, achieve, lock(FName));
  ??granted(FName);
  write(Text, FName);
  .send(server, achieve, unlock(FName)).
```

Fig. 7. Modified client agents, using the "??" operator

6   The Reasoning Cycle of eJason Agents

The introduction of the new language constructs and semantics described above alters the interpreter of the agent, i.e., the number of state transitions in the Jason reasoning cycle have increased. In Fig. 8 the new transitions are depicted as dashed lines. The different steps that compose the reasoning cycle of a Jason agent are the following:

- **ProcMsg:** during this initial step, the agent obtains information from its environment (perception) and from the messages received from other agents. This information may update the belief base and provide new goals, generating the corresponding events in each case.
- **SelEv:** one of the unprocessed events is chosen to be processed during the current iteration. Such event is selected using an agent-specific *event selection function*.
- **RelPl:** the set of relevant plans for the event selected in the previous step is computed. If there is no relevant plan either the event is discarded (in the case of belief additions/deletions) or a failure event is generated (in the case of goal additions).
- **ApplPl:** the set of applicable plans is computed from the set of relevant plans. If the set of applicable plans is empty, either the selected event is discarded or a failure event is generated (for the same cases as before).
- **SelAppl:** one, and only one, of the applicable plans is selected using the agent-specific *option selection function*.
- **AddIM:** if the selected event possesses a related intention (i.e., it is a subgoal added during the execution of an instruction in the body of another plan), the selected applicable plan is put on top of such intention (recall that an intention is a stack of plans). Otherwise, a new intention, only containing the selected applicable plan, is added to the set of intentions.
- **SelInt:** if the set of intentions is empty, then a transition to the initial step is taken. Otherwise, an agent-specific *intention selection function* selects one intention from the set of intentions of the agent. Note that each intention represents a different focus of attention of the agent.
- **ExecInt:** the first formula in the body of the plan on top of the intention stack is executed, triggering some modification of the mental state or its environment (e.g., adding a new belief or sending a message), along with the generation of the corresponding event. If the formula executed is not a goal addition of type !g or ?g, such formula is removed from the body of the plan. Otherwise, the execution of the intention is suspended until the subgoal introduced is fully executed (the suspended intention appears as a related intention to the corresponding goal addition event). Note that only one formula is executed in each iteration of the cycle.
- **ClearInt:** if the body of the plan on top of the intention is not empty (i.e., the plan has not been fully executed) the intention is returned to the set of intentions and a new iteration starts. Otherwise, such plan is removed from the top of the intention stack. If there are more plans left in the intention, a transition to the initial step is taken. If the intention is empty, it is completely removed and a new iteration starts.

The new transitions, depicted in Fig. 8 as dashed transitions, are the following:

- When there are no relevant plans for either an achievement goal or a test goal introduced using the operator "??", the transition k is taken.
- During the execution of a critical section no new events are selected. After executing an action within a critical section, the transition l is taken.

- During the execution of a critical section, the focus of attention does not change. After the addition of the intended means for a goal within a critical section, the transition m is taken.
- During the execution of critical sections, the presence of failures introduces new transitions. The absence of relevant plans for an event causes transition n. The emptiness of the set of applicable plans causes transition o.

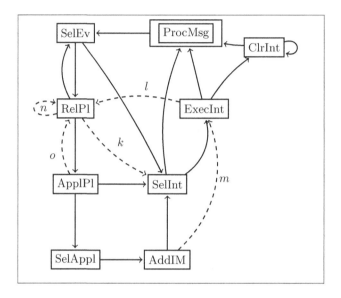

Fig. 8. Possible state transitions within a reasoning cycle in eJason.

7   Conclusions

In this chapter we have analysed a number of Jason mechanisms for controlling intra-agent concurrency and communication, and have identified a number of potential pitfalls these mechanisms can cause an inexpert Jason programmer. Moreover, we have suggested alternatives to these mechanism, which, in our opinion, may make the task of controlling and coordinating the concurrent activities of Jason (intra-agent) intentions easier.

For two of these mechanisms we advocate changing the standard Jason semantics. An alternative to doing so is to *configure* a standard Jason implementation by replacing e.g., the standard intention selection function with a custom one. However, we argue that there are dangers in such customizations too, as a (concurrent) Jason program cannot then be judged correct by itself, but must be judged in conjunction with the particular configuration it is designed to be run under.

In future work we aim to revise the Jason semantics to account for these new mechanisms, without relying on external customization functions.

Acknowledgments. This work has been partially funded by the Spanish MINECO project TIN2012-39391-C04-02 *STRONGSOFT*, and the Madrid Regional Government grant S2013/ICE-2731 *N-GREENS*. The authors would also like to thank Rafael H. Bordini for his useful comments.

References

1. Bordini, R.H., Wooldridge, M., Hübner, J.F.: Programming Multi-Agent Systems in AgentSpeak using Jason. Wiley Series in Agent Technology. Wiley, Chichester (2007)
2. Collier, R.W., Russell, S., Lillis, D.: Reflecting on agent programming with AgentSpeak (L). In: Chen, Q., Torroni, P., Villata, S., Hsu, J., Omicini, A. (eds.) PRIMA 2015. LNCS (LNAI), vol. 9387, pp. 351–366. Springer, Cham (2015). https://doi.org/10.1007/978-3-319-25524-8_22
3. Díaz, Á.F., Earle, C.B., Fredlund, L.Å.: eJason: an implementation of Jason in Erlang. In: Dastani, M., Hübner, J.F., Logan, B. (eds.) ProMAS 2012. LNCS (LNAI), vol. 7837, pp. 1–16. Springer, Heidelberg (2013). https://doi.org/10.1007/978-3-642-38700-5_1
4. Díaz, A.F.: eJason: a framework for distributed and fault-tolerant multi-agent systems. Ph.D. thesis, Universidad Politécnica de Madrid (2018)
5. Fredlund, L.Å., Mariño, J., Alborodo, R.N., Herranz, Á.: A testing-based approach to ensure the safety of shared resource concurrent systems. Proc. Inst. Mech. Eng. Part O: J. Risk Reliab. **230**(5), 457–472 (2016). https://doi.org/10.1177/1748006X15614231
6. Rao, A.S.: AgentSpeak(L): BDI agents speak out in a logical computable language. In: Van de Velde, W., Perram, J.W. (eds.) MAAMAW 1996. LNCS, vol. 1038, pp. 42–55. Springer, Heidelberg (1996). https://doi.org/10.1007/BFb0031845
7. van Riemsdijk, M.B., Dastani, M., Meyer, J.C.: Goals in conflict: semantic foundations of goals in agent programming. Auton. Agents Multi-Agent Syst. **18**(3), 471–500 (2009). https://doi.org/10.1007/s10458-008-9067-4
8. Shapiro, S., Sardiña, S., Thangarajah, J., Cavedon, L., Padgham, L.: Revising conflicting intention sets in BDI agents. In: van der Hoek, W., Padgham, L., Conitzer, V., Winikoff, M. (eds.) International Conference on Autonomous Agents and Multi-agent Systems, AAMAS 2012, Valencia, Spain, 4–8 June 2012, vol. 3, pp. 1081–1088. IFAAMAS (2012). http://dl.acm.org/citation.cfm?id=2343851
9. Thangarajah, J., Padgham, L.: Computationally effective reasoning about goal interactions. J. Autom. Reason. **47**(1), 17–56 (2011). https://doi.org/10.1007/s10817-010-9175-0
10. Zatelli, M.R., Hübner, J.F., Ricci, A., Bordini, R.H.: Conflicting goals in agent-oriented programming. In: Proceedings of the 6th International Workshop on Programming Based on Actors, Agents, and Decentralized Control, AGERE 2016, pp. 21–30. ACM, New York, NY, USA (2016). https://doi.org/10.1145/3001886.3001889

AgentSpeak(ER): Enhanced Encapsulation in Agent Plans

Alessandro Ricci[1]([⊠]), Rafael H. Bordini[2], Jomi F. Hübner[3], and Rem Collier[4]

[1] DISI, University of Bologna, Cesena, Italy
a.ricci@unibo.it
[2] POLI-PUCRS, Porto Alegre, Brazil
r.bordini@pucrs.br
[3] Federal University of Santa Catarina, Florianópolis, Brazil
jomi.hubner@ufsc.br
[4] University College of Dublin, Dublin, Ireland
rem.collier@ucd.ie

Abstract. In this chapter, we introduce AgentSpeak(ER), an extension of the AgentSpeak(L) language tailored to support encapsulation. The AgentSpeak(ER) extension allows for significantly improving the style of BDI agent programming along relevant aspects, including program modularity and readability, failure handling, and reactive as well as goal-based reasoning. The chapter introduces the novel language based on AgentSpeak, illustrates the features of the language through examples, and discuss results of a case study based on the implementation of the proposed language.

1 Introduction

AgentSpeak(L) has been introduced in [28] with the purpose of defining an expressive, abstract language capturing the main aspects of the Belief-Desire-Intention architecture [7,19], featuring a formally defined semantics and an abstract interpreter. The starting point to define the language were real-world implemented systems, namely the Procedural Reasoning System (PRS) [22] and the Distributed Multi-Agent Reasoning System (dMARS).

AgentSpeak(L) and PRS have become a main reference for implementing concrete Agent Programming Languages based on the BDI model: main examples are Jason [2,6] and ASTRA [14]. Besides Agent Programming Languages, the AgentSpeak(L) model has been adopted as the main reference to development several BDI agent-based frameworks and technologies [3,4] as well as serving as inspiration for theoretical work aiming to formalise aspects of BDI agents and agent programming languages [5,17,33].

Existing Agent Programming Languages extended the language with constructs and mechanisms making it practical from a programming point of view [2]. Besides, proposals in literature extended the model in order to make it effective for specific kinds of systems—e.g. real-time systems [32] – or to improve the structure of programs, e.g. in terms of modularity [23,26].

© Springer Nature Switzerland AG 2019
D. Weyns et al. (Eds.): EMAS 2018 Workshops, LNAI 11375, pp. 34–51, 2019.
https://doi.org/10.1007/978-3-030-25693-7_3

Along this line, in this chapter we describe a novel extension of the **AgentSpeak(L)** language—called **AgentSpeak(ER)**[1]—featuring *plan encapsulation*, i.e. the possibility to define plans that fully encapsulate the strategy to achieve the corresponding goals, integrating both the pro-active and the reactive behaviour. The motivation for this extension comes from authors' experience in applying such agent-oriented programming platforms in both academic and real-world projects (examples are described in [10, 14, 15]).

The extension is aimed at bringing a number of important benefits to agent programming based on the BDI model, namely:

- improving the overall readability of the agent source code, reducing fragmentation and increasing modularity;
- promoting a more goal-oriented programming style, enforcing yet preserving the possibility to specify purely reactive behaviour, properly encapsulated into plans for goals;
- improving intention management, enforcing a one-to-one relation between intentions and goals—so every intention is related to a (top-level) goal;
- improving failure handling, in particular simplifying the management of failures related to plans that react to environment events.

A first prototype implementation of the new language has been developed on top of Jason and ASTRA.

The remainder of the chapter is organised as follows: first we describe in details the motivations that lead to the proposal of a new AgentSpeak extension (Sect. 2). We then introduce **AgentSpeak(ER)**, defining the main concepts, syntax and informal semantics (Sect. 3). A case study about the implementation of the Minority Game is then used to discuss the approach (Sect. 4). Finally we conclude the chapter discussing related work (Sect. 5) and sketching future work (Sect. 6).

2   Motivation

The main motivation behind **AgentSpeak(ER)** comes from the experience using agent programming languages based on the **AgentSpeak(L)** model, **Jason** and ASTRA in particular. Yet, these issues are relevant for any language based on the BDI architecture.

In the BDI model, plans are meant to specify some means by which an agent can satisfy an end [28]. In **AgentSpeak(L)**, a plan consists of a rule of the kind e : c <- b. The head of a plan consists of a triggering event e and a context c. The triggering event specifies why the plan was triggered, i.e., the addition or deletion of a belief or goal. In the following, we refer to plans triggered by event goals as *g-plans*, and plans triggered by belief change (including percepts) as *e-plans*. The context specifies those beliefs that should hold given the agent's current belief base if the plan is to be triggered. The body of a plan is a sequence of actions or (sub-)goals.

In this approach—as well as in planning, in general—the *means* to achieve a goal (i.e., the plan body) is meant to be fully specified in terms of the actions the agent

---

[1] The ER suffix stands for "Encapsulated Reactivity".

should execute and the (sub-)goals the agent should achieve or test. In practice, when programming such systems, it is often the case that the strategy (the means) adopted to achieve some goal (the end) naturally includes reactions—i.e., reacting to events asynchronously perceived from the environment, including changes in the beliefs. This reflects more than just the ability of an agent to change/adapt its course of actions; it allows the integration of reactivity as a core ingredient of the strategy to achieve some goal. This revised notion of a plan is not just a programming feature; it also occurs naturally in human activity. For example, a fisherman with the goal of catching fish waits for the event of a tug on their line indicating a fish is on the hook. Reactivity is a key ingredient of many activities that we perform to achieve specific goals, not only to handle events that represents errors or unexpected situations (for the current courses of actions). It follows naturally that this is also an opportunity to extend the plan model so as to fully *encapsulate* reactions that are part of the strategy to achieve the goal, as well as the subgoals that are specific to that particular goal.

The use of e-plans to achieve goals is actually an important conceptual brick of the AgentSpeak(L) model. Let us consider the robot cleaning example used to describe plans in [28]. One of the plans is:

```
+location(waste,X) : location(robot,X) & location(bin,Y)
  <- pick(waste); !location(robot,Y); drop(waste).
```

That is, as soon as the robot perceives that there is waste at its location, then it can pick it up and bring it to the bin. This e-plan is an essential brick of the overall strategy to achieve the goal of cleaning the environment. The problem here is that it is an implicit rather than explicit goal of the agent (since it is an e-plan, it is executed regardless of the agent currently having the goal of keeping the environment clean). In practice, we adopt a maintenance goal [18] to clean the environment, which includes reacting to cleaning up waste when we see it. In the above program, this notion cannot be represented and remains in the mind of the programmer/designer; as there is no g-plan for it, there is no explicit trace in the agent mental structures about this goal.

This problem can also be illustrated with the following scenario. Consider an agent that includes a set of plans (a module written by a third party) to handle social obligations. The module has several e-plans for different types of obligations:

```
+obligation(Ag,committed(Goal)) : .my_name(Ag)       <- ...
+obligation(Ag,achieve(Goal))   : .my_name(Ag)       <- ...
-obligation(Ag,Goal) : .my_name(Ag) & .intend(Goal) <- ...
```

If for some reason during its execution an agent decides not to follow these plans anymore (e.g. it chooses to become disobedient), it is difficult to "disable" the behaviour of the above plans. Either these plans have to be changed to consider a particular state of the agent or the agent removes all these plans from its plan library. Neither option is simple to program. Although we can solve the problem, the lack of an explicit goal stating that the agent intends to be obedient is the cause of this problem.

Besides maintenance goal, also for achievement goals we see benefits in encapsulating the reactive behaviour in the corresponding plans. Let's consider, as a very simple example, yet capturing the point, the goal of printing down all the numbers between N and 1, stopping if/when a 'stop' percept is perceived. In AgentSpeak(L) this task can be effectively tackled using only g-plans:

```
+!print_nums(0).
+!print_nums(_) : stop.
+!print_nums(N) : not stop <- println(N); !print_nums(N-1).
```

The action `println` is meant to print the number on standard output. Here we exploit the fact that the BDI reasoning cycle automatically updates beliefs from percepts, and this allows us to write down structured plans with courses of actions that change according to the environment, by exploiting goals/subgoals and contexts. More generally, in AgentSpeak(L) the suggested approach to realise structured activities whose flow can be environment dependent is by means of (sub-)goals and corresponding plans with a proper context. In some cases however this approach is not fully effective, and *e-plans* are needed, in particular every time we need to react *while executing the body of a plan*. A typical case occurs when we have actions (or subgoals) in a plan that could take a long time to complete. For instance, suppose that instead of simply printing we have a long-term `elab` goal (it could be even an action):

```
+!print_nums(0).
+!print_nums(N) : stop.
+!print_nums(N) : not stop <- !elab(N); !print_nums(N-1).
```

Suppose that, realistically, we cannot spread/pollute plans about the goal `!elab` with a stop-dependent behaviour. To solve this problem, using AgentSpeak(L) and in BDI architectures an e-plan can be introduced, using e.g. internal actions to act on the current ongoing intention:

```
+!print_nums(0).
+!print_nums(N) <- !elab(N); !print_nums(N-1).
+stop <- .drop_intention(print_nums(_)).
```

The problem here is that the e-plan `+stop <- ...` is part of the strategy to achieve the goal `!print_nums`, however it is encoded as a separate unrelated plan.

Finally, the encapsulation of also impacts plan failures handling, which is a very important aspect of agent programming. In the Jason dialect of AgentSpeak(L), we can define plans that handle the failure of the execution of g-plans (generating the event `-!g`), but not of e-plans. For example, if there is a problem in the println action in:

```
+stop <- println("stopped").
```

the plan execution fails, without any possibility to react and handle the failure. In order to handle this, a programmer is forced to structure every e-plan with failure handling using a subgoal:

```
+stop <- !manage_stop.
+!manage_stop <- println("stopped").
-!manage_stop <- println("failure").
```

This contributes to making the program longer and verbose, besides increasing the number of plans to be managed by the interpreter.

To summarise, this is the set of key issues identified for the basic plan model in the practice of agent programming:

Lack of encapsulation: The strategy to achieve a goal is fragmented among multiple plans, not explicitly related to each other.

Implicit vs. Explicit goals: Some parts of an agent program may have plans for which the goal is implicit.

Difficult failure handling: Failures/errors generated in the body of e-plan cannot be directly captured.

Besides the pure programming perspective, it is worth noting that these issues can affect the software engineering process for agent development. In particular, at the design perspective, it is natural to specify coarse-grained plans fully encapsulating the strategy to achieve or maintain goals. It would be important then to keep as much as possible the same level of abstraction when going from the design to programming, and at runtime too, to support agent reasoning.

3   The AgentSpeak(ER) Proposal

To overcome the problems discussed above, we consider two key changes in the plan model. The first one is to extend the plans beyond the simple sequence of actions and goals, so as to include also the possibility to specify reactive behaviour encapsulated within the plan. Coherently, with the AgentSpeak(L) model, such a behaviour can be expressed in terms of e-plans. Accordingly, a plan becomes the *scope* of (*i*) a sequence of actions (referred as *body actions*), (*ii*) a set of *e-plans*, specifying a reactive behaviour which is active at runtime only when the plan is in execution, and (*iii*) a set of *g-plans*, specifying plans to achieve subgoals that are relevant only in the scope of this plan. The e-plans and g-plans are referred to as *sub-plans*. The sub-plans may include also reactions to failures occurring when the plan is executed.

The second change is enforcing that e-plans—as pieces of reactive behaviours—must always be defined in the context of a g-plan. We are thus enforcing the principle that an agent does (and reacts) always because of a goal to achieve or maintain. This ensures that programmers explicitly specify what is the goal to achieve even when defining a purely reactive behaviour. In so doing, at runtime every intention[2] has an associated goal being pursued.

In the remainder of the section, we first describe in detail the syntax and informal semantics of the new plan model, including simple examples, and then we discuss the key benefits.

3.1   Informal Syntax and Semantics

At the top level, an AgentSpeak(ER) program is a collection of g-plans, whose syntax is exemplified below:

---

[2] As in AgentSpeak(L), an intention is the result of the deliberation to commit to some desire. Briefly, if the agent has an applicable plan for a goal event (i.e. a desire), it commits to it by creating an intention based on that plan and starts executing it.

```
/*  g-plans to achieve goal g in context c */

+!g : c <: gc {

  <- a; b; ?g1; !g1; !!g2. // plan body (optional).

  /* e-plans */

  +e1 : c1 <- b1.
  +e2 : c2 <- b2.

  /* e-plans catching failures */

  -!g[error(ia_failed)] : ...
    <- ... catches from failures

  /* further g-plans */

  +!g1 : c1 <: gc1 { ... }

  +!k : true <: b(10) {
    <- a,b,c.
    +e3 : c3 <- b3. // possible old-style plans
  }
}
```

Like in AgentSpeak(L), a g-plan is defined with a head and a body. Besides the triggering event and the context, in AgentSpeak(ER) the head has a third new element: a *goal condition*, optionally written after <:, with the same syntax as the context. While the context is a pre-condition to select a plan as applicable for an event, the goal condition is a post-condition that defines when the goal can be considered as achieved[3]. Any goal created based on this g-plan is considered achieved if and only if this condition holds. If no goal condition is specified, the goal is considered achieved as soon as the body execution completes, as usual in AgentSpeak(L). If the case that no plan body is specified as well, then the goal condition is considered false—it is the case of never-ending maintenance goal. However, if a goal condition is defined, having finished the body execution is not sufficient to deactivate the goal. Notice that if the goal condition becomes true while the body actions are being executed, the execution ceases immediately, since the goal being achieved means no further action would be necessary.

In AgentSpeak(ER) the body defines the g-plan scope enclosed by '{' and '}' and is composed of the body actions (after '<-' and before '.') as well as sub-plans. Like in AgentSpeak(L), as soon as a g-plan is instantiated, the body actions start to execute. The body actions can be empty—this is the case of g-plans expressing a purely

---

[3] Or considered impossible to achieve, or the motivation for the goal no longer holds, etc. Programmers can use this for any condition that implies the goal should no longer be pursued. Note that, when programming declaratively, this condition is likely to include the goal in the triggering event itself (as believed to be true).

reactive behaviour. The sub-plans of the g-plan are considered as relevant only for events produced by the g-plan execution, since they are in the scope of the g-plan.

While a g-plan is executing, it can be *interrupted* by events relevant for its e-plans. When the agent perceives an event and an e-plan from g-plan is applicable according to its specified context, then the execution of the g-plan body is suspended until the body of the e-plan finishes its execution. In AgentSpeak(L), other plans do also interrupt the execution of a plan in the case of subgoals. For example, in the body "a1; a2; !g1; a3", g1 is a sub-goal and thus the action a3 is executed after g1 is achieved. The plan body execution in interrupted synchronously. In AgentSpeak(ER) this uniformly occurs also with any kind of events, not only sub-goal events; that is, the body actions can be interrupted to react to events coming from the environment. However, in this case the interruption is *asynchronous* – the point where the body actions is interrupted is unknown, and depends on the environment, at runtime.

3.2   Examples

To give a more concrete taste of the language, we consider again the examples seen in Sect. 2, now rewritten in AgentSpeak(ER). The robot cleaning example becomes:

```
+!clean_env  {
   +location(waste,X) : location(robot,X) & location(bin,Y)
      <- pick(waste); !location(robot,Y); drop(waste).
}
```

We can give an explicit reason for the reactive behaviour by encapsulating the e-plan inside a g-plan, with an explicit goal clean_env. Setting the goal condition to false means that the plan execution is going to last forever. It is a way of implementing some form of maintenance goal. This is also a particular case where the body of the g-plan does not have any actions.

The print_nums example seen before can be rewritten to fully encapsulate the strategy in the same g-plan:

```
+!print_nums(0)  :- +done.
+!print_nums(N) <: stop | done  {
   <- !elab(N); !print_nums(N-1).
   +!elab(M) <- ...
}
```

The goal print_nums is achieved either by the perception of stop or done by the execution of its body actions. In case we want to take some action to react to stop, we can introduce an e-plan as follows:

```
+!print_nums(0).
+!print_nums(N) <: done {
   <- !elab(N); !print_nums(N-1).
   +!elab(N) <- ...
   +stop <- println("stopped"); +done.
}
```

For the example of plans to handle social obligations, we can define an explicit goal by encapsulating the e-plans in a g-plan as follows:

```
+!be_obedient {
    +obligation(Ag,committed(Goal)) : .my_name(Ag)         <- ...
    +obligation(Ag,achieve(Goal))   : .my_name(Ag)         <- ...
    -obligation(Ag,Goal) : .my_name(Ag) & .intend(Goal) <- ...
}
```

Now the agent can disable these plans by simply performing . drop_ intention(be_obedient), and resuming its obedient behaviour by adopting the goal !be_obedient, and it can also check whether it is being obedient by testing .intend(be_obedient).

With the new language, we can program different kinds of commitments to goals [13,34] by exploiting the goal condition. For instance, the Single Minded Commitment for goal g can be programmed as:

```
+!g <: g | f {
    ...
}
```

where f states when the goal becomes impossible. The agent commits to achieve g until g is believed either true or impossible to achieve. To program this kind of commitment in AgentSpeak(L), we have to follow some programming patterns requiring extra plans (three extra plans as shown in [21]).

3.3 Failure Management

Failures generated by the execution of actions of sub-plans for a goal g can be handled and managed by:

– subplans of type -!g listed in the body of the g-plan;
– plans at the same level of +!g, if the event is not managed within the body.

In terms of the new language style, we can keep the failure plans within the scope of the g-plan. However, it is also reasonable that if we define a plan for +!g at a certain level of a g-plan tree[4], it might make sense for the programmer if the plans for -!g are all placed at the same level (specially if the programmer is influenced by the style of the Jason variant of AgentSpeak).

3.4 Key Points

We conclude this section by summarising the key points brought out by AgentSpeak(ER):

Encapsulation – The strategy to achieve a goal is encapsulated in one or multiple g-plans, each embedding also the reactive behaviour which is part of the strategy. The effect is to reduce code fragmentation, improving its understanding.

---

[4] Note that g-plans within g-plans now implicitly form a plan tree for a top-level goal, and the plan library is thus a forest of such trees.

Explicit goals – Every behaviour of the agent is now explicitly related to some goal to achieve. This promotes a more goal-oriented programming style, yet preserving the possibility to easily define g-plans based on purely reactive strategies; this allows the agent to better *manage* its intentions. For instance, a programmer can now do a simple .drop_intention(g) to disable the behavior of e-plans embedded in the corresponding g-plans. In AgentSpeak(L), the relation goal-intention is not one-to-one. AgentSpeak(L) can have intentions from e-plans and so intentions without a explicitly represented goal. In AgentSpeak(ER) there is a one-to-one relation between goals and intentions. All intentions come from goals (only explicit goals are allowed). Primitives to handle goals can thus handle *all* intentions. In AgentSpeak(L), primitives to handle goals can manage a limited set of the intentions (those created from goal addition plans).

Failure handling – Thanks to explicit goals, failures generated in the body of an e-plan can now be directly captured and managed by failure recovery plans defined for g-plan, without the need for auxiliary goals and plans to be introduced.

Coarse-grained intentions – In AgentSpeak(L), each e-plan in execution has its own intention/stack, which runs concurrently to the other intentions. Conceptually, this follows the idea that the management of environment events are not part of an existing overall plan to achieve some goal. In the new model instead, an e-plan inside a g-plan is meant to specify a behaviour that is useful for achieving the goal of the g-plan, so part of the same intention. For this reason, if an e-plan (sub-plan) inside a g-plan in execution is triggered, no new intentions are generated and the body of the sub-plan is placed on the top of the stack of the same intention. The new model leads then to more coarse-grained intentions.

As a final remark, the choice of constraining the definition of e-plans to be inside g-plans deserves some further clarification. Apparently, it may seems a limitation, making the approach not capable of capturing purely reactive behaviour, enforcing a designer to define artificial goals. However, in software development a designer has always a goal in mind when writing down the behaviour of an agent: this is true also for purely reactive agents. This is not true if we consider e.g., agent-based modelling and simulation, where the definition of the behaviour of an agent could be driven by the description of a real-world phenomena, a local behaviour. The extension presented in this chapter is explicitly targeted to the design and programming of agents as software components responsible of autonomously performing some tasks. The extension then allows to enforce a better discipline, enforcing the designer to give always an explicit representation (at the programming level) about the tasks (goals) she/he has in mind.

4   First Implementation and Discussion

In order to play with the new language and do a first evaluation, a first prototype implementation has been developed on top of both Jason [2] and ASTRA [14][5]. The Jason extension has been used to implement the examples used in this chapter. The ASTRA extension is syntactically different to the examples provided in Sect. 3, being it adapted to the syntactic style adopted in ASTRA. An example follows:

---

[5] The Jason extension is available here: https://github.com/agentspeakers/jason-er.

```
g-plan +!g() : c <: gc {
  body {
    // main plan body goes here...
    a; b; !g1(); !!g2();
  }

  /* e-plans */
  rule +e1 : c1 { b1; }
  rule +e2 : c2 { b2; }
}
```

The different syntax however does not impact the associated semantics. In the remainder of this section we show the benefits of **AgentSpeak(ER)** by considering an existing program, rewritten with the new language. ASTRA is adopted as implementation language—however the same discussion would apply by considering Jason as implementation language.

4.1 Minority Game

We have adapted a simulation of the Minority Game (MG), a well-known model for evaluating collective behaviour of agents competing for finite resources [24]. The game involves an odd number of agents competing for a resource over a series of rounds. For a round, each agent makes a binary decision (yes/no). At the end of the round, the bids are counted, and the agents that are in the minority win. The game has been applied mainly in the areas such as modelling financial markets [11] and traffic simulation [12].

The existing implementation (see Fig. 1) consists of 3 types of agent: the *compere* agent, who is responsible for managing the game (starting rounds, evaluating bids, ...); the *player* agents, who implement a set of MG strategies; and the *main* agent, which is responsible for configuring the game (creating and configuring the compere and player agents). Interaction between the compere and the players is through a shared game-board artifact implemented using CArtAgO [29].

The existing implementation currently consists of 2 types of plan: *configuration plans*, one of which is called when the agent is created; and *strategy plans* which implement the various potential strategies that the agent can use. A subset of the ASTRA implementation of the *player* agent is given below:

```
rule +!main(["bestplay", [int t, int h]]) {
  -+strategy("bestplay"); !setup_tactic(t, h); !setup();
}
rule +!main([string strategy, []]) {
  -+strategy(strategy); !setup();
}
rule +!setup_tactic(0,int h) {}
rule +!setup_tactic(int t2, int h) {
  list hist = [];
  int i=0;
  while (i<h) {
    hist = hist + [M.randomInt()
    i++;
```

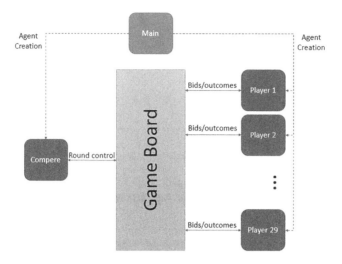

Fig. 1. Minority game agent architecture

```
    }
    +strategy(t2, hist, M.randomInt()
    +score(t2, 0);
    !setup_tactic(t2-1, h);
}

rule $cartago.signal(string id, play()) : strategy("bestplay") {
    cartago.results(java.util.ArrayList history);

    int max_len = -1; int max_choice = -1; int max_score = -1;
    foreach (strategy(int s, list hist, int c) & score(s, int sc)) {
        cartago.match(history, P.fromASTRAList(hist), int len);
        if ((len > max_len) | ((len == max_len) & (max_score < sc))) {
            max_choice = c; max_score = sc; max_len = len;
        }
    }
    cartago.bid(S.name(), max_choice);
}

rule $cartago.signal(string id, winner(int bid)) : strategy("bestplay") {
    foreach (strategy(int s, list hist, bid) & score(s, int sc)) {
        -score(s, sc); +score(s, sc+1);
    }
}
```

In the above code, the !main(...) plans are the configuration plans. The !setup_tactic(...) plans are part of the bestplay strategy but are also used for configuration. This is because, unlike simpler strategies such as *Random Bid* and *Tit-for-Tat*, the best play strategy requires that a set of random strategies be created as part of its configuration. In best play, a random strategy is a randomly generated set of h outcomes combined with a recommended next move. Each strategy has an associated score which is used to help determine how successful each strategy is.

The strategy plans are the $cartago.signal(...) plans, which handle the play() and winner(...) signals respectively. These signals are generated by the game board when the *compere* agent performs operations on it (e.g. when a round starts/ends). For bestplay, the play() signal triggers a behaviour where the agent compares the game outcome history against its strategies and picks the strategy that best fits the history (longest matching subsequence). The corresponding next move is played (via the bid() artifact operation). Conversely, the winner(...) signal triggers a behaviour where the agent updating the score for all strategies that lead to bid being selected.

Some of the key points to note when reviewing the above code are: (i) a custom plan is needed to handle the !main(...) goal in the case of the bestplay strategy because it requires some custom initialisation; (ii) a strategy belief is required to enable the identification of the plans that are relevant to the selected strategy; and (iii) there is no guarantee that these plans will be grouped together in the implemented agent. They could be spread throughout the agents codebase making it difficult to read and understand the overall behaviour.

In the AgentSpeak(ER) implementation, we still maintain the two types of plan, however instead on needing multiple plans to capture a strategy, the entire strategy is now encapsulated within a single g-plan (of course the other plans still exist as subplans of the g-plan). The snippet of code below contains the AgentSpeak(ER) code to the ASTRA example given above:

```
rule +!main([string strategy, list config]) {
  !win(strategy, config);
}

g-rule +!win("bestplay", [int t, int h]) {
  body {
    !setup_tactic(t);
  }

  rule +!setup_tactic(0) {}
  rule +!setup_tactic(int t2) {
    list hist = [];
    int i=0;
    while (i<h) {
      hist = hist + [M.randomInt()
      i++;
    }
    +strategy(t2, hist, M.randomInt()
    +score(t2, 0);
    !setup_tactic(t2-1);
  }

  rule $cartago.signal(string id, play()) {
    cartago.results(java.util.ArrayList history);
```

```
    int max_len = -1; int max_choice = -1; int max_score = -1;
    foreach (strategy(int s, list hist, int c) & score(s, int sc)) {
      cartago.match(history, P.fromASTRAList(hist), int len);
      if ((len > max_len) | ((len == max_len) & (max_score < sc))) {
        max_choice = c; max_score = sc; max_len = len;
      }
    }
    cartago.bid(S.name(), max_choice);
  }

  rule $cartago.signal(string id, winner(int bid)) {
    foreach (strategy(int s, list hist, bid) & score(s, int sc)) {
      -score(s, sc); +score(s, sc+1);
    }
  }
}
```

As can be seen from the above snippet of code. The implementation of the two types of agent is quite similar. In fact many of the rule implementations have not changed significantly. However, there are a few interesting observations regarding the revised implementation: *(i)* the complexity of the plan contexts were simplified when using g-plans because the g-plan itself provided some of the context; *(ii)* the number of arguments passed as parameters was reduced, again because the scope of the parameters of the g-plan was the plan body *and* all of its sub-plans; *(iii)* the total number of rules under consideration on each iteration was significantly less because only the rules within an active g-plan were considered by the agent. This means that, when an agent has multiple strategies, only the rules relating to the active strategy will be considered, whereas in ASTRA, all rules are always considered.

4.2 A Note on Performance

After reviewing our new language, it became apparent that (i) it was reducing the number of plans that need to be evaluated on each iteration; but (ii) the introduction of a goal condition introduces a significant new overhead because it must be evaluated on each iteration. As a result, it was decided that a comparison of the new and old languages be carried out. Initially, we compared interpreter cycle execution time and the number of iterations based on a single configuration of the MG with 29 players and 1000 rounds. For our results, we averaged the values across all 29 players and repeated the experiment 5 times.

Results of our initial comparison can be found in Table 1. The difference in the number of cycles is due primarily to the scheduling algorithm used by ASTRA, which suspends agents that have no sensors (perceptors) and whose event and intention queues

Table 1. Comparing ASTRA and AgentSpeak(ER)

	ASER	ASTRA
Cycle time (ms)	0.0017	0.0036
Cycles	293,772	62,880
Elapsed execution time (ms)	495.22	229.29
Unix (timed)	16 s	15 s

are empty. The impact of this is that ASTRA is generally more efficient than AgentSpeak(ER). Due to the small but consistent difference in performance between the unix timing of the two experiments, we then explored how increasing the number of rounds affected performance. Results for this are shown in Table 2.

Table 2. ASTRA vs AgentSpeak(ER) performance

	1000	2000	3000	4000	10000
ASER (s)	15.514	30.251	44.202	57.736	140.059
ASTRA (s)	14.893	28.232	42.168	56.453	137.379
Diff. (%)	4.2%	6.8%	4.8%	2.3%	2.0%

This second table shows that the introduction of g-rules in AgentSpeak(ER) has only a small impact on performance. Here, it is almost linear. Further, ASTRA shows a marginal performance improvement of between 2–6%.

While this is not intended to be a thorough evaluation of AgentSpeak(ER), it is useful because it hints that the use of goal conditions does not significantly impact the performance of the language. It must also be noted that the prototype implementation is not as mature as the ASTRA implementation—interpreter optimisations could further reduce the difference in performance.

5   Related Work

AgentSpeak(ER) is primarily related to work in literature focusing on improving cognitive BDI agent programming [3,4]. A main aspect widely discussed and developed in the literature is *modularity* [8,9,16,20,23,25–27,30]. Modules are typically used as a mechanism to structure agent programs in separate parts (modules), each encapsulating cognitive components such as beliefs, goals, and plans that together model a specific functionality and can be used to handle specific situations or tasks [16]. From a software engineering point of view, modules allow a programmer to focus on those skills that are required to handle a situation [20]. In this perspective, AgentSpeak(ER) improves modularity in BDI-based agent programming languages based on the PRS and AgentSpeak(L) model by devising coarse-grained plans encapsulating goal-oriented *and* reactive behaviour. This approach can be integrated with existing more comprehensive proposal about modularity in AgentSpeak(L) such as [23], where a module is meant to be a composable subset of the functionality of an agent, represented by a functional unit encapsulating goals, beliefs and plans.

Besides research works on modularity, AgentSpeak(ER) is related to existing BDI agent programming languages extending the basic plan model as found in the original proposal of AgentSpeak(L). In this context, a main reference is CANPlan [31], a BDI-style agent-oriented programming language enhancing usual BDI programming style with declarative goals, look-ahead planning, and failure handling. It allows programmers to mix both procedural and declarative aspects of goals, enabling reasoning about properties of goals and decoupling plans from what these plans are meant to achieve. The lookahead planning makes it possible to guarantee goal achievability and avoid undesirable situations. The plan model adopted in CANPlan is analogous to the AgentSpeak(L) one. Each plan is characterised by a plan rule $e(t) : \psi (xt, y) \leftarrow P(xt, y, z).$, where P is a "reasonable strategy" to follow when ψ is believed true in order to resolve/achieve the event. P can be a rich composition of actions but not reactions. Reactive behaviours can be expressed instead—like in AgentSpeak(L) and in the basic BDI—as separate plans handling belief updates corresponding to environment events.

6   Conclusion

In this chapter, we introduced AgentSpeak(ER), a novel extension of the classical AgentSpeak(L) language. The language provides encapsulation for agent goals, which clearly improves legibility and reusability of AgentSpeak code. Furthermore, the new language improves some of the shortcomings of AgentSpeak in regards to goal orientation and declarative goals by ensuring that all reactive plans are also associated with general goals, providing a "goal condition" which means goals can be still active even though presently there is no action for the agent to take towards that goal, and allowing external events (i.e. reactions to changes in beliefs) to trigger various plans, for all the goals it might be relevant. The proposal was implemented and on top of both the ASTRA and the Jason platforms.

As with any new programming language, there is much future work, some in fact ongoing. We are currently refining both the ASTRA and Jason implementation, trying to make a few optimisations to improve the evaluation results we reported in this chapter. A comparison of the performances of the two implementations might lead to insights that might improve the implementation of the platforms themselves.

More generally, full understanding and evaluation of a programming language takes many years. We expect in the long term to use AgentSpeak(ER) in the practical development of multi-agent systems, both for real-world systems and also academic ones (e.g., for the multi-agent programming contest [1]). However, besides the actual programming practice, we expect AgentSpeak(ER) to contribute to formal work as well. Assessing how formal verification of AgentSpeak(ER) systems compares to the original language is also planned as future work.

References

1. Ahlbrecht, T., Fiekas, N., Dix, J.: Multi-agent programming contest 2016. Int. J. Agent-Oriented Softw. Eng. **6**(1), 58–85 (2018). https://doi.org/10.1504/IJAOSE.2018.089597
2. Bordini, R.H., Hübner, J.F.: BDI agent programming in AgentSpeak using *Jason*. In: Toni, F., Torroni, P. (eds.) CLIMA 2005. LNCS (LNAI), vol. 3900, pp. 143–164. Springer, Heidelberg (2006). https://doi.org/10.1007/11750734_9
3. Bordini, R.H., Dastani, M., Dix, J., El Fallah Seghrouchni, A. (eds.): Multi-Agent Programming: Languages, Platforms and Applications. Multiagent Systems, Artificial Societies, and Simulated Organizations, vol. 15. Springer, Boston (2005). https://doi.org/10.1007/b137449
4. Bordini, R.H., Dastani, M., Dix, J., El Fallah Seghrouchni, A. (eds.): Multi-Agent Programming: Languages, Tools and Applications. Springer, Boston (2009). https://doi.org/10.1007/978-0-387-89299-3
5. Bordini, R.H., Fisher, M., Visser, W., Wooldridge, M.: Verifying multi-agent programs by model checking. Auton. Agents Multi-Agent Syst. **12**(2), 239–256 (2006). https://doi.org/10.1007/s10458-006-5955-7
6. Bordini, R.H., Hübner, J.F., Wooldrige, M.: Programming Multi-Agent Systems in AgentSpeak Using Jason. Wiley Series in Agent Technology. Wiley, Chichester (2007). http://jason.sf.net/jBook
7. Bratman, M.E., Israel, D.J., Pollack, M.E.: Plans and resource-bounded practical reasoning. Comput. Intell. **4**, 349–355 (1988). https://doi.org/10.1111/j.1467-8640.1988.tb00284.x
8. Braubach, L., Pokahr, A., Lamersdorf, W.: Extending the capability concept for flexible BDI agent modularization. In: Bordini, R.H., Dastani, M.M., Dix, J., El Fallah Seghrouchni, A. (eds.) ProMAS 2005. LNCS (LNAI), vol. 3862, pp. 139–155. Springer, Heidelberg (2006). https://doi.org/10.1007/11678823_9
9. Busetta, P., Howden, N., Rönnquist, R., Hodgson, A.: Structuring BDI agents in functional clusters. In: Jennings, N.R., Lespérance, Y. (eds.) ATAL 1999. LNCS (LNAI), vol. 1757, pp. 277–289. Springer, Heidelberg (2000). https://doi.org/10.1007/10719619_21
10. Cardoso, R.C., Krausburg, T., Baségio, T.L., Engelmann, D.C., Hübner, J.F., Bordini, R.H.: SMART-JaCaMo: an organization-based team for the multi-agent programming contest. Ann. Math. Artif. Intell. **84**(1–2), 75–93 (2018)
11. Challet, D., Marsili, M., Zhang, Y.C., et al.: Minority games: interacting agents in financial markets. OUP Catalogue (2013)
12. Chmura, T., Pitz, T.: Minority game: experiments and simulations of traffic scenarios. Technical report, Bonn Econ Discussion Papers (2004)
13. Cohen, P.R., Levesque, H.J.: Intention is choice with commitment. Artif. Intell. **42**, 213–261 (1990)
14. Collier, R.W., Russell, S., Lillis, D.: Reflecting on agent programming with AgentSpeak(L). In: Chen, Q., Torroni, P., Villata, S., Hsu, J., Omicini, A. (eds.) PRIMA 2015. LNCS (LNAI), vol. 9387, pp. 351–366. Springer, Cham (2015). https://doi.org/10.1007/978-3-319-25524-8_22
15. Croatti, A., Montagna, S., Ricci, A.: A personal medical digital assistant agent for supporting human operators in emergency scenarios. In: Montagna, S., Abreu, P.H., Giroux, S., Schumacher, M.I. (eds.) A2HC/AHEALTH -2017. LNCS (LNAI), vol. 10685, pp. 59–75. Springer, Cham (2017). https://doi.org/10.1007/978-3-319-70887-4_4
16. Dastani, M., Steunebrink, B.: Modularity in BDI-based multi-agent programming languages. In: 2009 IEEE/WIC/ACM International Joint Conference on Web Intelligence and Intelligent Agent Technology, vol. 2, pp. 581–584, September 2009

17. Dennis, L.A., Farwer, B., Bordini, R.H., Fisher, M., Wooldridge, M.: A common semantic basis for BDI languages. In: Dastani, M., El Fallah Seghrouchni, A., Ricci, A., Winikoff, M. (eds.) ProMAS 2007. LNCS (LNAI), vol. 4908, pp. 124–139. Springer, Heidelberg (2008). https://doi.org/10.1007/978-3-540-79043-3_8

18. Duff, S., Harland, J., Thangarajah, J.: On proactivity and maintenance goals. In: Proceedings of the Fifth International Joint Conference on Autonomous Agents and Multiagent Systems, AAMAS 2006, pp. 1033–1040. ACM, New York (2006). http://doi.acm.org/10.1145/1160633.1160817

19. Georgeff, M.P., Lansky, A.L.: Reactive reasoning and planning. In: Proceedings of the Sixth National Conference on Artificial Intelligence - Volume 2, AAAI 1987, pp. 677–682. AAAI Press (1987), http://dl.acm.org/citation.cfm?id=1863766.1863818

20. Hindriks, K.: Modules as policy-based intentions: modular agent programming in GOAL. In: Dastani, M., El Fallah Seghrouchni, A., Ricci, A., Winikoff, M. (eds.) ProMAS 2007. LNCS (LNAI), vol. 4908, pp. 156–171. Springer, Heidelberg (2008). https://doi.org/10.1007/978-3-540-79043-3_10

21. Hübner, J.F., Bordini, R.H., Wooldridge, M.: Programming declarative goals using plan patterns. In: Baldoni, M., Endriss, U. (eds.) DALT 2006. LNCS (LNAI), vol. 4327, pp. 123–140. Springer, Heidelberg (2006). https://doi.org/10.1007/11961536_9

22. Ingrand, F.F., Georgeff, M.P., Rao, A.S.: An architecture for real-time reasoning and system control. IEEE Expert. Intell. Syst. Their Appl. **7**(6), 34–44 (1992). https://doi.org/10.1109/64.180407

23. Madden, N., Logan, B.: Modularity and compositionality in Jason. In: Braubach, L., Briot, J.-P., Thangarajah, J. (eds.) ProMAS 2009. LNCS (LNAI), vol. 5919, pp. 237–253. Springer, Heidelberg (2010). https://doi.org/10.1007/978-3-642-14843-9_15

24. Moro, E.: The minority game: an introductory guide. arXiv preprint cond-mat/0402651 (2004)

25. Novák, P., Dix, J.: Modular BDI architecture. In: Proceedings of the Fifth International Joint Conference on Autonomous Agents and Multiagent Systems, AAMAS 2006, pp. 1009–1015. ACM, New York (2006). http://doi.acm.org/10.1145/1160633.1160814

26. Nunes, I.: Improving the design and modularity of BDI agents with capability relationships. In: Dalpiaz, F., Dix, J., van Riemsdijk, M.B. (eds.) EMAS 2014. LNCS (LNAI), vol. 8758, pp. 58–80. Springer, Cham (2014). https://doi.org/10.1007/978-3-319-14484-9_4

27. Ortiz-Hernández, G., Hübner, J.F., Bordini, R.H., Guerra-Hernández, A., Hoyos-Rivera, G.J., Cruz-Ramírez, N.: A namespace approach for modularity in BDI programming languages. In: Baldoni, M., Müller, J.P., Nunes, I., Zalila-Wenkstern, R. (eds.) EMAS 2016. LNCS (LNAI), vol. 10093, pp. 117–135. Springer, Cham (2016). https://doi.org/10.1007/978-3-319-50983-9_7

28. Rao, A.S.: AgentSpeak(L): BDI agents speak out in a logical computable language. In: Van de Velde, W., Perram, J.W. (eds.) MAAMAW 1996. LNCS, vol. 1038, pp. 42–55. Springer, Heidelberg (1996). https://doi.org/10.1007/BFb0031845

29. Ricci, A., Piunti, M., Viroli, M., Omicini, A.: Environment programming in CArtAgO. In: Bordini, R.H., Dastani, M., Dix, J., El Fallah Seghrouchni, A. (eds.) Multi-Agent Programming: Languages, Tools and Applications, Chap. 8, pp. 259–288. Springer, Boston (2009). https://doi.org/10.1007/978-0-387-89299-3_8

30. van Riemsdijk, M.B., Dastani, M., Meyer, J.J.C., de Boer, F.S.: Goal-oriented modularity in agent programming. In: Proceedings of the Fifth International Joint Conference on Autonomous Agents and Multiagent Systems, AAMAS 2006, pp. 1271–1278. ACM, New York (2006)

31. Sardina, S., Padgham, L.: A BDI agent programming language with failure handling, declarative goals, and planning. Auton. Agents Multi-Agent Syst. **23**(1), 18–70 (2011)

32. Vikhorev, K., Alechina, N., Logan, B.: Agent programming with priorities and deadlines. In: The 10th International Conference on Autonomous Agents and Multiagent Systems - Volume 1, AAMAS 2011, pp. 397–404. International Foundation for Autonomous Agents and Multiagent Systems, Richland (2011). http://dl.acm.org/citation.cfm?id=2030470. 2030529

33. Winikoff, M., Padgham, L., Harland, J., Thangarajah, J.: Declarative & procedural goals in intelligent agent systems. In: Fensel, D., Giunchiglia, F., McGuinness, D.L., Williams, M. (eds.) Proceedings of the Eights International Conference on Principles and Knowledge Representation and Reasoning (KR 2002), Toulouse, France, 22–25 April 2002, pp. 470–481. Morgan Kaufmann (2002)

34. Winikoff, M., Padgham, L., Harland, J., Thangarajah, J.: Declarative and procedural goals in intelligent agent systems. In: Proceedings of the Eighth International Conference on Principles of Knowledge Representation and Reasoning (2002)

Agent-Oriented Software Engineering

Improving the Usability of a MAS DSML

Tomás Miranda[1], Moharram Challenger[2], Baris Tekin Tezel[2,3],
Omer Faruk Alaca[2], Ankica Barišić[1], Vasco Amaral[1], Miguel Goulão[1],
and Geylani Kardas[2(✉)]

[1] NOVA LINCS, DI, FCT, Universidade NOVA de Lisboa, Lisbon, Portugal
{tr.miranda,a.barisic}@campus.fct.unl.pt,
{vma,mgoul}@fct.unl.pt
[2] International Computer Institute, Ege University, Izmir, Turkey
{moharram.challenger,geylani.kardas}@ege.edu.tr,
omerfarukalaca@gmail.com
[3] Department of Computer Science, Dokuz Eylul University, Izmir, Turkey
baris.tezel@deu.edu.tr

Abstract. Context: A significant effort has been devoted to the design and implementation of various domain-specific modeling languages (DSMLs) for the software agents domain.

Problem: Language usability is often tackled in an ad-hoc way, with the collection of anecdotal evidence supporting the process. However, usability plays an important role in the productivity, learnability and, ultimately, in the adoption of a MAS DSML by agent developers.

Method: In this chapter, we discuss how the principles of The "Physics" of Notations (PoN) can be applied to improve the visual notation of a MAS DSML, called SEA_ML and evaluate the result in terms of usability.

Results: The evolved version of the language, SEA_ML++, was perceived as significantly improved in terms of icons comprehensibility, adequacy and usability, as a direct result of employing the principles of PoN. However, users were not significantly more efficient and effective with SEA_ML++, suggesting these 2 properties were not chiefly constrained by the identified shortcomings of the SEA_ML concrete syntax.

Keywords: Usability · Multi-agent systems ·
Domain specific modeling language · Physics of Notations · SEA_ML

1 Introduction

Software agents with the capability of both being autonomous and performing reactive/proactive behaviors, interact with each other in a Multi-agent system (MAS) to solve problems in a competitive or collaborative manner within an environment. To eliminate the complexity and the difficulty of MAS development, the researchers in agent-oriented software engineering (AOSE) field have significant efforts on design and implementation of various domain-specific modeling languages (DSMLs) such as DSML4MAS [19], FAML [4], SEA_ML [7],

© Springer Nature Switzerland AG 2019
D. Weyns et al. (Eds.): EMAS 2018 Workshops, LNAI 11375, pp. 55–75, 2019.
https://doi.org/10.1007/978-3-030-25693-7_4

MAS-ML [10], and JADEL [3]. Those DSMLs are specific to the agent domain and provide appropriate integrated development environments (IDEs) in which both modelling and code generation for system-to-be-developed can be performed properly [25].

To be effective, the proposed agent DSMLs need to meet the various stakeholder concerns and the related quality criteria for the corresponding MASs. Unfortunately, very often the evaluation of the DSML, especially covering the language components and the use of the DSML during design and implementation of agent-based systems, is completely missing or has been carried out with an idiosyncratic approach [8]. Specifically, the usability, which plays an important role on the adoption of a MAS DSML by agent developers, needs to be taken into consideration preferably during language design and improved to better align the DSML with developer expectations. Hence, in this chapter, we focus on the usability of DSMLs for MAS and propose an approach for promoting the usability of such languages by applying the principles of The "Physics" of Notations (PoN) [30]. For this purpose, the visual notation of a MAS DSML, called SEA_ML [7], is evaluated and its usability is improved by employing each principle of PoN. Hence, it is possible to enrich SEA_ML's visual notation and its correlation to the linked semantic constructs. A comparative assessment of the improved language is also performed with 2 different experiments using end-users that are defined by the domain experts. SEA_ML is an open source language and it is easy to achieve both abstract and concrete syntax specifications. Moreover, reflecting the changes according to the conducted PoN experiments and generating the new version of the language become much easier since the required source code is available online. These are the main reasons of selecting SEA_ML as the application language in our work.

The rest of the chapter is organized as follows: Sects. 2 and 3 discuss SEA_ML and the principles of PoN respectively. The analysis of SEA_ML and improving its visual notation by using PoN principles are given in Sect. 4. Comparative evaluation of the new language is discussed in Sect. 5. Related work is given in Sect. 6 and Sect. 7 concludes the chapter.

2   SEA_ML

SEA_ML [7] is a MAS modeling language which enables the developers to model agent systems in a platform independent level and then automatically generate codes and related documents required for the execution of the modeled MAS on target MAS implementation platforms. In addition to these capabilities, SEA_ML also supports the model-driven design and implementation of autonomous agents who can evaluate semantic data and collaborate with semantically-defined entities of the Semantic Web [35], like Semantic Web Services (SWSs). Within this context, it includes new viewpoints which specifically pave the way for the development of software agents working on the Semantic Web environment. Modeling agents, agent knowledge-bases, platform ontologies, SWS and interactions between agents and SWS are all possible in SEA_ML.

To support MAS experts when programming their systems, and to be able to fine-tune them visually, SEA_ML covers all aspects of an agent system from the internal view of a single agent to the complex MAS organization.

To this end, SEA_ML's metamodel is divided into 8 viewpoints, each of which represents a different aspect for developing Semantic Web enabled MASs.

– Agent's Internal Viewpoint is related to the internal structures of semantic web agents (SWAs) and defines entities and their relations required for the construction of agents.
– Interaction Viewpoint expresses the interactions and the communications in a MAS by taking messages and message sequences into account.
– MAS Viewpoint solely deals with the construction of a MAS as a whole. It includes the main blocks which compose the complex system as an organization.
– Role Viewpoint delves into the complex controlling structure of the agents and addresses role types.
– Environmental Viewpoint describes the use of resources and interaction between agents with their surroundings.
– Plan Viewpoint deals with an agent Plan's internal structure, which is composed of Tasks and atomic elements such as Actions.
– Ontology Viewpoint addresses the ontological concepts which constitute agent's knowledge-base (such as belief and fact).
– Agent-SWS Interaction Viewpoint defines the interaction of agents with SWS including the definition of entities and relations for service discovery, agreement and execution. A SWA executes the semantic service finder Plan (SS_FinderPlan) to discover the appropriate services with the help of a special type of agent called SSMatchMakerAgent who executes the service registration plan (SS_RegisterPlan) for registering the new SWS for the agents. After finding the necessary service, one SWA executes an agreement plan (SS_AgreementPlan) to negotiate with the service. After negotiation, a plan for service execution (SS_ExecutorPlan) is applied for invoking the service.

Appendix A lists the important SEA_ML concepts (meta-entities) and their brief descriptions for the comprehension of the corresponding visual notations used in the diagrams throughout this chapter.

SEA_ML instances are given as inputs to a series of modelto-model and model-to-text transformations to achieve executable artifacts of the system-to-be-built for JADEX [33] agent platform and semantic web service description documents conforming to Web Ontology Language for Services (OWL-S) ontology [28].

To demonstrate the modeling and implementation environment provided by SEA_ML, let us consider the development of a MAS for stock exchange software in which Investor (Buyer and/or Seller), Broker and Stock Trade Manager agents take role in a computerized stock trading system. All of the user agents including investors and brokers cooperate with stock trade manager agent to access the stock market. Also, the user agents interact with each other, for instance, investor A and investor B can cooperate with a broker in order to exchange the stock for which the broker is an expert. Figure 1 is a screenshot taken from SEA_ML modeling environment which shows the modeling of such a stock exchange MAS which is composed of 6 semantic web agent instances, 1 trade manager, 2 brokers, and 3 investors. The given model only considers the overview of the system from SEA_ML MAS viewpoint. However, it is also possible to model all specifications and components of the system considering the other SEA_ML viewpoints again inside the same IDE. Interested readers may refer to [7] for an extensive discussion on SEA_ML and [24] for complete design and implementation of this agent-based stock exchange system with SEA_ML.

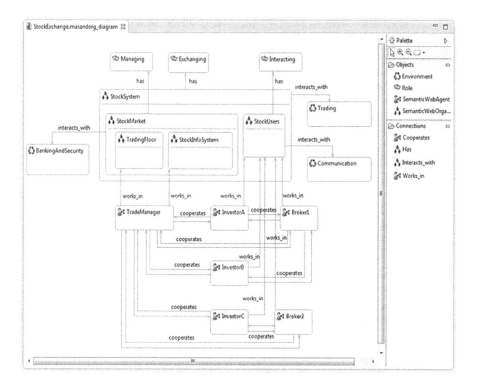

Fig. 1. MAS and organization diagram for stock exchange system in SEA_ML

3   Physics of Notations

The Physics of Notations (PoN) [30] is a design theory which focuses on the perceptual (physical) properties of notations rather than their semantic (logical) properties. It is based on a set of 9 principles which form a prescriptive theory for designing cognitively effective visual notations, defined (and measured) as the speed, ease, and accuracy with which a given representation can be processed by the human mind. This principles can be used to evaluate, compare and ultimately enhance the communication properties of a given language when designing its visual concrete syntax.

Table 1. PoN principles

Principle	Comment
Semiotic Clarity	There should be a 1:1 correspondence between semantic constructs and graphical symbols
Perceptual Discriminability	Different symbols should be clearly distinguishable from each other
Semantic Transparency	The appearance of visual representations should suggest their meaning
Complexity Management	Explicit mechanisms for dealing with complexity should be included
Cognitive Integration	There should be explicit mechanisms to support the integration of information from different diagrams
Visual Expressiveness	The full range of capacities and visual variables should be used
Dual Coding	Text should be used to complement graphics
Graphic Economy	The number of symbols presented in the notation may affect the handling of the tool
Cognitive Fit	Different dialects should be used for different tasks and audiences

The principles were synthesized from theory and empirical evidence about cognitive effectiveness of visual representations. Each principle was defined by its Name (named in a positive sense) and Semantic (theoretical) definition (A imperative statement of what it means), listed in Table 1. Further, each principle contains Operational (empirical) definition, which gives evaluation procedures and/or metrics; Design strategies, Exemplars and Counter exemplars.

4   Applying Physics of Notations Principles to SEA_ML

We proposed notation improvements for all 8 viewpoints of SEA_ML by following 9 PoN principles given in Table 1. These improvements are employed in the development of the new version of SEA_ML, called SEA_ML++. Table 2 synthesizes the conclusions derived from review of PoN principles which is detailed in [29]. Plus (+) refers that SEA_ML currently conforms to the presented principle, while a minus (−) refers that SEA_ML has room for improvement under that principle.

SEA_ML notation conforms to *Semiotic Clarity* as for each SEA_ML viewpoint, different symbols are presented, representing a different semantic construct. There is no such case where two symbols represent the same semantic construct, or when they are not connected to a semantic construct.

Table 2. Review of SEA_ML visual notation according to each principle of PoN

Principle	Room for improvement
Semiotic Clarity	+
Perceptual Discriminability	-
Semantic Transparency	-
Complexity Management	+/-
Cognitive Integration	+
Visual Expressiveness	-
Dual Coding	-
Graphic Economy	+
Cognitive Fit	-
+ **OK** — - can be improved	

Based on *Perceptual Discriminability* principle, SEA_ML can be improved, as some symbols only differ by a label, which is proven to be cognitively ineffective. The distance between visual symbols is too short, as predefined by the language editor when generating the tool.

Regarding *Semantic Transparency* principle we identify 19 visual notations of SEA_ML that could represent better intended meaning and provided improvement suggestions for each symbol (see [29]).

Complexity Management is not applicable, as SEA_ML does not have any direct mechanism for dealing with the complexity of the viewpoints.

SEA_ML conforms to *Cognitive Integration* principle, as it requires a name for every diagram and label used during the modelling. Every procedure is verified to be connected to some entity.

SEA_ML presents similar colours and symbols to similar semantic constructs. Some semantic figures are only differentiated by a letter, which is not conforming to *Visual Expressiveness* principle since the icons should be presented using different visual variables to automatically distinguish each semantic construct only looking to visual notation.

Based on the *Dual Coding* principle, SEA_ML has eleven visual notations that are only differentiated through letters or textual differences that are difficult to see, which are impossible to differentiate without it.

The user is presented with a palette of icons which are allowed to be used on each viewpoint, therefore conforming to the *Graphic Economy* principle.

Regarding *Cognitive Fit*, some of the proposed visual notation can be improved in order to have a better relation with other similar symbols presented on the SEA_ML language, which may turn the language easier to understand and to be worked for novice users.

Concept	Current Notation	New Notation	Concept	Current Notation	New Notation	Concept	Current Notation	New Notation
Goal			Message			Effect		
Capability			Message Sequence			Architecture Role		
Fact			DomainRole			Ontology Mediator Role		
Plan			Agent State			Semantic Web Organization		
Semantic Service Register Plan			Resource			Role Ontology		
Semantic Service Finder Plan			Web Service			Organization Ontology		
Semantic Service Agreement Plan			Semantic Web Service			Service Ontology		
Semantic Service Executor Plan			Grounding			Interaction		
Send			Process			Behavior		
Receive			Interface			Agent Type		
Action			Precondition					

Fig. 2. SEA_ML vs SEA_ML++ notations

Some SEA_ML visual notations were not modified as these notations reflect correctly its semantic constructs and they conform to *PoN* principles. Of the 43 symbols (44 including the symbol for arrows that relate each entity), 32 symbols were modified (see Fig. 2 for the current (SEA_ML) and new (SEA_ML) notations). With respect to the proposed SEA_ML++ notation, the justification for each new symbol is defined below:

1. **Goal** - The new notation adds color to the target, making it more appropriate to be selected when using viewpoints that use this semantic construct;
2. **Capability** - The current visual notation may induce users wrong. The new notation reflects that users have a set of capabilities in order to solve their problems;
3. **Fact** - The current notation is similar to other notations present in SEA_ML. The new notation (check mark) reflects something that is correct and concrete;
4. **Plan** - The notation addresses a plan to reach a goal from X to Y;
5. **Semantic Service Register Plan (SSRP)** - The current notation has 4 similar symbols, being distinguished through different letters. The new notation adds the SWS notation and a person registering to a customer's list;
6. **Semantic Service Finder Plan (SSFP)** - The current notation has 4 similar symbols, being distinguished through different letters. The new notation adds the "Semantic Web Services" notation and a magnifying glass;

7. **Semantic Service Agreement Plan (SSAP)** - The current notation has 4 similar symbols, being distinguished through different letters. The new notation adds the "Semantic Web Services" notation and a handshake between 2 people;

8. **Semantic Service Executor Plan (SSEP)** - The current notation has 4 similar symbols, being distinguished through different letters. The new notation adds the "Semantic Web Services" notation and a "Play" icon;

9. **Send** - It is not clear what the current notation is addressing. The new notation states clearly that the message is going to be sent elsewhere;

10. **Receive** - It is not clear what the current notation is addressing. The new notation states clearly that the message is going to be received;

11. **Action** - Removed the round border. The clapperboard is enough to understand the semantic construct;

12. **Message** - The new notation attempts to be similar to the new notations adopted in "Message Sequence", "Send" and "Receive";

13. **Message Sequence** - Similar to the notations presented in "Send" and "Receive", the new notation hints a sequence of message being transmitted by those parties;

14. **ODMOWLClass** - The new notation is similar to the previous "Plan" symbol. It tries to remove two similar element from the visual notation (as the "Plan" symbol is totally different from the original one);

15. **DomainRole** - The current visual notation does not have any relation with a domain. The metaphor tried on the new notation aims at reflecting the web domains, inserting its roles on a web browser window;

16. **Agent State** - The current visual notation does not have any relation with an Agent State. The new notation attempts to add a "Secret Agent" to a typical rounded "State Icon" that appears on some loading screens;

17. **Resource** - The new notation reflects a box full of resources, which reflects more what the semantic construct is;

18. **Web Service** - The new notation adds a gear to an icon that relates to the web;

19. **Grounding** - Proposed by the MAS developers having experience on MAS and SWS;

20. **Process** - Proposed by the MAS developers having experience on MAS and SWS;

21. **Interface** - Proposed by the MAS developers having experience on MAS and SWS;

22. **Precondition** - Proposed by the MAS developers having experience on MAS and SWS;

23. **Effect** - The current visual notation does not have any direct relation with Effect. The new notation tries to adapt the "Magic" metaphor for an effect cause;

24. **Architecture Role** - The current visual notation does not have any direct relation with an "ArchitectureRole". The new icon adds the "Role" symbol to a common architecture plan;

25. **Ontology Mediator Role** - Proposed by the MAS developers having agent programming experience;
26. **Semantic Web Organization (SWO)** - The current visual notation does not have any direct relation with a SWO. The new symbol adds that relation;
27. **Role Ontology** - The new visual notation adapts to the new ODMOWL-Class proposed above;
28. **Organization Ontology** - The new visual notation adapts to the new ODMOWLClass and "Semantic Web Services" proposed above;
29. **Service Ontology** - The new notation adapts to the new ODMOWLClass proposed above;
30. **Interaction** - Although it is perceptible what the current visual notation proposes, there is room for improvement by adding a clearer symbol;
31. **Behavior** - The current visual notation does not have any relation with the "Behavior" semantic construct. The new symbol tries to apply a metaphor related to the human behavior;
32. **Agent Type** - Proposed by the MAS developers having agent programming experience.

5 Evaluation

5.1 Experiment Planning

Goals. Broadly, we aim to compare the impact of using the evolved version of the MAS DSML (*SEA_ML++*) when contrasted with the previous version (*SEA_ML*), focusing, one at a time, in different quality criteria for the language assessment. We present our evaluation goals following the GQM research goals template [2], which is shared among all our goals, with the exception of the term *concrete quality criterion*, which varies from one goal to the next.

In general, our goal is to **analyse** the effect of evolving from *SEA_ML* to *SEA_ML++*, **for the purpose of** evaluation, **with respect to** the *semantics transparency* of the symbols used in the concrete syntax, **from the viewpoint of** researchers, **in the context of** an experiment conducted with participants with limited or no experience with MAS at Universidade Nova de Lisboa (UNL) in Portugal and EGE University in Turkey.

More specifically, our first goal is concerned about the *comprehensibility* of the symbols used on the concrete syntax, leading to the following formulation: Our first goal (G1) is to **analyse** the effect of evolving from *SEA_ML* to *SEA_ML++*, **for the purpose of** evaluation, **with respect to** the *comprehensibility* of the symbols used in the concrete syntax, **from the viewpoint of** researchers, **in the context of** an experiment conducted with participants with limited or no experience with MAS at UNL and EGE University. Our second goal (G2) is concerned about the *perceived usability* of the concrete syntax. Our third goal (G3) is concerned about the *effectiveness* of the concrete syntax. Finally, our fourth goal (G4) is concerned about the *efficiency*.

Table 3. Experimental design. Key: MT = Music Trading; EF = Expert Finder

Sequence	Task 1	Task 2	Task 3	Task 4
Group 1	MT/SEA_ML++	MT/SEA_ML++	EF/SEA_ML	EF/SEA_ML
Group 2	EF/SEA_ML	EF/SEA_ML	MT/SEA_ML++	MT/SEA_ML++
Group 3	MT/SEA_ML	MT/SEA_ML	EF/SEA_ML++	EF/SEA_ML++
Group 4	EF/SEA_ML++	EF/SEA_ML++	MT/SEA_ML	MT/SEA_ML

All materials for the conducted evaluation, including experiment setup, result sets and statistics are also available in this chapter's online repository[1].

Tasks. To achieve *(G1)*, (1) each participant read and signed a consent letter regarding the data collected in the experiment. This letter was only used for the purpose of this study. All participants remained anonymous. Then (2) each participant selected the symbol (s)he found more suitable for each of the 33 *SEA_ML++* concepts identified in the PoN assessment reported in Sect. 4. Finally, (3) participants filled in a background questionnaire.

We recruited a different, non-intersecting, group of participants for the remaining tasks. Again, (1) each participant read and signed a consent letter regarding the data collected, similar to the letter used in the other experiment. Then (2) each participant completed 4 exercises, 2 covering *SEA_ML* and 2 covering *SEA_ML++*. Each exercise ended with the user filling in a questionnaire about it. We had a crossover design with 4 possible sequences, as represented in Table 3. The goal was to mitigate any potential learning effects and balance the number of participants working with each example in each of the possible sequence positions. Finally, (3) participants filled in a background questionnaire.

Experimental Material. We provided each participant with a consent letter and a background questionnaire, which were the same for both experiments. In the symbol selection experiment, the participant also received a questionnaire where (s)he was asked to match each concept definition with the symbol that would best represent its concrete syntax. For the second experiment, the participants received 4 different scenarios with a corresponding challenge, each followed by a questionnaire about the notation they had just used. 2 of those scenarios were related with music trading among software agents, while the other 2 involved an agent-based expert finding system. Each of these scenarios had 2 versions, one with *SEA_ML* and the other with *SEA_ML++*. Each participant received 2 different scenarios for each concrete syntax.

---

[1] https://doi.org/10.5281/zenodo.1288390

Participants. Johnson [23] suggests that six individuals per subset of the population are the minimum required for a controlled experiment. It is sensible to take a larger number, but the costs should be kept to a minimum. Regarding the usability study, Nielsen [32] claims that testing with 5 people lets us find almost as many usability problems as by using many more test participants. However, when performing the quantitative studies, Nielsen suggests testing at least 20 users to get statistically significant numbers.

All the participants in our studies have formal University training in Informatics. For the symbol selection experiment, 25 participants (all undergraduate students) were involved. All of these participants are current or former students at Universidade Nova de Lisboa (UNL). 11 of those had some basic knowledge of MAS (in the context of a course), but not of SEA ML++. For the evaluation experiment, a total of 36 participants were included. That experiment was run in 2 replicas: The first one was conducted at UNL with 24 participants, including 12 with some basic knowledge of MAS. The second one was conducted at EGE University with 12 participants, all graduate students with some basic knowledge of MAS. All participants were selected through convenience sampling.

It is worth noting that the domain of agents interacting with SWSs is not an established professional occupation field and we could have limited number of researchers in the evaluation. Such professional evaluators are familiar with the concepts and their relations which makes the development and subsequently the evaluation more real. Because of this shortcoming, we have a small size society for the evaluation.

Table 4. Hypotheses

H_{0G1}	The concrete syntax of SEA_ML++ is **as comprehensible as** the one of SEA_ML
H_{1G1}	The concrete syntax of SEA_ML++ is **more comprehensible than** the one of SEA_ML
H_{0G2}	The concrete syntax of SEA_ML++ is **perceived as usable as** the one of SEA_ML
H_{1G2}	The concrete syntax of SEA_ML++ is **perceived as more usable** than the one of SEA_ML
H_{0G3}	The concrete syntax of SEA_ML++ is **as effective as** the one of SEA_ML
H_{1G3}	The concrete syntax of SEA_ML++ is **more effective than** the one of SEA_ML
H_{0G4}	The concrete syntax of SEA_ML++ is **as efficient as** the one of SEA_ML
H_{1G4}	The concrete syntax of SEA_ML++ is **more efficient than** the one of SEA_ML

Hypotheses, Parameters and Variables. Overall, we hypothesize that the proposed SEA_ML++ has a *better* concrete syntax than SEA_ML. In order to make this more concrete, we anchor our formalized hypotheses on the research goals defined in Sect. 5.1, as presented in Table 4. For each of the high-level goals, we define the null (H_0Gi) and alternative (H_1Gi) hypotheses (where i denotes the specific goal).

For all hypotheses, the independent variable is the *concrete syntax*, which can be SEA_ML++ or SEA_ML. The dependent variables are different for each of the tested hypothesis.

Comprehensibility. Graphical symbols' *comprehensibility* can be assessed by measuring hit rates, *i.e.*, the percentage of correct responses [21,22]. In this case, we measure the *hit rate* (percentage of answers where the correct symbol was chosen) for each concept in each of the concrete syntaxes.

Perceived Usability. In order to assess the *perceived usability* we asked our participants to fill in a *System Usability Scale* [5] questionnaire. This questionnaire consists of 10 questions, each with 5 response options, ranging from *"Strongly Disagree"* to *"Strongly Agree"*. The scores are then converted to a scale of 0-100. The threshold of 68 points is considered as the *"average usability"* [5]. Lower scores indicate below average usability, while higher scores are considered above average. In addition, we asked our participants to classify the following 3 statements:

- **S1:** The symbols on the user interface (UI) were easy to **understand**.
- **S2:** The symbols on the UI are **adequate** to the MAS constructions they are linked to.
- **S3:** The symbols on the UI **helped** me solve the exercise in less time.

We deliberately used the term *"symbols on the UI"* (User Interface) rather than *"concrete syntax"*, as a simplification for our participants, who were not necessarily familiar with the notion of *"concrete syntax"*. For each of these sentences, the participants had to select from a five-point ordinal scale, ranging from 1 *"Strongly Disagree"* to 5 *"Strongly Agree"*.

Effectiveness. We use the *correctness* of the answers of our participants to measure how effectively they were able to solve the exercises.

Efficiency. We recorded the *duration* of the working sessions to measure how fast our participants were able to complete their assigned tasks.

5.2   Analysis

Descriptive Statistics. In this section, we present descriptive statistics for the metrics collected to answer our research questions (Table 5). For each data row, we identify the corresponding **goal** (ranging from *G1* to *G4*), the *dependent variable* (the quality focus for a particular goal), the *independent variable*, *i.e.* the *concrete syntax* followed by the descriptive statistics: the *mean, standard deviation (SD), skewness (Skew), kurtosis (Kurt)* and the *p-value* for the

Table 5. Selection rate descriptive statistics

Goal	Dependent	Independent	Mdn.	Mean	S.Dev.	Skew.	Kurt.	S-W
G1	Preference	SEA_ML++	.44	.45	.14	−.10	.07	.457
		SEA_ML	.16	.19	.14	.20	−1.18	.018
G2	SUS	SEA_ML++	61.25	59.38	19.97	−.20	−.24	.409
		SEA_ML	57.50	54.17	20.62	−.20	.19	.268
	Understandability	SEA_ML++	4	3.96	1.09	−1.15	.83	.000
		SEA_ML	3	2.92	1.25	−.04	−.98	.001
	Adequacy	SEA_ML++	4	3.65	1.02	−.10	−1.10	.000
		SEA_ML	3	2.96	1.03	−.16	−.11	.001
	Speed	SEA_ML++	4	3.83	1.10	−.86	.23	.000
		SEA_ML	3	2.85	1.29	−.09	−.95	.000
G3	Correctness	SEA_ML++	1.00	.84	.32	−1.763	1.724	.000
		SEA_ML	1.00	.80	.32	−1.509	1.096	.000
G4	Duration	SEA_ML++	11:51	13:20	06:12	1.520	2.434	.000
		SEA_ML	12:24	14:48	09:32	2.784	8.463	.000

Shapiro-Wilk normality test $(S\text{-}W)$. In most of these variables, the assumption of normality is **not** reasonable $(p - value < 0.05)$, as confirmed by the visual inspection of boxplots in Fig. 3, Q-Q plots and kernel density plots, omitted for the sake of brevity.

Hypotheses Testing. We now present the results of our hypotheses tests.

G1: RQ1: Are participants more likely to select the correct elements from the PoN-based concrete syntax of SEA_ML++ or the baseline SEA_ML concrete syntax elements? A Wilcoxon Signed-Ranks test was run and the output indicated that SEA_ML++ scores $(Mdn = .44)$ were statistically significantly higher than SEA_ML scores $(Mdn = .16)$, $Z = 4.573$, $p < .001$, $r = .83$. This supports our hypothesis that participants were more likely to select the SEA_ML++ elements.

G2: RQ2: Do participants using SEA_ML++ perceive it as more usable than SEA_ML? In order to answer this question, we look at this from 2 different perspectives. We use a standard usability test – the System Usability Scale (SUS) – and a set of 3 questions to gather more detailed feedback (Fig. 3).

SUS: Is SEA_ML++ perceived as more usable than SEA_ML? The usability did not differ significantly, according to Welch's t test, $t(141.854) = 1.539$, $p = .126$ from SEA_ML++ $(M = 59.38, SD = 19.97)$ to the usability of SEA_ML $(M = 54.17, SD = .20.62)$ (Fig. 3a).

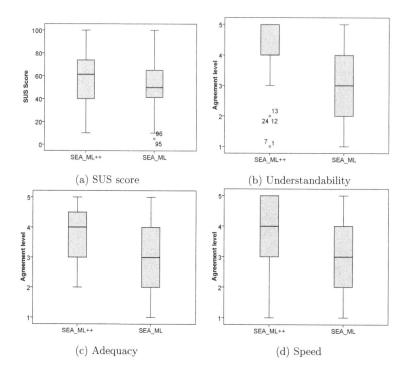

(a) SUS score

(b) Understandability

(c) Adequacy

(d) Speed

Fig. 3. Perceived usability of SEA_ML vs SEA_ML++

Understandability: The symbols on the user interface (UI) were easy to understand. Because the data was skewed for both variables, a Wilcoxon Signed-Ranks Test was run and the output indicated that *SEA_ML++* scores ($Mdn = 4$), were statistically significantly higher than *SEA_ML* scores ($Mdn = 3$), $Z = 3.683$, $p < .001$, $r = .53$ (Fig. 3b).

Adequacy: The symbols on the UI are adequate to the constructs they are linked to. Because the data was skewed for both variables, a Wilcoxon Signed-Ranks Test was run and the output indicated that *SEA_ML++* scores ($Mdn = 4$) were statistically significantly higher than *SEA_ML* scores ($Mdn = 3$), $Z = 2.939$, $p < .003$, $r = .42$. These results suggest that participants found *SEA_ML++* more adequate than *SEA_ML* to the constructs they were linked to (Fig. 3c).

Speed: The symbols on the UI helped me solve the exercise in less time. Because the data was skewed for both variables, a Wilcoxon Signed-Ranks Test was run and the output indicated that *SEA_ML++* scores ($Mdn = 4$) were statistically significantly higher than *SEA_ML* scores ($Mdn = 3$), $Z = 3.324$, $p < .001$, $r = .48$ (Fig. 3d). These results suggest that participants perceived using *SEA_ML++* had helped them solving the exercise faster than using *SEA_ML*.

G3: We applied the Welch t-test, which is robust to deviations from normality within groups and when variance homogeneity among groups may not be assumed. The correctness does not differ significantly, according to Welch's t-test, $t(141.968) = .417$, $p = .519$ from the SEA_ML ($M = .80$, $SD = .32$) to the SEA_ML++ ($M = .84$, $SD = .32$) concrete syntax. These results suggest that there was no difference between the 2 concrete syntaxes, in terms of *complexity*.

G4: As in *G3*, we applied the Welch t-test. The duration does not differ significantly, $t(122.030) = 1.180$, $p = .280$ from the SEA_ML ($M = 14 : 48$, $SD = 09 : 32$) to SEA_ML++ ($M = 13 : 20$, $SD = 06 : 12$) concrete syntax. These results suggest that there was no difference between the 2 concrete syntaxes, in terms of *duration*.

5.3   Discussion

Evaluation of the Results and Implications. By using the PoN to guide a redesign of the concrete syntax of SEA_ML, we proposed SEA_ML++. We found that (RQ1) the participants in our study were better at correctly identifying the symbols with SEA_ML++. They found the SEA_ML++ syntax (RQ2) easier to *understand*, more *adequate* to the MAS constructs it represents and helpful for performing *faster*, when compared to the SEA_ML syntax. However, in practice, (RQ3) participants were neither significantly able to use the language more correctly, (RQ4) nor significantly faster using it. So, overall, although the perception of language usage has improved with the new concrete syntax (and, with it, the developer experience), its implications for the actual usage of the language in agent development did not translate into improved effectiveness or efficiency (the small improvements observed were not significant). While it was certainly the case that there was room for improvement of the concrete syntax, the PoN-based improvements only took us as far as improving the perceived developer experience. Other alternative techniques, such as the sign production technique used successfully with other languages, such as $i*$ [6], could potentially further improve the developer experience. That said, it seems more likely that the effectiveness and efficiency in using SEA_ML++ are mostly constrained by the semantics of the language. Further research is ongoing to explore this hypothesis.

Threats to Validity. The selection of participants is a potential threat. They are mostly representative of practitioners who are relatively inexperienced with MAS and, therefore, a good match for the main target population of this study. Most of the participants have less than 1 year experience on software agent development and only 5 participants in EGE University can be said experienced with having more than 3 years of MAS knowledge and implementation. As with many other languages, experts will cope better with the peculiarities of a given concrete syntax than newbies. The results obtained in the 2 replications were very similar, which increases our confidence on their external validity for other inexperienced MAS developers.

A second validity threat concerns the representativeness of the models used for this evaluation. While these models are good representatives of the complexity one would discuss with inexperienced MAS developers in the course of a training activity, further empirical evaluations with models of different complexities will increase the representativeness of this evaluation.

6 Related Work

In the last decade, several MAS modeling languages and DSMLs [4,9,11,14,17] were proposed to support development of MASs. For example, DSML4MAS [19] introduces a general MAS metamodel with various viewpoints that enable the development of MAS for many application domains. As another example study, in [20], the authors develop a DSML and its supporting tool, called ERE_ML, for MAS working in emergency response environments. However, most of these DS(M)Ls proposed for MASs have been evaluated by just providing a case study demonstrating how the related language can be used for design and implementation of MAS. A quantitative analysis and/or qualitative evaluation considering e.g. the development time performance, generation performance, and/or the usability of the language are not considered in these studies.

In [8], an evaluation framework is proposed which provides the systematic assessment of both the language constructs and the use of agent DSMLs according to various dimensions and criteria. The study also provides an assessment of SEA_ML [7], however, it does not take into account the usability of the language, i.e. usefulness regarding the needs of language users. This evaluation framework is adopted in [26], [24] and [12] for the assessment of the proposed MAS DSMLs. Another MAS DSML evaluation feature exists in [3] for a textual DSL, JADEL, providing 4 abstractions, namely agents, behaviours, communication ontologies, and interaction protocols to JADE agent development framework. However, the study only evaluates JADEL's code generation performance.

The mentioned studies evaluate their MAS DS(M)Ls to some extent with or without using a structured evaluation framework. However, none of them addresses the usability of the MAS DS(M)Ls considering both the end-user perspective and the improvement of the visual language notation which, we argue that, is critical for the adoption of such languages in AOSE. In this sense, this study contribute to the literature by assessing the usability of an available MAS DSML, namely SEA_ML, and improving its new version.

In general, despite the fact that it is usually claimed that DSLs are more usable and leading to productivity gains, in [13] it has been identified a generalized lack of practice of reporting their usability assessment. The Software Language Engineering community has been seeking for adequate and systematic approaches to evaluating the usability of DSLs [1]. Work was reported [31] on how i^* concrete syntax was evaluated using PoN and a new symbol set was proposed for it. In the sequence of this, in [6], it is compared the proposed concrete syntax with alternatives produced by novices (a stereotype and a prototype concrete syntaxes) and the standard i^* concrete syntax.

Several modelling languages, for example, BPMN 2.0 [16], Use Case Maps [15], WebML [18], and misuse cases [34], use PoN to evaluate and identify improvement opportunities. It is possible to observe consistently similar conclusions concerning the challenges in most visual notations from a PoN perspective [30]. Other studies assess the i^* and KAOS modelling languages [27], using interviews, creation of models, and evaluation of those models and the modelling language and found clarity problems in the semantics definition of those languages.

7   Conclusion and Future Work

There are many modeling languages and DSMLs for MAS. Although there are a few studies addressing the evaluation of MAS DSMLs and their performances, the usability of these DSMLs is not investigated in a systematic way. In this study, the principles of The "Physics" of Notations are applied on a MAS DSML, called SEA_ML. By applying 9 principles, 43 notations of SEA_ML are evaluated and 32 of them are modified which are used in the development of the new version of SEA_ML called, SEA_ML++. In this way the notations in the graphical concrete syntax of the DSML are improved leading to the improvement of SEA_ML++. This hypothesis is examined under 4 research goals covering comprehensiveness, usability, effectiveness, and efficiency. The experiment conducted by the participants shows that the participants were more likely to select the SEA_ML elements and the symbols were easy to understand. However, the results show that there was no significant difference between the 2 concrete syntax, in terms of complexity and duration. Finally, it is worth indicating that this study mainly focuses on evaluating the use of notations/symbols in the DSML and does not cover the other issues (e.g. diagram complexity, scalability) which PoN can be utilized. These can be addressed in the future work.

Acknowledgment. The authors would like to thank the followings: (i) the Scientific and Technological Research Council of Turkey (TUBITAK) under grant 115E591, and (ii) Portuguese grants NOVA LINCS Research Laboratory (Grant: FCT/MCTES PEst UID/ CEC/04516/2013) and DSML4MA Project (Grant: FCT/MCTES TUBITAK/0008/2014).

Appendix A. Descriptions of the Selected SEA_ML Concepts

Icon.	Concept	Description
	Semantic Web Agent (SWA)	Semantic web agent in the SEA_ML stands for each agent which is a member of semantic web-enabled MAS. It is an autonomous entity which can interact with both the other agents and the semantic web services, within the environment.
	Semantic service matchmaker agent (SSMatchmakerAgent)	It is a SWA extension. This meta-element represents matchmaker agents which store the SWS' capabilities list in a MAS and compare it with the service capabilities required by the other agents, in order to match them.
	Belief	Beliefs represent the informational state of the agent, in other words its knowledge about the world (including itself and other agents).
	Goal	A goal is a desire that has been adopted for active pursuit by the agent.
	Role	An agent plays different roles to realize different behaviors in various situations, such as organizations, or domains.
	Capability	Taking BDI agents into consideration, there is an entity called Capability which includes each agent's Goals, Plans and Beliefs about the surroundings.
	Fact	The statement about the agent's environment which can be true. Agents can decide based on these facts.
	Plan	Plans are sequences of actions that an agent can perform to achieve one or more of its intentions.
R	Semantic service register plan (SS_RegisterPlan)	The Semantic Service Register Plan (SS_RegisterPlan) is the plan used to register a new SWS by SSMatchmakerAgent.
F	Semantic service finder plan (SS_FinderPlan)	Semantic Service Finder Plan (SS_FinderPlan) is a Plan in which automatic discovery of the candidate semantic web services take place with the help of the SSMatchmakerAgent.
A	Semantic service agreement plan (SS_AgreementPlan)	Semantic Service Agreement Plan (SS_AgreementPlan) is a concept that deals with negotiations on quality of service (QoS) metrics (e.g., service execution cost, duration and position) and contract negotiation.
E	Semantic service executor plan (SS_ExecutorPlan)	After service discovery and negotiation, the agent applies the Semantic Service Executor Plan (SS_ExecutorPlan) to invoke appropriate semantic web services.
	Send	An action to transmit a message from an agent to another. This can be based on some standard such as FIPA_Contract_Net
	Receive	An action to collect a message from an agent. This can be based on some standard such as FIPA_Contract_Net
	Task	Tasks are groups of actions which are constructing a plan in an agent.
	Action	An action is an atomic instruction which constitutes a task.
	Message	A package of information to be send from an agent to another; possibly to deliver some information or instructions. Two special types of actions, namely Send and Receive, are used to handle these messages.
	Agent state	This concept refers to certain conditions in which agents are present at certain times. An agent can only have one state (Agent State) at a time, e.g., waiting state in which the agent is passive and waiting for another agent or resource.

	Resource	It refers to the system resources that the MAS is interacting with. For example, the database.
	Service	Any computer-based service presented to the users.
	Web Service	Type of service which is presented via web.
	Semantic Web Service	Semantically defined web services which can be interpreted by machines.
	Process	It describes how the SWS is used by defining a process model. Instances of the SWS use the process via described_by to refer to the service's ServiceModel.
	Interface	This document describes what the service provides for prospective clients. This is used to advertise the service, and to capture this perspective, each instance of the class Service presents a Service Interface.
	Grounding	In this document, it is described how an agent interact with the SWS. A grounding provides the needed details about transport protocols. Instances of the class Service have a supports property referring to a Service Grounding.
	Input	Defines the inputs for processes and interfaces of a SWS.
	Output	Defines the output for processes and interfaces of a SWS.
	Precondition	Defines the pre-conditions for processes and interfaces of a SWS.
	Effect	Defines the post-conditions or effects for processes and interfaces of a SWS.
	Semantic web organization	Refers to an organized group of semantic web agents (SWAs).
	Interaction	For communication and collaboration of agents, they can use series of messages via a message sequence which results to an agent interaction.
	Environment	The agent's surroundings including digitized resources, fact, and services.
	Registration Role	A specialized type of architectural role which is used to register SWSs in the multi agent systems.
	Behavior	In re-active agents, a behavior is a re-action of an agent towards an external or internal stimulus.
	Agent type	The agents in a multi-agent system can have different types taking various responsivities and representing various stakeholders.

References

1. Barišić, A., Amaral, V., Goulão, M.: Usability driven DSL development with USE-ME. Comput. Lang. Syst. Struct. (ComLan) **51**, 118–157 (2017). https://doi.org/10.1016/j.cl.2017.06.005
2. Basili, V., Caldiera, G., Rombach, H.: Goal question metric paradigm. Encycl. Softw. Eng. **1**, 528–532 (2001)

74 T. Miranda et al.

3. Bergenti, F., Iotti, E., Monica, S., Poggi, A.: Agent-oriented model-driven development for JADE with the JADEL programming language. Comput. Lang. Syst. Struct. **50**, 142–158 (2017)
4. Beydoun, G., et al.: FAML: a generic metamodel for mas development. IEEE Trans. Softw. Eng. **35**(6), 841–863 (2009)
5. Brooke, J.: SUS-a quick and dirty usability scale. Usability Eval. Ind. **189**(194), 4–7 (1996)
6. Caire, P., Genon, N., Heymans, P., Moody, D.L.: Visual notation design 2.0: towards user comprehensible requirements engineering notations. In: RE 2013, pp. 115–124. IEEE (2013)
7. Challenger, M., Demirkol, S., Getir, S., Mernik, M., Kardas, G., Kosar, T.: On the use of a domain-specific modeling language in the development of multiagent systems. Eng. Appl. Artif. Intell. **28**, 111–141 (2014)
8. Challenger, M., Kardas, G., Tekinerdogan, B.: A systematic approach to evaluating domain-specific modeling language environments for multi-agent systems. Softw. Qual. J. **24**(3), 755–795 (2016)
9. Ciobanu, G., Juravle, C.: Flexible software architecture and language for mobile agents. Concurr. Comput. Pract. E **24**(6), 559–571 (2012)
10. Da Silva, V.T., Choren, R., De Lucena, C.J.: MAS-ML: a multiagent system modelling language. IJAOSE **2**(4), 382–421 (2008)
11. Demirkol, S., Challenger, M., Getir, S., Kosar, T., Kardas, G., Mernik, M.: Sea_l: a domain-specific language for semantic web enabled multi-agent systems. In: 2012 Federated Conference on Computer Science and Information Systems (FedCSIS), pp. 1373–1380. IEEE (2012)
12. Faccin, J., Nunes, I.: A tool-supported development method for improved BDI plan selection. Eng. Appl. Artif. Intell. **62**, 195–213 (2017)
13. Gabriel, P., Goulão, M., Amaral, V.: Do software languages engineers evaluate their languages? In: Proceedings of the XIII Congreso Iberoamericano en "Software Engineering" (CIbSE 2010) (2011)
14. Gascueña, J.M., Navarro, E., Fernández-Caballero, A.: Model-driven engineering techniques for the development of multi-agent systems. Eng. Appl. Artif. Intell. **25**(1), 159–173 (2012)
15. Genon, N., Amyot, D., Heymans, P.: Analysing the cognitive effectiveness of the UCM visual notation. In: Kraemer, F.A., Herrmann, P. (eds.) SAM 2010. LNCS, vol. 6598, pp. 221–240. Springer, Heidelberg (2011). https://doi.org/10.1007/978-3-642-21652-7_14
16. Genon, N., Heymans, P., Amyot, D.: Analysing the cognitive effectiveness of the BPMN 2.0 visual notation. In: Malloy, B., Staab, S., van den Brand, M. (eds.) SLE 2010. LNCS, vol. 6563, pp. 377–396. Springer, Heidelberg (2011). https://doi.org/10.1007/978-3-642-19440-5_25
17. Gonçalves, E.J.T., et al.: MAS-ML 2.0: supporting the modelling of multi-agent systems with different agent architectures. J. Syst. Softw. **108**, 77–109 (2015)
18. Granada, D., Vara, J.M., Brambilla, M., Bollati, V., Marcos, E.: Analysing the cognitive effectiveness of the webML visual notation. Softw. Syst. Model. **16**(1), 195–227 (2017)
19. Hahn, C.: A domain specific modeling language for multiagent systems. In: Proceedings of the 7th international joint conference on Autonomous agents and multiagent systems, vol. 1, pp. 233–240 (2008)
20. Hosein Doost, S., Adamzadeh, T., Zamani, B., Fatemi, A.: A model-driven framework for developing multi-agent systems in emergency response environments. Softw. Syst. Model. **18**, 1–28 (2017)

21. ISO: Standard graphical symbols: Safety colours and safety signs-registered safety signs (ISO 7010: 2003). International Standards Organisation (ISO): Geneva, Switzerland (2003)
22. ISO: ISO standard graphical symbols: Public information symbols (ISO 7001:2007). International Standards Organisation (ISO): Geneva, Switzerland (2007)
23. Johnson, P.: Human Computer Interaction: Psychology, Task Analysis, and Software Engineering. McGraw-Hill, London (1992)
24. Kardas, G., Bircan, E., Challenger, M.: Supporting the platform extensibility for the model-driven development of agent systems by the interoperability between domain-specific modeling languages of multi-agent systems. Comput. Sci. Inf. Syst. **14**(3), 875–912 (2017)
25. Kardas, G., Gomez-Sanz, J.J.: Special issue on model-driven engineering of multi-agent systems in theory and practice. Comput. Lang. Syst. Struct. **50**, 140–141 (2017)
26. Kardas, G., Tezel, B.T., Challenger, M.: Domain-specific modelling language for belief-desire-intention software agents. IET Softw. **12**(4), 356–364 (2018)
27. Matulevičius, R., Heymans, P.: Comparing goal modelling languages: an experiment. In: Sawyer, P., Paech, B., Heymans, P. (eds.) REFSQ 2007. LNCS, vol. 4542, pp. 18–32. Springer, Heidelberg (2007). https://doi.org/10.1007/978-3-540-73031-6_2
28. McGuinness, D.L., van Harmelen, F.: OWL web ontology language overview. W3C (2004)
29. Miranda, T.R.: Software language engineering : interaction and usability modeling of language editors. MSc thesis, Universidade Nova de Lisboa, Faculdade de Ciências e Tecnologia, Monte Caparica, Portugal (2017)
30. Moody, D.: The "physics" of notations: toward a scientific basis for constructing visual notations in software engineering. IEEE Trans. Softw. Eng. **35**(6), 756–779 (2009)
31. Moody, D.L., Heymans, P., Matulevičius, R.: Visual syntax does matter: improving the cognitive effectiveness of the i* visual notation. Requir. Eng. **15**(2), 141–175 (2010)
32. Nielsen, J.: How many test users in a usability study. Nielsen Norman, vol. 4, no. 06 (2012)
33. Pokahr, A., Braubach, L., Walczak, A., Lamersdorf, W.: JADEX-engineering goal-oriented agents. In: Developing multi-agent systems with JADE, pp. 254–258 (2007)
34. Saleh, F., El-Attar, M.: A scientific evaluation of the misuse case diagrams visual syntax. Inform. Softw. Tech. **66**, 73–96 (2015)
35. Shadbolt, N., Berners-Lee, T., Hall, W.: The semantic web revisited. IEEE Intell. Syst. **21**(3), 96–101 (2006)

Designing Multi-Agent Systems
from Ontology Models

Artur Freitas$^{(\boxtimes)}$, Rafael H. Bordini, and Renata Vieira

PUCRS, Porto Alegre, Brazil
artur.freitas@acad.pucrs.br, {rafael.bordini,renata.vieira}@pucrs.br
http://smart-pucrs.github.io/

Abstract. This chapter presents our proposal for the development of
multi-agent systems designed as ontology models supporting code generation and reasoning. The foundation of such work takes into consideration ontologies for agent-oriented software engineering aligned with
the JaCaMo framework. These techniques are implemented in a tool
that supports multi-agent systems core code generation for JaCaMo. The
underlying ontology also allows for reasoning about the multi-agent systems models under development. Such comprehensive approach, therefore, spans through the modelling, programming, and verification of
agent-oriented software.

Keywords: Ontologies for agents ·
Reasoning in agent-based systems ·
Development techniques, methodologies, tools and platforms

1 Introduction

The design of complex systems, such as Multi-Agent Systems (MAS), should
consider models that are clear to communicate, provide support during programming, and allow reuse and reasoning over the specification [6]. The use
of modelling methodologies help us to understand complex problems and their
potential solutions through abstractions. Thus, in this context, research investigating ontologies to support the modelling of MAS has been carried out [6,11,16].
Well-known MAS development frameworks, such as JaCaMo [1], integrate different technologies and languages for the design of MAS. In this chapter, we
propose an ontology-based MAS development approach where a common basic
language is used to present and specify a MAS, resulting in the integration of
their different aspects and also serving for core code generation in JaCaMo [1].

It should be noted from the start that, although the general approach can
be applied to any agent-oriented platform, the fact that there is not overall
agreement on concepts and terms used in Agent-Oriented Software Engineering
(AOSE), we need specific ontologies for each platform. While we here concentrate
on the well-known JaCaMo framework [1], work on alignment with upper ontologies might in the future facilitate also the integration of different approaches to
agent-oriented development.

© Springer Nature Switzerland AG 2019
D. Weyns et al. (Eds.): EMAS 2018 Workshops, LNAI 11375, pp. 76–95, 2019.
https://doi.org/10.1007/978-3-030-25693-7_5

An important contribution of agent-oriented programming as a new paradigm was to provide ways to help programmers in developing autonomous systems. For example, agent programming languages typically have high-level programming constructs which facilitate (compared to traditional programming languages) the development of systems that are continuously running and reacting to changes in the dynamic environments where such autonomous systems usually operate [1]. Agent-oriented paradigms are normally used to develop very complex systems, where not only are many autonomous entities present in a shared environment but also they need to interact in complex ways and need to have social structures and norms to regulate the overall social behaviour that is expected of them.

This chapter is organised as follows. Section 2 focuses on alternative modelling approaches for engineering MAS. Section 3 introduces the topic of programming such systems using JaCaMo. Section 4 presents our model-based techniques to support code generation for JaCaMo. Section 5 explores the issue of reasoning with ontology models. In Sect. 6 we discuss the results of an experiment that was conducted to evaluate the proposed framework. Section 7 concludes this chapter and highlights some research directions for future work.

2   Multi-Agent Systems Modelling Approaches

Current AOSE methodologies (such as Prometheus [12]) are usually deficient in at least one area of MAS development [15], such as agent internal design, interaction design, or organisation modelling. Also, currently we have separate approaches to address the modelling and programming of MAS, resulting in gaps and conceptual divergences in AOSE [6,7]. While JaCaMo [1] is a programming platform that uses three *different* formalisms for coding, Prometheus [12] is an agent modelling approach that does not apply or explore any formal (logic-based) representation as part of its technique. This work addresses issues stemming from those facts investigating an ontology-based model-driven engineering approach as an integrated global model of MAS characteristics, where ontology models support MAS verification and programming. Although the advantages of ontologies for agents are clear, few MAS platforms currently integrate ontology techniques [6,15]. Limited ontological support is provided by a number of existing AOSE methodologies since they do not incorporate ontologies throughout the entire development lifecycle nor consider ways in which ontologies can be used to account for interoperability and verification during design [15].

Several models and methodologies can be found in literature to formalise and define the processes of MAS design and implementation. For example, Prometheus [12] is one of the best-known MAS modelling methodology for developing intelligent agent systems. It defines a development process with associated deliverables for assisting developers to design, document, and build agent systems based on concepts such as goals, beliefs, plans, and events. The Prometheus [12] methodology encompasses three phases: *system specification*, *architectural design*, and *detailed design*. Among future work for Prometheus [12] there is the introduction of social concepts to improve its current models, however these improvements are not available yet in the latest official version of the Prometheus Design Tool (PDT). Therefore, some aspects of MAS are not covered by the models of Prometheus, which also does not explore the use of formal or explicit ontologies as part of its approach. Ontologies for MAS are being proposed and investigated to support programming and reasoning over specifications, and they can also offer code generation features and help in organising the many concepts involved in the modelling, development, and verification of MAS. In this direction, ontologies have been considered in several different approaches in AOSE [6,11,16]. Ontologies are defined as knowledge representation structures composed of concepts, properties, individuals, relationships, and axioms.

It is possible to find in literature ontologies for the environments of MAS [11]. Environments play an essential role in MAS, and their semantic representation improves the way agents reason about the objects with which they interact and the overall environment where they are situated. This is important because most agent-oriented programming languages are weak in allowing the developer to model the environment within which the agents will execute [2]. The use of an environment ontology adds three important features to existing multi-agent approaches [11]: *(i)* ontologies provide a common vocabulary to enable environment specification by agent developers (since it explicitly represents the environment and agent essential properties, defining environments in ontologies facilitates and improves the development of multi-agent simulations); *(ii)* an environment ontology is useful for agents acting in the environment because it provides a common vocabulary for communication within and about the environment (it allows interoperability of heterogeneous systems); and *(iii)* environment ontologies can be defined in ontology editors with graphical user interfaces, making easier for those unfamiliar with programming to understand and design such ontologies.

Research on ontologies for MAS environments [11] had already foreseen the relationship between the environment and other MAS dimensions, since they mention the intention of looking at higher-level aspects of environments, i.e., social environment aspects of agents, such as the specification of social norms and organisations in agent societies. In fact, on the MAS organisation dimension, there is a semantic description of MAS organisations [16] to specify an ontology for organisational characteristics of the Moise meta-model. This approach helps agents in becoming aware, querying, and reasoning about their social and organisational context in a uniform way, making possible to convert between ontology and Moise specifications, thus providing more flexibility for modelling and developing in this domain. This semantic description of Moise [16] provides other benefits such as increased modularisation, knowledge enriching with metadata, reuse of specifications, and easier integration. With the semantic web effort aiming to represent the information in semantic formats, the MAS community can take advantage of these new technologies in AOSE development tasks such as to integrate organisational models, to monitor organisations, and to analyse agent societies [16].

Next section introduces the JaCaMo as a unified programming framework for these MAS characteristics recently discussed.

3   Programming in JaCaMo

MAS programming in JaCaMo [1] requires the development of code in Jason [3], CArtAgO [14], and Moise [9]. Jason [3] is an AgentSpeak language implementation that focuses on agent actions and mental concepts and provide to programmers features such as speech-act based agent communication, plan annotation, architecture customisation, distributed execution, extensibility through internal actions, among other functionalities. On the environment side of agent systems, CArtAgO [14] is a platform to support the artifact notion in MAS. Artifacts are function-oriented computational devices which provide services that agents can exploit to support their individual and social activities [14]. Lastly, the specification of agents at the organisation level can be achieved using an organisation modelling language, such as Moise [9]. Moise explicitly decomposes the specification of an organisation into its structural, functional, and normative dimensions.

JaCaMo resulted from one of the earliest approaches aimed at explicitly investigating the integration of all the dimensions of MAS from a design and programming point of view. Most previously existing approaches had considered either only the agent-organisation dimensions, or the agent-environment dimensions [1]. The combination of these dimensions of MAS into a single programming paradigm with a concrete working platform has a major impact on the ability to program complex distributed systems. The authors of JaCaMo pointed out, as future work, the desire for an Integrated Development Environment (IDE) to facilitate the process of design, development, and execution of JaCaMo applications, potentially reusing and integrating existing Jason, CArtAgO, and Moise tools and technologies [1]. Thus, recognising the importance achieved by JaCaMo, this research direction is one of the motivations in this chapter.

JaCaMo is one of the few fully operational platforms combining all three dimensions of MAS, to the best of our knowledge, and arguably one of the best-known (e.g., given it is highly cited). Thus, our proposed techniques for modelling and code generation address the design of MAS with an eye on implementations using JaCaMo as the target programming platform specifically. However, as noted earlier, the overall approach could also be recreated for other agent development platforms as well. Other frameworks for MAS development provide some support for environments, or some organisational notions such as roles, but without including a fully-fledged organisational model and first-class environment abstractions that are provided by JaCaMo.

4   Code Generation Techniques for Multi-Agent Systems Designed as Ontology Models

In our work we present two different techniques for code generation based on models specified using an ontology of MAS obtained from the literature [5,6]. One technique is the iterative drag-and-drop of elements from ontology to transform them into the different parts of code that compose a JaCaMo project: Jason, CArtAgO, Moise, or the jcm file. The other technique is the automatic generation of the initial files and code of JaCaMo projects that match the ontology-specified content. Both techniques are implemented in our tool called Onto2JaCaMo. Our work employs the ontology of MAS obtained from [5,6] as the basis for the code generation techniques, and we refer to it as OntoMAS. For details about the ontology, we refer to its references, so that we can focus here on its applications. When using an ontology for modelling MAS, the underlying idea is that the MAS project conception should start by its modelling as an ontology. This is done by extending the ontology top-level concepts, and adding new classes, instances and relationships in order to specify the corresponding desired project to be implemented in terms of agent-oriented concepts [6].

In OntoMAS, a particular MAS begins to be modelled by *extending* the ontology, which is done by creating new subclasses to its top-level concepts. Then, individuals are created in the process of *instantiating* the extended ontology. From an instantiated model, it is possible to perform *reasoning* and obtain an inferred specification, which can be explored for *verification* purposes such as, for example, in model checking approaches. Then, a model specified using OntoMAS can be used in our techniques for supporting MAS *programming*, which are incorporated into the Onto2JaCaMo tool. Such an approach also allows designers to gradually refine from high-level abstract views to elements directly available in concrete features of MAS programming platforms. The designers may apply the desired level of completeness in their models, which will later result in a code with a corresponding detailing. Figure 1 illustrates how OntoMAS and Onto2JaCaMo fit in the phases of AOSE in the proposed methodology. Currently, an ontology editor tool, such as Protégé [10], should be used to interact with OntoMAS during the MAS modelling. OntoMAS is currently formalised in OWL (Web Ontology Language), which is a computational logic-based Semantic Web language designed to represent rich and complex knowledge about things, groups of things, and relations between things. Future research, besides, could consider new languages to be used for OntoMAS if they offer some sort of advantages in terms of knowledge representation and reasoning.

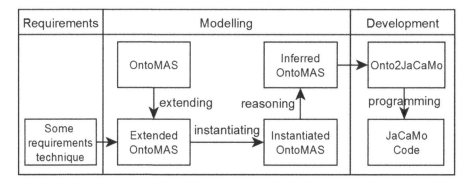

Fig. 1. Methodology using OntoMAS and Onto2JaCaMo.

4.1   Mapping Elements from the MAS Ontology to JaCaMo Code

Initially, lets make a mapping of where elements from OntoMAS [5,6] are usually found in a JaCaMo project. There are concepts to deal with the *Agent Dimension* with a clear relation to Jason (such as *Agent*, *Plan*, and *Belief*), concepts to deal with the *Environment Dimension* to establish a relation with CArtAgO (such as *Artifact*, *Space*, and *Operation*), and concepts to deal with the *Organisation Dimension* to address Moise specifications (such as *Group*, *Role*, and *Norm*).

From the agent dimension, we are not interested in defining any possible and generic characteristics of any kind of agent, such as physical agents. Instead, we are interested in specifying only the concepts of virtual agents that make sense in the context of programming for this dimension. Thus, the OntoMAS ontology contains the following 6 top-level concepts to represent the agent dimension: *Agent*, *Plan*, *Action*, *AgentGoal*, *Belief*, and *Message*. Figure 2 summarises the main concepts, subclasses and properties in the agent dimension of OntoMAS.

As already mentioned, the use of OntoMAS ontology sometimes requires to create subclasses that specialise the given top-level domain concepts. A subclass of *Agent* represents a type of agent, such as for example, *Player*. When defining a given concept as a subclass of *Agent*, this concept represents all individual agents of that kind. Subclasses of *Agent* are usually found in JaCaMo as the .asl files. An instance of a subclass of *Agent* represents an individual agent of that corresponding type, such as for example *playerJohn*. Instances, such as *playerJohn*, are usually found in JaCaMo as individual agents defined by an agentID in the .jcm file.

A *Plan* is a procedure composed of actions and it is triggered inside agents. The definition of each plan should be represented as an instance of the *Plan* concept. Thus, instances of plans represent the specification of a plan, such as for example *chooseMovement*. The specification of a plan is found in JaCaMo inside the .asl code of the type of agent that contains such plan. From this modelling perspective adopted in OntoMAS, the designer does not need to create subclasses of *Plan*, but this possibility is allowed. There are classes in this dimension that can be applied just by creating instances, which we argue that is the most simple way. However, the modeller is allowed to create subclasses to achieve an additional layer of expressiveness.

There are two kinds of *Actions* represented in OntoMAS: *ExternalAction* and *InternalAction*. An *ExternalAction* is what the agent does that affects the environment, such as the act of opening a door. An *InternalAction* is how an agent act to manipulate its mental state, for example, forgetting some belief. While internal actions may be defined by local actions in the agent's state, external actions may refer to performing operations of artifacts that are situated in an environment. The definition of an action is represented by creating an instance of *Action*, such as for example *openDoor*. Actions are usually found in JaCaMo in the body of agents' plans. Similarly with plans, the designer does not need to create further subclasses of *Action*, but this possibility is allowed. For example, the subclass *openDoor* could have two different instances according to different door handles, *openDoor-barhandle* and *openDoor-knobshandle*.

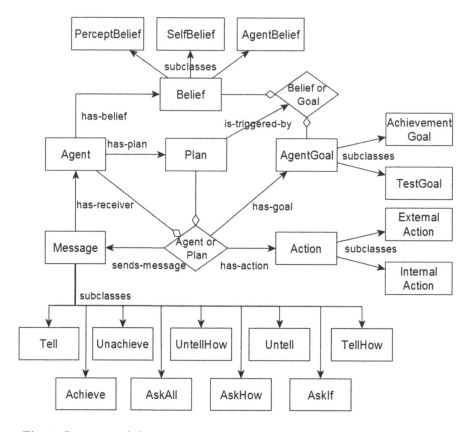

Fig. 2. Concepts, subclasses and properties in the agent dimension of OntoMAS.

An *AgentGoal* represents some agent individual desire to be achieved. Goals can be in one of the two following types. An *AchievementGoal* represents a state of the world (objective) that an agent can have intention to attain, such as having the door opened. A *TestGoal* is a check on the agent's beliefs in order to verify if a given belief holds, for example, querying the belief about the door being closed. Both achievement and test goals may fail, but for any plan that is using them in order to continue its execution and finish with success, its goals must be completed. The definition of a type of goal that agents may pursue is represented by creating an instance of *AgentGoal*, such as for example to achieve *doorOpened*. Goals are usually found in JaCaMo inside agent code (`.asl` files).

The *Belief* encodes the knowledge of agents, which can be one of the three types, as follows. *PerceptBeliefs* are obtained from environment perception, for example, the belief *stoveLit* to represent the state perceived from a device. *AgentBeliefs* are beliefs obtained from some other agent, for example, when an agent is told by other about something. *SelfBeliefs* are obtained by internal agent reasoning, for example, when an agent believes in something but not because it was perceived from the environment nor it was told by other agent. The definition of a type of belief is specified by creating an instance of *Belief*, such as for example *preferredMove*, which can be a *SelfBelief*. Beliefs are usually found in JaCaMo inside the code of agents (`.asl` files).

A *Message* is a communication that goes from one agent to another. The definition of a type of message is represented by creating an instance of *Message*, such as for example *informLocation*. Sending a *Message* may be a part of a plan in agents. The message types correspond to which performative is part of the *sender* agent's intention, for example, if it is delegating a goal (*AchieveMessage*), informing a belief (*TellMessage*), requesting a plan (*AskHowMessage*), etc. There are 9 different types that a message can assume, each representing its illocutionary force, all of them depicted in Fig. 2 as subclasses of *Message*.

After explaining the concepts illustrated in Fig. 2, we can now discuss other topic depicted there, namely the properties that take place in relationships among concepts of the agent dimension. Plans may contain actions, which means that when a given plan is being executed, its corresponding actions may be performed. This is represented by connecting instances of these concepts using the *has-action* property, for example, *chooseMovement has-action openDoor*. The same is true for plans that may start the pursue of goals, defined through the property *has-goal*, as exemplified by *chooseMovement has-goal doorOpened*. Also about plans, they may be triggered by an event involving a belief or a goal, which is given by the property named *is-triggered-by*. To indicate that a given plan sends a specific message, the *sends-message* property may be used. There is no need to specify for agents the *has-action* and *sends-message* properties if they were all specified for plans, a general rule can make inferences to check if an agent contains plans that have actions and send messages, in such case the agent will also present these properties too. We refer to Sect. 5 for more details about rules and reasoning over OntoMAS models.

Some properties work with the concept of *Agent* as its domain or range. We have explained that the *Agent* concept may have both subclasses (e.g., *Player*) and instances (e.g., *playerJohn*). When it is desired to use a property to connect between instances, the semantic is the same as explained in the previous paragraph. For example, agents may have beliefs, as expressed by the *has-belief* property. If *playerJohn* has some belief, lets call *preferredMove*, then these instances have to be connected using the mentioned *has-belief* property. However, if all agents of that type (*Player*) have such belief, then a "subclass of" restriction should be used in that concept. This is represented as: *Player* is a subclass of *has-belief value preferredMove*. The same principles are applied to: the *has-goal* property, which indicates the goals of agents; the *has-plan* for indicating the plans of agents; and the *sends-message* property, which indicates which messages the agent sends. To connect an instance of message with an instance of agent that should receive it, the property *has-receiver* can be applied (e.g., *informLocation has-receiver playerJohn*).

We point out to reference [5] for further details on the ontology meta-model that are not tackled here in this chapter. However, we next briefly explain the dimensions of environment and organisation, but not with the same level of detail employed above to show the concepts and properties of the agent dimension.

Each subclass of *Artifact* is found in CArtAgO as a Java class, and instances of *Artifact* subclasses represents an object/tool/resource of that type, which may be found in JaCaMo in the .jcm file that describes the initial artifacts of a system; however, other artifacts instances may be created after the initialisation of the MAS. *Spaces* are initialised in the JaCaMo project file, but agents may make reference to spaces in their code too. *Operations* are found in CArtAgO as methods of the artifact that implements such procedures. Instances of *Percept* (*ObservableProperty* or *ObservableEvent*) are found in the Java code of artifacts through methods provided by the CArtAgO API to manipulate them (such as *defineObsProperty*, *getObsProperty*, *updateObsProperty*, and *signal*).

Subclasses of *Group* can be found in the XML that specifies an organisation in Moise, and their instances take place in the JaCaMo project file, as well as in the code of agents in Jason that can make references to groups (e.g., join_group). Instances of *Role* are found in the Moise XML file, and the code of Jason agents can make reference to such roles too (e.g., adopt_role). Instances of *OrganisationGoal* are also found in the Moise file, and the code of agents in Jason can make references to those goals (for example, agents may have plans to act when a goal is assigned to them by the organisation). Lastly, instances of *Missions* and *Norms* are defined in the Moise XML file of a JaCaMo system.

The classes and properties in OntoMAS are modelled in three sub-ontologies, one for each dimension: agent, environment, and social organisation. The integration and connections among concepts in the dimensions of OntoMAS are encoded by means of concepts, object properties, and rules which determine how elements are allowed to relate among each other. To illustrate, in order to specify the location of agents' instances in spaces from the environment dimension, the property *is-in* may be used, such as, for example *playerJohn is-in classRoom* (considering *classRoom* an instance of *Space*). The property *is-focused* connects an agent with an instance of artifact in which that agent is focused, such as *playerJohn is-focused homeComputer* (considering *homeComputer* an instance of *Artifact*). Then, some properties may be obtained by inference over elements from different dimensions. If an agent (*?a*) is in a space (*?s*), and this space provides some percept (*?p*), then this agent can have such percept (*?a can-perceive ?p*). This is specified through the following rule:

$$is\text{-}in(?a, ?s), provides\text{-}percept(?s, ?p) \rightarrow can\text{-}perceive(?a, ?p).$$

As another example to illustrate important things to represent in the ontology, when relating concepts from the dimensions of agent and organisation, we may desire to specify that a given agent is adopting a role. This may be done with the property *adopts-role*. If a characteristic affects only some individuals of a group, then it should be defined as an object property in those affected instances. In this case, for example, supposing *redSoccerTeam* as an instance of the *Group* concept, if the *redSoccerTeam* contains the *playerJohn* agent, then these instances should be related using the object property *contains-agent*.

4.2 Drag-and-Drop Transformation Technique from the Multi-Agent Systems Ontology to JaCaMo

The idea of using an ontology for providing drag-and-drop operations from models to code in JaCaMo has been already mentioned in literature [5,6]. In this chapter we explain how the elements of an ontology model can be dragged to generate code for the different parts of JaCaMo, such as Jason, CArtAgO, Moise, or the JaCaMo project file that defines the specification that initialises the corresponding system. Each element from an ontology model can be transformed in MAS code in several different ways.

To exemplify the drag-and-drop conversions, let us take a look at how instances of the *ObservableProperty* concept may be employed in the code of each of the different parts of JaCaMo. Suppose there is an instance of *ObservableProperty* called *temperature*, defined at the *Environment Dimension*. If a programmer makes a drag-and-drop of *temperature* in this dimension, a code automatically created as suggestion may be to update the value of such observable property. Thus, the following code can be created:

```
getObsProperty(temperature).updateValue(newValue);
```

In Jason, making a drag-and-drop using this same instance of *ObservableProperty* may give origin to a plan triggered by the observation of such property:

```
+temperature : true <- planBody.
```

However, if dropped in the middle of a plan, then just the corresponding belief identified by *temperature* is generated. When a JaCaMo system is running, the observable properties provided by environmental artifacts become beliefs to agents that are focusing on those artifacts, and when they become beliefs, some plans may be triggered by the belief addition event. Instances of observable properties are not applicable for drag-and-drop code transformations in the case of Moise or JaCaMo project file. We have summarised the information about the drag-and-drop operations provided by Onto2JaCaMo for transforming from the ontology to JaCaMo code in Table 1. This table shows the generation when the desired outcome is the *Agent Dimension* of JaCaMo (i.e., Jason). Similarly, there are strategies to convert the ontology to the *Environment Dimension* of JaCaMo (CArtAgO), to the *Organisation Dimension* (Moise), and also to the initialisation setup of JaCaMo (the .jcm file). However, the tables illustrating these other mappings were not included in this chapter for the sake of space (see reference [5] for further details).

4.3 Core Code Generation Technique from OntoMAS to JaCaMo

The technique proposed in this subsection is related to the idea of using an ontology for the automatic generation of skeleton code for each of the JaCaMo languages. Elements from an ontology of MAS should have their resulting code counterparts in Jason, CArtAgO, and Moise. Therefore, it would be possible to directly transform an ontology-based MAS specification into initial code for JaCaMo. While when using drag-and-drop programmers are iteratively transforming elements from their ontology model into code, this code generation technique uses another perspective, which is to generate an initial structure of a corresponding project in JaCaMo to what is specified in the ontology model.

The generation of initial agent files and code for Jason considers mainly the subclasses and instances of the *Agent Dimension* of the employed ontology. For example, each subclass of *Agent* becomes an .asl file with its corresponding plans, actions, goals, beliefs, and messages. However, characteristics defined at other dimensions, such as the environment, although not directly applicable to generate the initial code at the agent level, may be considered to suggest implementation alternatives for programmers (at least for them to be aware of). For example, for an agent that is expected to receive a given percept, a plan triggered by the addition event of that percept may be suggested as a situation that programmers are likely to have to handle.

Similarly, the initial files of the CArtAgO part of a JaCaMo project derive mainly from the *Environment Dimension* of the ontology in use, and the Moise initial code is generated based on the *Organisation Dimension*. Subclasses of *Artifact* become the Java files with their corresponding operations as methods, and observable properties are initialised. All the organisation elements (subclasses, instances, and relationships) are considered in the generation of the initial XML file of a Moise organisation. Lastly, the JaCaMo project file considers characteristics from all the three dimensions, and relationships from their integration.

To exemplify the initial project generation, consider the *ObservableProperty* instance used in previous examples, *temperature*. If it is said that an artifact type (e.g., *computer*) has this property, then such observable property definition must compose the *init*() method of the *computer* artifact class in the format:

```
defineObsProperty("temperature", initialValue);
```

Considering Jason, Moise, or .jcm files, instances of observable properties are not directly applicable for the automatic code generation in this case. However, a plan triggered by the addition event of the related observable property could be suggested to the agents' programmers as a situation worth to be handled.

How each element from OntoMAS models can be transformed into the initial structure of files and code for Jason is shown in Table 2. This same principle is applied to CArtAgO, Moise, and the project file, albeit, it is not possible to illustrate all those tables in this chapter. However, we have complete definitions for OntoMAS models as starting point to generate skeleton code for each part of JaCaMo programming (Jason, CArtAgO, Moise, and the .jcm project file).

The so-called core code generation technique presented in this subsection creates the first skeleton code for a JaCaMo project that was modelled using the OntoMAS ontology. The drag-and-drop technique is a way to complement and iteratively evolve the programming of such systems. Compared to a fully handwritten code, developers would lack tools that could provide means to integrate the modelling and programming of their MAS.

Table 1. Drag-and-drop code generation for Jason (*Agent Dimension*) from ontology elements.

Instance of the Ontology Element	Drag-and-Drop Code for Jason	Explanation
Agent Dimension		
ExternalAction	`actionName();`	an external action invocation inside a plan's body representing an agent acting in the environment.
InternalAction	`.actionName();`	an internal action invocation inside a plan's body representing an action that an agent performs mentally.
Agent	`agentName`	the identification of the individual agent in order to send messages, or perform some other tasks.
Belief	`+beliefName[source(value)];`	a belief addition event with source's value defined by the belief's subtype: self, percept, or other agent.
AchievementGoal	`!achievementGoalName;`	an initial goal for that agent; or a goal that has to be achieved during the execution a plan.
TestGoal	`?testGoalName;`	a goal that has to be tested during the execution of a plan.
Message	`send(receiver,illocutionaryForce, propositionalContent);`	the act of sending the corresponding instance of message
Plan	`is_triggered_by : true <- actions; goals.`	a plan with its triggering condition, context (that by default is true), and a body composed (mainly) of actions and goals.
Environment Dimension		
Space	`joinWorkspace("workspaceName");`	an action for that agent to join the corresponding workspace.
Artifact	`focus(artifactName);`	the action of focusing on that instance of artifact.
Operation	`operationName();`	the invocation of the corresponding operation in the body of a plan representing the execution of that operation by an agent.
ObservableProperty	`+propertyName : true <- planBody.`	a plan triggered by the observation of the corresponding property.
ObservableEvent	`+eventName : true <- planBody.`	a plan triggered by the observation of the corresponding event.
Organisation Dimension		
Group	`join_group(groupName);`	an action of joining in the given group.
Role	`adopt_role(roleName,groupName);`	the action to adopt the given role in the specified group.
Mission	`commit_mission(missionName, schemeId);`	an action to commit with the instance of mission in the given scheme.
Norm	`+normName: true <- planBody.`	a plan triggered by the perception of the given norm.
OrganisationGoal	`+!goalName : true <- planBody.`	a plan triggered by the addition event of the specified goal.

4.4   The Onto2JaCaMo Tool for Multi-Agent Systems Development

For effective and efficient software development, preferably all tasks and activities during the development process should be adequately supported by tools [13]. The quality of any software tool support can be assessed by considering the degree of support for the different phases and tasks [13], e.g., design tools, which besides the creation and editing of design models also often support consistency checking and/or code generation.

We have implemented the techniques previously explained in Subsects. 4.2 and 4.3 in a software tool to support MAS development, which we refer to as Onto2JaCaMo. It consists of a plug-in for Eclipse that loads instantiated models based on the ontology of MAS obtained from [5,6] to provide code generation for JaCaMo. Eclipse [4] is an open source software development project that provides an IDE in which a basic unit of function, or a component, is called a plug-in. Eclipse is already the standard IDE for JaCaMo development, and it was indeed an interesting choice since Eclipse is recognised as a mature IDE, and one of the most widely used by programmers [13].

Onto2JaCaMo is easily installed by adding its .jar file in the Eclipse plug-ins folder. It can be activated to appear visually in the graphical interface of Eclipse by following this sequence: $Window \rightarrow Show\ View \rightarrow Other... \rightarrow JaCaMo\ Ontology \rightarrow Ok$. When it is enabled, Onto2JaCaMo requests to be informed about the OWL file corresponding to an instantiated ontology so that it can be loaded. The plug-in was designed to be used in the "JaCaMo Perspective" of Eclipse (or related perspectives, such as Jason). The tool loads OWL ontologies and provides three model-based programming features to generate MAS code: drag-and-drop, conversion from ontology to code, and auto-complete from instantiated ontologies.

In the drag-and-drop functionality, the developer can visualise and navigate through the ontology concepts, instances, and properties. These elements from the model can be dragged to the code in files being edited in Eclipse. For example, the programmer may perform a dragging and dropping operation using the action **pass_ball** to be inserted in a plan of agents of type "player". Similarly, it is possible to provide developers the auto-complete feature from ontology to agent code, which is activated when the developer is typing MAS code (or press the auto-complete shortcut: "ctrl + space"). Then, the available options based on the ontology are presented to programmers as suggestions. One example is when coding the plan's context, which may be composed of ontology-based queries (e.g., verifying if an individual belongs to a concept).

The Onto2JaCaMo tool is able to generate code fragments based on design information, which is known as forward engineering [13]. This is in the opposite direction of extracting design information out of existing application code, the so called reverse engineering. A drawback of forward or reverse engineering techniques is that after a generated artifact has been changed manually, forward or reverse engineering cannot be reapplied without losing the changes, as stated in the called "post editing problem". The combined support of forward and reverse engineering, such that changes in one artifact can always be merged into the other without compromising consistency or losing changes, is referred to as round-trip engineering [13]. The Onto2JaCaMo tool presented in this work does not address such advanced and complex concepts of synchronisation as yet; these are, however, interesting topics for future work.

5   Ontology-Based Reasoning Support for Agent Systems

Model verification refers to the processes and techniques that the model developer uses to ensure that their model is correct and matches any agreed-upon specifications and assumptions. OntoMAS can be explored with its available reasoning mechanisms to implement model verification in the context of MAS. The literature reports that most practical approaches for verification of MAS are done on code, and most of the work done on model checking within the MAS research area is quite theoretical [2]. However, there are approaches that use model checkers typically to verify properties of particular aspects of a given MAS. While this has the advantage of proving properties of systems that will be deployed, it is also often useful to check properties during systems' design.

Considering this context, semantic reasoners may provide, for example, consistency checking and inferences about the MAS specified as an ontology. Ontologies empower the execution of semantic reasoners that provide functionalities such as *consistency checking*, *concept satisfiability*, *classification*, and *realisation*. In other words, reasoners are able to automatically infer logical consequences from a set of axioms. The possibility to reason about the model can provide support for various consistency checks during the MAS project design and implementation. For example, when considering only MAS organisations, it is possible to check for conflicts considering the existing norms, roles, and missions. When an instantiation of MAS organisation is combined with instantiated agents, it is possible to check for other kinds of inconsistencies integrating information from more than one dimension, such as whether the agents contain the required capabilities to achieve the existing organisation goals. Organisation goals are assigned to agents playing the organisation roles, and an agent playing a specific role may not have the required plans to achieve the goals that the organisation will assign to it. Reasoning can be applied also to verify consistency among the norms in the organisation. The combination of some norms can result in contradictions, for example, when a prohibition occurs together with an obligation or permission. These contradictions can appear when considering the missions of just one isolated role, or when combining the missions of two or more roles.

When analysing the knowledge about the environment, it can be checked whether agent actions are valid in a given environment configuration. If there is an agent action that does not exist in the environment, the invocation of such an action in run-time will result in failure. Thus, the verification of characteristics over an instantiated model at design time may prevent future errors to happen during the execution time of the corresponding JaCaMo specified project.

The use of ontology enables the creation of *rules*, which can be coded in the Semantic Web Rule Language (SWRL). Such rules can be inherited from the base

OntoMAS ontology, and new ones can be added specifically for an extension and instantiation of OntoMAS, when defining a desired MAS scenario. All elements in the ontology are taken into consideration when semantic reasoners are executed for making inferences. For example, one general rule is that if an agent a is in a space s, and this space s can provide an observable property p, then it can be inferred that the agent a is able to perceive p if it chooses to do so. This rule is coded as follows:

```
is-in(?a,?s), provides-percept(?s,?p) -> can-perceive(?a,?p).
```

In such reasoning mechanism it is possible to relate elements from any dimension (e.g., agent) with elements from other dimensions (e.g., environment). Lets suppose now a more complex example for inferences about a modelled MAS. We already commented that agents join organisations by playing organisation-defined roles, and it is expected that such agents have in their codes the required plans to handle the goals that the organisation may assign to them. Organisation goals are assigned to agents, for example, if there is an obligation norm on that role, and an agent that adopts such role should have a plan for achieving that goal. Lets represent this with a new property to specify that Agents should-have-plan-for Goals. This can be inferred, for example, if there is an obligation norm n that targets a role r, and there is an agent a that adopts the role r, then, the conclusion is that the agent a should have a plan for the goal g, where g is a goal from mission m, which is the mission for the obligation norm n. The following rule exemplifies how to make this inference:

```
ObligationNorm(?n), targets-role(?n,?r), adopts-role(?a,?r),
targets-mission(?n,?m), has-goal(?m,?g) ->
                              should-have-plan-for(?a,?g).
```

As we have exemplified using some rules in this subsection, more complex information can be incrementally inferred from the basic conceptualisation proposed by OntoMAS. Also, it allows extensions to be made on top of it, by including for example new concepts, properties, and so on.

As another example, it can be inferred which operations and percepts can be obtained from each space based on which artifacts are situated in it (the concept of *Space* from the ontology refers to the called *Workspaces* of CArtAgO). A rule may be used as follows:

```
contains-artifact(?s,?a), provides-percept(?a,?p) ->
                              provides-percept(?s,?p).
```

This rule can be read as: if the space s contains an artifact a, and a provides a percept p, then s provides p. The same reasoning principle applies to operations from artifacts that are located in some space. Moreover, another general rule about environments is that the percepts and operations of sub-spaces are also provided by the spaces that contain them.

6 Evaluating Onto2JaCaMo

Our initial evaluation of Onto2JaCaMo indicates that it facilitates coding in JaCaMo, mainly for beginners or for those who are not fully aware about how to implement some agent concepts. Users have reported that it improves the understanding about the operation of JaCaMo and how to program particular behaviours. Also, Onto2JaCaMo helps avoid syntactical errors as it provides code templates, which is important because the auto-complete shortcut from Eclipse ("ctrl + space") does not work in all JaCaMo extensions. Thus, more agility can be obtained in JaCaMo code generation. Lastly, during development, it is interesting to visualise the system's ontology, so that the idea defined in models may be followed easier when programming. Most importantly, it avoids some of the most common types of bugs made by programmers such as mistyping names since now the ontology provides the vocabulary to be used in the code.

Before starting our experiments regarding the evaluation of the programming techniques implemented in Onto2JaCaMo, the participants received the required prior instructions on these topics in order to perform the tasks with the minimum required knowledge, such as, for example, how to load and how to use ontology models in Onto2JaCaMo. The participants received the Onto2JaCaMo plug-in, where they had to load their previously instantiated ontology models and use the tool to support the model-based development of their agent code. Each participant had previously defined their own application scenario to work with. After finishing the programming of their MAS using the drag-and-drop provided by Onto2JaCaMo, the participants were surveyed by means of questionnaires to extract their perceptions and opinions about the techniques and tool according with statements that followed a 5-point Likert scale. Some criteria have received only positive evaluations from all participants, such as that Onto2JaCaMo is easy to understand, provides coding support, offers advantages for programming, and enables a better understanding of JaCaMo.

Thus, we observe that the proposed plug-in helps in code consistency (e.g., it facilitates coding using the same terms), and it prevents developers from using terms outside the ontology-based model. In summary, such approach provides an overview about agent systems to be visualised within the programming context, combined with features of dragging content from models to MAS code. As lessons learned from our practical experiences, we have observed that more MAS code could be generated from the proposed modelling approach, and that the ontology could be used in a technique to constrain the MAS coding (i.e., to indicate errors or mismatches between model and code). Also as future work, we have noticed that Onto2JaCaMo could provide model editing features (for example, to include new instances), which would discard the need of an ontology editing tool to update the ontology model. Another point for improvement that was highlighted by our practices, although a very complex one, is the automatic update of the ontology when the MAS code changes [6], in the direction of synchronising model and code. This might be solved by implementing features to highlight mismatches between MAS code and its corresponding model in order to keep both aligned.

In a last part of our experiments, the participants created theirs models and later programmed manually their code, which means without using the core code generation mechanism. That allowed us to compare the code that our technique creates automatically from the ontology models with the code actually programmed by the participants. Through these comparisons, we have observed the correspondences and similarities between elements in the code that was automatically generated from the specification in contrast with the code that was manually programmed. These similarities between these two sources of code are indicative of the correctness of the proposed model-based code generation technique. We have analysed that some key elements in the ontology models created by the participants, the corresponding code that was automatically generated from these elements by using the proposed techniques, and the code actually programmed by them. We were able to confirm that the model-based technique for generating code is indeed offering a program reasonably similar to the code structured created by the programmer[1], given the analysed aspects. We argue that if the starting codes were created based on converting their corresponding models, then it would be easier for programmers to align their initial code with the design and continue their programming based on that. The similarities between what can be automatically generated with what was manually created indicate that the code generation is in the correct direction and it provides more agility for developers that have their systems modelled before they start coding. We point out to our reference [5] for further details on our evaluations that would not be possible to tackle here in this chapter.

7   Final Remarks

In this chapter, we have proposed development techniques focusing on the JaCaMo platform, on the basis of ontologies that support the modelling and programming of MAS. Our proposal considers MAS designed as ontology models as the foundation for a MAS engineering process that allows core code generation. We have explored the research direction of reasoning with these ontology models, which allows the implementation of inference mechanisms in agent-based systems such as, for example, to reason about action, plans, knowledge, beliefs, goals, and norms in MAS. Producing software code for complex and highly detailed systems directly in programming environments by first using a specification, modelling, or design mechanism may avoid many problems. Without a proper modelling, it may be difficult to find potential bugs when they eventually appear in the implementation. Features derived from our approach are techniques for: *(i)* integrating design and code; *(ii)* supporting MAS programming with automatic code generation through model-based development; and *(iii)* performing verification with focus on the use of semantic reasoning and model checking.

---

[1] The model is at a higher abstraction level than the code, so sometimes only a structure or code skeleton can be created and programmers have to complete it in order to obtain a fully executable and running system.

Ontologies that serve as the basis of agent models could also inform agents in reasoning about their own system or even other systems or projects. These would allow agents to be able to share their implementation with others, or to execute inferences about its own implementation. In this context, an approach that provides for MAS the ability to interact with ontologies may be applied [8]. As future experiments, it would be interesting to consider more complex and distributed scenarios of software development, for example where teams of software engineers need to work together to develop a single MAS. These teams would be composed of persons playing different roles such as requirement engineer, designer, programmer, etc. In this context, it should be investigated how much a modelling and programming approach that is based on an ontology would help the team to communicate, synchronise, and coordinate the development of the desired MAS. Moreover, a viewpoint that should also be considered in future work is the comparison between using and not using the approach proposed in this chapter (similar to what is done with experiments conducted on the basis of a control group). Moreover, as we have highlighted in this chapter, new features may be added to Onto2JaCaMo, such as refactoring mechanisms for model and code synchronisation. Another related point would be to automatically identify mismatches between current MAS code and its corresponding model. That would contribute towards implementing round-trip engineering features in the context of MAS development (combined use of forward and reverse engineering).

For the sake of better explaining our approaches through examples, Sect. 4 discussed mostly the possibility of extending the OntoMAS ontology by creating new subclasses. We claim that the approach is more extensible than shown here, for example, one may decide to add new classes, properties or even rules, but in these cases, the consistency of the obtained ontology may be a major problem to deal with, especially in terms of future research directions. However, it is not an easy task to extend an ontology if the users do not have any solid prior knowledge about it. For example, Sect. 5 depicted general rules of agent systems which can be refined and extended for specific domains, which means that OntoMAS is extensible not only by adding new subclasses but in every part of its components. Literature often claims that it is worth considering what someone else has done and checking if existing sources can be refined and extended for the required particular domain and task. Reusing existing ontologies may be a requirement if a system needs to interact with other applications that have already committed to particular ontologies or controlled vocabularies. Lastly, the OntoMAS ontology[2] and the Onto2JaCaMo plug-in[3] can be found in the addresses given as footnotes.

Acknowledgements. This study was financed in part by the Coordenação de Aperfeiçoamento de Pessoal de Nivel Superior – Brasil (CAPES) – Finance Code 001.

---

[2] OntoMAS ontology: http://www.inf.pucrs.br/linatural/wordpress/index.php/recur sos-e-ferramentas/ontomas/.

[3] Onto2JaCaMo plug-in: http://www.inf.pucrs.br/linatural/wordpress/index.php/re cursos-e-ferramentas/onto2jacamo/.

References

1. Boissier, O., Bordini, R.H., Hübner, J., Ricci, A., Santi, A.: Multi-agent oriented programming with JaCaMo. Sci. Comput. Program. **78**(6), 747–761 (2013)
2. Bordini, R.H., Dastani, M., Winikoff, M.: Current issues in multi-agent systems development. In: O'Hare, G.M.P., Ricci, A., O'Grady, M.J., Dikenelli, O. (eds.) ESAW 2006. LNCS (LNAI), vol. 4457, pp. 38–61. Springer, Heidelberg (2007). https://doi.org/10.1007/978-3-540-75524-1_3
3. Bordini, R.H., Hübner, J.F., Wooldridge, M.: Programming Multi-Agent Systems in AgentSpeak Using Jason. Wiley, Chichester (2007)
4. Budinsky, F.: Eclipse Modeling Framework: A Developers Guide. The Eclipse Series. Addison-Wesley, Boston (2004)
5. Freitas, A.: Model-driven engineering of multi-agent systems based on ontology. Ph.D. thesis, Pontifícia Universidade Católica do Rio Grande do Sul, Porto Alegre, RS, Brazil (2017). http://tede2.pucrs.br/tede2/handle/tede/7930
6. Freitas, A., Bordini, R.H., Vieira, R.: Model-driven engineering of multi-agent systems based on ontologies. Appl. Ontol. J. **12**, 157–188 (2017)
7. Freitas, A., Cardoso, R.C., Vieira, R., Bordini, R.H.: Limitations and divergences in approaches for agent-oriented modelling and programming. In: Baldoni, M., Müller, J.P., Nunes, I., Zalila-Wenkstern, R. (eds.) International Workshop on Engineering Multi-Agent Systems, pp. 88–103 (2016)
8. Freitas, A., Panisson, A.R., Hilgert, L., Meneguzzi, F., Vieira, R., Bordini, R.H.: Applying ontologies to the development and execution of multi-agent systems. Web Intell. J. **15**(4), 291–302 (2017)
9. Hübner, J.F., Boissier, O., Kitio, R., Ricci, A.: Instrumenting multi-agent organisations with organisational artifacts and agents. Auton. Agents Multi-Agent Syst. **20**(3), 369–400 (2010)
10. Musen, M.A.: The Protégé project: a look back and a look forward. AI Matters **1**(4), 4–12 (2015)
11. Okuyama, F.Y., Vieira, R., Bordini, R.H., da Rocha Costa, A.C.: An ontology for defining environments within multi-agent simulations. In: Workshop on Ontologies and Metamodeling in Software and Data Engineering (2006)
12. Padgham, L., Winikoff, M.: Prometheus: a methodology for developing intelligent agents. In: Giunchiglia, F., Odell, J., Weiß, G. (eds.) AOSE 2002. LNCS, vol. 2585, pp. 174–185. Springer, Heidelberg (2003). https://doi.org/10.1007/3-540-36540-0_14
13. Pokahr, A., Braubach, L.: A survey of agent-oriented development tools. In: Fallah-Seghrouchni, A.E., Dix, J., Dastani, M., Bordini, R.H. (eds.) Multi-Agent Programming, Languages, Tools and Applications, pp. 289–329. Springer, Boston (2009). https://doi.org/10.1007/978-0-387-89299-3_9
14. Ricci, A., Viroli, M., Omicini, A.: CArtAgO: an infrastructure for engineering computational environments in MAS. In: Weyns, D., Parunak, H.V.D., Michel, F. (eds.) International Workshop Environments for Multi-Agent Systems, pp. 102–119 (2006)
15. Tran, Q.N.N., Low, G.: MOBMAS: a methodology for ontology-based multi-agent systems development. Inf. Softw. Technol. J. **50**(7–8), 697–722 (2008)
16. Zarafin, A.M.: Semantic description of multi-agent organizations. Master's thesis, Automatic Control and Computers Faculty, Computer Science and Engineering Department - Politehnica University of Bucharest (2012)

Engineering Self-adaptive Systems: From Experiences with MUSA to a General Design Process

Massimo Cossentino[1], Luca Sabatucci[1(✉)], and Valeria Seidita[1,2]

[1] Consiglio Nazionale delle Ricerche, Istituto di Calcolo e Reti ad Alte Prestazioni,
Palermo, Italy
{massimo.cossentino,luca.sabatucci}@icar.cnr.it
[2] Dip. dell'Innovazione Industriale e Digitale, Università degli Studi di Palermo,
Palermo, Italy
valeria.seidita@unipa.it

Abstract. Designing and developing complex self-adaptive systems require design processes having specific features fitting and representing the complexity of these systems. Changing requirements, users' needs and dynamic environment have to be taken in consideration, also considering that, due of the self-adaptive nature of the system, the solution is not fixed at design time but it is a run-time outcome. Traditional design approach and life cycles are not suitable to design software systems where requirements continuously change at runtime.

A new design process paradigm is needed to design such systems. In this Chapter, we present a retrospective analysis based on three projects developed in the last five years with the middleware MUSA in order to identify specific features of the design process for supporting continuous change and self-adaptation. The result is a general approach allowing to reduce the gap between design time and run-time.

Keywords: Adaptive management · Continuous change · Design process

1 Introduction

Today, there are several trends that are forcing application architectures to evolve. Users expect a rich, interactive and dynamic user experience on a wide variety of clients including mobile devices. Customers expect frequent rollouts, even multiple times a day, to keep pace with their informational and service requirements. Moreover, customers want to significantly reduce technology costs and are unwilling to fund technology changes that do not result in direct customer benefits.

In traditional software life-cycles, a single change can affect multiple components, creating a complicated testing effort, requiring testers to understand various code interdependencies or test the entire application for each change. IT

© Springer Nature Switzerland AG 2019
D. Weyns et al. (Eds.): EMAS 2018 Workshops, LNAI 11375, pp. 96–116, 2019.
https://doi.org/10.1007/978-3-030-25693-7_6

organizations demand a paradigm shift: from monolithic applications (that puts all user interfaces, business logic and data in a single process) toward applications that enable architectural extensibility.

The level of adaptability to changing requirements is managed at design time using ad-hoc life cycle or process models. Developing self-adaptive systems using a systematic approach requires to consider several factors that may be summarized in: changing operational context and changing environment.

Even though different kinds of approaches for engineering self-adaptive systems exist - they span from control theory to service-oriented and from agent-based approaches to nature-inspired ones - today some possible good approaches seem to be those exploiting models-at-run-time and reflection. Nevertheless, a disciplined and systematic design process for developing self-adaptive systems, able to consider changing operational context and changing environment, still lacks.

A need for new design paradigms arises. Design paradigms where continuous changes are managed through continuous delivery or adaptation of new portions of the system during its operations.

The aim of this Chapter is to identify a general design process for self-adaptive systems. For pursuing this objective, we started from our experience with MUSA (Middleware for User-Driven Service Adaptation), the middleware we created for developing self-adaptive systems. We explored the way in which MUSA works, to identify and to analyze which are the elements of the process involved in that. We considered a five years experience in employing MUSA on three projects. The analysis has been conducted focusing on the design activities and three different measures to gain insights on the effort spent in the design and the aptitude of the system to autonomously find solutions. The results have, then, been used for generalizing a design approach.

The rest of the Chapter is organized as follows: Section 2 discusses the need for a new design paradigm, Sect. 3 illustrates some existing middleware for self-adaptive systems, Sect. 4 discusses the retrospective analysis on MUSA; in Sect. 5 the obtained results are discussed and in Sect. 6 we discuss them and we propose a general design approach; finally in Sect. 7 some conclusions are drawn.

2   Continuous Changes and Self-adaptation

A self-adaptive system is a system able to modify its behavior and/or its structure in order to respond to changes perceived from the environment it is working on or from inside the system itself. Changes are considered to occur while the system is working. System requirements and also system ability to adapt depend by all the actors that interact with the system, the environment whose changes are affected by and affect the system. The system behavior itself is a source of changes and adaptation. Adaptive behavior is prone to three types of dependency: actor-dependency, system-dependency, and environment-dependency.

Designing and developing self-adaptive systems have to consider the following factors: requirements are identified at runtime, environment conditions continuously change, users heavily and continuously interact with the system and the global behavior of the system emerges at runtime.

Traditional software engineering approaches cannot be used for developing self-adaptive systems. They prescribe a very disciplined process that follows a well-specific life-cycle; the main aim is to make the software development as more predictable as possible. All the requirements have to be identified and analyzed in the very early activities of the design process and then transformed into code.

A software system is a solution to a problem, regardless the level of complexity of the problem and the software, and the level of adaptivity to changing requirements is managed at design time using ad-hoc life cycles or process models. Several process models may be used: waterfall, iterative and incremental and so on. This way of working has been well established since years for all those systems that do not require particular changes and do not work in changing conditions.

Different kinds of approaches for engineering self-adaptive systems exist [14,22,41], they span from control theory [10] to service-oriented [29] and from agent-based approaches [19,40] to nature-inspired ones [43]. They all map to the so-called MAPE cycle [38]: monitoring, analyzing, planning and executing. In [42], for instance, authors propose five patterns of interacting MAPE loops to be used for implementing decentralized control.

A promising approach to manage complexity in runtime environments is to develop adaptation mechanisms that involve software models. This is referred to as models@run.time. The idea is to extend the model produced using MDE approaches to the run-time environment. The authors of models@run.time emphasize the importance that software models (artifacts) may play at runtime stating that *if a system changes the representation of the system should change and vice versa.* Another approach aims at managing complexity in runtime environments and at implementing MAPE cycle by developing adaptation mechanisms that involve software models (artifacts). Blair et al. [6] emphasize the importance that software models may play at runtime. They use the mechanism of reflection inducing that the necessary adaptation is performed at the model level rather than at the system level.

This vision is opposite to the traditional design approaches that prescribe the system be stopped each time a new requirement or a new goal occurs or the environmental conditions change. Conventional processes also prescribe that changes have to be inserted in the system while it is not working; there are several methods in literature for facing changes, from simple software maintenance to software evolution [39]. In any case, a new design activity is necessary during which the system cannot work; someone says that in this case, the system is offline.

In our work, we consider that designing and developing self-adaptive systems require continuous delivery and designing while the system is working; we accept the idea the system has to be always online.

Baresi et al. [3] introduce the need of bringing near the design time to the runtime: "The clear separation between development-time and run-time is blurring and may disappear in the future for relevant classes of applications". This allows some changing activities to be shifted from design and development to runtime and some changing responsibilities to be assigned to the system itself instead of to the analysts or designers. Thus, realizing and implementing adaptation [1,9].

Several scientists agree [2,13] self-adaptation is closely related to the ability of reasoning about the inner world beyond than the outer. In other words, self-awareness is the key for self-adaptation. In previous work, we adopted agent's knowledge to implement run-time artifacts for modeling user's requirements and norms [32].

We claim that the maintenance of complex distributed software is a mix of continuous delivery and continuous integration. Automation is indeed one way to enable constant changes. In particular, we are interested in exploring the automation that supports continuous changes. Hence, continuous changes may be handled at runtime with the aid of an automatic tool.

Our intuition is that the life cycle of a self-adaptive system, or of one of its components, starts with its design and does not terminate with its deployment [25] and testing. The life-cycle continues with some monitoring phases aiming at identifying and handling new or emergent requirements and/or needs from users. This implies that self-adaptation allows making run-time changing and the self-adaptive system itself supports the further development phase aiding, or better substituting, designers. In so doing, we overcome the limits of traditional design methodologies: they are not adequate for a self-adaptive system because they do not consider the run-time.

In the following sections, we identify the characteristics of a design process for supporting self-adaptive middleware. To investigate this topic we exploit the experience gained with MUSA, a self-adaptive middleware, and then we generalize some of the obtained results.

3   MUSA: A Middleware for Self-adaptation

MUSA (Middleware for User-driven Service Adaptation) [34] is a middleware for orchestrating distributed services according to unanticipated and dynamic user needs. It has been conceived for managing evolution and adaptivity of dynamic workflows [33]. MUSA provides basic concepts to model a software system able to detect and react to exceptional events, failures and resources unavailability.

Key enablers of MUSA are: (a) representing *what the system will do* and *how the system can do* as a couple of first-class entities (respectively *Goals* and *Capabilities*) [36]; (b) providing goals and capabilities and run-time artifacts the system can reason on by representing them through a common formalism, based on a grounding semantic [17]; (c) providing a flexible and configurable planning system [31] for dynamically generating workflows of capabilities to address the specified goals.

In the following, we compared MUSA with some of the middleware for self-adaptation in the literature. The remaining sub-section will discuss which steps are necessary for engineering a system with MUSA.

3.1 Middlewares for Self-adaptation

Literature provides an increasing number of middlewares for developing and managing the self-adaptive characteristics of a system under development. These approaches are highly heterogeneous, yet one can usually classify them as component or service-based [4,29], agent-based [14,31], or bio-inspired [20,43].

The benefits of these middlewares are that they provide basic functionalities for rapid prototyping of many self-adaptation features such as monitors and actuators. The common factor of almost all these different infrastructures is the idea of exploiting the mechanism of reflection to take run-time strategic decisions. They support some run-time entities and models, i.e., high-level abstractions of the software system. By maintaining these abstractions at run-time, the software system could be able to perform reflection, and it may predict/control certain aspects of its behavior for the future.

Kramer and Magee [8,24] propose MORPH, a reference architecture for self-adaptation, inspired to robotics, that includes (i) a control layer, a reactive component consisting of sensors, actuators and control loops, (ii) a sequencing layer which reacts to changes from the lower levels by modifying plans to handle the new situation and (iii) a deliberation layer that consists in time consuming planning which attempts to produce a plan to achieve a goal. The main difference with our architecture is that we introduce a layer for handling goals evolution. The architecture is suitable for implementing a self-adaptive system able to deal with anticipated changes by selecting among pre-computed adaptation strategies.

SeSaMe (SEmantic and Self-Adaptive MiddlewarE) [5] is a self-organizing distributed middleware that uses semantic technologies to harmonize the interaction of heterogeneous components. In SeSaMe, components self-connect at runtime, without any prior knowledge of the topology. The dynamic architecture grants system's reliability even when multiple components leave or fail unexpectedly, and dynamically alters the system's topology to cope with message congestion. The main difference is that SeSaMe focuses on structural/component-based abstractions (groups, roles, components) whereas MUSA concentrates more on functional requirements. In SeSaMe, adaptation consists in modifying the topology of connections among the components, whereas in MUSA it consists in changing the workflow by removing/replacing infeasible tasks.

SAPERE (Self-aware Pervasive Service Ecosystems) [43] is inspired to natural ecosystems to model dynamism and decentralization in pervasive networks. In SAPERE various agents coordinate through spatially-situated and environment-mediated interactions, to serve their own needs as well as the sustainability of the overall ecology. The environment is modeled as a spatial substrate where agents' interactions are managed as virtual chemical reactions. The main difference is that SAPERE is focused more on emergence and evolution rather than on control. The collaboration between agents is incidentally due to the current context and to underlying eco-laws. Emergence is programmed via eco-laws, i.e. natural metaphors that specify how agents will interact.

As a final remark, independently from the kind of middleware chosen for a specific purpose, all of them imply a methodological shift in which some design models move from the design-time towards run-time artifacts.

3.2 Using MUSA for Engineering a Self-adaptive System

The use of MUSA for building a self-adaptation system consists basically in providing a model of goals and a model of capabilities to the MUSA instance, thus enabling its proactive means-end reasoning. However, there exist a preliminary activity to be done: the analysis of the domain for building a common ontological background for goals and capabilities.

The *Problem Ontology Description* (POD) is a design fragment [28] that allows describing the problem domain elements and their relationships in a formal way. This activity grounds on an ontology used as an analysis (i.e. descriptive) model for representing the reality of problem domains typically addressed by agent-oriented technologies. This ontology is described by the Problem Ontology metamodel. The Problem Ontology metamodel, we employ, has been inspired by the FIPA (Foundation for Intelligent Physical Agents)[1] standard and ASPECS [16] ontology. Thus, similarly, our meta-ontology describes what are the elements of interest in a domain (*Concept*) with their properties (*Predicate*) and how they act in the domain (*Action*) and it introduces some new elements in order to explicitly model intentional behaviors.

Requirement Analysis and Goals. Traditionally, when specifying system requirements, analysts crop the solution space in order to define the expected system behavior in a deterministic way. However, the characteristics of being autonomous and proactive make the agents able to explore a wider solution space, even when this space dynamically changes or contains uncertainty [40]. The novelty of our approach consists in making some constraints of the solution less rigid, thus allowing more degrees of freedom to the system.

Several methods exist in literature to conduct a goal-oriented requirement analysis. We do not suggest to use a specific one, providing the output is rendered via the GoalSPEC language [37]. It has been specifically conceived to support MUSA with a run-time artifact for dealing with user's requirements, some of its most interesting features will be presented in the following.

GoalSPEC Supports Adaptivity. GoalSPEC provides some domain-independent keywords but it offers a powerful plug-in mechanism for providing different ontology groundings. It is fully compatible with the Problem Ontology Description fragment, thus goals can be expressed as desired states of the world, defined in the POD as concepts and predicates.

GoalSPEC Supports Evolution. GoalSPEC allows MUSA agents to reason and commits to the specified goals. Goals are run-time artifacts, therefore agents perceive them as part of the environment. This run-time nature of goals allows they can change during system lifecycle, thus supporting a global evolution of the system.

---

[1] Available at: http://www.fipa.org/specs/fipa00086.

Services and Capabilities. The concept of capability comes from AI (planning actions [21]), software engineering (contracts [18]) and service-oriented architecture (micro-services [26]). Indeed, this composite nature is well represented by the separation we adopt between *abstract capability* – a description of the effect of an action that can be performed – and *concrete capability* – a small, independent, composable unit of computation that produces some concrete service.

Implementing system functionalities as capabilities provides some benefits:

– each capability is relatively small, and therefore easier for a developer to implement,
– it can be deployed independently from other capabilities,
– it is easier to organize the overall development effort around multiple teams,
– it supports self-adaptation because of improved fault isolation.

An example of description of capabilities is provided in [34] where the smart travel domain is considered. In this context, each capability encapsulates a web service for reserving some kind of travel service (hotel, flight, local events).

Moreover, we focused on the idea that capabilities make it easier to deploy new versions of the software frequently. Providing capabilities (as well as goals) as run-time entities contributes to enable continuous changes and self-adaptation. Supporting this claim is one of the objectives of this Chapter. In the remaining section, we used data about the implementation of three different applications for getting some findings of the easiness of continuously evolving a system.

4   A Retrospective Analysis of MUSA

This section presents a retrospective analysis of the design activities with MUSA and discusses some emerging results.

Empirical Study Design. We selected MUSA [34] because we gained a practical experience of use, due to its adoption in several applications.

In the last years, MUSA has been employed in research projects and case studies with very different application domains. Table 1 gives an overview of the sources from where data have been collected.

The empirical study mainly focuses on the design activities for producing ontology, capabilities and goals for the selected projects of Table 1. The design process we followed in all the projects follows three main activities:

– As it happens in traditional requirement analysis, we suggest every MUSA project started with a good understanding of the domain. We adopt an ontology to record and represent this knowledge. For this reason measuring the evolution of the **ontology** model may be interesting for this study.

Table 1. Summary of research projects and case studies where the MUSA middleware has been employed between 2013 and 2016.

Acronym	Type	App. Name	Description
IDS	Research Project	Innovative Document Sharing	The aim has been to realize a prototype of a new generation of a digital document solution that overcomes current operating limits of the common market solutions. MUSA has been adopted for managing and balancing human operations for enacting a digital document solution in a SME
OCCP	Research Project	Open Cloud Computing Platform	The aim was the study, design, construction and testing of a prototype of cloud infrastructure for delivering services on public and private cloud. MUSA has been employed, in the demonstrator, in order to implement an adaptive B2B back-end service for a fashion company
Smart Travel	Case Study	Travel Agency System	MUSA provides the planning engine that creates a travel-pack as the composition of several heterogeneous travel services. The planning activity is driven by traveler's goals

- The second step is understanding and representing customer's requirements. In MUSA, they must be translated into significant states of the system to be addressed. In some circumstances, this activity may require a revision of the ontology to adjust some of the concepts. For this reason, the study includes an evaluation of the evolution of the **goal** model.
- A third step concerns the development of the services the system may employ in the emerging solution. In MUSA, capabilities are run-time artifacts that describe how to employ available services to compose a solution. As well as goal modeling, defining the capabilities may require a revision of the ontology. Therefore, we decided to include the analysis of the available **capabilities**.

For comparison reasons, for each project, we identified three main iterations, in which the application received substantial changes. In different projects, iterations have been deduced by considering the delivery of functionalities, therefore they may have a variable duration between 1 to 2 months. In each iteration, we have considered either which artifacts have been produced or how they have been modified with respect to the previous iteration (versioning history).

For each artifact, we planned a set of measurements.

- The first measurement is the **size** of the model. It is calculated by employing the system metamodel as illustrated in [7]. The metamodel provides the language for describing models of the system. It contains elements and relationships underpinning and guiding the design process activities used for developing a specific system. During the design activities, designers use the metamodel as a trace for instantiating elements in the models. The **size** of the model is a measure of the effort spent on instantiating models from the metamodel. It refers to introducing new elements, relationships, attributes and so on.
- The second measurement is the **effort** (in man-hours) spent in the model. This measure is calculated by considering the number of commits done for

the specific artifact. To be more precise, we asked the involved developers to confirm or adjust the values. In any case we considered a possible error in this measure, thus we considered significant the differences of effort rather than their absolute values.

– The last measurement is done on the running system. After injecting the new set of goals and capabilities (by replacing the previous ones), MUSA calculates a new space of configurations and extracts a number of solutions to be used to provide the requested functionality. The measurement is done on the space of configuration as a value of the degree of freedom of the adaptation mechanism. It provides two values: the **number of** different **solutions** computed by the system for solving the problem.

5   Interpretation of Results

Table 2 reports the empirical data extracted from the three projects during their initial three iterations. Data is also summarized in three charts, as shown in Fig. 1.

The use of MUSA implies, at the very beginning, to perform some classical design activities. After the first injection, the self-adaptive application is online and every required change may be handled while it is running. We use the empirical data for identifying duration/effort of the various release phases of the process necessary for delivery a self-adaptive application with MUSA.

Before examining data, it is useful to provide some additional details about how MUSA works. MUSA is based on the paradigm of collaborating agents and artifacts [27]. Figure 2 depicts the main stakeholders, agents and artifacts involved in this process. According to the classic vision, an agent can perceive the environment and act in order to change it. In addition, MUSA agents are self-aware of which capabilities they own and how to use them for producing a result. MUSA agents share a main goal: 'to address users' run-time goals' (i.e. requirements). Therefore they continuously monitor either goal injection or goal changes.

When the designer specifies a set of goals to be addressed (or update them), then the agent groups called *solution explorer* is ready to collaborate to find one or more abstract solutions (as workflow of abstract capabilities). These form a run-time model called *Solutions* artifact (Fig. 4). The algorithm is described in [31,35].

Now, we use data from Table 2 to specify how these participants (humans and agents) collaborate during design-time and run-time (Fig. 4). It is worth noting that we should address two different system layers in studying MUSA applications: the MUSA middleware and the MUSA application:

1. The MUSA middleware provides runtime facilities for goal-models and capabilities, and enables agents for solution-discovery and adaptive-orchestration.
2. The MUSA (self-adaptive) application is the result of employing the MUSA middleware in building a set of user's requested functionalities. It is able to adapt to a changing domain.

Table 2. Summary of the empirical data by retrospective analysis of research projects in which the MUSA middleware has been adopted for engineering a self-adaptive system

Project	iteration 1	iteration 2	iteration 3
IDS	first injection	bugfix+evolution	evolution
size (number of model elements)			
ontology	6	9	10
capability	4	6	7
goal	4	6	7
effort (man hours)			
ontology	10	7	3
capability	30	23	7
goal	14	7	1
design total effort	54	35	21
space of configuration (number of solutions)			
	1	6	6
OCCP	first injection	evolution	bugfix+evolution
size (number of model elements)			
ontology	10	10	10
capability	5	8	12
goal	8	8	9
effort (man hours)			
ontology	30	10	7
capability	70	40	50
goal	7	7	4
design total effort	107	57	61
space of configuration (number of solutions)			
	1	9	18
Smart Travel	first injection	bugfix+evolution	bugfix+evolution
size (number of model elements)			
ontology	12	12	14
capability	3	5	8
goal	5	7	7
effort (man hours)			
ontology	7	7	14
capability	40	25	20
goal	100	14	1
design total effort	147	46	35
space of configuration (number of solutions)			
	5	5	5

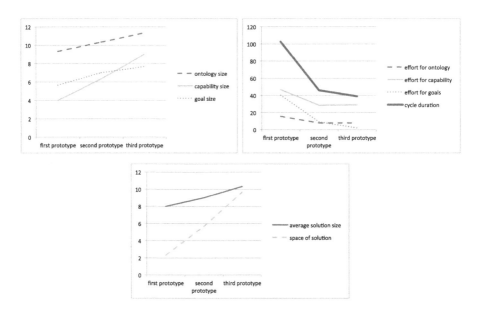

Fig. 1. Charts reporting average data, along three iterations, as extracted for the three projects. Top-left diagram shows the average increase of the complexity of the ontology, the capability model and the goal model. Top-right diagram shows the corresponding effort (in man hours) required to complete the iteration. Finally, bottom diagram highlights the growth of the space of solutions.

Design-time and run-time phases are represented in Fig. 3 in which we highlight the MUSA middleware and the MUSA (self-adaptive) application areas.

Design-time, generally speaking, is the moment in which taking design choices concerning the characteristics of the application. The *design-time of the MUSA Middleware* is out the scope of this Chapter. We work under the hypotesys that MUSA is complete and always running.

Therefore, Fig. 3 focuses on MUSA Middleware run-time phase (right-side of the box on the bottom). The box on the top represents the two phases of the MUSA application: design-time and run-time.

The *design-time for MUSA applications* concerns the definition of an ontology and, subsequently, of a couple of artifacts: goals and capabilities. As shown in Fig. 3, this design-time of the MUSA application occurs during MUSA middleware run-time, indeed the designer may exploit some simulation facilities offered by the middleware for evaluating the degree of adaptation of the application as a consequence of the new specifications.

The *run-time of the MUSA application* is shown in the top-right box of Fig. 3. It includes two possible states: online and offline. Offline is when the application is executing background operations but it not provides a working response to user expectations; on the other side, online means the application is providing the expected functionalities. The application is offline before the

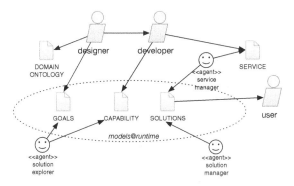

Fig. 2. The Human-Agent collaboration for the development of a MUSA self-adaptive application.

first injection (of goals and capabilities) and after any future injections for bug-fixing or functionality evolution: during this phase the middleware layer provides functionalities for solution-discovery. When the application layer is online, the middleware operates with an adaptive orchestration.

It is worth noting that, in the fashion of a continuous software delivery, the red line of Fig. 3, i.e. the boundary between MUSA application design-time and run-time, is less clear than the blue one. Indeed, after the first injection, designing the MUSA application may be an activity performed during application is online. Clearly, when changing the specifications at runtime, a short interruption of service occurs due to the adaptation activity.

MUSA Application

Design-Time			Run-Time	
ONTOLOGY	GOALS	CAPABILITIES	OFFLINE	ONLINE

MUSA Middleware

SIMULATION			SOLUTION DISCOVERY	ADAPTIVE ORCHESTRATION

Design-Time	Run-Time

Fig. 3. States of MUSA run-time execution. (Color figure online)

In Fig. 4, the alignment represents the design activities corresponding to a particular artifact (ontology, goals, capabilities and architecture). Indeed, MUSA agents support designer and developer, respectively, (1) by evaluating the degree of freedom of the set of goals and capabilities that are going to be built, and, (2) by verifying the compliance of the service under development with the corresponding capability. Figure 4 highlights this collaboration by coupling humans and agents in a design activity (designer with solution explorer and developer with service manager).

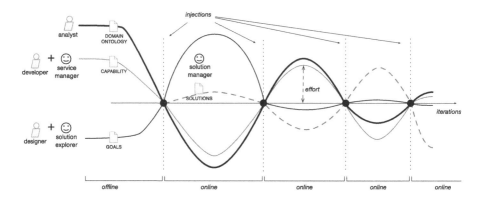

Fig. 4. Outcome of the retrospective analysis.

According to previously reported data, we identified three iterations (or release cycles) that begin and terminate with an injection. In Fig. 4, the amplitude of lines are proportional to the effort required for refining the correspondent artefact.

Results of the retrospective analysis are summarized in Fig. 4 and resumed in the following findings.

Injections. The boundary between the offline and online design is marked by the first injection, that is the moment in which the self-adaptive application begins. Time before the first modification point, the left part of the figure, represents when analyst, developer and customer designed the first version of the system for solving a specific problem with the aid of some agents working in MUSA. The short time interval soon after an injection is used by MUSA for acquiring occurring changes in the operating condition and for releasing new configurations of the system.

Boundary between MUSA Application Design-Time and Run-Time. The developer designs a first set of capabilities the system has to own and the designer designs a first set of goals the system has to pursue by using the right capabilities. These two design-time activities are performed respectively, with the aid of the service manager agent and the solution explorer agent. In particular, the solution explorer aids the designer in evaluating if available capabilities are enough for addressing the set of goals, also indicating the degree of freedom for future adaptations. The classical boundary between design-time and run-time is going to disappear.

Solution as a Model at Run-Time. Once the self-adaptive application is online, agents collaborate in order to achieve the goals and to monitor the environment. They exploit the available capabilities of the selected solution. The solution is a run-time artifact that only agents are responsible for (no human role is involved). They may change it for adaptation purpose.

Convergence. After each modification point, each design iteration takes a short time and less effort to be completed; on the other hand, the space of solutions increases. We observed that the self-adaptation property contributes in reducing the design effort. This because, iteration after iteration, the ontology domain description becomes stable and the repository of capability increases. As a consequence, the self-adaptive application is able to endorse a higher number of deviations from standard situations. Every time a modification occurs in the running/operating conditions (for instance, a new goal, a change in the environment or a change in the way the user uses the system), it is less frequent designers start a new design iteration. However, when a manual change is required, the ontology allows to quickly refine goals and to specify new capabilities. In practice, in the long run, designers and agents will interact less and for short time.

6   Discussion

In this section, starting from the results of the retrospective analysis, we propose a skeleton of a design process for engineering self-adaptive systems. We will achieve this objective by extracting a schematic design process from our previous experience with MUSA and then trying to generalize it.

6.1   The Design Process Adopted in MUSA Applications

It is a matter of fact that exploring the new world of adaptive system has brought many research groups to move in a new context where old methodologies have soon proved to be not applicable. Similarly, when starting our experiences with MUSA we tried to employ design activities and related artifacts coming from our agent-oriented software engineering background. Notably we considered influences coming from PASSI [15], Agile PASSI [12], and ASPECS [16]. Some of them influenced not only our way to use MUSA but, as it was expectable, the development of MUSA itself. For this reason, we will find some of them in the process we are trying to sketch as a suggested approach to the design of self-adaptive systems. Another relevant issue to be considered when looking at the way we designed our MUSA-based solutions is that MUSA itself was quickly and drastically evolving. Mostly in the first part of this 5-years long observation period. The fundamental concepts MUSA is based on (goals, capabilities, agents' hierarchical organization and so on) remained unchanged but their contribution to the middleware implementation significantly evolved over time. Looking at how we effectively developed the solutions required in the different projects where we employed MUSA, we can see the constant presence of the following design activities:

- Ontology definition
- Goals definition (and injection)
- Capability definition (and injection)

– Problem Solution
– Adaptation loop

These activities will be detailed in what follows.

Ontology Definition. One of the key ideas at the basis of MUSA is to let different modules contribute to find a solution to a problem even if they have not been conceived for that. In order to do that all the system parts (at least those involved in the solution of a specific problem, others may exist that are not involved on this but will contribute to another) need a common semantics for sharing information. Following the influences coming from our past experiences in software design we decided to provide that by using a methodology. Such methodology not only describes the concepts in the solution domain (and their status by using predicates) but also actions allowed in the domain itself.

Goals Definition (and Injection). In order to employ MUSA for solving a problem the designer has to communicate the problem requirements to MUSA. This is done by using goals and more specifically by injecting them in the (already) running middleware. Such goals will be received by a Solution Explorer agent who will be in charge of pursuing them as already depicted in Figs. 2 and 4. Goals will be expressed by referring to the problem ontology produced by the previous activity.

Capability Definition (and Injection). In our projects, capabilities often come from the real world. For instance, existing web or cloud services. A great part of the capabilities construction effort therefore consisted in wrapping them in order to ensure a semantically effective interaction with MUSA.

Problem Solution. This is the moment when MUSA is asked to solve the problem. MUSA uses its reasoning algorithms in order to find an abstract solution (employing abstract capabilities) and if feasible binds that to executables modules/services (concrete capabilities).

Adaptation Loop. There are several reasons that may trigger this loop: the execution of a concrete capability may not reach the expected result, the module/service wrapped by the capability is no more working or the proactive means-end reasoning module does not find a solution to the injected set of goals. MUSA reacts to such situations in two different ways: firstly, it tries to overcome the obstacle by replanning the solution (at the concrete or abstract level), finally, if the other ways did not solve the issue, MUSA involves the user in the loop by asking for its collaboration in terms of goals changing, constraints relaxing or injection of new capabilities.

According to our experiences these activities are all crucial and constantly applied in the design of our systems. Because of that we think these activities may be the pillars for building a more general design process as it will be discussed in the next subsection

6.2   A Generalised Design Process

A crucial part for any design process is to define its application scope. We think our experience is representative for the following category of systems and problems. First, the system is composed of two layers:

1. A middleware layer providing assembling/orchestrating/coordinating features of existing pieces of functionalities (software) and providing adaptation features to cope with unforeseeable changes.
2. An application layer running upon the middleware one. This layer directly interacts with the user providing the required functionalities/solutions.

Elementary pieces of functionalities assembled in the solution may be described in a semantically coherent way. The problem may be described in terms of functional and non-functional requirements that may change during system execution and that may be expressed in a machine understandable language. The problem requires the system to adapt to unforeseeable changes in the environment and in the system itself (requirements included) so that it can find solutions that may employ different strategies/portions of software/parameter settings.

For such a category of problems/systems we think the following process skeleton may be successfully applied.

1. Define problem and solution taxonomy or other semantic description. This creates an operational abstraction where the problem may be consistently described in terms of requirements and solution elements (composition/employment of existing pieces of software, data types, etc.).
2. Define problem model in a machine-readable language. Problem requirements cannot be expressed in conventional design languages (for instance UML) since the application-layer of the system has to be aware of them, both at the functional and non-functional level of detail.
3. Collect and wrap existing functionalities. The result will be a repository of semantically interoperable pieces of software that the adaptation middleware may compose to obtain the solution.
4. Validate functionalities repository towards requirements satisfaction. To this purpose, some relevant works on certification of self-adaptive systems may be found in literature [11,30]. Another challenge for adaptive systems is to ensure that enough pieces of functionality are available to face the demands of change proposed by the environment, changing user needs, system failures and so on. This check is a relevant issue and we think each middleware should interact with the designers (for instance using simulation features) in order to verify if the existing repository ensures a sufficient degree of adaptation. The specific algorithms used by the middleware may deeply affect the results of this validation.
5. Run the application layer. This may be roughly compared to the conventional running phase of a traditional software. The application layer needs the models produced in the previous phase in order to learn and pursue the specified

objectives. If the solution is not found or when it fails after succeeding for a while, the next activity will follow.

6. Adaptation. According to different implementation philosophies (and problem constraints) this phase may involve the human or not. For instance, when sensitive decisions have to be taken, a human supervision is usually required before swerving from a straightforward solution. Adaptation may involve the employment of alternative pieces of functionalities in pursuing the same plan, a replanning of the solution strategy or other approaches (for instance evolutionary ones) according to the specific middleware.

6.3 Limits of This Analysis

The data extracted could be a bit biased because in these three projects, engineers developed both the MUSA middleware and the MUSA application for the specific domain problem. In the reported retrospective analysis the most complex part was separating the time required for fixing the middleware from the time required to implement the application (ontology, goals and capabilities).

Moreover, we have restricted the retrospective analysis to the first three iterations. However, some projects were developed in more iterations that were not considered in this analysis. This choice was done in order to make them comparable. In any case, Fig. 1 shows that the trend of the curves is quite regular. So we can hypothesize the sample is quite respectful of the reality.

7   Conclusions

Due to the features of self-adaptive systems and the fact that, nowadays, systems are more interconnected and various than before, designers have not the right means to anticipate and design interactions among different components, interaction among users and the system. Indeed, (self-adaptive) software system properties are effectively known when all the relationships among the software components and between the software and the environment have been expressed and have been made explicit. Such issues have to be dealt with at runtime; modeling and monitoring users and the environment is the key for enabling software to be adaptive [13,23].

Self-adaptation deals with requirements that vary at run-time. Therefore it is crucial that requirements lend themselves to be dynamically observed, i.e., during execution. Middlewares for self-adaptation constitute the right tools for easing complex systems development and for providing a form of model@runtime. A methodological approach for developing self-adaptive systems supporting runtime continuous change still lacks.

In this Chapter, we illustrated the results of a retrospective analysis conducted on our middleware (MUSA) to identify the characteristics of a design process for developing self-adaptive systems.

We started from the hypothesis that changes occurring at run-time have to be handled by the system itself; like it were part of the team of designers. We reached this objective in MUSA by employing a well-specific agent architecture.

The analysis mainly highlighted that, using MUSA, supporting self-adaptive solutions implies a design process where humans and agents collaborate. Goals and capabilities are run-time entities that constitute the continuous data exchange between human and agents. Human and agents collaborate until the system (all the agents) possesses the useful knowledge for reaching the defined objectives by its own. Moreover, the collaboration between humans and agents and the fact that a run-time model exists until the system is running, guarantee the required system behaviour modifications during subsequent releases.

Finally, we deeply analyzed the way in which a system is developed by using MUSA and we identified some principal design activities a design approach for engineering self-adaptive system has to contain. The analysis of the use of MUSA covered five years. One of the most important insights we realized, also comparing that with other self-adaptive middleware systems, is that activities devoted to identifying the ontology of the system, the goals, and the capabilities are necessary to build a tool providing the right automation for supporting continuous changes.

The most relevant result of this analysis is the identification of the design process we used in developing MUSA applications. This process supports continuous change and strongly induce human and agents to collaborate in pursuing the solution. From this process we generalised a wider scope process for the design of self-adaptive applications based on the employment of a middleware layer providing assembling/orchestrating/coordinating features of existing pieces of functionalities (software) and providing the required adaptation features to cope with unforeseeable changes.

References

1. Andersson, J., et al.: Software engineering processes for self-adaptive systems. In: de Lemos, R., Giese, H., Müller, H.A., Shaw, M. (eds.) Software Engineering for Self-Adaptive Systems II. LNCS, vol. 7475, pp. 51–75. Springer, Heidelberg (2013). https://doi.org/10.1007/978-3-642-35813-5_3
2. Aßmann, U., Götz, S., Jézéquel, J.-M., Morin, B., Trapp, M.: A reference architecture and roadmap for Models@run.time systems. In: Bencomo, N., France, R., Cheng, B.H.C., Aßmann, U. (eds.) Models@run.time. LNCS, vol. 8378, pp. 1–18. Springer, Cham (2014). https://doi.org/10.1007/978-3-319-08915-7_1
3. Baresi, L., Ghezzi, C.: The disappearing boundary between development-time and run-time. In: Proceedings of the FSE/SDP workshop on Future of software engineering research, pp. 17–22. ACM (2010)
4. Baresi, L., Guinea, S.: A3: self-adaptation capabilities through groups and coordination. In: Proceedings of the 4th India Software Engineering Conference, pp. 11–20. ACM (2011)
5. Baresi, L., Guinea, S., Shahzada, A.: SeSaMe: towards a semantic self adaptive middleware for smart spaces. In: Cossentino, M., El Fallah Seghrouchni, A., Winikoff, M. (eds.) EMAS 2013. LNCS (LNAI), vol. 8245, pp. 1–18. Springer, Heidelberg (2013). https://doi.org/10.1007/978-3-642-45343-4_1
6. Blair, G., Bencomo, N., France, R.B.: Models@ run.time. Computer **42**(10), 22–27 (2009)

7. Bonjean, N., Gleizes, M.-P., Chella, A., Migeon, F., Cossentino, M., Seidita, V.: Metamodel-based metrics for agent-oriented methodologies. In: Proceedings of the 11th International Conference on Autonomous Agents and Multiagent Systems-Volume 2, pp. 1065–1072. International Foundation for Autonomous Agents and Multiagent Systems (2012)

8. Braberman, V., D'Ippolito, N., Kramer, J., Sykes, D., Uchitel, S.: Morph: a reference architecture for configuration and behaviour self-adaptation. In: Proceedings of the 1st International Workshop on Control Theory for Software Engineering, pp. 9–16. ACM (2015)

9. Buckley, J., Mens, T., Zenger, M., Rashid, A., Kniesel, G.: Towards a taxonomy of software change. J. Softw. Maint. Evol. Res. Pract. **17**(5), 309–332 (2005)

10. Calinescu, R., Gerasimou, S., Banks, A.: Self-adaptive software with decentralised control loops. In: Egyed, A., Schaefer, I. (eds.) FASE 2015. LNCS, vol. 9033, pp. 235–251. Springer, Heidelberg (2015). https://doi.org/10.1007/978-3-662-46675-9_16

11. Calinescu, R., Weyns, D., Gerasimou, S., Iftikhar, M.U., Habli, I., Kelly, T.: Engineering trustworthy self-adaptive software with dynamic assurance cases. IEEE Trans. Softw. Eng. **44**(11), 1039–1069 (2018)

12. Chella, A., Cossentino, M., Sabatucci, L., Seidita, V.: Agile passi: an agile process for designing agents. Int. J. Comput. Syst. Sci. Eng. **21**(2), 133–144 (2006)

13. Cheng, B.H.C., et al.: Software engineering for self-adaptive systems: a research roadmap. In: Cheng, B.H.C., de Lemos, R., Giese, H., Inverardi, P., Magee, J. (eds.) Software Engineering for Self-Adaptive Systems. LNCS, vol. 5525, pp. 1–26. Springer, Heidelberg (2009). https://doi.org/10.1007/978-3-642-02161-9_1

14. Cheng, S.-W.: Rainbow: cost-effective software architecture-based self-adaptation. ProQuest (2008)

15. Cossentino, M.: From requirements to code with the passi methodology. Agent-Oriented Methodol. **3690**, 79–106 (2005)

16. Cossentino, M., Gaud, N., Hilaire, V., Galland, S., Koukam, A.: ASPECS: an agent-oriented software process for engineering complex systems. Auton. Agents Multi-Agent Syst. **20**(2), 260–304 (2010)

17. Cossentino, M., Sabatucci, L., Seidita, V.: Towards an approach for engineering complex systems: agents and agility. In: Proceedings of the 18th Workshop on "From Objects to Agents", 1867, pp. 1–6 (2017)

18. Curbera, F.: Component contracts in service-oriented architectures. Computer **40**(11), 74–80 (2007)

19. De La Iglesia, D.G., Calderón, J.F., Weyns, D., Milrad, M., Nussbaum, M.: A self-adaptive multi-agent system approach for collaborative mobile learning. IEEE Trans. Learn. Technol. **8**(2), 158–172 (2015)

20. Fernandez-Marquez, J.L., Serugendo, G.D.M., Montagna, S.: BIO-CORE: bio-inspired self-organising mechanisms core. In: Hart, E., Timmis, J., Mitchell, P., Nakamo, T., Dabiri, F. (eds.) BIONETICS 2011. LNICST, vol. 103, pp. 59–72. Springer, Heidelberg (2012). https://doi.org/10.1007/978-3-642-32711-7_5

21. Gelfond, M., Lifschitz, V.: Action languages. Comput. Inf. Sci. **3**(16), 1–41 (1998)

22. Haesevoets, R., Weyns, D., Holvoet, T.: Architecture-centric support for adaptive service collaborations. ACM Trans. Softw. Eng. Methodol. (TOSEM) **23**(1), 2 (2014)

23. Inverardi, P.: Software of the future is the future of software? In: Montanari, U., Sannella, D., Bruni, R. (eds.) TGC 2006. LNCS, vol. 4661, pp. 69–85. Springer, Heidelberg (2007). https://doi.org/10.1007/978-3-540-75336-0_5

24. Kramer, J., Magee, J.: Self-managed systems: an architectural challenge. In: 2007 Future of Software Engineering, FOSE 2007, pp. 259–268. IEEE (2007)
25. Malek, S., Mikic-Rakic, M., Medvidovic, N.: A decentralized redeployment algorithm for improving the availability of distributed systems. In: Dearle, A., Eisenbach, S. (eds.) CD 2005. LNCS, vol. 3798, pp. 99–114. Springer, Heidelberg (2005). https://doi.org/10.1007/11590712_8
26. Namiot, D., Sneps-Sneppe, M.: On micro-services architecture. Int. J. Open Inf. Technol. **2**(9), 24–27 (2014)
27. Omicini, A., Ricci, A., Viroli, M.: Artifacts in the A&A meta-model for multi-agent systems. Auton. Agents Multi-Agent Syst. **17**(3), 432–456 (2008)
28. Ribino, P., Cossentino, M., Lodato, C., Lopes, S., Sabatucci, L., Seidita, V.: Ontology and goal model in designing bdi multi-agent systems. WOA@ AI* IA, **1099**, 66–72 (2013)
29. Rouvoy, R., et al.: MUSIC: middleware support for self-adaptation in ubiquitous and service-oriented environments. In: Cheng, B.H.C., de Lemos, R., Giese, H., Inverardi, P., Magee, J. (eds.) Software Engineering for Self-Adaptive Systems. LNCS, vol. 5525, pp. 164–182. Springer, Heidelberg (2009). https://doi.org/10.1007/978-3-642-02161-9_9
30. Rushby, J.: A safety-case approach for certifying adaptive systems. In: AIAA Infotech@ Aerospace Conference and AIAA Unmanned... Unlimited Conference, page 1992 (2009)
31. Sabatucci, L., Cossentino, M.: From means-end analysis to proactive means-end reasoning. In: Proceedings of 10th International Symposium on Software Engineering for Adaptive and Self-Managing Systems, 18–19 May 2015
32. Sabatucci, L., Cossentino, M., Lodato, C., Lopes, S., Seidita, V.: A possible approach for implementing self-awareness in JASON. EUMAS **13**, 68–81 (2013)
33. Sabatucci, L., Lodato, C., Lopes, S., Cossentino, M.: Towards self-adaptation and evolution in business process. In: AIBP@ AI* IA, pp. 1–10. Citeseer (2013)
34. Sabatucci, L., Lodato, C., Lopes, S., Cossentino, M.: Highly customizable service composition and orchestration. In: Dustdar, S., Leymann, F., Villari, M. (eds.) ESOCC 2015. LNCS, vol. 9306, pp. 156–170. Springer, Cham (2015). https://doi.org/10.1007/978-3-319-24072-5_11
35. Sabatucci, L., Lopes, S., Cossentino, M.: A goal-oriented approach for self-configuring mashup of cloud applications. In: 2015 International Conference on Cloud and Autonomic Computing (ICCAC) (2016)
36. Sabatucci, L., Lopes, S., Cossentino, M.: Self-configuring cloud application mashup with goals and capabilities. Clust. Comput. **20**(3), 2047–2063 (2017)
37. Sabatucci, L., Ribino, P., Lodato, C., Lopes, S., Cossentino, M.: GoalSPEC: a goal specification language supporting adaptivity and evolution. In: Cossentino, M., El Fallah Seghrouchni, A., Winikoff, M. (eds.) EMAS 2013. LNCS (LNAI), vol. 8245, pp. 235–254. Springer, Heidelberg (2013). https://doi.org/10.1007/978-3-642-45343-4_13
38. Schmidt, D.C.: Model-driven engineering. IEEE Comput. Soc. **39**(2), 25 (2006)
39. Sommerville, I., et al.:: Software engineering. Addison-Wesley, Reading (2007)
40. Weyns, D., Georgeff, M.: Self-adaptation using multiagent systems. IEEE Softw. **27**(1), 86–91 (2010)
41. Weyns, D., Haesevoets, R., Helleboogh, A., Holvoet, T., Joosen, W.: The macodo middleware for context-driven dynamic agent organizations. ACM Trans. Auton. Adapt. Syst. (TAAS) **5**(1), 3 (2010)

42. Weyns, D., et al.: On patterns for decentralized control in self-adaptive systems. In: de Lemos, R., Giese, H., Müller, H.A., Shaw, M. (eds.) Software Engineering for Self-Adaptive Systems II. LNCS, vol. 7475, pp. 76–107. Springer, Heidelberg (2013). https://doi.org/10.1007/978-3-642-35813-5_4
43. Zambonelli, F., Castelli, G., Mamei, M., Rosi, A.: Programming self-organizing pervasive applications with SAPERE. In: Zavoral, F., Jung, J., Badica, C. (eds.) Intelligent Distributed Computing VII. Studies in Computational Intelligence, vol. 511. Springer, Cham (2014). https://doi.org/10.1007/978-3-319-01571-2_12

Stellar: A Programming Model for Developing Protocol-Compliant Agents

Akın Günay and Amit K. Chopra[✉]

Lancaster University, Lancaster LA1 4WA, UK
{a.gunay,amit.chopra}@lancaster.ac.uk

Abstract. An interaction protocol captures the rules of encounter in a multiagent system. Development of agents that comply with protocols is a central challenge of multiagent systems. Our contribution in this chapter is a programming model, Stellar, that simplifies development of agents compliant with information protocols specified in BSPL. A significant distinction of Stellar from similar approaches is that it does not rely upon extracting control flow structures from protocol specifications to ensure compliance. Instead, Stellar provides a set of fundamental operations to programmers for producing viable messages according to the correct flow of information between agents as specified by a protocol, enabling flexible design and implementation of protocol-compliant agents. Our main contributions are: (1) identification of a set of programming errors that commonly occur when developing agents for protocol-based multiagent system, (2) definition of Stellar's operations and a simple yet effective pattern to develop protocol-compliant agents that avoid the identified errors, and (3) demonstration of Stellar's effectiveness by presenting concrete agents in e-commerce and insurance policy domains.

1 Introduction

Interaction protocols capture the rules of encounter in multiagent systems by defining operational constraints on the occurrence and ordering of messages between agents. Effective interaction of agents in a multiagent system depends on their compliance with the system's protocol. However, development of protocol-compliant agents is challenging in practical settings where communication is asynchronous.

There are several approaches to specify and implement interaction protocols, such as HAPN [14], Scribble [5,15], BPMN in conjunction with BPEL [10], and business artifacts [6,9]. These approaches mainly use procedural control flow structures (e.g., sequencing, branching, etc.) to specify interactions of agents, whose implementations reflect the protocol's control flow to ensure compliance. This is mostly achieved by developing agents on top of rigid code skeletons that are extracted from the protocol specifications. As a result, protocol specifications and implementations of agents who enact them become tightly coupled.

© Springer Nature Switzerland AG 2019
D. Weyns et al. (Eds.): EMAS 2018 Workshops, LNAI 11375, pp. 117–136, 2019.
https://doi.org/10.1007/978-3-030-25693-7_7

An imminent drawback of this approach is the lack of flexibility in agent design, which is a critical limitation particularly in open multiagent systems, where independent parties implement their own agents according to their private business requirements and logic. Another technical drawback of this approach is the need for synchronization between agents to ensure correct ordering of messages, which is hard to achieve in asynchronous decentralized environments.

Several information-based protocol languages [3, 11, 13] have been proposed in the recent years to overcome limitations of the procedural protocol specification approaches. These languages specify protocols in a declarative way with respect to the correct flow of information between the agents, rather than specifying rigid messages sequences. Hence, information-based languages do not impose a control flow for implementing protocol-compliant agents. As a result, independent parties can design their own agents as they see fit according to their own requirements, as long as their agents emit messages complying with the protocol's flow of information. Consequently, information-based languages do not rely on synchronization and inherently support asynchronous and decentralized communication.

In this chapter we focus particularly on BSPL [11] which constitutes the base for all later information-based languages. Although BSPL provides a rich protocol specification language, it does not define a systematic methodology for developing protocol-compliant agents. Our contribution, namely Stellar, addresses this issue with a simple yet effective programming model. To this end, Stellar defines a set of fundamental operations and a software pattern over these operations that enables developers to build compliant agents. Hence, developers can focus on the business logic of their agents without worrying about compliance with protocols. Thanks to BSPL's declarative approach, Stellar does not rely on control flow structures (e.g., no code skeleton is created), which enables maximum flexibility when designing and implementing agents. Our main contributions are as follows. One, we identify common pitfalls of protocol-compliant agent development in decentralized multiagent systems. Two, we develop Stellar's pro gramming model, describe its programming pattern, and define its operations. Three, we demonstrate Stellar's effectiveness by developing agents in e-commerce and insurance policy domains.

2   BSPL

In this section we provide an overview of BSPL to establish the necessary background. BSPL [11] is an information-based protocol specification language. The main difference of BSPL from procedural protocol specification approaches is its way of characterizing operational constraints with respect to causality and flow of information between agents. We explain BSPL's main features using an example purchase protocol that we present in Listing 1.

Listing 1. A BSPL protocol for purchase.

```
Purchase {
  roles B, S // buyer, seller

  parameters out pID key, out item, out price, out result

  B ↦ S: rfq [out pID, out item]
  S ↦ B: quote [in pID, in item, out price]
  B ↦ S: accept [in pID, in item, in price, out result]
  B ↦ S: reject [in pID, in item, in price, out result]
}
```

A BSPL protocol is composed of a name, a set of roles, a set of public parameters, and a set of message schemas. BSPL is a declarative language and hence the ordering of message schemas in a protocol specification is irrelevant. The name of the protocol in Listing 1 is Purchase. It includes two roles, B and S corresponding to a buyer and a seller, respectively. Purchase has four public parameters pID, item, price, and result, which describe the protocol's interface, intuitively corresponding to the identifier of the protocol, an item to purchase, price of the item, and the outcome of the interaction, respectively. A protocol's enactment is complete when all of its public parameters are bound. BSPL protocols can be composed using their interfaces to build complex interactions. However, we do not consider composite protocols in this chapter for brevity. Each message schema in the form of $s \mapsto r : m[P]$ has a sender s and a receiver r role, a message name m, and a set of parameters P.

For instance, the name of the first message schema in Listing 1 is rfq, corresponding to a request for a quote, in which the sender is B, the receiver is S, and the parameters are pID and item. Instances of message schemas are relational tuples that represent the bindings of message parameters. For instance, Table 1 shows three instance of quote. In the rest of the chapter we use "message" to refer to both a message schema and message instance when there is no ambiguity.

Table 1. Instances of quote message.

pID	item	price
1	*book*	5
2	*bike*	10
3	*phone*	20

An *enactment* of a protocol corresponds to the set of messages that are exchanged between the agents with respect to a unique key. Each unique enactment of a protocol is identified by one or more key parameters. In our example the only key parameter is pID. Hence, each distinct enactment of Purchase must have a unique binding for pID. The uniqueness constraints of typical relational models apply to the bindings of keys in each message instance (i.e., no two instances of a message can have the same binding for a key), and each parameter across the messages (i.e., a parameter has the same binding for the same key in the instances of different messages).

Agents can enact multiple instances of a protocol concurrently. To this end, each agent keeps its own *local history*, which is the set of sent and received messages by the agent in all enactments. Table 2 shows an example local history of an agent who enacts the buyer role. In Table 2, there are four enactments of Purchase (i.e., one for each distinct binding of pID). Note that only the enactments in which pID is bound to 1 and 2 are complete. That is, all the public parameters of Purchase are bound in these two enactments. The local history of an agent is sufficient for the agent to carry out its interactions with other agents complying with a protocol. In other words, an agent does not need any information about the states of the other agents to interact with them. Hence, BSPL protocols can be enacted by agents in a fully decentralized way without referring to any global state.

Table 2. Local history of an agent enacting the buyer role.

(a) rfq

pID	item
1	*book*
2	*bike*
3	*phone*
4	*pen*

(b) quote

pID	item	price
1	*book*	5
2	*bike*	10
3	*phone*	20

(c) accept

pID	item	price	result
1	*book*	5	*OK*

(d) reject

pID	item	price	result
2	*bike*	10	*NOK*

Given an agent's local history, we say that a parameter's binding is *known* to the agent in an enactment of a protocol, if the agent's local history includes a message with a binding of the parameter for that particular enactment. Otherwise, we say that the parameter's binding is *unknown* to the agent in that particular enactment. For instance, according to the local history of the buyer in Table 2, binding of price is known (as 5) to the buyer for the enactment of Purchase where pID is bound to 1. This is due to the quote message that is received by the buyer for this enactment. However, the binding of price is unknown to the buyer for the enactment where pID is bound to 4, since there is no message in the buyer's local history with a binding of price for that enactment.

As we have stated earlier, the key idea of BSPL is to specify operational constraints of a protocol in terms of correct flow of information among agents, instead of using procedural control structures. BSPL models the flow of information in a protocol by adorning parameters with ⌜in⌝, ⌜out⌝, or ⌜nil⌝.

Parameters that are adorned ⌜in⌝ in a message correspond conceptually to the inputs of the message, whose bindings must be known to the sender before sending the message. For instance, the seller must know the bindings of pID and item before sending a quote. Parameters that are adorned ⌜out⌝ correspond conceptually to the outputs of a message, whose bindings are produced by the sender when sending the message. For instance, the seller must produce the binding of price when sending a quote. Agents cannot violate integrity of information when sending messages. That is, a sender cannot change the known binding of a parameter when sending a message. As a consequence, if two or more message share the same ⌜out⌝ adorned parameter, only one of these messages can be sent in an enactment to ensure integrity, meaning that the messages that share ⌜out⌝ adorned parameters are mutually exclusive (e.g., accept and reject due to ⌜out⌝ adorned parameter outcome). Lastly, if a parameter is adorned ⌜nil⌝ in a message, the sender must not know the binding of the parameter and also must not produce a binding for the parameter when sending the message.

BSPL formalizes the correct flow of information in a protocol by defining *viability* of messages in an enactment. A message is viable for a sender in an enactment, if and only if (1) the sender knows the bindings of all the ⌜in⌝ adorned parameters of the message, and (2) there is no earlier message in the sender's local history that already binds any of ⌜out⌝ or ⌜nil⌝ adorned parameters of the message. Agents comply with a protocol, if they exchange only viable messages in an enactment of the protocol. For instance, considering the local history of the buyer in Table 2, the instance $(3, phone, 20, OK)$ of accept is viable for the buyer, since the bindings of all its ⌜in⌝ adorned parameters are known (due to the earlier rfq and quote messages that are exchanged in the enactment) and the binding of the ⌜out⌝ adorned result is unknown to the buyer for the enactment where pID is 3. Hence, the buyer can send this message by producing the binding of result, which is OK in our case. Similarly, the reject message instance $(3, phone, 10, NOK)$ is also viable.

On the other hand, there is no viable accept message for the enactment where pID is bound to 2, since the ⌜out⌝ adorned result is already bound to NOK in this enactment as a result of the prior reject message (i.e., the value of an ⌜out⌝ adorned parameter is known). Similarly, there is no viable reject message for the enactment where pID is bound to 1, since the ⌜out⌝ adorned result is already bound to OK in this enactment because of the prior accept message. For the enactment where pID is bound to 4, the buyer does not know the binding of price, which is adorned ⌜in⌝ in accept and reject messages. Hence, there are no viable accept or reject messages for this enactment.

3   Pitfalls of Developing Protocol-Compliant Agents

Development of a protocol-compliant agent for an information-based protocol is a challenging task due to factors such as concurrent enactments of the protocol and asynchronous communication between agents. Without a well-defined methodology, developers may easily fail to identify subtle details of a protocol and implement non-compliant agents. In this section we identify such potential pitfalls of agent development for information-based protocols using our Purchase example from the previous section. Although our example is specified in BSPL, the issues that we discuss here are general and occur when developing agents for protocols that are specified in any language.

Let us start by examining some interactions between a protocol-compliant buyer and seller for our Purchase protocol. Figure 1 shows two such interactions. In both cases, the buyer first sends an rfq in which pID and item are bound to 1 and *book*, respectively. Then, the seller replies with a quote that binds price to 5. Finally, the buyer either sends an accept as in Fig. 1(a) or a reject as in Fig. 1(b) in response to the received quote. Now we identify several issues that induce non-compliant implementation of agents.

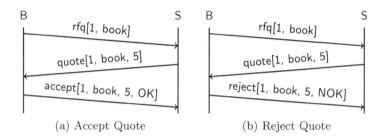

(a) Accept Quote   (b) Reject Quote

Fig. 1. Compliant interactions between the buyer (B) and seller (S).

Information Integrity: Protocol-compliant agents must ensure integrity of the exchanged information when interacting according to an information-based protocol. An agent may easily violate information integrity (maliciously or accidentally) by either creating information that does not exist or by altering known information. Figure 2(a) shows an interaction that corresponds to the former case, where the buyer sends an accept message to the seller without receiving a quote message by creating the binding of price as 3 even tough price is adorned ⌜in⌝ for accept. Figure 2(b) shows an interaction that corresponds to the latter case, where the buyer alters the binding of the item to *bike* when sending the accept message, which should actually be *book* as in the prior rfq message that she sent to the seller earlier.

In both cases, the integrity of the exchanged information is violated by the buyer leading to a non-compliant enactment of the protocol. These kind of mistakes occur especially when an agent is implemented for concurrently enacting multiple instances of a protocols. For instance, consider a buyer that interacts concurrently with multiple sellers to purchase the cheapest copy of a book. This normally can be achieved by executing multiple instances of the buyer agent concurrently (e.g., in separate threads), each handling a separate enactment of Purchase with a different seller. If each concurrent instance of the buyer code can be executed in complete isolation, the errors we identify cannot happen. However, in most realistic applications, instances of an agent cannot be fully isolated since they must access to some shared data. In our example, the instances of buyer agent must share the price information they receive from different buyers. A developer may make a mistake when developing the buyer agent, which may cause the price that is received in one enactment to be used in another enactment as we demonstrate in Fig. 2.

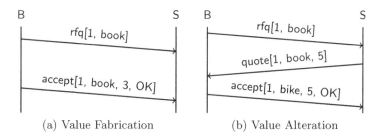

(a) Value Fabrication   (b) Value Alteration

Fig. 2. Violation of information integrity.

Mutual Exclusion: Realistic information-based protocols usually involve mutually exclusive messages. For instance, when the buyer receives a quote message from the seller, she must either send an accept or reject message, but not both. Figure 3(a) shows violation of the mutual exclusion by the buyer, who sends first an accept message and then a reject message after receiving a quote message. Note that, in this example mutual exclusion is local to the buyer. That is, emission of the accept and reject messages are local choices of the buyer. Hence, violation of mutual exclusion can be avoided by ensuring the buyer's compliance with the protocol.

However, mutual exclusion may also be non-local [7]. Suppose that in an extended version of our purchase protocol the seller may cancel its quote by sending a cancel message, which binds result, between the quote and accept messages. Therefore, if there is a cancel message, there should not be an accept message and vice versa. However, these message are emitted by different agents (i.e., mutual exclusion is non-local) and violation of mutual exclusion may occur as Fig. 3(b) shows even though the agents are protocol-compliant. In general, non-local mutual exclusion cannot be satisfied unless behaviors of agents are synchronized, which is costly and hard to achieve (if not impossible) in realistic systems. A protocol is called *safe* if it does have any enactments where two agents may bind the same parameter, and in this chapter we only consider safe protocols.

Concurrency: As we have discussed in information integrity issues, in many practical multiagent systems, agents concurrently enact multiple instances of protocols. For instance, in our purchase scenario, the buyer may concurrently

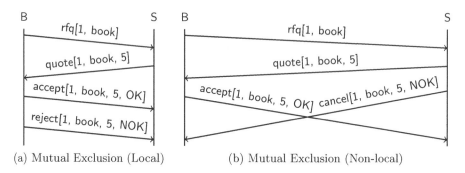

Fig. 3. Violation of mutual exclusion.

send multiple quote requests to the seller for different items in different enact-ments. Besides, the buyer (and also seller) can interact with multiple sellers (buyers) concurrently in different enactments of the purchase protocol. In such situations, in addition to the integrity issues that we have discussed, develop-ers should also deal with interleaved asynchronous emission and reception of messages in different enactments. To this end, developers normally use multi-threading mechanisms (i.e., each concurrent protocol instance is executed in a separate thread). However, this requires the use of complex synchronization mechanisms between the threads to properly handle interleaving messages from different enactments. For instance, the seller must check if there are sufficient quantity of goods when making concurrent quotes. Achieving such synchroniza-tion is an error-prone task and if not done correctly may easily cause agents to act in a non-compliant manner or event stop operating due to deadlock issues.

4   Stellar

Stellar[1] is a programming model to develop protocol-compliant agents for BSPL protocols. Stellar eliminates the pitfalls of protocol-compliant agent development that we have discussed in Sect. 3. To this end, Stellar provides a a set of well-defined operations around a software pattern for developing agents to enact roles in a protocol. If an agent's interactions are implemented using the operations of Stellar following its software pattern, the developed agent is guaranteed to be protocol-compliant.

We implement Stellar as a Java framework. The implementation provides, (1) a code generation tool, which, given a BSPL protocol, automatically gener-ates a protocol-specific code library that includes classes to represent the roles, messages, and parameters of the given protocol, and (2) a static core library that provides the operations to apply Stellar's software patterns.

The workflow for developing a protocol-compliant agent using Stellar is as follows. First, a BSPL protocol for which an agent is intended to be developed is

---

[1] Stellar is available on https://github.com/akingunay/stellar.

specified. Second, the protocol is provided to Stellar's code generation tool, which automatically generates a library of classes corresponding to the roles, messages, and parameters of the given protocol. Third, programmers develop their agents using the static core library and the automatically generated protocol-specific library and by following Stellar's software pattern.

Before explaining Stellar's details, we first highlight its key features for developing protocol-compliant agents using the following Java snippet, which shows a possible implementation of the seller agent in Purchase protocol to handle the reception of an rfq message and respond with the corresponding quote message.

Listing 2. Handling of a received rfq message by a seller.

```
1   public void handleRfq(Rfq rfq)
2   {
3     // create a query to define a criteria for message retrieval
4     Query query = new Query("pID", Query.EQ, rfq.get(Rfq.pID));
5
6     // use adapter to retrieve an enabled message according to the criteria
7     Quote quote = adapter.retrieveEnabled(Quote.class, query).getFirst();
8
9     // seller's business logic to determine the requested item's price
10    String price = priceMap.get(quote.get(Quote.ITEM));
11
12    // send the enabled message by binding necessary parameters
13    quote.send(price);
14  }
```

Stellar follows BSPL's declarative approach. Hence, it does not impose a control flow for developing protocol-compliant agents. Instead, Stellar uses an event-driven model, where viable messages are created and sent according to the local history of an agent when certain events happen. In this regard, the above code snippet shows an event handler for the reception of an rfq message. A key class of Stellar is a role adapter, which provides operations to retrieve and exchange viable messages during enactment of protocols. In our code snippet the seller's adapter is referred via the variable adapter, which is created during the initialization of the seller agent as we will demonstrate later.

A fundamental feature of an adapter is to provide operations for retrieving *enabled* messages from an agent's local history. In an enabled message, all ⌜in⌝ adorned parameters are bound according to the local history of the agent, and all ⌜out⌝ and ⌜nil⌝ parameters are unbound. Hence, the programmer can easily create a viable message from an enabled message, which is retrieved from its local history using the role adapter, simply by producing bindings for all unbound ⌜out⌝ parameters according to the business logic of the agent. In this way Stellar ensures that agents send only viable messages and accordingly guarantees compliance of an agent's implementation with a protocol.

To exemplify, in Line 7 of Listing 2, adapter object's retrieveEnabled method retrieves an enabled quote object of Quote class, which corresponds to a quote message of Purchase protocol, to create a viable response to the received rfq message. The retrieval operation takes a query to determine which particular enabled message(s) it should retrieve. In our example, a single object corresponding to the enabled quote message is retrieved as a response to the received rfq, using the identifier of the received message in the query that is provided to retrieveEnabled. Finally, in Line 13, the send method of the retrieved Quote object is used to send the actual message to its recipient (i.e., the buyer who sent the received rfq message), which is automatically set by the adapter when retrieving the Quote object from the sender's local history. Note that, in order to make the corresponding message viable, the send method takes a price argument, whose value is determined by the seller's business logic.

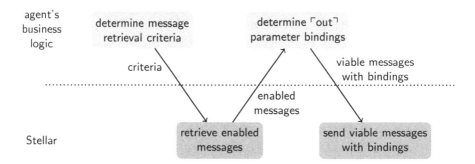

Fig. 4. Pattern to implement protocol-compliant agents using Stellar.

Figure 4 shows an abstract representation of Stellar's software pattern that we use in the above code snippet in Listing 2 to ensure compliance of the seller agent. First, the agent's business logic determines the criteria to retrieve a certain type of enabled message(s) from its local history. Then, the agent uses Stellar to retrieve the enabled message(s) that satisfy its criteria. Next, the agent's business logic determines the bindings of the ⌜out⌝ adorned parameters of the retrieved enabled message(s), and provide them to Stellar. Finally, Stellar compiles viable messages using the enabled messages and the provided bindings for the ⌜out⌝ adorned parameters, and sends them to their recipients.

4.1   Developing Agents Using Stellar

In this section we present details of Stellar using an example in which we implement a buyer agent for the Purchase protocol in Listing 1.

Structure of an Agent: Listing 3 shows the overall structure of the Buyer class, which we use to implement the buyer agent. The object adapter of class BAdapter is the buyer's role adapter which is generated by Stellar from the specification of the Purchase protocol. Buyer class implements QuoteHandler interface, which is also generated by Stellar, with a single method handleQuote, which is called by adapter when the buyer receives a Quote message. Note that QuoteHandler could also be implemented by a separate class to enhance modularity. Buyer class may have other variables and methods as usual to represent the buyer's business logic. Also note that Buyer is a programmer defined class and it is not generated by Stellar. That is, Stellar does not require developers to inherit a certain base class or use a certain code skeleton when implementing their agents.

Listing 3. Structure of the buyer's agent.

```
1  public class Buyer implements QuoteHandler
2  {
3
4    private BAdapter adapter;
5
6    // class variables and methods to represent buyer's business logic
7    ...
8
9    // object initialization
10   ...
11
12   public void handleQuote(Quote quote)
13   {
14     ...
15   }
16
17 }
```

Initialization of Agent: Listing 4 shows the constructor of Buyer class. The object adapter of class BAdapter is initialized using the factory method newAdapter according to a Configuration object, which includes information about the buyer's deployment such as its own and other agents network addresses. We discuss these concepts in detail in Sect. 4.2. Next, the created Buyer object registers itself as the handler for the received Quote messages.

Listing 4. Initialization of the buyer's agent.

```
1  public Buyer(Configuration configuration)
2  {
3    adapter = BAdapter.newAdapter(configuration);
4    adapter.registerQuoteHandler(this);
5
6    // initialization of other class variables
7    ...
8  }
```

Initialization of Interaction: Listing 5 shows how the buyer agent initiates its interaction with a seller agent. The code first retrieves an enabled rfq message object calling the method retrieveEnabled of adapter. Remember that in the Purchase protocol the rfq message does not have any ⌜in⌝ adorned parameters. Hence, this message corresponds to an entry point for a new enactment of the protocol. Therefore, the buyer can send this message at any time to initiate a new enactment by setting its ⌜out⌝ adorned parameters. In other words, an rfq message is always viable. When retrieveEnabled method is called for such a message, Stellar automatically assigns values to the key parameter(s) of the message to create a unique key for initiating a new enactment ensuring information integrity. Hence, the only thing the buyer should do is to determine the item, for which it intends to request a quote, and call the send method of the retrieved rfq object.

Listing 5. Initialization of interaction by the buyer's agent.

```
1  Rfq rfq = adapter.retrieveEnabled(Rfq.class);
2  String item = ... // set by buyer's business logic
3  rfq.send(item);
```

This code snippet can be part of any programmer-defined method that captures the buyer agent's business logic. For instance, if the buyer agent is provided a list of items to buy, it can iterate over the list and execute the snippet for each item in effect imitating a new (concurrent) enactment of the Purchase protocol. Note that, although the buyer can enact multiple protocols concurrently, it is executed as a single thread, avoiding pitfalls of concurrency. Agents that are developed using Stellar process a single message at a time (similar to actors model). Hence, an agent is always implemented as a single thread even if it enacts multiple protocols concurrently.

Handling of Messages: The next two code snippets show handling of received quotes. Listing 6 shows the interface that is generated by Stellar from the specification of Purchase and Listing 7 shows the implementation of the interface by the buyer's agent.

Listing 6. Specification of QuoteHandler interface.

```
1   public interface QuoteHandler
2   {
3     public void handleQuote(Quote quote);
4   }
```

For simplicity, suppose that the business logic of the buyer is to accept quotes below 50 and reject others. The code in Listing 7 first creates a Query object to represent the buyer's acceptance criteria for the received quotes. The first part of the query calls the get method to determine the identifier of the enactment for which the quote is received (Line 3), and then defines the buyer's criterion for the acceptable value of the price (Line 4). Next, the code calls the retrieveEnabled method to retrieve an enabled Accept message object that matches the given query.

Listing 7. Implementation of QuoteHandler interface by buyer's agent.

```
1    public void handleQuote(Quote quote)
2    {
3      Condition c1 = new Condition("pID", Query.EQ, quote.get(Quote.pID));
4      Condition c2 = new Condition("price", Query.LT, 50));
5      Query aQuery = new Query(new AndCondition(c1, c2));
6
7      Accept accept = adapter.retrieveEnabled(Accept.class,
                  aQuery).getFirst();
8
9      if (accept != null) {
10       accept.send("OK");
11     } else {
12       Query rQuery = new Query("pID", Query.EQ, quote.get(Quote.pID));
13       Reject reject = adapter.retrieveEnabled(Reject.class,
                  rQuery).getFirst();
14       reject.send("NOK");
15     }
16   }
```

Note that there can only be one enabled accept message for every enactment with a particular binding of pID. However, retrieveEnabled returns a MessageSet object, which implements the Set interface with additional convenience methods. In Line 7, getFirst is one of these convenience methods that retrieves a single message if the set is a singleton and null otherwise.

If there is an enabled accept message that matches the query (i.e., the quoted price is below 50), the code sends the retrieved Accept message using its send method, providing "OK" as the binding of result parameter (Lines 9–10). Otherwise (i.e., the quoted price is above 50 and hence accept is null), the code sends a Reject message, which is retrieved by calling the retrieveEnabled method with the corresponding query (Lines 11–14).

Remember that the buyer should either send an accept or a reject message for a received quote to comply with Purchase (i.e., accept or reject are mutually exclusive). Let us explain how this is guaranteed by Stellar. Suppose that the programmer of buyer agent made a mistake an wrote the following code to handle received quote messages instead of the code in Listing 7.

```
1   public void handleQuote(Quote quote)
2   {
3     ...
4     Accept accept = adapter.retrieveEnabled(Accept.class,
          aQuery).getFirst();
5     if (accept != null) {
6       accept.send("OK");
7     }
8     Query rQuery = new Query("pID", Query.EQ, quote.get(Quote.pID));
9     Reject reject = adapter.retrieveEnabled(Reject.class,
          rQuery).getFirst();
10    if (reject != null) {
11      reject.send("NOK");
12    }
13    ...
```

This piece of code tries to send first an accept and then a reject message for the same pID binding. However, when an accept message for a pID binding is sent (Line 6), the parameter result is bound for the pID binding, which makes the reject message for the same pID binding disabled, since result is adorned ⌜out⌝ in reject. Accordingly, retrieveEnabled always returns null when it is called to retrieve a Reject object for a binding of pID for which an accept message is already sent (Line 9). Hence, the agent still complies with the Purchase protocol, event though its business logic is not correctly implemented.

4.2   Implementation of Stellar

Management of Local Histories: Stellar stores local history of an agent in a local relational database. Stellar hides the details of the particular database system from programmers. In fact, the programmer should not access the local history of the agent directly. Instead, the programmer should use only the retrieve and send methods provided by Stellar. Our implementation currently uses MySQL to store local histories of agents, however any relational database system that supports fundamental relational operations can be easily adopted.

Emission and Reception of Viable Messages: Stellar uses asynchronous message passing for agent communication, which we implemented using UDP. The messages that are exchanged over the network are serialized into parameter-value pairs and represented in JSON format. Emission of messages is enabled only via the send methods of the generated message classes. The aim of these methods is to ensure that agents send only viable messages by binding all of the necessary parameters. Otherwise, these methods throw exception. Reception of messages and their insertion into an agent's local history is handled by the adapters of Stellar. Hence, Stellardoes not provide any method to programmers for manual message reception. Instead, the programmers should implement handlers of the messages that they want to react, which are automatically called by the adapters of Stellar when a message is received. This simplifies programming of agents in asynchronous settings.

Retrieval of Enabled Messages: Here we provide Stellar's algorithm for the retrieval of enabled messages from an agent's local history. Below, we use, $\mathbb{P}$ for a BSPL protocol, p for individual parameters, P, Q, K for lists (or sets if their ordering is not important) of parameters. We use calligraphic capital letters for relations in the local history of an agent, and apply standard relational algebra operators Π for projection, σ for selection, $\bowtie$ for natural join, $\bowtie$ for full outer join, and $\bowtie$ for left outer join. We also use the utility methods `allParams`, `keyParams`, `inParams`, `nilParams`, and `outParams` with a relation and protocol argument to access the set of all, key, ⌜in⌝, ⌜nil⌝, and ⌜out⌝ adorned parameters of the relation, respectively.

Algorithm 1. retrieveEnabled($\mathcal{M}, \phi, \mathbb{P}$)

---

1 $P_{in} \leftarrow \texttt{inParams}(\mathcal{M}, \mathbb{P})$ // ⌜in⌝ adorned parameters of $\mathcal{M}$
2 $P_{nil} \leftarrow \texttt{nilParams}(\mathcal{M}, \mathbb{P})$ // ⌜nil⌝ adorned parameters of $\mathcal{M}$
3 $P_{out} \leftarrow \texttt{outParams}(\mathcal{M}, \mathbb{P})$ // ⌜out⌝ adorned parameters of $\mathcal{M}$
4 $K \leftarrow \texttt{keyParams}(\mathcal{M}, \mathbb{P})$ // key parameters of $\mathcal{M}$
5 $\mathcal{W}_I \leftarrow \emptyset$
6 **if** P_{in} *is* $\emptyset$ **then**
7 $\quad$ | $\quad$ **return** $\{()\}$
8 $\mathcal{W}_I \leftarrow \bigcup_{\mathcal{N} \in \mathbb{P}} \Pi_K(\mathcal{N})$
9 **foreach** $p \in P_{in}$ **do**
10 $\quad$ | $\quad Q \leftarrow K \cup \{p\}$
11 $\quad$ | $\quad \mathcal{W}_p \leftarrow \texttt{createRelation}(Q)$
12 $\quad$ | $\quad$ **foreach** $\mathcal{N} \in \mathbb{P}$ *such that* $p \in \texttt{allParams}(\mathcal{N}, \mathbb{P})$ **do**
13 $\quad$ | $\quad$ $\quad \lfloor \mathcal{W}_p \leftarrow \Pi_Q(\mathcal{N}) \cup \mathcal{W}_p$
14 $\quad$ | $\quad \mathcal{W}_I \leftarrow \mathcal{W}_I \bowtie_K \mathcal{W}_p$
15 $\mathcal{W}_E \leftarrow \bigcup_{\mathcal{N} \in \mathbb{P}} \Pi_K(\mathcal{N})$
16 **foreach** $p \in P_{out} \cup P_{nil}$ **do**
17 $\quad$ | $\quad Q \leftarrow K \cup \{p\}$
18 $\quad$ | $\quad \mathcal{W}_p \leftarrow \texttt{createRelation}(Q)$
19 $\quad$ | $\quad$ **foreach** $\mathcal{N} \in \mathbb{P}$ *such that* $p \in \texttt{allParams}(\mathcal{N}, \mathbb{P})$ **do**
20 $\quad$ | $\quad$ $\quad \lfloor \mathcal{W}_p \leftarrow \Pi_Q(\mathcal{N}) \cup \mathcal{W}_p$
21 $\quad$ | $\quad \mathcal{W}_E \leftarrow \mathcal{W}_E \bowtie_K \mathcal{W}_p$
22 $\mathcal{W} \leftarrow \sigma_{P_{out}=null \wedge P_{nil}=null}(\mathcal{W}_I \bowtie_K \mathcal{W}_E)$
23 **return** $\sigma_\phi(\mathcal{W})$

Algorithm 1 defines retrieval of enabled messages, given the relation $\mathcal{M}$ that corresponds to a message schema (e.g., a quote message schema), the user defined query ϕ, and the protocol specification $\mathbb{P}$. Note that the algorithm returns a relation (not actual message objects in Java), where each tuple of the relation corresponds to the parameter bindings of an enabled instance of the message schema $\mathcal{M}$. A Stellar adapter uses this relation to create the corresponding message objects and return them as the result of a retrieveEnabled method call as we demonstrated in earlier examples.

Algorithm 1 can be divided into three phases. In the first phase (from lines 8 to 14), the algorithm builds the relation $\mathcal{W}_I$ where all ⌜in⌝ adorned parameters of $\mathcal{M}$ are bound. In the second phase (from lines 15 to 21), the algorithm builds another relation $\mathcal{W}_E$ where one or more ⌜out⌝ or ⌜nil⌝ adorned parameters of $\mathcal{M}$ are bound. In the last phase (lines 22–23), the algorithm removes the tuples from $\mathcal{W}_I$ for which there is a matching tuple (i.e., identified by the same key) in $\mathcal{W}_E$. Hence, each tuple of the resulting relation corresponds to an enabled message (i.e., all ⌜in⌝ parameters are bound and all ⌜out⌝ and ⌜nil⌝ parameters are unbound). Note that this operation removes the tuples that would cause violation of mutual exclusion. If a message $\mathcal{M}'$ that is mutually exclusive to $\mathcal{M}$ is already emitted in an enactment, then there are tuples in $\mathcal{W}_E$ with bindings of the parameters that are adorned ⌜out⌝ in both $\mathcal{M}$ and $\mathcal{M}'$, and accordingly the corresponding tuples in $\mathcal{W}_I$ are removed. Hence, the messages that can cause to violation of mutual exclusion are not enabled. The algorithm applies the given query ϕ to the resulting relation $\mathcal{W}$ to filter the tuples.

4.3   Revisiting Pitfalls

Stellar's retrieval and emission operations ensure causality and information integrity. Specifically, retrieval operations ensure integrity of ⌜in⌝ adorned parameters by binding them permanently to the corresponding values according to the agent's local history. Hence, a programmer cannot fabricate or alter ⌜in⌝ adorned parameters of a message. The send operations ensure integrity of ⌜out⌝ and ⌜nil⌝ adorned parameters by enforcing the programmer to assign values to only ⌜out⌝ adorned parameters when needed. Hence, the programmer cannot omit assignment of mandatory parameters and thus break integrity. Further, Stellar handles creation of bindings for key parameters ensuring their uniqueness, which prevents key related integrity issues.

Stellar's retrieval operations prevent emission of mutually exclusive messages. That is, if two (or more) messages are mutually exclusive in a protocol and an agent has already sent one of these messages in an enactment of the protocol, the retrieval operation does not consider the other mutually exclusive message(s) as enabled in the same enactment. Hence, the agent cannot retrieve and send mutually exclusive messages. Stellar does not directly handle non-local mutual exclusion. However, safety of a BSPL protocol, which means that the protocol is free from non-local mutual exclusion, can be verified automatically [12] at design time to avoid non-local mutual exclusion issues.

Communication in Stellar is fully asynchronous. Hence a single-threaded agent can easily enact multiple protocols at the same time using Stellar. That is, an agent's execution is never blocked when sending or receiving messages. Further, Stellar's programming model handles one incoming message at a time.

Hence, developers can implement their agents without any thread synchronization that deals with interleaving reception of multiple messages in different enactments. This feature of Stellar substantially simplifies design of an agent, as our case study in Sect. 5 demonstrates. Note that UDP, which is used in our implementation, is an unreliable protocol (i.e., it does not guarantee delivery of emitted messages), which may compromise liveness of an interaction. This issue can be avoided using a reliable alternative, such as RUDP, TCP, or message queues. However, these alternatives provide features (e.g., ordered message delivery), which are not needed by Stellar. We chose UDP for our implementation to show that lack of such features do not affect protocol-compliance of agents. We will address liveness of interactions in our future work.

5 Case Study

To demonstrate the use of Stellar in a more comprehensive case, where an agent should consider multiple messages for decision making, we use a claim handling scenario from insurance domain. We list the protocol that represents this scenario in Listing 8. In this scenario there is a policy subscriber and an insurer. The subscriber can make multiple claims (claim message) by sending an incident's details and the claimed amount to the insurer. The insurer either approves (approve message) or rejects a claim (reject message). In case of approval, the insurer pays the claimed amount to the subscriber. The insurer can pay its balance immediately for each claim or as lump sum for several claims (pay message). For brevity, we omit some policy aspects such as premium payments.

Listing 8. An insurance policy claim protocol.

```
Insurance {
 roles I, S //insurer, subscriber

 parameters out sID key, out cID key, out pID key, out subscriber, out
     period,
       out type, out date, out incident, out cAmount, out outcome, out pAmount

 S ↦ I: subscribe[out sID, out subscriber, out period, out type]
 I ↦ S: register[in sID, in subscriber, in period, in type, out date]
 S ↦ I: claim[in sID, out cID, out incident, out cAmount]
 I ↦ S: approve[in sID, in cID, in incident, in cAmount, out outcome]
 I ↦ S: reject[in sID, in cID, in incident, in cAmount, out outcome]
 I ↦ S: pay[in sID, out pID, out pAmount]
}
```

Listing 9 shows the implementation of ClaimHandler interface by the insurer agent to handle claim messages when enacting Insurance. As we explained earlier, ClaimHandler interface is generated by Stellar from the specification of Insurance and consists of a single method handleClaim, which is used to define the insurer's business logic for handling claims. Suppose that the insurer handles a claim in two steps. In the first step, the insurer decides whether the received claim is valid or not. In the second step, if the claim is valid and the insurer's policy balance exceeds a minimum payable amount, the insurer pays its balance. Otherwise, the insurer does not make any immediate payment.

The method processClaim (Lines 8–21) captures the first step. The method first decides whether the received claim is valid by calling isValidClaim (Line 12), which returns true for valid and false for invalid claims. We do not present the details of isValidClaim since they are not relevant to our demonstration. Depending on the validity of the claim, processClaim retrieves and sends either the enabled Approve (Lines 13–15) or Reject (Lines 17–19) message. Finally, processClaim returns true or false depending on the validity of the claim.

If the claim is approved (Line 3), handleClaim calls payBalance (Line 4), which captures the second step (Lines 23–30). The method payBalance first computes the insurer's total balance for the policy using approvedClaimAmount and paid-ClaimAmount methods (Line 24). We describe these methods later in Listing 10. If the insurer's balance is more that the minimum payable amount, processClaim retrieves and sends the enabled Pay message to pay the insurer's balance (Lines 25–29).

Listing 9. Implementation of ClaimHandler interface by the insurance agent.

```
1   public void handleClaim(Claim claim)
2   {
3     boolean isApproved = processClaim(claim);
4     if (isApproved) {
5       payBalance(claim.get(Claim.sID));
6     }
7   }
8
9   private void processClaim(Claim claim)
10  {
11    Condition c1 = new Condition("sID", Query.EQ, claim.get(Claim.sID));
12    Condition c2 = new Condition("cID", Query.EQ, quote.get(Claim.sID));
13    Query query = new Query(new AndCondition(c1, c2));
14
15    if (isValidClaim(claim)) {
16      Approve msg = adapter.retrieveEnabled(Accept.class, query).getFirst();
17      msg.send("APPROVED");
18      return true;
19    } else {
20      Reject msg = adapter.retrieveEnabled(Reject.class, query).getFirst();
21      msg.send("REJECTED");
22      return false;
23    }
24  }
25
26  private void payBalance(String sId)
27  {
28    int balance = payableClaimedAmount(sId) - totalPaidAmount(sId);
29
30    if(MIN_PAYABLE_AMOUNT <= balance) {
31      Query query = new Query("sID", Query.EQ, sId);
32      Pay msg = adapter.retrieveEnabled(Pay.class, query);
33      msg.send(balance);
34    }
35  }
```

Computation of the insurer's balance for a policy requires consideration of multiple messages. That is, we should first compute the total payable claimed amount for the policy according to the approved claims. Then we should compute the total paid amount for the policy according to the previous payments, and subtract it from the total payable claimed amount. The method payableClaimedAmount in Listing 10 (Lines 1–9) computes the total payable claimed amount. It first retrieves all the sent Approve messages for the policy, which is identified by sId, from the insurer's message history calling retrieveMessage method (Line 3). Note that this is a different method than retrieveEnabled. Next, the total payable amount is computed by iterating over all the retrieved Approve messages and summing up the claimed amount of each message. The method totalPaidAmount (Lines 11–19) repeats the same process to compute the total paid amount for the policy using Pay messages (instead of Approve messages) and corresponding paid amounts in those messages.

Listing 10. Computation of total claimed and paid amounts.

```
1   private int payableClaimedAmount(String sId)
2   {
3     Query query = new Query("sID", Query.EQ, sId);
4     MessageSet<Approve> msgs = adapter.retrieveMessage(Approve.class,
          query);
5
6     int sum = 0;
7     for (Approve msg : msgs) {
8       sum += (int) msg.get(Approve.cAmount);
9     }
10    return sum;
11  }
12
13  private int totalPaidAmount(String sId)
14  {
15    Query query = new Query("sID", Query.EQ, sId);
16    MessageSet<Pay> msgs = adapter.retrieveMessage(Pay.class, query);
17
18    int sum = 0;
19    for (Pay msg : msgs) {
20      sum += (int) msg.get(Pay.pAmount);
21    }
22    return sum;
23  }
```

6 Discussion

We summarize our contributions, relate them to the literature, and discuss directions for future work.

6.1 Summary

This chapter presented Stellar, a programming model for developing protocol-compliant agents for BSPL. Stellar's main idea is to ensure compliance of agents by allowing exchange of only viable messages between them. To this end, Stellar provides a simple yet effective software pattern for retrieving enabled messages from an agent's local history and for sending them ensuring their viability. Communication in Stellar is fully asynchronous. Further, Stellar implicitly ensures information integrity of interaction, prevents emission of locally mutually exclusive messages, and enables concurrent enactment of protocols without relying on multithreading mechanisms. Accordingly, Stellar simplifies agent development in decentralized settings ensuring their compliance. Stellar is different from programming models that ensure agent compliance using control flow structures (i.e., code skeletons), and more distantly related to distributed programming models without interaction protocols.

6.2 Related Work

Scribble [15] enforces design-time adherence to protocols that specify typed message signatures and messaging constraints with explicit control flow. Scribble [5] extracts state machines from protocol specifications to generate APIs for endpoints. Sending or receiving a message returns a protocol state object and each protocol state object provides message sending and receiving operations that comply with correct subsequent state transitions. Stellar provides more flexibility to developers, since it does not impose a control flow for ensuring compliance when implementing agents. Developers are free to design their agents as they see fit, without being distracted about the state of their interactions. Stellar's retrieve and send pattern ensures exchange of only viable messages and accordingly ensures compliance of agent, which is independent from a control flow.

Business-oriented approaches for web services propose the use of high-level processes according to which correct interactions are enforced in code. Business Process Modeling Notation (BPMN) has been used to specify processes that are then translated into the Business Process Execution Language [10] (BPEL), an executable language for externally invoking web services and their interactions based on event occurrences. The BPMN-BPEL approach is inherently process-oriented and depends on the correct realization of workflows. Stellar is information-oriented and uses a declarative approach without imposing any workflow. Business artifacts [9] are high-level representations of both processes, interaction, and the relational data that they operate on. Artifact interoperation hubs [6] enforce correct messaging with business processes by acting as central communication points between web services. Stellar only uses local information and does not rely on any centralized communication artifacts to ensure compliance.

Programming models for distributed systems generally do not consider protocols, e.g., functional reactive programming [2], the Sunny Event-driven programming model [8], and the Actor programming model [4] implemented in Akka [1]. These programming models support interaction derived from internal system or actor code, without a protocol specification against which correct implementations must comply. In Stellar, we focus on supporting independent agent development against protocol specifications, where programmers are protected from violating protocol compliance and integrity of information.

6.3 Future Work

Stellar is a first step toward declarative agent programming based on declarative information-based protocols. A fuller exploration of agent programming would need to consider abstractions for agent policies and how they fit with Stellar. Another interesting direction would be to explore how normative abstractions (e.g., commitments) may be used alongside Stellar, especially since norms represent the meaning of information communicated via protocols.

Acknowledgments. Munindar P. Singh and Thomas C. King gave valuable suggestions that helped improve this chapter. Akın Günay and Amit Chopra were supported by the EPSRC grant EP/N027965/1 (Turtles).

References

1. Akka: 2.5.6 (2017). http://akka.io
2. Bainomugisha, E., Carreton, A.L., van Cutsem, T., Mostinckx, S., de Meuter, W.: A survey on reactive programming. ACM Comput. Surv. **45**(4), 52:1–52:34 (2013)
3. Chopra, A.K., Christie V., S.H., Singh, M.P.: Splee: a declarative information-based language for multiagent interaction protocols. In: Proceedings of the 16th Conference on Autonomous Agents and MultiAgent Systems, pp. 1054–1063 (2017)
4. Hewitt, C., Bishop, P., Steiger, R.: A universal modular actor formalism for artificial intelligence. In: Proceedings of the 3rd International Joint Conference on Artificial Intelligence, IJCAI 1973, pp. 235–245. Morgan Kaufmann Publishers Inc., San Francisco (1973)
5. Hu, R., Yoshida, N.: Hybrid session verification through endpoint API generation. In: Stevens, P., Wąsowski, A. (eds.) FASE 2016. LNCS, vol. 9633, pp. 401–418. Springer, Heidelberg (2016). https://doi.org/10.1007/978-3-662-49665-7_24
6. Hull, R., Narendra, N.C., Nigam, A.: Facilitating workflow interoperation using artifact-centric hubs. In: Baresi, L., Chi, C.-H., Suzuki, J. (eds.) ICSOC/ServiceWave -2009. LNCS, vol. 5900, pp. 1–18. Springer, Heidelberg (2009). https://doi.org/10.1007/978-3-642-10383-4_1
7. Ladkin, P.B., Leue, S.: Interpreting message flow graphs. Formal Aspects Comput. **7**(5), 473–509 (1995)
8. Milicevic, A., Jackson, D., Gligoric, M., Marinov, D.: Model-based, event-driven programming paradigm for interactive web applications. In: Proceedings of the 2013 ACM International Symposium on New Ideas, New Paradigms, and Reflections on Programming and Software, Onward! 2013, pp. 17–36. ACM, New York (2013)
9. Nigam, A., Caswell, N.S.: Business artifacts: an approach to operational specification. IBM Syst. J. **42**(3), 428–445 (2003)
10. Ouyang, C., Dumas, M., van der Aalst, W.M.P., Hofstede, A.H.M., Mendling, J.: From business process models to process-oriented software systems. ACM Trans. Softw. Eng. Methodol. **19**(1), 2:1–2:37 (2009)
11. Singh, M.P.: Information-driven interaction-oriented programming: BSPL, the Blindingly Simple Protocol Language. In: Proceedings of the 10th International Conference on Autonomous Agents and MultiAgent Systems, pp. 491–498 (2011)
12. Singh, M.P.: Semantics and verification of information-based protocols. In: Proceedings of the 11th International Conference on Autonomous Agents and Multiagent Systems, pp. 1149–1156 (2012)
13. Singh, M.P.: Bliss: specifying declarative service protocols. In: Proceedings of the 2014 IEEE International Conference on Services Computing, pp. 235–242 (2014)
14. Winikoff, M., Yadav, N., Padgham, L.: A new hierarchical agent protocol notation. Auton. Agents Multi-Agent Syst. **32**(1), 59–133 (2018)
15. Yoshida, N., Hu, R., Neykova, R., Ng, N.: The Scribble protocol language. In: Abadi, M., Lluch Lafuente, A. (eds.) TGC 2013. LNCS, vol. 8358, pp. 22–41. Springer, Cham (2014). https://doi.org/10.1007/978-3-319-05119-2_3

Formal Analysis and Techniques

Slicing Agent Programs for More Efficient Verification

Michael Winikoff[1]([⊠]), Louise Dennis[2], and Michael Fisher[2]

[1] Victoria University of Wellington, Wellington, New Zealand
michael.winikoff@vuw.ac.nz
[2] Liverpool University, Liverpool, UK
{l.a.dennis,mfisher}@liverpool.ac.uk

Abstract. Agent programs are increasingly used as the core high-level decision-making components within a range of autonomous systems and, as the deployment of such systems in safety-critical scenarios develops, the need for strong and trustworthy *verification* becomes acute. Formal verification techniques such as model-checking provide this high level of assurance yet they are typically both complex and slow to deploy. In this chapter we introduce, develop and evaluate a *program slicing* technique that significantly improves the efficiency of such verification, hence providing more effective routes to the assurance of safety, reliability, and ethics in autonomous systems.

Keywords: Formal verification · Program analysis ·
Agent-oriented programming languages

1 Introduction

The study of agent programming languages is becoming increasingly important not just from an academic viewpoint but because agent programs now play a central role in many *autonomous systems*. The need for transparency and explainability, in particular, is leading to the development of *hybrid agent architectures* for autonomous systems whereby a *rational agent* [29] provides the core high-level decision-making capabilities within the autonomous systems architecture. This approach leads naturally to clarity, flexibility and verifiability [12,15]. Specifically, a rational agent is not only able to take independent decisions but has explicit notions of the *motivations* that lead it to select one option over another. The predominant model of rational agency, and one that we follow here, is the BDI model ('Beliefs', 'Desires', and 'Intentions') [7], in which the agent's assessments about the state of the world (and itself) are captured

Michael Winikoff–This paper is written while the author was at University of Otago, Dunedin, New Zealand

Work supported in the UK by EPSRC through the projects EP/L024845, EP/R026084, and EP/R026092.

© Springer Nature Switzerland AG 2019
D. Weyns et al. (Eds.): EMAS 2018 Workshops, LNAI 11375, pp. 139–157, 2019.
https://doi.org/10.1007/978-3-030-25693-7_8

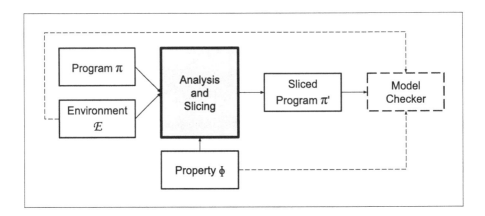

Fig. 1. High-level view of the process

as *beliefs*, the agent's long-term motivations are captured as *desires*, while the agent's partially instantiated plans are captured as *intentions* [22].

There is a wide range of programming languages that use the idea of rational agency, often the BDI approach, as their central model, for example PRS [16,18], AgentSpeak [23], Jason [5], GOAL [17], JACK [27], GWENDOLEN [11], and others [2,3]. As these become deployed in increasingly sophisticated and complex scenarios, there is increased need for much greater assurance through *verification and validation*. Although the most common approach to software verification is through *testing*, [1], Winikoff *et al.* [25,28] show how assurance of agent programs cannot feasibly be carried out using traditional software testing, leading us to *formal verification*.

Formal verification is a mathematically well-founded process for proving that a specification given in formal logic matches the system in question. For a specific logical property, ϕ, there are many different approaches to this [6,9,14], ranging from deductive verification against a logical description of the system ψ_S (i.e., $\vdash \psi_S \Rightarrow \phi$) to the algorithmic verification of the property against a model of the system, M_S (i.e., $M_S \models \phi$). The latter has been extremely successful in Computer Science and Artificial Intelligence, primarily through the *model checking* approach [8]. This takes a description of the system in question, capturing all possible executions, and then checks the logical property against this description (and, hence, against all possible executions).

If (rational) agents are to be used at the core of increasingly sophisticated autonomous systems, it therefore seems natural to explore the model checking of these agent programs. There have been several developments in this direction [19,21], with the most well-developed being that of AJPF/MCAPL [12,15]. This verification approach has been used throughout a range of work tackling applications in autonomous aircraft, spacecraft and road vehicles [10,12,20,24], where a (central) rational agent is verified using model-checking in order to assess all high-level decision-making.

While very useful, such formal verification can be extremely slow, even for relatively small programs [12]. Around a decade ago, there was initial work by Bordini *et al.* [4] aiming to improve the efficiency of agent program model checking by using *slicing*. The basic idea (see Fig. 1) is that instead of model-checking a property ϕ with respect to program π situated in environment $\mathcal{E}$, we instead model-check a *sliced program* π'. The sliced program is a simplified version of π where (some) parts of the program that do not affect the truth of ϕ have been removed. This can result in a program π' that is smaller and substantially faster to model check. For example, Bordini *et al.* [4] found a 61% reduction in run-time to check a particular property of a particular program.

This chapter advances the 2009 paper, updating the algorithm for a contemporary verification framework and proposing a new, and improved, slicing method. We begin by briefly introducing required background material, including reviewing the slicing algorithm of Bordini *et al.* We then present the new slicing method, provide evaluation results, and conclude with a brief discussion of future work (which includes a formal proof of corectness).

2   Background

We briefly review required background, including the specific BDI language we use, GWENDOLEN [11] (Sect. 2.1), the mapping from a BDI program to a graph structure (Sect. 2.2), and the slicing method proposed by Bordini *et al.* [4] (Sect. 2.3).

2.1   BDI Programming Languages and GWENDOLEN

The common core of BDI languages is that an agent program is a collection of *plans*. Each plan $t : c \leftarrow s_1; \ldots; s_n$ comprises a *trigger* t (e.g. posting a sub-goal, denoted $+!g$, or a change to the agent's beliefs, denoted $+b$ or $-b$), a *context condition* c that indicates in which situation the plan is applicable, and a *plan body*. The plan body is a sequence of steps s_i (or more generally a program). Steps include belief updates (adding a belief $+b$ or removing a belief $-b$), testing conditions ($?c$), posting sub-goals $!g$ (but $+!g$ in GWENDOLEN), and actions a.

The core execution cycle is that when a trigger t' is posted, all the *relevant* plans (those whose triggers t unify with t') are collected. A relevant plan is *applicable* if its context condition currently holds. An applicable plan is selected, and that plan's body is executed. Execution is interleaved with processing of other incoming percepts/events and with parallel execution of other plans, in response to other triggers. Details vary between languages (e.g. see Winikoff [26]). We assume the common practice of considering relevant plans in sequential order.

Many BDI languages incorporate a failure handling mechanism where if a step fails (e.g. an action's preconditions are not met), the plan body it is a part of fails. Failure handling then considers the trigger for that plan, and seeks to use alternative plans to handle it. This is done by re-posting the trigger.

In the remainder of this chapter we use the GWENDOLEN notation, where a plan is written: "$t : \{c\} \leftarrow s_1, \ldots, s_n;$". Context conditions are logical

```
:Reasoning Rules:                                                          1
can_accelerate :– safe, ˜ driver_accelerates, ˜ driver_brakes;            2
                                                                          3
:Initial Goals:                                                           4
at_speed_limit [achieve]                                                  5
                                                                          6
:Plans:                                                                   7
+! at_speed_limit [achieve] : {B can_accelerate}                          8
  ← perf(accelerate), wait;                                               9
+! at_speed_limit [achieve] : {˜B safe} ← *safe;                         10
+! at_speed_limit [achieve] : {B driver_accelerates}                     11
  ← *˜driver_accelerates;                                                12
+! at_speed_limit [achieve] : {B driver_brakes}                          13
  ← *˜driver_brakes;                                                     14
+at_speed_limit: {B can_accelerate, B at_speed_limit}                    15
  ← perf(maintain_speed);                                                16
−at_speed_limit: {˜G at_speed_limit [achieve],                           17
  ˜B at_speed_limit} ← +! at_speed_limit[achieve];                       18
−safe: {˜B driver_brakes, ˜B safe} ← perf(brake);                       19
+driver_accelerates: {B safe, ˜B driver_brakes,                          20
  B driver_accelerates} ← perf(accelerate);                              21
+driver_brakes: {B driver_brakes} ← perf(brake);                         22
```

Fig. 2. GWENDOLEN program for cruise control.

combinations ("," denotes conjunction, and "˜" denotes negation) of beliefs ("B") and goals being pursued ("G"). The notation $\mathsf{perf}(a)$ denotes performing an action, and $*c$ means "wait for condition c". Figure 2 shows a simple GWENDOLEN program implementing a cruise control, taken from the GWENDOLEN distribution. Note that the annotation [achieve] indicates an achievement goal, which can be explained in terms of the following[1] "meta-plan": $+!achieve(G) : \{B\ G\}. +!achieve(G) : \{^{\sim}\ B\ G\} \leftarrow +!G; +!achieve(G)$, i.e. keep trying $+!G$ until G is believed. The language is described by the following grammar, where u is a term, and an agent program includes a sequence of plans $\pi_1 \ldots \pi_m$:

$$\pi ::= t : \{c\} \leftarrow s_1; \ldots; s_n$$
$$t ::= +!u \mid +u \mid -u$$
$$c ::= \mathsf{B}\ t \mid \mathsf{G}\ u \mid {}^{\sim}c \mid c_1 \wedge c_2$$
$$s ::= +u \mid -u \mid +!u \mid *c \mid \mathsf{perf}(u)$$

It is important to note that although the presentation in this chapter uses the GWENDOLEN notation, the language features are very similar to those of other

---

[1] An empty plan body is indicated by eliding the "←".

BDI languages, and changing this chapter to apply to another BDI language would require only two very minor changes[2].

An agent exists in an *environment*, which needs to be modelled for verification purposes. Whereas Bordini *et al.* model the environment using a collection of plans that connect each action to its post-conditions, we instead follow Dennis *et al.* [12] and do not define a direct link between actions and their post-conditions. Instead, we define a collection of possible exogenous belief updates that can occur. This representation is more realistic, since often, in real domains, there is a delay between an action being commenced, and the effects of that action manifesting. Additionally, the effects of an action are not usually guaranteed. For example, performing an accelerate action does not necessarily result in being at the speed limit, instead, at some future point the sensors may indicate that the car has reached the speed limit. We define for a given MAS a set of *exogenous belief updates*, $\mathcal{B}$. For instance, for the cruise control example the set of relevant exogenous belief updates is $\mathcal{B} = \{\mathsf{at\_speed\_limit}, \mathsf{safe}, \mathsf{driver\_accelerates}, \mathsf{driver\_brakes}\}$. For each $b \in \mathcal{B}$ a percept $+b$ or $-b$ can occur at any time.

For verification, we define a simple language based on the property specification language used in MCAPL/AJPF:

$$\psi ::= \mathsf{Bel}\ a\ p \mid \mathsf{Des}\ a\ p \mid \mathsf{Int}\ a\ p \mid \mathsf{Does}\ a\ p \qquad (1)$$

$$\varphi :: \psi \mid \varphi \wedge \varphi \mid \phi \vee \varphi \mid \neg\varphi \mid \varphi \rightarrow \varphi \mid \Box\varphi \mid \Diamond\varphi \qquad (2)$$

The full semantics of this language is given by Dennis *et al.* [12]. It is based on Propositional Linear Temporal Logic (PLTL) [13] defined over program traces where the expressions in (2) are as standard in presentations of PLTL and $\mathsf{Bel}\ a\ p$ means that p appears in the belief base of agent a, $\mathsf{Des}\ a\ p$ means that p appears in the goal base of agent a, $\mathsf{Int}\ a\ p$ means that p appears in the goal base of agent a *and also* that a plan has been selected to handle the goal, and $\mathsf{Does}\ a\ p$ means that agent a has executed $\mathsf{perf}(p)$.

2.2 Mapping to a Graph Structure

We map each program clause of the form $t : c \leftarrow s_1, \ldots, s_n$ to a graph that has a trigger node[3] t, a context node c, and step nodes s_i ($1 \leq i \leq n$). We assume that each node has a unique ID (which allows the occurrence of, for instance, a step such as $\mathsf{perf}(\mathsf{accelerate})$ in multiple places in the program to be represented by multiple nodes with unique identifiers, but the same name). We denote the name of a node as $\widehat{N}$ where N is the node's unique ID.

---

[2] Specifically, there is a minor change to the graph construction, noted in a later footnote, and the definition of a belief link would change very slightly (replacing "*" with "?").

[3] There is one slight difference between our mapping and that used by Bordini *et al.*: we do not have a trigger node for each plan, instead we use a single common trigger node for plans that share the same trigger.

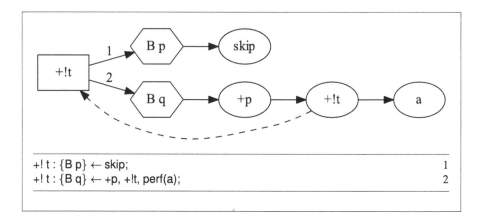

+! t : {B p} ← skip;   1
+! t : {B q} ← +p, +!t, perf(a);   2

Fig. 3. Simple program and the corresponding graph

We then represent the plan's structure by defining *basic edges* (denoted $A \to B$) from c to s_1 and from each s_i to s_{i+1}. We also define *numbered edges* (denoted $A \xrightarrow{n} B$) from t to each plan's context condition. The initial mapping is extended with *triggering edges* (denoted $A \dashrightarrow B$) from step s_i to trigger t where[4] $\widehat{s_i} = \widehat{t}$). Figure 3 shows the graph plan structure corresponding to a simple program[5]. In the figure, the trigger node is a rectangle, step nodes are ovals, and context nodes are hexagons. The dashed line indicates a triggering edge, and the numbers are numbered edges (as explained above).

Finally, we rename each agent's beliefs and plans so that when the plans are combined, each agent's plans, goals, and beliefs, are uniquely named.

2.3 Original Slicing Method

The approach of Bordini *et al.*, which is inspired by a slicing algorithm for a concurrent logic programming language [30], comprises three stages:

1. Create a *literal dependence net* (LDN);
2. Mark nodes relevant to checking the property of interest ϕ [4, Algorithm 1, Page 1405]; and
3. Remove any plans that are not marked, yielding π'.

Building the LDN: The LDN takes, as a starting point, the basic mapping described in the previous subsection. It modifies this by: (i) instead of linking each step to the next step ($s_i \to s_{i+1}$), it instead has a link from the context condition directly to each step ($c \to s_i$ for each $s_i, 1 \le i \le n$); and (ii) it adds

---

[4] For AgentSpeak we would need to adjust this slightly, since the trigger node for a sub-goal is named $+!g$ but the step is named $!g$.
[5] This artificial program was constructed to illustrate features of the graph representation.

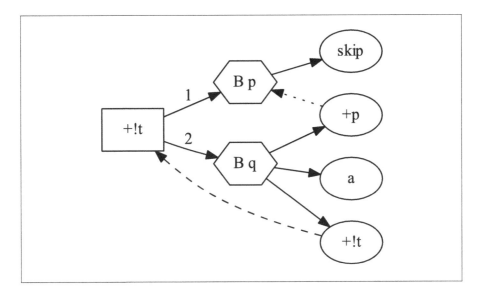

Fig. 4. Simple graph showing original slicing method's construction

belief links, representing dependencies via the belief base: there is a link from each belief update to any context condition (or test) that depends on that belief[6]. Figure 4 shows the graph constructed for the same simple example. As before, a dashed line is a triggering edge. A dotted edge denotes a belief link. Observe that information about the order of steps, e.g. in the second plan body, is not preserved.

Marking Nodes: Nodes are marked to indicate whether they affect the property ϕ being verified. The marking process considers every plan. Let *te* be the node corresponding to the trigger of the plan[7]. Then the marking has four cases, one for each case for ψ:

Bel *ag p*: If the property of interest ϕ contains Bel *ag p*, then the plan is marked iff there is a node with name $+p$ or $-p$ that is reachable from *te* in the LDN. This is because that is the step that affects the truth of Bel *ag p*.

Des *ag g*: If the property of interest contains Des *ag g* then the plan is marked iff there is a *step* node with name $+!g$ reachable from *te*. A reachable step posting the goal in question is enough for the agent to have the goal, and hence for Des *ag g* to be affected.

Int *ag g*: If the property of interest contains Int *ag g* then the plan is marked iff a *trigger* node with name $+!g$ is reachable from *te*. This is stronger than the previous case, in that it requires not only that the goal be able to be posted,

---

[6] Handling reasoning rules requires additional complexity.
[7] We actually use the context condition, since we do not have a unique trigger node for each plan.

but that there exist a plan for handling it. Having a goal with an associated plan corresponds to the agent having an intention. Note that the difference between Des $ag\ p$ and Int $ag\ p$ is that the latter requires a path to a trigger node, whereas the former only requires a path to a step node posting the goal.

Does $ag\ p$: Finally, if the property of interest contains Does $ag\ p$ then the plan is marked iff a *step* node with name perf(p) is reachable from *te*. In other words, a step that performs the action in question is reachable.

For instance, given[8] $\phi = \Box$(Does car accelerate $\rightarrow$ Bel car safe), in the context of the example given in Fig. 2, the nodes of interest are those corresponding to the action perf(accelerate) or to a belief update that affects safe (but since this is updated exogenously, it does not appear in any plan). Therefore, the plans that are marked are those that have a path from their context condition to a perf(accelerate) node.

3   Improved Slicing Method

The slicing algorithm proposed by Bordini *et al.* [4] has a number of "missed opportunities" where it does not take into account information that is available. These include:

1. the ordering of execution, e.g. the sequence of steps, is not exploited, nor is the order of the plans, or knowledge about failure handling;
2. the initial goals are ignored, which means that even if a node cannot be reached in achieving these goals, it is still considered; and
3. the structure of ϕ is not considered: the algorithm for marking plans [4, Algorithm 1, Page 1405] considers only the presence of sub-formulae of the form Bel $ag\ b$, Des $ag\ b$, Int $ag\ g$ and Does $ag\ a$ (and atomic b). It does not consider the logical structure of ϕ.

To illustrate where the original slicing algorithm misses out on useful distinctions consider a program that includes one plan with body "?p; perf(a)"[9] where the action a is of interest (i.e. ϕ includes Does $ag\ a$), and a second plan with body "$-p$". Now, the second plan is clearly important: its execution may prevent the first plan from progressing beyond its first step. However, it is possible that the second plan will never be executed before the first plan. The original slicing method does not take this into account.

Our proposed slicing process addresses the first two of these missed opportunities. Firstly, it constructs a dependency graph based on the language's semantics, including modelling failure handling, and handling GWENDOLEN language features. This allows sequencing information to be exploited in the slicing analysis. Secondly, we distinguish between parts of the agent program that are

---

[8] The '$\Box$' is the standard temporal operator meaning "at all points in the future".

[9] Where ?p tests whether p holds, failing if it does not. This differs from the GWENDOLEN construct *p which suspends the plan until p becomes true.

unreachable, and hence simply removed, and parts that are reachable, but can be compressed and simplified without affecting the verification outcome. Our analysis is therefore more fine-grained in that it allows *parts* of a plan to be removed. This turns out to provide a substantial efficiency gain.

The slicing process comprises four steps: constructing the dependency graph (Sect. 3.2), removing nodes that are not reachable (Sect. 3.3), marking nodes that are incompressible (Sect. 3.4), and compressing nodes that are unmarked (Sect. 3.5). However, before we begin the process, we need to deal with certain language features, which we do by transforming them away.

3.1   Transforming the Program

A number of language features pose challenges, as the earlier slicing algorithm is not clear how they should be dealt with. Specifically, the earlier paper does not explain how the algorithm deals with these constructs, and how to deal with them is not obvious. For instance, the example program used by Bordini *et al.* included use of the .dropDesires built-in action, but it is not clear how this is handled in the LDN.

First Feature: *Achievement Goals.* As noted earlier, an achievement goal in GWENDOLEN can be explained in terms of a "meta plan". For each achievement goal G we introduce meta-plans with trigger $+!achieve(G)$, and replace $+!G[achieve]$ with $+!achieve(G)$.

Second Feature: *Context Conditions that Test Goals.* In GWENDOLEN a context condition can include not only tests of whether certain beliefs are held ("B p"), but also tests of whether a goal is held by the agent ("G g"). This poses a challenge, because the slicing analysis needs to know about the steps that can affect the truth of a context condition, but whereas changes that affect belief conditions are explicit, whether a goal is held by the agent is affected by the goal being posted or achieved, and this is not always explicit.

We therefore need to transform the program to make goal status changes explicit. We do this using beliefs of the form $goal\_G$, associated with each goal G that appears in a test (e.g. a context condition), this mechanism requires us to associate changes to this belief both with the explicit posting of new goals and with the implicit removal of goals. This is achieved as follows. First, when a goal is posted, we also update the corresponding belief, i.e. we replace all occurrences of $+!G$ with $+goal\_G, +!G$. Next, whenever a goal is dropped, we add an explicit $-goal\_G$. A goal is dropped when any one of its plans concludes, so given a goal that is tested for, we add to each of its plans a final step $-goal\_G$. Note that a special case is when a plan for G ends with a recursive sub-goal $+!G$: in this case the belief $goal\_G$ is not modified. Another special case is achievement goals, for which the goal is dropped only in the first meta-plan, and where we replace $+!G[achieve]$ with $+goal\_G, +!achieve(G)$. Finally, we replace the condition G G with B $goal\_G$. It can be easily seen that these transformations preserve the semantics of the program.

The code below shows the transformed program for the example (showing only the parts that were changed). The changes are: (i) the achievement goal has been realised by adding a meta-plan and removing "[achieve]" (not shown); and (ii) the condition G at_speed_limit has been replaced with B goal_at_speed_limit, and that belief about a goal is updated in the first plan (where it is dropped) and in the last plan (where the goal is adopted). An additional change (not shown) is that the reasoning rule (line 2 of Fig. 2) is handled by unfolding it: this replaces can_accelerate with its definition of "safe, ˜ driver_accelerates, ˜ driver_brakes".

+! achieve_at_speed_limit:{B at_speed_limit} ← −goal_at_speed_limit.	1
+! achieve_at_speed_limit : {˜B at_speed_limit}	2
← +! at_speed_limit, +!achieve_at_speed_limit;	3
−at_speed_limit : {˜B goal_at_speed_limit, ˜B at_speed_limit}	4
← +goal_at_speed_limit, +! achieve_at_speed_limit;	5

Third Feature: *Explicitly Dropping Goals.* Explicit goal dropping ("$-!G$") is not used in the example. We deal with this not by transforming the program, but by having an additional case for generating belief links when constructing the graph (see end of Sect. 3.2).

3.2   Constructing the Dependency Graph

We define the dependency graph as follows. We start with the initial mapping of the program presented in Sect. 2.2. We then define a *control link* (denoted $A \Rightarrow B$) as existing between two nodes under any of the conditions below[10]. The definition of the dependency graph in essence follows the semantics of the language. The basic principle is that there should be a control link from A to B exactly when after doing A, the next thing to be done is B. And there should be a failure link from A to B precisely when the next thing that happens when A fails is B.

1. As previously, we have $A \Rightarrow B$ from a step A to the relevant trigger node B (formally: $A \Rightarrow B$ if $A \dashrightarrow B$).
2. Rather than linking a context condition to *all* steps in the plan body, we link the steps of the plan body in sequence. Additionally, we correctly capture sub-goals by not having a link from posting a sub-goal to the next step. Instead, the link to the next step is from where the sub-goal is achieved (i.e. the last step of·each plan that achieves it).
   Specifically, this means that we have $A \Rightarrow B$ when there is a basic edge $A \rightarrow B$ from a context node or from a step other than a sub-goal (formally: $A \Rightarrow B$ if $A \rightarrow B \wedge (context(A) \vee (step(A) \wedge \neg subgoal(A)))$).
   In the case where $A' \rightarrow B$ and A' is a sub-goal, then instead of having a control link from A' to B, we find the plans that are triggered by A', and

---

[10] We assume predicates $context(N)$, $step(N)$, $subgoal(N)$, as well as $last(N)$ (true iff N is the last step in a plan), $getContext(A, C)$ (true iff C is the context condition of the plan in which A appears), and $canFail(A)$ (true iff the step A can fail).

have links from the last step of each such plan to B. In other words, we also have $A \Rightarrow B$ if A is the last step of a plan that is triggered by $+!G$, and B is the next step after the posting of the goal G. (formally: $A \Rightarrow B$ if $step(A) \wedge (\neg subgoal(A)) \wedge last(A) \wedge getCaller(A, D) \wedge next(D, B)$, where $getCaller(A, D)$ is true when D is the identifier of a step that has the same name as the trigger node of the plan containing A, and $next(D, B)$ is true when B is the next step after D, taking account of control-flow returning from the end of a plan[11])

3. We capture plan order by linking from the trigger goal to only the *first* plan's context condition. Specifically $A \Rightarrow B$ when there is a basic edge numbered 1 from a trigger to the *first* context condition. (formally: $A \Rightarrow B$ if $A \xrightarrow{1} B$).

4. We capture failures, including in plans other than the first, by having failure links. We link each context condition that can fail (i.e. excluding a plan condition that is "true") to the next plan's context condition (if there is one). We also link each step in a plan body to the next plan's context condition, unless the plan step is one that cannot fail. Formally: $A \Rightarrow B$ if $\exists C, G : ((context(A) \wedge \widehat{A} \neq \text{"true"} \wedge G \xrightarrow{n} A) \vee (step(A) \wedge canFail(A) \wedge getContext(A, C) \wedge G \xrightarrow{n} C)) \wedge G \xrightarrow{n+1} B$

In addition to control links, we also define *belief links* (denoted $A \Rightarrow_B B$) between A and B if A updates a belief that can affect the truth of a context condition or test/wait B, where B contains the belief that A updates. While this definition does not cater for reasoning rules, we have: $A \Rightarrow_B B$ if $step(A) \wedge (context(B) \vee (step(B) \wedge \widehat{B} = *C)) \wedge contains(\widehat{B}, getBelief(\widehat{A}))$ where $getBelief(+b) = getBelief(-b) = b$, and $contains(\phi, b)$ is true iff ϕ contains b.

Finally, as mentioned earlier, we need to also add belief links that relate to explicitly dropping a goal ("$-!G$"). Semantically, dropping a goal explicitly is problematic. This is because it creates a situation where the execution of a plan can be aborted at any point. Consider the simple program below. Suppose that $+!g1$ is being pursued. At any point in the execution of the first, or the second plan, a percept may update b, resulting in $g1$ being dropped, and its plan aborted. This means that there is a dependency between $-!g1$ and *every* node that follows on from the body of a plan to handle $+!g1$. We therefore define that there is also a belief link from $-!g$ to any node N such that $+!g \Rightarrow^* N$, where N is a step, $+!g$ is a trigger node, and $\Rightarrow^*$ denotes the transitive closure of $\Rightarrow$.

$+! g1 \leftarrow +! g2.$	1
$+! g2 \leftarrow s1, s2.$	2
$+b \leftarrow -!g1.$	3

We exclude belief links if there is no possibility that A can influence B. In other words, if B *cannot* occur after A, then we suppress the belief link from A to B. This makes sense because, in this situation, even though A can change b,

---

[11] Formally: $next(A, B) \equiv \exists D : A \rightarrow B \vee (last(A) \wedge getCaller(A, D) \wedge next(D, B))$ and $getCaller(A, D) \equiv getContext(A, C) \wedge G \xrightarrow{n} C \wedge step(D) \wedge \widehat{G} = \widehat{D}$.

which occurs in the condition of B, the change cannot occur before b is checked, and therefore there is no dependency. The definition of when B cannot occur after A is somewhat complex. In essence, B and A must have the same initial goal or exogenous event (otherwise they occur in parallel), and there cannot be a control edge path from A to B.

Figure 5 shows the graph for the same simple program. The numbers on edges refer to the numbered items in Sect. 3.2, with $2'$ denoting the second case of the second numbered item.

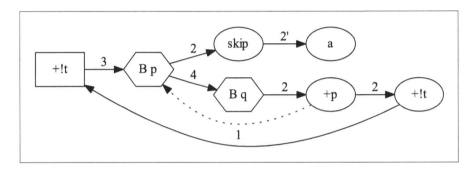

Fig. 5. Simple graph showing new slicing method's construction

3.3 Removing Unreachable Nodes

We analyse the graph to remove *unreachable* nodes. A node is *reachable* if there is a control link path to it from either the initial goal, or from an exogenous update. If neither of these is the case, then the node cannot be reached, and will never play a role in execution. It can therefore safely be removed from the graph. Note that since there is a control link path from each context condition to each step in its plan, if a step node is unreachable, that means that the whole plan is unreachable, and can be deleted, although a well-constructed program is unlikely to have unreachable plans.

3.4 Marking the Graph

Next, we mark nodes that play an essential role in determining the outcome of verification of the desired property ϕ. These are nodes that must be retained. Other atomic step nodes that remain unmarked are reachable, but can be *compressed* (i.e. replaced by a null-action "skip"). There are two ways in which a node can play an essential role, and hence be incompressible.

Firstly, a node A can directly affect the truth of ϕ (denoted *directlyAffects*(A, ϕ)). For example, if ϕ includes the atomic property Bel a b then both $+b$ and $-b$ are marked as directly affecting ϕ. Similarly, following Bordini *et al.*, we define the same cases for desire, intention, and performing actions (see Sect. 2.3).

Secondly, a node can *indirectly* affect the truth of ϕ by changing a belief that can affect the subsequent execution. In order for this change to matter, it must occur before a subsequent node that directly affects ϕ. Changing a belief that affects subsequent execution corresponds to the notion of belief link, defined above, so this second case can be defined as $indirectlyAffects(A, \phi) \equiv \exists B, C :$ $A \Rightarrow_B B \wedge B \rightrightarrows^* C \wedge directlyAffects(C, \phi)$ where $B \rightrightarrows C \equiv B \Rightarrow C \vee B \Rightarrow_B C$ and $\rightrightarrows^*$ is the usual "path of length 0 or more" operator. Note that in this case both A and B are marked: A can affect ϕ by changing a condition that affects the execution of B, and B can affect ϕ by allowing execution to take more than one possible path, depending on the condition modified by A.

We then propagate markings. The basic idea is that an unmarked step should be marked if it triggers a plan that can lead to a marked node. Formally we mark node A when $step(A) \wedge trigger(B) \wedge \widehat{A} = \widehat{B} \wedge B \Rightarrow^* C \wedge marked(C)$.

3.5 Compressing the Graph

Having marked the nodes that can affect ϕ, directly or indirectly, we can now simplify the program by "compressing" nodes that have not been marked. This is done via the following transformations, which are justified on semantic grounds. Note that since GWENDOLEN does not support disjunctions in context conditions, or the test step $?c$, the 3rd transformation cannot be done, and the 4th can only be done when $\bigvee c_i \equiv$ true, in which case no test is needed.

1. If a step is unmarked then replace it with the no-effect step "skip". Justification: If the step is unmarked, then its execution does not affect the verification property ϕ, nor does it affect the future path of execution in a way that may affect ϕ. It therefore can be safely replaced with a "do nothing" step.
2. Replace "S, skip" or "skip , S" with just "S". This is a basic semantic equivalence, as long as the environment is *numerically ahistorical*, i.e. the result of performing an action does not depend on the number of actions performed. For example, consider an environment that includes a counter that is incremented each time an action a is performed. In this scenario, the result of executing $a; a$ is different to that of executing a. As long as the counter can play a role in the eventual truth of ϕ, we cannot compress or remove instances of a. Note that in verification one approach is to define an environment that at each point simply returns a nondeterministic subset of possible percepts [12]. This environment satisfies the assumption.
3. Any two adjacent plans which have bodies that are simply a single "skip" can be combined: $+!g : c_1 \leftarrow$ skip. $+!g : c_2 \leftarrow$ skip $\Rightarrow$ $+!g : c_1 \vee c_2 \leftarrow$ skip. This clearly preserves the execution semantics.
4. When a sub-goal has only relevant plans of the form "$+!g : c_i \leftarrow$ skip" then the plans can be deleted, and the sub-goal $+!g$ replaced with a simple test $?(\bigvee c_i)$ (if $\bigvee c_i$ is just "true" then $+!g$ can be replaced with "skip"). Again, this clearly preserves the semantics.
5. A plan triggered by an exogenous update that has a plan body that is just "skip" can be deleted, since, semantically, this has no effect: responding to an event by doing nothing is equivalent to ignoring the event.

Note that we only remove plans with empty ("skip") plan bodies if there are no other plans to handle that trigger. This differs from Bordini *et al.* The reason is that when considering failure handling, the presence of these plans can make a difference. For example, in Fig. 6, if the context condition (lines 7 and 16) fails, then there is no alternative plan to attempt. In GWENDOLEN's semantics the failure to find *any* applicable plan forces the program into a tight loop in which perception is no longer polled[12]. The plans in lines 18–20 prevent this tight loop occurring.

Finally, note that while, for analysis purposes, we expand achievement goals using a meta-plan, when generating the final GWENDOLEN program we remove the meta-plans and go back to using achievement goals.

4   Evaluation

The previous section has presented the definitions of a new slicing analysis. Although this chapter does not present a formal proof of correctness, we have explained along the way why the slicing algorithm works. In other words, we have given a sketch of correctness by construction. Further work includes a formal statement of correctness, along with a proof.

We have written software that takes a representation of a transformed GWENDOLEN program, and implements the slicing method described in the previous section[13]. Specifically, the program transformation (Sect. 3.1) is done manually, but the graph generation, reachability analysis, and marking are all automated. The final compression step (Sect. 3.5) is performed manually. The software also implements the original slicing analysis of Bordini *et al.*, for comparison purposes. It is important to appreciate that the parts of the process that have been implemented are the complex parts of the analysis, whereas the manual parts are simple local and compositional steps. It is also worth noting that the implementation was done by transliterating the formal definitions given earlier into Prolog. This means that it is easy to see that the implementation correctly captures these definitions. However, the implementation is not efficient. Developing an efficient implementation is future work.

We applied the slicing method to two programs from the GWENDOLEN distribution. Both programs have been verified. The first was selected initially since it is simpler than other verified GWENDOLEN programs, so was a good starting point. The second was selected as a representative larger, and more complex, program. There are not many verified GWENDOLEN programs, and slicing and timing more programs is future work.

Applying the slicing method to the cruise control example results in the sliced program shown in the bottom part of Fig. 6. The middle part of the figure shows

---

[12] This feature of the language is not common in BDI languages and it is possible that Bordini *et al.* had not come across such behaviour when they were designing their algorithm.

[13] This program and logs of our evaluation runs are available from http://datacat. liverpool.ac.uk/id/eprint/576.

:Reasoning Rules:	1
can_accelerate :− safe, ˜ driver_accelerates, ˜ driver_brakes;	2
:Initial Goals:	3
at_speed_limit [achieve]	4
	5
:Plans: // Bordini slicing	6
+! at_speed_limit [achieve] : {B can_accelerate} ←	7
perf(accelerate),	8
wait;	9
−at_speed_limit: {˜G at_speed_limit [achieve],	10
˜B at_speed_limit} ← +! at_speed_limit[achieve];	11
+driver_accelerates: {B safe, ˜B driver_brakes,	12
B driver_accelerates} ← perf(accelerate);	13
	14
:Plans: // New slicing	15
+! at_speed_limit [achieve] : {B can_accelerate} ←	16
perf(accelerate);	17
+! at_speed_limit [achieve] : {˜B safe}; // ← skip	18
+! at_speed_limit [achieve] : {B driver_accelerates} ;	19
+! at_speed_limit [achieve] : {B driver_brakes} ;	20
−at_speed_limit: {˜G at_speed_limit [achieve],	21
˜B at_speed_limit} ← +! at_speed_limit[achieve];	22
+driver_accelerates: {B safe, ˜B driver_brakes,	23
B driver_accelerates} ← perf(accelerate);	24

Fig. 6. Sliced GWENDOLEN program

the plans resulting from applying the old slicing method. Comparing the two slicing methods, we observe: (1) That the original slicing method appears to be overly eager to slice away plans that are essential to the execution (e.g. the first meta-plan that terminates the recursion is sliced away [not shown in the Figure]); and (2) That when the original slicing method retains a plan, it retains the whole plan, whereas the improved method can simplify the plan (e.g. removing the wait comparing lines 8–9 with line 17).

Property $\phi = \Box(\mathsf{Does}\ car\ \mathsf{accelerate} \rightarrow \mathsf{Bel}\ car\ \mathsf{safe})$ was verified using AJPF[14] against the original GWENDOLEN program, the program sliced using the Bordini et al. method, and the program sliced using the new method. The original program (which, as shown in Fig. 2, has 9 plans) took 12.388 s to verify (user+sys time), whereas the sliced programs took respectively 5.116 and 5.26 s to verify (see Fig. 7). As shown in Fig. 6, the original slicing method slices away 6 plans, keeping 3, whereas the new slicing method keeps 6 plans, but is able to slice away parts of the plans' bodies.

We also manually analysed a larger program which manages the physical configuration of a collection of autonomous Low Earth Orbit (LEO) satellites

---

[14] On a 3.2 GHz Intel Core i5 iMac with 16 GB RAM running OSX 10.10.3; each number is the result of a single run.

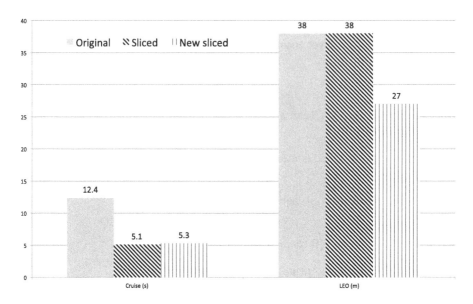

Fig. 7. Verification time (left: cruise control program in seconds, right: LEO program in minutes)

[12, Section 4]. The LEO program, which has 35 plans, is in the GWENDOLEN distribution, and the property that we verified is theorem 18, which states that "if the planning process succeeds then either the agent eventually believes it is maintaining the position or it believes it has a broken thruster". For this program and property, slicing using the old method (yielding a program with 24 plans) makes no difference to model checking performance. However, the new method (also yielding a program with 24 plans) is able to reduce the execution from around 38 min (117554 states) to around 27 min (67670 states). The reason why the new method does substantially better is that it is able to remove parts of plans, which the old method is not able to do. For this program, this considerably reduces the search space for the model checker.

5   Discussion

We have extended the work of Bordini *et al.* [4] by updating it for the GWENDOLEN framework, defining a graph that reflects the execution semantics of the language (including failure handling), and using a more precise slicing method that is able to simplify plan bodies. We emphasise that this chapter provides a full and precise formalisation of the method, and that we have implemented the complex parts of the process. By contrast, Bordini *et al.* do not actually define the precise construction of the LDN, instead they refer to Zhao *et al.* Additionally, they did not implement the method, performing their slicing entirely by hand.

Future work includes:

1. Defining the belief link constraint "can influence", and extending to properly handle reasoning rules, which requires revising the definition of *contains* to account for indirect effects via reasoning rules;
2. Exploiting the logical structure of ϕ, for instance, consider $\phi = \Box(\text{Does } ag\ a \rightarrow \text{Bel } ag\ b)$, i.e. whenever ag does a it must believe b. The original slicing algorithm considers any step that modifies b to be relevant, but the belief b is only relevant when action a is done. So for instance, in the (special but not unusual) case where a only occurs as the first step of a plan whose context condition checks b, then no other plan is relevant to model checking ϕ;
3. Further evaluation, including investigating what characteristics of particular agent programs make them more or less likely to benefit from slicing, and implementing the transformation and compression steps;
4. Implementing an efficient algorithm[15], and analysing its complexity; and
5. Completing the proof of correctness.

References

1. Ammann, P., Offutt, J.: Introduction to Software Testing. Cambridge University Press, Cambridge (2008)
2. Bordini, R.H., Dastani, M., Dix, J., El Fallah Seghrouchni, A. (eds.): Multi-Agent Programming: Languages, Platforms and Applications. Springer, Boston (2005). https://doi.org/10.1007/b137449
3. El Fallah Seghrouchni, A., Dix, J., Dastani, M., Bordini, R.H. (eds.): Multi-Agent Programming. Springer, Boston (2009). https://doi.org/10.1007/978-0-387-89299-3
4. Bordini, R.H., Fisher, M., Wooldridge, M., Visser, W.: Property-based slicing for agent verification. J. Log. Comput. **19**(6), 1385–1425 (2009). https://doi.org/10.1093/logcom/exp029
5. Bordini, R.H., Hübner, J.F., Wooldridge, M.: Programming Multi-Agent Systems in AgentSpeak Using Jason. Wiley, Chichester (2007)
6. Boyer, R.S., Moore, J.S. (eds.): The Correctness Problem in Computer Science. Academic Press, London (1981)
7. Bratman, M.E.: Intentions, Plans, and Practical Reason. Harvard University Press, Cambridge (1987)
8. Clarke, E.M., Grumberg, O., Peled, D.A.: Model Checking. The MIT Press, Cambridge (2000). ISBN 978-0-262-03270-4
9. DeMillo, R.A., Lipton, R.J., Perlis, A.J.: Social processes and proofs of theorems of programs. ACM Commun. **22**(5), 271–280 (1979)
10. Dennis, L., Fisher, M., Slavkovik, M., Webster, M.: Formal verification of ethical choices in autonomous systems. Robot. Auton. Syst. **77**, 1–14 (2016). https://doi.org/10.1016/j.robot.2015.11.012
11. Dennis, L.A.: Gwendolen semantics: 2017. Technical report ULCS-17-001, Department of Computer Science, University of Liverpool (2017)

---

[15] We know that this can be done, because the slicing analysis only considers the static program structure, and involves defining links and checking for paths, which can be done efficiently.

12. Dennis, L.A., Fisher, M., Lincoln, N.K., Lisitsa, A., Veres, S.M.: Practical verification of decision-making in agent-based autonomous systems. Autom. Softw. Eng. **23**(3), 305–359 (2016). https://doi.org/10.1007/s10515-014-0168-9

13. Emerson, E.A.: Temporal and modal logic. In: van Leeuwen, J. (ed.) Handbook of Theoretical Computer Science, pp. 996–1072. Elsevier, Amsterdam (1990)

14. Fetzer, J.H.: Program verification: the very idea. ACM Commun. **31**(9), 1048–1063 (1988)

15. Fisher, M., Dennis, L.A., Webster, M.: Verifying autonomous systems. ACM Commun. **56**(9), 84–93 (2013)

16. Georgeff, M.P., Lansky, A.L.: Procedural knowledge. Proc. IEEE Spec. Issue Knowl. Represent. **74**, 1383–1398 (1986)

17. Hindriks, K.V., de Boer, F.S., van der Hoek, W., Meyer, J.-J.C.: Agent programming with declarative goals. In: Castelfranchi, C., Lespérance, Y. (eds.) ATAL 2000. LNCS (LNAI), vol. 1986, pp. 228–243. Springer, Heidelberg (2001). https://doi.org/10.1007/3-540-44631-1_16

18. Ingrand, F.F., Georgeff, M.P., Rao, A.S.: An architecture for real-time reasoning and system control. IEEE Expert **7**(6), 34–44 (1992)

19. Jongmans, S.-S.T.Q., Hindriks, K.V., van Riemsdijk, M.B.: Model checking agent programs by using the program interpreter. In: Dix, J., Leite, J., Governatori, G., Jamroga, W. (eds.) CLIMA 2010. LNCS (LNAI), vol. 6245, pp. 219–237. Springer, Heidelberg (2010). https://doi.org/10.1007/978-3-642-14977-1_17

20. Kamali, M., Dennis, L.A., McAree, O., Fisher, M., Veres, S.M.: Formal verification of autonomous vehicle platooning. Sci. Comput. Program. **148**, 88–106 (2017). https://doi.org/10.1016/j.scico.2017.05.006

21. Lomuscio, A., Qu, H., Raimondi, F.: MCMAS: a model checker for the verification of multi-agent systems. In: Bouajjani, A., Maler, O. (eds.) CAV 2009. LNCS, vol. 5643, pp. 682–688. Springer, Heidelberg (2009). https://doi.org/10.1007/978-3-642-02658-4_55

22. Rao, A.S., Georgeff, M.P.: An abstract architecture for rational agents. In: Proceedings of 3rd International Conference on Principles of Knowledge Representation and Reasoning (KR), pp. 439–449 (1992)

23. Rao, A.S.: AgentSpeak(L): BDI agents speak out in a logical computable language. In: Van de Velde, W., Perram, J.W. (eds.) MAAMAW 1996. LNCS, vol. 1038, pp. 42–55. Springer, Heidelberg (1996). https://doi.org/10.1007/BFb0031845

24. Webster, M., Cameron, N., Fisher, M., Jump, M.: Generating certification evidence for autonomous unmanned aircraft using model checking and simulation. J. Aerosp. Inf. Syst. **11**(5), 258–279 (2014)

25. Winikoff, M., Cranefield, S.: On the testability of BDI agent systems. J. Artif. Intell. Res. (JAIR) **51**, 71–131 (2014). https://doi.org/10.1613/jair.4458

26. Winikoff, M.: An AgentSpeak meta-interpreter and its applications. In: Bordini, R.H., Dastani, M.M., Dix, J., El Fallah Seghrouchni, A. (eds.) ProMAS 2005. LNCS (LNAI), vol. 3862, pp. 123–138. Springer, Heidelberg (2006). https://doi.org/10.1007/11678823_8

27. Winikoff, M.: Jack^{TM} intelligent agents: an industrial strength platform. In: Bordini, R.H., Dastani, M., Dix, J., Fallah-Seghrouchni, A.E. (eds.) Multi-Agent Programming: Languages, Platforms and Applications, Multiagent Systems, Artificial Societies, and Simulated Organizations, vol. 15, pp. 175–193. Springer, Boston (2005). https://doi.org/10.1007/0-387-26350-0_7

28. Winikoff, M.: BDI agent testability revisited. J. Auton. Agents Multi-Agent Syst. (JAAMAS) **31**(5), 1094–1132 (2017). https://doi.org/10.1007/s10458-016-9356-2

29. Wooldridge, M., Rao, A. (eds.): Foundations of Rational Agency. Applied Logic Series. Kluwer Academic Publishers, Dordrecht (1999). https://doi.org/10.1007/978-94-015-9204-8
30. Zhao, J., Cheng, J., Ushijima, K.: Literal dependence net and its use in concurrent logic programming environment. In: Proceedings of the Workshop on Parallel Logic Programming (Held with FGCS 1994), pp. 127–141 (1994)

Belief Shadowing

Łukasz Białek[1], Barbara Dunin-Kęplicz[1], and Andrzej Szałas[1,2(✉)]

[1] Institute of Informatics, University of Warsaw, Warsaw, Poland
{bialek,keplicz,andrzej.szalas}@mimuw.edu.pl
[2] Department of Computer and Information Science, Linköping University,
Linköping, Sweden

Abstract. Adapting beliefs to new circumstances, like belief change, update, revision or merging, typically requires deep and/or complex adjustments of belief bases even when adaptations happen to be transient. We present a novel, lightweight and tractable approach to a new kind of beliefs' interference which we call *belief shadowing*. Put simply, it is a transient swap of beliefs when part of one belief base is to be shadowed by another belief base representing new observations and/or beliefs of superior agents/teams. In this case no changes to belief bases are needed. This substantially improves the performance of systems based on doxastic reasoning. We ensure tractability of our formal framework, what makes it suitable for real-world applications.

The presented approach is based on a carefully chosen four-valued paraconsistent logic with truth values representing truth, falsity, incompleteness and inconsistency. Moreover, potentially undesired or forbidden conclusions are prevented by integrity constrains together with their shadowing machinery.

As an implementation environment we use $4QL^{Bel}$, a recently developed four-valued query language based on the same underlying logic and providing necessary reasoning tools. Importantly, the shadowing techniques are general enough to be embedded in any reasoning environment addressing related phenomena.

1 A New Perspective on Belief Change

When agents act in dynamic environments, belief change/revision/update/ merging is inevitable, creating a multitude of problems of theoretical and applied nature [7,27,35]. In the case of group beliefs, like in teamwork, the situation becomes even more complex [13]. In real-world applications, beliefs are contextual, and affected socially, psychologically and emotionally. Some, like "do not harm", are hardly mutable but others, like "avoid slippery surfaces", meant as an indication, are flexible. In fact, known theories of belief update/change/revision/merging do not distinguish between the rigid and transient beliefs. However, in everyday activities we temporarily adjust our beliefs to specific situations with no intention to

Supported by the Polish National Science Centre grant 2015/19/B/ST6/02589, the ELLIIT network organization for Information and Communication Technology, and the Swedish Foundation for Strategic Research (SymbiKBot Project).

© Springer Nature Switzerland AG 2019
D. Weyns et al. (Eds.): EMAS 2018 Workshops, LNAI 11375, pp. 158–180, 2019.
https://doi.org/10.1007/978-3-030-25693-7_9

change them radically. Such a shallow change, not requiring a deeper revision, has not been addressed in the literature.

Our research is devoted to a new belief change method inspired by a discussion in [11] where it is pointed out that:

"In contrast to many existing approaches, we do not assume that an agent entering a group changes its beliefs. However, group beliefs prevail over individual ones [...] When the group is dismissed, agents continue to act according to their individual beliefs. These can be revised to reflect information acquired during cooperation."

When beliefs are flexible or do change frequently, it hardly makes sense to adjust the entire belief base accordingly. A better choice is to suspend them for the time being. The belief interference we address is a potentially transient swap of beliefs, further called *belief shadowing*. For example, when two belief bases participate in reasoning, one of them may turn out to be more important or up to date. Then, the conflicting part of the "weaker" base may be shadowed by the "stronger" one. With such phenomena we deal frequently during teamwork and other forms of cooperation. Individuals joining a group are expected to accept the group beliefs and suspend their conflicting ones. Therefore, a swap from individual to group beliefs, and then perhaps back, is needed. Importantly, the ability of shadowing rather than updating, revising or merging beliefs can result in a substantial improvement of the performance of agent systems relying on doxastic reasoning what is particularly important from the systems' engineering point of view.

As a lightweight form of belief change, shadowing may introduce inconsistencies. In our approach inconsistencies are first class citizens, so much heavier belief revision, often meant as a remedy for inconsistencies, is not required. Another phenomenon of realistic environments, calling for an attention, is the unavoidable information incompleteness. Therefore, both paraconsistent and paracomplete reasoning is needed in the spirit of [22]:

"Inconsistency robustness is information system performance in the face of continually pervasive inconsistencies – a shift from the previously dominant paradigms of inconsistency denial and inconsistency elimination attempting to sweep them under the rug. Inconsistency robustness is a both an observed phenomenon and a desired feature: [...] an observed phenomenon because large information-systems are required to operate in an environment of pervasive inconsistency. [...] a desired feature because we need to improve the performance of large information system."

Belief bases represent snapshots of the environment and the agents' mindsets, both evolving over time. In AI systems this evolution should be supervised, especially when rules are machine learned or data mined in a human-free manner. We decided to achieve this by introducing integrity constraints. Though they are well-known in database systems, their shadowing is novel, pertaining admissible modes of behavior at desired abstraction levels, in a semantically meaningful manner. A coherent, tractable and comprehensive framework to belief shadowing that we aim for, amounts to:

- introducing a lightweight belief shadowing framework;
- introducing integrity constraints and their shadowing;
- providing a tractable reasoning engine for pragmatic applications.

The belief shadowing framework is *lightweight*: (i) the shadowing operator is efficient, (ii) does not require changes in the belief bases involved, and (iii) does not assume agents' familiarity with details of other agents' belief bases. The requirement (i) is crucial for systems' performance and for efficient swapping between contexts in which different shadowings apply. The requirements (ii) and (iii) are vital in cooperation/teamwork of heterogeneous agents designed by separate parties. To our best knowledge no other research realizes these goals: the presented solution is original and general enough to be embedded in many programming frameworks. As a computational engine for belief bases we adopt and extend the $4QL^{Bel}$ four-valued rule language, recently developed in [6]. The presented ideas are implemented in an open-source interpreter inter4QL 4.0, available via http://4ql.org.

The rest of the chapter is structured as follows. Section 2 introduces a scenario used to illustrate important and novel features of our approach. Next, Sect. 3 presents belief bases and discusses their role. Then, Sect. 4 presents the underlying logic and Sect. 5 briefly recapitulates the rule-based language $4QL^{Bel}$. In Sect. 6 we extend $4QL^{Bel}$ to $4QL^{Bel+}$ by adding constraints. Section 7 introduces the shadowing operator formally. In Sect. 8 we illustrate the introduced language formalizing the scenario of Sect. 2. Section 9 presents properties of shadowing, in particular its complexity. In Sect. 10 we discuss related work. Finally, Sect. 11 concludes the chapter.

2   An Emergency Room Scenario

To illustrate the approach, we shall consider a hospital ER (Emergency Room) service which specializes in handling emergency situations. ER is usually operated by several emergency physicians delivering basic professional treatments.

As a common practice, emergency physicians consult a therapy with other specialists. Simple cases are dealt with internally or after a single consultation. More difficult ones may require gathering an MDM (Multidisciplinary Meeting). While MDM participants may propose a variety of treatments, the chosen one prevails and is applied. In terms of different beliefs this means that the physician's beliefs may be defeated, though not necessarily revised. On the other hand, patients naturally follow their individual beliefs, Specifically, they may reject various treatments, like those violating their religious convictions. The refusal of blood transfusion or organ transplants is a typical case. Also, according to legal regulations valid in many countries, patients may refuse life-sustaining treatments what, on the other hand, may be obligatory for medical staff.

The main goal of an emergency physician on duty, Mark, is to apply necessary treatments to patients brought to the ER. Mark can either decide on his own or call an MDM. Finally, the selected treatment may be unacceptable to the patient. We will show that belief shadowing is useful in modeling such situations (see Sect. 8).

3   Belief Bases

A bottom concept underlying our approach to belief bases, initiated in [11,12], is that of a *world*. Worlds are sets of ground literals (i.e., variable-free atomic formulas) representing feasible states of affairs. For example, an accident witness could report a victim's shallow breathing and leg injury, not being sure how serious the injury is: 3 or 4, in a given scale. In this case, the following two worlds may represent patient's conditions, where integers from 0 to 9 represent the severity degree:

$$\{\text{symptom(victim, leg, injury, 3)}, \text{symptom(victim, breathing, shallow, 6)}\}, \quad (1)$$

$$\{\text{symptom(victim, leg, injury, 4)}, \text{symptom(victim, breathing, shallow, 6)}\}. \quad (2)$$

Gathering the worlds (1) and (2) together, we obtain a belief base $\{(1), (2)\}$ representing the two alternatives. It can be augmented with information about the heart failure and its severity:

$$\{(1), (2), \{\text{symptom(victim, heart, failure, 7)}\}\}. \quad (3)$$

Note that worlds can represent alternatives and/or add new information, perhaps originating from another source. However, belief base designers do not indicate whether a world provides an alternative or augments other worlds. This implicitly follows from the worlds' contents.

In many papers, e.g., related to the AGM theory of belief revision (for survey see [35]),[1] a belief base consists of a set of formulas of the underlying logic, not necessarily closed on consequences. Here we do not consider the consequence relation. By restricting formulas to ground literals we are able to use querying machinery assigning truth values to the results. This allows us to obtain a tractable framework also when we allow rules, making the specification of belief bases more uniform and concise.

As we use a paraconsistent and paracomplete four-valued logic, involving truth values t (true), f (false), i (inconsistent) and u (unknown), a belief base becomes a compact structure, capable of storing beliefs originating from nondeterministic environments. Belief bases are systems' passive components reacting on requests and queries via a suitable query processing engine. In order to formally define belief bases, we extend the definition of [11,12] by assuming that

---

[1] AGM is an acronym referring to names of originators of the theory: Alchourrón, Gärdenfors and Makinson [2].

constraints are their inherent parts. Let *Const* be a fixed finite set of constants, *Var* be a fixed finite set of variables and *Rel* be a fixed finite set of relation symbols. By a *positive literal* we understand an expression of the form $r(\bar{e})$, where $r \in Rel$ and $\bar{e}$ is a vector consisting of variables and/or constants. A *negative literal* is an expression of the form $\neg \ell$, where ℓ is a positive literal. Literals without variables are called *ground*. We always identify $\neg\neg\ell$ with ℓ. In the rest of the chapter we sometimes use $3i$ as an abbreviation for *incomplete* and/or *inconsistent* information. In particular, by $3i$-*worlds* we shall understand finite sets of ground literals with all constants belonging to *Const*.

Definition 1. *By a* belief base over a set of constants *Const we understand any pair $\mathcal{B} = \langle \Delta, \mathcal{C} \rangle$ consisting of:*

- $\Delta = \{M_1, \ldots, M_k\}$, *where* $k \geq 1$ *and for* $i = 1, \ldots, k$, M_i *is a $3i$-world;*
- $\mathcal{C}$, *called* constraints *of $\mathcal{B}$, being a finite set of (universally closed) formulas of the underlying logic, which are true in Δ (for formal definitions, see Sect. 4).* ◁

Each M_i in a belief base represents a feasible or augmenting (perhaps still incomplete and/or inconsistent) view of the world. In the ER scenario Mark's beliefs can be represented by a belief base $\mathtt{mark} = \langle \Delta_M, \mathcal{C}_M \rangle$ with Δ_M containing several $3i$-worlds with initial observations, results of medical tests and measurements, etc. These observations lead to alternative diagnoses which, in turn, may result in alternative treatments. Therefore, Δ_M includes modules, like:

- `doctor`, containing general medical knowledge;
- `patient` containing data coming from various sources, like Mark's observations, measurement and test results, patients' medical files (if accessible), etc.

and Mark's constraints, $\mathcal{C}_M$, may contain statements like:

"if the patient's life is not at risk and he/she is conscious, his/her permissions regarding treatments are obeyed."

As a result of an MDM, some of Mark's beliefs and constraints may be shadowed by beliefs and constraints of others. Moreover, Mark can disregard some beliefs of his patients if they are hazardous to their health and lives.

Constructions presented in the sequel provide means for formal and executable specifications of a vast variety of scenarios. Belief shadowing deliver means for clear specifications and the detection of integrity constraints' violations.

4   A Logic of Beliefs

In the syntax of the underlying logic we assume truth constants t, f, i and u, propositional connectives $\neg, \vee, \wedge, \rightarrow$, quantifiers $\forall, \exists,$[2] operators $A \in T, A = t,$

---

[2] In fact, in implementation we allow restricted quantifiers, where we have to specify a domain the variable bound by the quantifier ranges over.

where A is a formula, $T \subseteq \{\mathsf{t}, \mathsf{f}, \mathsf{i}, \mathsf{u}\}$, $t \in \{\mathsf{t}, \mathsf{f}, \mathsf{i}, \mathsf{u}\}$ and belief operator $\mathrm{Bel}_{\mathcal{B}}(A)$ where $\mathcal{B}$ is a belief base. To define semantics of the logic let us start with *truth ordering* on truth values, denoted by $\leq_t$, being the reflexive and transitive closure of ordering: $\mathsf{f} < \mathsf{u} < \mathsf{i} < \mathsf{t}$.[3] For $t, t_1, t_2 \in \{\mathsf{f}, \mathsf{u}, \mathsf{i}, \mathsf{t}\}$, the semantics of $\neg, \wedge, \vee$ is given by:

$$\neg \mathsf{f} \stackrel{\text{def}}{=} \mathsf{t}, \quad \neg \mathsf{u} \stackrel{\text{def}}{=} \mathsf{u}, \quad \neg \mathsf{i} \stackrel{\text{def}}{=} \mathsf{i}, \quad \neg \mathsf{t} \stackrel{\text{def}}{=} \mathsf{f}; \tag{4}$$

$$t_1 \wedge t_2 \stackrel{\text{def}}{=} \min\{t_1, t_2\}; \quad t_1 \vee t_2 \stackrel{\text{def}}{=} \max\{t_1, t_2\}; \quad t_1 \to t_2 \stackrel{\text{def}}{=} \neg t_1 \vee t_2; \tag{5}$$

$$\mathrm{Bel}_{\mathcal{B}}(t) \stackrel{\text{def}}{=} t, \tag{6}$$

where $\min, \max$ are the minimum and maximum wrt $\leq_t$. The *truth value* of a literal ℓ wrt a $3i$-world M and an assignment $v : \textit{Var} \longrightarrow \textit{Const}$, denoted by $\ell(M, v)$, is defined as follows, where $v(\ell)$ denotes the ground literal obtained from ℓ by substituting all occurrences of every variable x in ℓ by $v(x)$:

$$\ell(M, v) \stackrel{\text{def}}{=} \begin{cases} \mathsf{t} & \text{if } v(\ell) \in M \text{ and } (\neg v(\ell)) \notin M; \\ \mathsf{i} & \text{if } v(\ell) \in M \text{ and } (\neg v(\ell)) \in M; \\ \mathsf{u} & \text{if } v(\ell) \notin M \text{ and } (\neg v(\ell)) \notin M; \\ \mathsf{f} & \text{if } v(\ell) \notin M \text{ and } (\neg v(\ell)) \in M. \end{cases}$$

Remark 1. Like other relations, in our approach domain membership is four-valued. Though typically the membership $a \in D$ is true or false, for some objects it may be unknown or inconsistent whether a belongs to D.   ◁

Table 1. Semantics of $\mathrm{Bel}()$-free formulas.

Let $v : \textit{Var} \longrightarrow \textit{Const}$ be an assignment, $\mathcal{B} = \langle \Delta, \mathcal{C} \rangle$ be a belief base, M be a $3i$-world and A, B be formulas. Then:

- $t(M, v) \stackrel{\text{def}}{=} t$ for $t \in \{\mathsf{f}, \mathsf{u}, \mathsf{i}, \mathsf{t}\}$;
- $(\neg A)(M, v) \stackrel{\text{def}}{=} \neg(A(M, v))$;
- $(A \odot B)(M, v) \stackrel{\text{def}}{=} A(M, v) \odot B(M, v)$, for $\odot \in \{\wedge, \vee, \to\}$;
- $(\forall x : D(A(x)))(M, v) \stackrel{\text{def}}{=} \min\{((a \in D) \to A(a))(M, v) \mid a \in \textit{Const}\}$;
- $(\exists x : D(A(x)))(M, v) \stackrel{\text{def}}{=} \max\{((a \in D) \wedge A(a))(M, v) \mid a \in \textit{Const}\}$;
- $(A \in T)(M, v) \stackrel{\text{def}}{=} \begin{cases} \mathsf{t} & \text{when } A(M, v) \in T; \\ \mathsf{f} & \text{otherwise}; \end{cases}$
- $(A = t)(M, v) \stackrel{\text{def}}{=} (A \in \{t\})(M, v)$;
- $A(\Delta, v) \stackrel{\text{def}}{=} A(\bigcup_{M \in \Delta} M, v)$;
- $(\mathrm{Bel}_{\mathcal{B}}(A))(v) \stackrel{\text{def}}{=} \begin{cases} \mathrm{LUB}\{ A(M, v) \mid M \in \Delta \} \text{ when} \\ \qquad \text{for all } C \in \mathcal{C},\ C(\Delta, v) = \mathsf{t}; \\ \mathsf{u} \qquad \text{otherwise}; \end{cases}$
- $A(\mathcal{B}, v) \stackrel{\text{def}}{=} \begin{cases} A(\Delta, v) \text{ when for all } C \in \mathcal{C}, C(\Delta, v) = \mathsf{t}; \\ \mathsf{u} \qquad \text{otherwise}. \end{cases}$

---

[3] For motivations behind $\leq_t$ see, e.g., [3,41].

The definition of truth value of a literal is extended to all formulas in Table 1 where *Lub* is the least upper bound wrt *information ordering* defined as the reflexive and transitive closure of the ordering shown in Fig. 1. Observe that C, being a constraint, does not contain free variables, so v in $C(\Delta, v)$ is redundant. In similar cases we will use $C(\Delta)$ rather than $C(\Delta, v)$, and $C(\mathcal{B})$ rather than $C(\mathcal{B}, v)$.

Fig. 1. Information ordering.

When the logic we consider is restricted to connectives $\neg, \wedge, \vee, \rightarrow$ and projected onto two- or three-valued calculi, it becomes one of well-known logic – see Table 2. This is well justified by the fact that Kleene three-valued logic K_3 is the standard choice for interpreting the third truth vale as u. K_3 is also a standard choice for interpreting the third value as i. Indeed, assuming that the reality is consistent, the value i can also be seen as an indicator of a lack of knowledge: we have contradictory claims that a given property is both t and f but it is (perhaps temporarily) unknown which claim is actually the right one.

Table 2. The relation of the $\mathrm{Bel}()$–free part of the considered logic to other logics.

Truth values	Logic
$\{\mathsf{t},\mathsf{f}\}$	Classical propositional logic
$\{\mathsf{t},\mathsf{u},\mathsf{f}\}$	Kleene three-valued K_3
$\{\mathsf{t},\mathsf{i},\mathsf{f}\}$	K_3 with Priest's interpretation of the third truth value as i

5   A Rule-Based Language for Beliefs

The 4QL^{Bel} language [6], an extension of 4QL [30,31,41], is a four-valued rule language designed for doxastic reasoning with paraconsistent and paracomplete belief bases. A unique feature of the 4QL-based language family is the presence of truth values t, f, i, u as well as the unrestricted use of negation in both conclusions and premises of rules while retaining intuitive results and tractable query evaluation. Though the full definition of 4QL^{Bel} is available in [6], for clarity we recall the most important constructs of the language.

```
1 module moduleName:
2 │   domains:...
3 │   relations:...
4 │   rules:...
5 │   facts:...
6 end.
```

Module 1: Syntax of 4QL^{Bel} modules.

Table 3 provides correspondences between logical syntax used in Sect. 4 and the syntax used in inter4QL. We also apply the standard convention that variables start with capital letters.

The language inherits a fair amount of elements from 4QL, including basic program syntax and semantics. The 4QL^{Bel} program consists of modules, structured as shown in Module 1. Sections **domains** and **relations** are used to specify domains and signatures of relations used in rules. 4QL^{Bel} rules, specified in the section **rules** have the following form, where $\langle Formula \rangle$ is an arbitrary formula of the logic presented in Sect. 4:

$$\langle Literal \rangle : - \langle Formula \rangle. \tag{7}$$

Table 3. Correspondences between logical syntax and the inter4QL syntax.

Logical syntax	Syntax of inter4QL
t f i u	true false incons unknown
$\neg \wedge \vee \rightarrow$	$-, \mid ->$
$\forall x$: dom	forall X: dom
$\exists x$: dom	exists X: dom
$\in T$	in T
$\text{Bel}_{\mathcal{B}}(\ )$	$\text{Bel}[\mathcal{B}](\ )$
$= \leq \geq$	math.eq math.leq math.geq
$< >$	math.lt math.gt

Facts, specified in the **facts** section, are rules with the empty $\langle Formula \rangle$ part (being **t**). In such cases we simply write $\langle Literal \rangle$. A rule of the form (7) is "fired" for its ground instantiations when the truth value of $\langle Formula \rangle$ is **t** or **i**.[4] As the effect:

– $\langle Literal \rangle$ is added to the set of conclusions when the truth value of
$\langle Formula \rangle$ is **t**; (8)

---

[4] That is, the value of $\langle Formula \rangle$ contains some truth.

- ⟨*Literal*⟩ and ¬⟨*Literal*⟩ are added to the set of conclusions when the truth value of ⟨*Formula*⟩ is **i**.   (9)

Note that ':−' is formalized in the 4QL-based languages by a generalization of the Shepherdson's implication [40] rather than by the → connective (see [41]). The implication → is more suitable for evaluating formulas while the former one reflects rule evaluation principles (8)–(9). To define the semantics of ':−' we use ordering $\leq_i$ which is reflexive and transitive closure of $\mathsf{f} = \mathsf{u} < \mathsf{t} < \mathsf{i}$. The implication ⤳, corresponding to ':−', is defined by:

$$(A \rightsquigarrow B)(L, v) \stackrel{\text{def}}{=} A(L, v) \leq_i B(L, v). \qquad (10)$$

When the set of truth values is restricted to $\{\mathsf{t}, \mathsf{f}, \mathsf{u}\}$ or $\{\mathsf{t}, \mathsf{f}, \mathsf{i}\}$, the implication ⤳ is the three valued implication of [40]. The semantics of rules is given by:

$$(C \mathbin{:-} B)(L, v) \stackrel{\text{def}}{=} B(L, v) \rightsquigarrow C(L, v). \qquad (11)$$

What distinguishes 4QL^{Bel} from 4QL, is a support for doxastic reasoning due to use the Bel() operator, enhancing advanced agents' reasoning. It will further be extended by providing means for belief and constraints shadowing.

Modules are primarily used for structuring belief bases. If m is a module name, $m.A$ expresses *references to m*. Semantically, one can view relation symbols within a module m as (implicitly) extended by prefix '$m.$'. In order to maintain a clear semantics and tractability, a certain form of acyclicity of references is required, close in spirit to stratification in logic programming and deductive databases [1] but concerning formulas with the operator '$\in T$' rather than negation.

Definition 2. *The* reference graph *of a set of modules Π consists of nodes labeled by names of modules occurring in Π, assuming that there is an edge between m and n iff premises of a rule in m contain an expression $A \in T$ or $A = \mathsf{t}$, where A is a formula containing a reference of the form $n.B$. A $4QL^{\mathrm{Bel}}$ program is set of modules whose reference graph is acyclic.*   ◁

The semantics of 4QL^{Bel} modules is given by *well-supported models* in the sense of [31]. A $3i$-world is a *model* of a module M if all rules of M, understood as implications (11), are true in the model. Intuitively, a model is well-supported when it consists of ground literals (if any) assuming that all literals it contains are conclusions of reasoning starting from facts. As shown in [6], for each 4QL^{Bel} program, its well-supported model exists, is uniquely determined, and can be computed in deterministic polynomial time wrt the size of all domains and number of modules.

Let us emphasize that well-supportedness requires the Open World Assumption (OWA): all conclusions have to be explicitly inferred. This is an opposite to the Closed World Assumption (CWA), where conclusions which are not inferred are assumed to be false. In the 4QL family of languages, a literal is false when its negation is a consequence of a rule. Otherwise it may be unknown. However, one can easily (partially or totally) close the world, as shown in Sect. 8.

Each $4QL^{Bel}$ module uniquely specifies its well-supported model, so it can be identified with a $3i$-world. That way:

$$QL^{Bel} \text{ modules have a very important role as a tool for concise}$$
$$\text{and uniform specification of } 3i\text{-worlds.} \qquad (12)$$

Indeed, when facts of a module are updated, its well-supported model is changed accordingly. Therefore, rather than list all facts constituting a $3i$-world, one can provide rules reflecting the way in which derived facts are obtained on the basis of given facts. For example, facts in a module may indicate patient's symptoms while rules may provide diagnoses. Taking the principle (12) into account, in the sequel modules can appear wherever $3i$-worlds are allowed, in particular as elements of Δ in a belief base $\langle \Delta, \mathcal{C} \rangle$. Whenever we specify the $4QL^{Bel}$ entities, we use the syntax developed in the inter4QL interpreter. Since $4QL^{Bel}$ extends 4QL, all 4QL constructs can be used as listed in Module 1. Belief bases are specified as in Belief Base 2.

```
1 beliefs beliefBaseName:
2   constraints:
3     | // see Section 6 ...
4   worlds:
5     | // list of 4QL^Bel modules specifying 3i-worlds
6 end.
```

Belief Base 2: Syntax of belief bases.

An important feature of belief bases is that domains of their worlds become their domains, accessible in their constraints. If, in different worlds, a domain 'dom' appears – the corresponding belief base's domain, 'dom', is the union of all

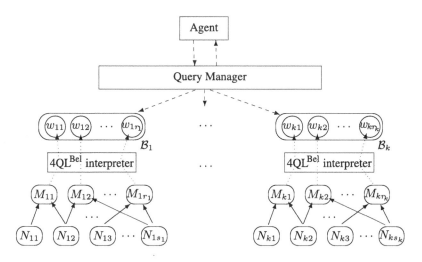

Fig. 2. High level agent's belief bases architecture.

domains 'dom' appearing in the belief base's worlds (assuming the same types of domain elements).

A high level agents' belief bases architecture is summarized in Fig. 2, where, for $1 \leq l \leq k$, $\mathcal{B}_l$ are belief bases, $M_{l1}, \ldots, M_{lr_l}, N_{l1}, \ldots, N_{ls_l}$ are 4QL^{Bel} modules, $w_{l1}, \ldots, w_{lr_l}$ are the $3i$-worlds being respectively well-supported models of modules $M_{l1}, \ldots M_{lr_l}$, solid lines represent queries among modules, dotted lines represent correspondences between modules and $3i$-worlds, and dashed lines represent agent's queries. Note that agents may use multiple belief bases, some of which may be private, some own by groups, and some may be available to all agents. Query manager may be a 4QL^{Bel} interpreter or another database querying engine.

6 Adding Integrity Constraints

Though belief bases, as introduced in Sect. 4, contain integrity constraints, their use in our framework deserves further discussion. In particular, belief shadowing, similarly to belief revision or update, may result in creating undesirable conclusions. For example, some treatments can cause complications when applied to patients of a specific characteristics. To avoid such risky cases one could construct a specific rule. A better idea, however, is to formulate a general integrity constraint preventing patients from risky complications.

The idea of constraints is not new in information systems (see, e.g., [8,23,26,36,38]), where a distinction between hard and soft constraints might be desirable [33]. Hard constraints cannot be violated while soft ones are flexible and often considered as preferences whose violation should be avoided as long as possible. In our case a distinction between non-shadowable ("hard") and shadowable ("soft") constraints also appears useful. To avoid terminological misunderstandings we shall further call them *rigid* and *flexible* ones, respectively. For example, a patient's constraint concerning refusal of blood transfusion, when rigid, could not be shadowed, making a transfusion unacceptable regardless the circumstances. When being a flexible one, it can be shadowed, allowing for blood transfusion.

In rule languages constraints are typically expressed by rules with empty heads expressing what is disallowed. Dually, in our approach constraints express what should always be true. The separation between constraints and rules gives the former ones an axiom-like flavor. Constraints can be specified in modules and in belief bases in two subsections, separating rigid and flexible ones, $\mathcal{C} = \mathcal{C}_R \cup \mathcal{C}_F$. Constraints are specified as shown in Module 3. By 4QL^{Bel} plus we will denote the rule language obtained from 4QL^{Bel} by allowing the constraints section.

```
1 module abc:
2     constraints:
3         rigid: ...
4         flexible: ...
5 end.
```

Module 3: Constraints specification.

The distinction between rigid and flexible constraints does not affect the semantics of $\mathcal{C}_R$ and $\mathcal{C}_F$ unless they appear in the context of the shadowing operator (see Sect. 7). Importantly, we require constraints to be true (cf. the last item of Table 1). This might seem restrictive in a four-valued framework. However, formulas of the form '$A \in T$' can be used, so requirements like "A is true or inconsistent" can easily be expressed by '$A \in \{\mathbf{t},\mathbf{i}\}$' being $\mathbf{t}$ when the truth value of A is in the set $\{\mathbf{t},\mathbf{i}\}$.

Though specified within modules, constraints may be local (limited to a single module) and global (span over multiple modules). Local constraints refer solely to relations in the same module. Accordingly, global constraints can contain literals referring to multiple, perhaps all, modules as long as references do not create cycles in the reference graph. Technically, to avoid cycles, additional modules/belief bases can be created as containers for constraints. Such additional structures can be viewed as being "above" modules referenced by non-local constraints. For an illustration of this approach see Sect. 8. We extend Definition 2 to deal with constraints as follows.

Definition 3. *By the* reference graph *of a set Π of modules with constraints we mean the reference graph for Π seen as a $4QL^{\text{Bel}}$ program (disregarding constraints), augmented with edges from m to n whenever constraints of m contain a reference to n, i.e., a subexpression of the form 'n.'.* ◁

Definition 4. *By a $4QL^{\text{Bel}+}$ program we mean a set of $4QL^{\text{Bel}}$ modules with constraints such that its reference graph (in the sense of Definition 3) is acyclic and all constraints in modules are true.* ◁

Note that for every $4QL^{\text{Bel}+}$ program Π, well-supported models of Π's modules do exist and, as in the case of $4QL^{\text{Bel}}$ programs, are uniquely determined. For a $4QL^{\text{Bel}+}$ module m, by $wsm(m)$ we denote the well-supported model of m. Using this correspondence between modules and well-supported models, being themselves $3i$-worlds, we can specify any belief base $\mathcal{B} = \langle \Delta, \mathcal{C} \rangle$ by:

$$\mathcal{B} = \langle m_1, \ldots, m_k \rangle, \tag{13}$$

where $m_1, \ldots, m_k$ are $4QL^{\text{Bel}+}$ modules. In such a case,

- $\Delta \stackrel{\text{def}}{=} \{wsm(m_1), \ldots, wsm(m_k)\}$;
- $\mathcal{C}$ consists of all rigid and flexible constraints collected from $m_1, \ldots, m_k$.

To simplify notation, we often identify single modules with belief bases, assuming that:

$$\text{module } m \text{ represents the belief base } \langle m \rangle. \tag{14}$$

Of course, specifications of belief bases of the form (13) inherit all advantages of rule-based specifications. In particular, comparing to Definition 1, $4QL^{\text{Bel}+}$-based specifications are typically much more concise and easier to understand and maintain.

7   The Shadowing Operator

To avoid semantical complexity, we treat shadowing as a formal expression rather than a belief base. However, to simplify presentation, syntactically we treat such formal expressions as belief bases. Thus, slightly abusing notation, we allow them to occur in the $\mathrm{Bel}()$ operator. Belief shadowing is defined by $\mathrm{Bel}_{\mathcal{B}_1 \text{ as } \mathcal{B}_2}(A)$ intuitively returning $\mathrm{Bel}_{\mathcal{B}_2}(A)$ when it is t, i or f, or $\mathrm{Bel}_{\mathcal{B}_1}(A)$, when $\mathrm{Bel}_{\mathcal{B}_2}(A)$ is u. However, suitable constraints have to be validated. If they are not, $\mathrm{Bel}_{\mathcal{B}_1 \text{ as } \mathcal{B}_2}(A)$ returns u for any query A.

Belief shadowing, denoted by 'as', is a left-associative operation. That is,

$$\mathcal{B}_1 \text{as } \mathcal{B}_2 \text{as } \mathcal{B}_3 \overset{\text{def}}{=} (\mathcal{B}_1 \text{as } \mathcal{B}_2) \text{as } \mathcal{B}_3.$$

To define belief shadowing we need an auxiliary operator $\bowtie$ allowing one to fuse beliefs. Let, in (15) and Definitions 5, 6, $\mathcal{B}^1 = \langle \Delta^1, \mathcal{C}_R^1 \cup \mathcal{C}_F^1 \rangle$ and $\mathcal{B}^2 = \langle \Delta^2, \mathcal{C}_R^2 \cup \mathcal{C}_F^2 \rangle$ be belief bases. Then:

$$\mathrm{Bel}_{\mathcal{B}_1 \bowtie \mathcal{B}_2}(A) \overset{\text{def}}{=} \begin{cases} \mathrm{Bel}_{\mathcal{B}_2}(A) \text{ when } \mathrm{Bel}_{\mathcal{B}_2}(A) \in \{\mathsf{t}, \mathsf{f}, \mathsf{i}\}; \\ \mathrm{Bel}_{\mathcal{B}_1}(A) \text{ when } \mathrm{Bel}_{\mathcal{B}_2}(A) = \mathsf{u}. \end{cases} \tag{15}$$

We are now ready to define integrity constraints and belief shadowing, $\mathcal{B}_1 \text{as } \mathcal{B}_2$, the central concepts of our approach.

Definition 5. *By* integrity constraints of $\mathcal{B}_1 \text{ as } \mathcal{B}_2$ *we understand the set* $\mathcal{C}_R^1 \cup \mathcal{C}_R^2 \cup \mathcal{C}_F^2$ *with* $\mathcal{C}_R^1 \cup \mathcal{C}_R^2$ *being* rigid constraints *and* $\mathcal{C}_F^2$ *being* flexible constraints *of* $\mathcal{B}_1 \text{ as } \mathcal{B}_2$. ◁

Definition 6. *The* belief operator *over belief base* $\mathcal{B}_1$ shadowed by *belief base* $\mathcal{B}_2$, $\mathrm{Bel}_{\mathcal{B}_1 \text{ as } \mathcal{B}_2}()$, *is defined by:*

$$\mathrm{Bel}_{\mathcal{B}_1 \text{ as } \mathcal{B}_2}(A) \overset{\text{def}}{=} \begin{cases} \mathrm{Bel}_{\mathcal{B}_1 \bowtie \mathcal{B}_2}(A) \text{ when for any } C \in \mathcal{C}_R^1 \cup \mathcal{C}_R^2 \cup \mathcal{C}_F^2, \\ \qquad\qquad\qquad\qquad C'(\mathcal{B}_1) = \mathsf{t} \\ \mathsf{u} \qquad\qquad\qquad otherwise, \end{cases}$$

where C' *is obtained from* C *by substituting references to* $\mathcal{B}_1$ *in subformulas of the form* $\mathrm{Bel}_{\dots \mathcal{B}_1 \dots}(\dots)$ *by* $\mathcal{B}_1 \bowtie \mathcal{B}_2$. ◁

Though constraints of belief bases are always true, as required in Definition 4, constraints of $\mathcal{B}_1 \text{as } \mathcal{B}_2$ may be unsatisfied for some $\mathcal{B}_1$ and $\mathcal{B}_2$. When this occurs, we assume that any query to $\mathcal{B}_1 \text{as } \mathcal{B}_2$ returns the empty set of tuples with the truth value u. Note that some queries may also return u when constraints are satisfied but $\mathcal{B}_1 \text{as } \mathcal{B}_2$ contains no facts supporting or denying such queries. These cases can be distinguished without recalculating constraints, e.g., using the query $\mathrm{Bel}_{\mathcal{B}_1 \text{ as } \mathcal{B}_2}(\mathsf{t})$ which returns t when constraints are satisfied and u otherwise.

8   Formalizing the ER Scenario

Let us now illustrate the introduced ideas formalizing the ER scenario of Sect. 2. For this purpose we shall assume that a woman, Pat, arrives to ER. We shall specify the following $4QL^{Bel+}$ modules and belief base:

- Module 4, gathering basic data about patients registered in the ER, in particular about their statuses, symptoms, refusals/acceptances of specific treatments and treatments prescribed at ER;
- Module 5, containing medical data about Pat's about symptoms diagnosed and treatments prescribed before she has been admitted to ER;
- Module 6, gathering beliefs of the MDM meeting called by Mark for the Pat's case;
- Module 7, gathering belies common to the ER doctors;
- Belief Base 8, representing Mark's beliefs.

Recall that $4QL^{Bel+}$ is based on the OWA. Listing all treatments accepted/refused by a patient in Module 4 would not be practical so many refusals would remain unknown. To close this gap one needs a default, like:

"a treatment is allowed unless it is explicitly refused by the patient"   (16)

One way to implement the default (16) is to close the world partially (affecting only relations 'accepts' and 'refuses'), as done by rules in Lines 19–21 of Module 4, where we assume that a treatment is assumed to be accepted by Pat if the belief as to its refusal is false, unknown or inconsistent, i.e., when:

- the patient explicitly accepted the treatment (making the refusal false);
- no information as to refusal is available (e.g., the patient is unconscious and there is no one to ask);
- information as to refusal is inconsistent (e.g., the patient is unconscious and authorized persons, like close relatives, provide contradictory claims).

Module 5 contains Pat's medical data, as gathered before Pat's arrival to ER. Medical information about Pat is collected in **patients** on the basis of information obtained from **pat** (Lines 26–27 of Module 4) and additional information collected during the examination at ER. This information allocation reflects reality where a patient has its medical history while diagnoses and basic treatments are within ER's responsibilities when an emergency case happens.

To simplify presentation and make it self-contained, MDM is represented by Module 6, containing final decisions rather than by a belief base consisting of modules representing MDM members equipped with a procedure of reaching the conclusion. This would require argumentation modeling being itself a wide research area.[5] Sample general doctors' beliefs are contained in Module 7. Mark's beliefs are formalized by Belief Base 8 aggregating beliefs and constraints from

---

[5] The use of 4QL-like approach to argumentation is investigated, e.g., in [9,10].

$3i$-worlds represented by modules **patients** and **doctor**. Due to OWA, in many cases the implications occurring in Line 4 of Module 7 and Line 5 of Belief Base 8 may be unknown. Therefore, these constraints are required to be true or unknown, excluding false and inconsistent.

Table 4. Sample queries and results.

	Query	Results
(1)	Bel[pat](accepts(pat,blood,T))	T: transplant = false
		T: transfusion = false
(2)	Bel[patients](accepts(pat,blood,T))	T: antibiotic = true
		T: transfusion = false
		T: transplant = false
		T: diuretics = true
		T: alpha-blocker = true
(3)	Bel[mark](prescribed(pat,O,T))	O: blood, T: transfusion = inconsistent
		O: blood, T: diuretics = true
		O: blood, T: alpha-blocker = true
		O: heart, T: massage = true
		O: heart, T: check = true
		O: kidney, T: antibiotic = true
(4)	Bel[mark as doctor](prescribed(pat,O,T))	O: blood, T: transfusion = false
		O: heart, T: check = true
(5)	Bel[mark as mdmMember](prescribed(pat,O,I))	O: blood, I: transfusion = true

To illustrate the use of $4QL^{Bel+}$ and inter4QL, Table 4 contains sample queries and their results, as provided by the interpreter, where the following notation is used:

- 'X:v' indicates that the value of variable 'X' is 'v';
- 'L = t' indicates that the tuple specified by the list of variable assignments 'L' satisfies the query with truth value 't'∈{true,incons,false}.[6]

Queries (1) and (2) show how the default (16) closes the relation 'accepts': the new facts are concluded since in the **pat** module they are unknown.

Belief base **mark** combines information from **patients** and **doctor**. The rule in Line 18 of Module 4 makes 'prescribed(pat,blood,transfusion)' true. According to **doctor**, the same conclusion is false. Therefore, **mark**'s the conclusion as to blood transfusion in the answer to query (3) is inconsistent. Due to shadowing, answers to queries (4) and (5) give preferences to **doctor**'s and **mdmMember**'s beliefs, respectively.

---

[6] Tuples for which the query is evaluated to **u** are not listed.

```
1  module patients:
2  │  constraints:
3  │  │  rigid: forall N:name (status(N,alive)).
4  │  domains:
5  │  │  literal name.       // patient's name
6  │  │  literal statusId.   // patient's status
7  │  │  literal organ.      // organ affected
8  │  │  literal issue.      // symptom description
9  │  │  integer severity.   // 0–9, 0 - lowest, 9 - highest
10 │  │  literal treatment.  // treatment type
11 │  relations:
12 │  │  status(name,statusId).            // patients status
13 │  │  symptom(name,organ,issue,severity). // symptoms observed
14 │  │  refuses(name,organ,treatment).      // treatments refused
15 │  │  accepts(name,organ,treatment).      // treatments accepted
16 │  │  prescribed(name,organ,treatment).   // prescriptions
17 │  rules:
18 │  │  prescribed(N,O,T) :– Bel[mdmMember](prescribed(N,O,T)).
19 │  │  accepts(pat,O,T) :– pat.refuses(pat,O,T) in {false, unknown,
   │  │  incons}.
20 │  │  -accepts(pat,O,T) :– pat.accepts(pat,O,T) = false.
21 │  │  refuses(pat,O,T) :– pat.refuses(pat,O,T) = true.
22 │  │  refuses(N,O,T) :– -accepts(N,O,T).
23 │  │  -refuses(N,O,T) :– accepts(N,O,T).
24 │  │  accepts(pat,O,transplant) :– symptom(pat,O,I,S), math.ge(S,8).
25 │  │  -accepts(pat,O,transplant) :– symptom(pat,O,I,S), math.le(S,7).
26 │  │  symptom(pat,O,I,S) :– pat.symptom(pat,O,I,S).
27 │  │  prescribed(pat,O,T) :– pat.prescribed(pat,O,T).
28 │  facts:
29 │  │  status(pat,alive).
30 │  │  status(pat,emergency).
31 │  │  symptom(pat,leg,injury,3).
32 │  │  symptom(pat,hand,injury,6).
33 │  │  symptom(pat,heart,failure,7).
34 │  │  prescribed(pat,heart,massage).
35 end.
```

Module 4: Module representing patients registered in the ER.

9   Properties of Shadowing

For any belief bases, $\mathcal{B}_1$, $\mathcal{B}_2$, the operator $\mathrm{Bel}_{\mathcal{B}_1 \text{ as } \mathcal{B}_2}()$ satisfies (KD45n) axioms.

Proposition 1. *For any belief bases,* $\mathcal{B}_1$, $\mathcal{B}_2$ *and formula* A,

$$\mathrm{Bel}_{\mathcal{B}_1\,as\,\mathcal{B}_2}\big(A\big) \rightarrow \neg\mathrm{Bel}_{\mathcal{B}_1\,as\,\mathcal{B}_2}\big(\neg A\big); \tag{17}$$

$$\mathrm{Bel}_{\mathcal{B}_1\,as\,\mathcal{B}_2}\big(A\big) \rightarrow \mathrm{Bel}_{\mathcal{B}_1\,as\,\mathcal{B}_2}\big(\mathrm{Bel}_{\mathcal{B}_1\,as\,\mathcal{B}_2}\big(A\big)\big); \tag{18}$$

$$\neg\mathrm{Bel}_{\mathcal{B}_1\,as\,\mathcal{B}_2}\big(A\big) \rightarrow \mathrm{Bel}_{\mathcal{B}_1\,as\,\mathcal{B}_2}\big(\neg\mathrm{Bel}_{\mathcal{B}_1\,as\,\mathcal{B}_2}\big(A\big)\big). \tag{19}$$

```
1  module pat:
2     constraints:
3        rigid: forall O:organ forall I:issue forall S:severity (
4                (symptom(pat,O,I,S),math.le(S,7)) ->
           refuses(pat,O,transplant)).
5        flexible: refuses(pat,blood,transfusion).
6     domains:
7        literal name.      // patient's name
8        literal organ.     // organ affected
9        literal issue.     // symptom description
10       integer severity.  // 0–9, 0 - lowest, 9 - highest
11       literal treatment. // treatment type
12    relations:
13       refuses(name,organ,treatment).
14       accepts(name,organ,treatment).
15       symptom(name,organ,issue,severity). // diagnosed before ER
16       prescribed(name,organ,treatment).   // prescribed before ER
17    rules:
18       accepts(pat,O,transplant) :- symptom(pat,O,I,S), math.ge(S,8).
19       -accepts(pat,O,transplant) :- symptom(pat,O,I,S), math.le(S,7).
20       accepts(pat,O,T) :- -refuses(pat,O,T).
21       -accepts(pat,O,T) :- refuses(pat,O,T).
22       refuses(pat,O,T) :- -accepts(pat,O,T).
23       -refuses(pat,O,T) :- accepts(pat,O,T).
24    facts:
25       refuses(pat,blood,transfusion).
26       symptom(pat,blood,hypertension,6).
27       symptom(pat,kidney,pain,7).
28       prescribed(pat,blood,diuretics).
29       prescribed(pat,blood,alpha-blocker).
30       prescribed(pat,kidney,antibiotic).
31 end.
```

Module 5: Module representing Pat.

Note, however, that axioms (17)–(19) do not have the classical meaning. For example, when the truth value of A is $\mathbf{i}$, the implication (17) holds but it does not mean that (an inconsistent) belief in A prevents (inconsistent) belief in $\neg A$. Indeed, in this case, both $\mathrm{Bel}_{\mathcal{B}_1\,as\,\mathcal{B}_2}(\mathbf{i})$ and $\neg\mathrm{Bel}_{\mathcal{B}_1\,as\,\mathcal{B}_2}(\neg\mathbf{i})$ are $\mathbf{i}$.

Complexitywise, similarly to [6], we have the following propositions, where for any $4QL^{Bel+}$ program Π, $\#D$ denotes the sum of the sizes of all domains of Π; $\#\Pi$ denotes the number of modules in Π.

Proposition 2. *For every* $4QL^{Bel+}$ *program* Π*, both:*

- *checking the existence of the well-supported models of modules of* Π*;*
- *computing well-supported models of modules of* Π*,*

can be done in PTIME in $\max\{\#D, \#\Pi\}$. ◁

```
1  module mdmMember:
2  |  domains:
3  |  |  literal name.        // patient's name
4  |  |  literal organ.       // organ affected
5  |  |  literal treatment.   // treatment type
6  |  relations: prescribed(name,organ,treatment).
7  |  facts: prescribed(pat,blood,transfusion).
8  end.
```

Module 6: A module representing members of the MDM called for the Pat's case.

```
1  module doctor:
2  |  constraints:
3  |  |  flexible: forall N:name forall O:organ forall T:treatment (
4  |  |       patients.refuses(N,O,T) -> -patient.prescribed(N,O,T)) in
   |  |     {true,unknown}.
5  |  domains:
6  |  |  literal name.        // patient's name
7  |  |  literal organ.       // organ affected
8  |  |  literal treatment.   // treatment type
9  |  relations:
10 |  |  prescribed(name,treatment).
11 |  rules:
12 |  |  prescribed(N,blood,transfusion) :-
   |  |  patients.symptom(N,O,injury,S), math.ge(S,7).
13 |  |  -prescribed(N,blood,transfusion) :-
   |  |  patients.symptom(N,O,injury,S), math.le(S,5).
14 |  |  prescribed(N,heart,transplant) :-
   |  |  patients.symptom(N,heart,failure,9).
15 |  |  prescribed(N,O,check) :- patients.symptom(N,O,I,S),
   |  |  math.ge(S,7).
16 end.
```

Module 7: General doctors' beliefs.

Proposition 3. *Given belief bases* $\mathcal{B}_1, \mathcal{B}_2$ *expressed using modules of a* $4QL^{Bel+}$ *program* Π*, the problem of computing queries involving expressions of the form* $\mathrm{Bel}_{\mathcal{B}_1 \, as \, \mathcal{B}_2}()$ *has deterministic polynomial time complexity in* $\max\{\#D, \#\Pi\}$. ◁

Since shadowing is defined in terms of belief base queries, as a consequence of the corresponding result of [6], we have the following proposition.

Proposition 4. *Assuming that domains are linearly ordered, every polynomially computable shadowing can be expressed in* $4QL^{Bel+}$.   ◁

From the perspective of systems' engineering, the above complexity results are important. However, even tractability does not guarantee scalability over big data. Belief shadowing can be made horizontally scalable when recursive queries are not allowed, assuming that all $4QL^{Bel}$ modules are already computed and belief bases consist of the resulting $3i$-worlds. In this case, $\mathrm{Bel}()$-free formulas are equivalent to first-order (and non-recursive SQL) queries which can be evaluated in a horizontally scalable manner. Queries involving belief operators can also be easily horizontally distributed (with a separate thread evaluating a given query in each $3i$-world of a given belief base).

```
1  beliefs mark:
2  │  constraints:
3  │  │  flexible:
4  │  │  │  forall N:name forall O:organ forall I:issue (
5  │  │  │  patients.symptom(N,O,I,9) -> doctor.prescribed(N,O,check))
   │  │  │  in {true,unknown}.
6  │  worlds:
7  │  │  patients.  // see Module 4
8  │  │  doctor.    // see Module 7
9  end.
```

Belief Base 8: Mark's belief base.

10   Related Work

Beliefs and their modifications are intensively tackled in many contexts. A fundamental issue is the definition of different kinds of beliefs [13,14,17,24,34,45] together with sophisticated structures like belief sets and belief bases [18,19,39]. Our approach builds on paraconsistent and paracomplete belief bases understood as in [11,12]. Moreover, we equip them with constraints, creating a convenient reasoning engine with built-in safety tools vital for maintaining belief bases. As we have shown, constraints are naturally applicable in belief shadowing and can be shadowed, too.

As agent systems act in dynamic environments, belief update and revision are in the mainstream of the area. For representative approaches see [21,28,29,32,35] and references there. Importantly, belief revision has been found one of the most fundamental research topics [16,20] aiming at consistent and deterministic solutions. Among others, the well known AGM [2] model was developed as a theoretical framework for adequate belief modification practices. It inspired a large body of work over many years. For surveys see [15] and references there. A significant amount of AGM extensions and improvements have been proposed, including paraconsistent ones [37,42,43]. Apart from undeniable profits, belief modifications can be computationally expensive, and create some other issues, like underdetermination (inability to determine rules to be defeated). Our belief shadowing significantly differs from belief update or revision and provides a remedy for these issues.

An alternative framework, belief merging, is addressed in many sources (for an overview see [27]). The authors study merging several belief bases in the presence of integrity constraints. The presented solutions do not allow inconsistent belief bases which forces the authors to look for consistency preserving belief merging operators. Our framework is more general: both input belief bases and the resulting beliefs can be inconsistent which offers flexibility of the specifications. Also, the complexity of belief merging is typically high (see [25]) while our framework guarantees tractability.

Another aspect of beliefs' dynamics is addressed in [11,12], where transformations of initial raw beliefs into more abstract, mature ones have been modeled. Belief dynamics is approached there via epistemic profiles permitting to model both beliefs related to states of the environment and deliberative processes of agents. Belief shadowing can contribute to express epistemic profiles flexibly and efficiently. Apart from the area of belief change, our approach is rooted in the field of paraconsistent reasoning [4,5]. It is based on a logic derived from [6,11,31,44].

11   Conclusions

We have provided a novel, tractable and natural framework for modeling everyday human-like belief shadowing. The framework focuses on belief changes in dynamic environments. We have identified a broad niche where known belief change techniques can be substantially improved by developing a lightweight method of belief shadowing.

Besides providing efficient solution to the addressed phenomena, belief shadowing is also meant to complement belief revision/update/merging when these methods are difficult or impossible to apply. Firstly, when an agent acts in an unknown environment, frequent belief revisions might be needed. As such revisions may be computationally demanding, the shadowing machinery can serve as a "buffer" gathering new observations. Deeper revisions could then be postponed till the proper moment. Secondly, belief revisions might be hardly applicable, for example, when many rules contribute to a particular conclusion contradicting the observed reality. Then, belief shadowing provides a more nuanced means than just to live with inconsistency. Dynamic reasoning with beliefs and their interferences calls for safety mechanism preventing from forbidden states. This is well visible in machine learning, in particular data/rule mining. To ensure the required properties of belief bases at various abstraction levels, we have defined a constraint shadowing technique.

Last but not least, to illustrate how belief and constraint shadowing may be embedded into an existing rule language, we have extended $4QL^{Bel}$ by adding constraints and shadowing operator. The obtained $4QL^{Bel+}$ language provides tractable querying machinery and is strong enough to express all shadowings computable in deterministic polynomial time. The language is implemented and its open-source interpreter inter4QL is available via `4ql.org`. Interestingly, $4QL^{Bel+}$ permits to combine paracomplete and paraconsistent reasoning with lightweight versions of nonmonotonic and doxastic reasoning. As we indicated, though this feature is not implemented in inter4QL, the language is horizontally scalable wrt non-recursive queries.

References

1. Abiteboul, S., Hull, R., Vianu, V.: Foundations of Databases: The Logical Level. Addison-Wesley, Boston (1995)
2. Alchourrón, C.E., Gärdenfors, P., Makinson, D.: On the logic of theory change: partial meet contraction and revision functions. J. Symb. Log. **50**(2), 510–530 (1985)
3. de Amo, S., Pais, M.: A paraconsistent logic approach for querying inconsistent databases. Int. J. Approx. Reason. **46**, 366–386 (2007)
4. Bertossi, L., Hunter, A., Schaub, T. (eds.): Inconsistency Tolerance. LNCS, vol. 3300. Springer, Heidelberg (2005). https://doi.org/10.1007/b104925
5. Béziau, J.Y., Carnielli, W., Gabbay, D. (eds.): Handbook of Paraconsistency. College Publications, London (2007)
6. Białek, Ł., Dunin-Kęplicz, B., Szałas, A.: Rule-based reasoning with belief structures. In: Kryszkiewicz, M., Appice, A., Ślęzak, D., Rybinski, H., Skowron, A., Raś, Z.W. (eds.) ISMIS 2017. LNCS (LNAI), vol. 10352, pp. 229–239. Springer, Cham (2017). https://doi.org/10.1007/978-3-319-60438-1_23
7. Bochman, A.: A Logical Theory of Nonmonotonic Inference and Belief Change. Springer, Heidelberg (2001). https://doi.org/10.1007/978-3-662-04560-2
8. Dechter, R.: Constraint Processing. Morgan Kaufmann, Burlington (2003)
9. Dunin-Kęplicz, B., Strachocka, A.: Paraconsistent argumentation schemes. Web Intell. **14**(1), 43–65 (2016)
10. Dunin-Kęplicz, B., Strachocka, A., Szałas, A., Verbrugge, R.: Perceiving speech acts under incomplete and inconsistent information. In: Barbucha, D., et al. (eds.) Proceedings of the 7th KES AMSTA Conference, pp. 255–264. IOS Press (2013)
11. Dunin-Kęplicz, B., Szałas, A.: Taming complex beliefs. In: Nguyen, N.T. (ed.) Transactions on Computational Collective Intelligence XI. LNCS, vol. 8065, pp. 1–21. Springer, Heidelberg (2013). https://doi.org/10.1007/978-3-642-41776-4_1
12. Dunin-Kęplicz, B., Szałas, A.: Indeterministic belief structures. In: Jezic, G., Kusek, M., Lovrek, I., J. Howlett, R., Jain, L.C. (eds.) Agent and Multi-Agent Systems: Technologies and Applications. AISC, vol. 296, pp. 57–66. Springer, Cham (2014). https://doi.org/10.1007/978-3-319-07650-8_7
13. Dunin-Kęplicz, B., Verbrugge, R.: Teamwork in Multi-Agent Systems: A Formal Approach. Wiley, Hoboken (2010)
14. Fagin, R., Halpern, J., Moses, Y., Vardi, M.: Reasoning About Knowledge. The MIT Press, Cambridge (2003)
15. Fermé, E., Hansson, S.O.: AGM 25 years: twenty-five years of research in belief change. J. Philosophical Logic **40**(2), 295–331 (2011)
16. Gärdenfors, P.: Conditionals and changes of belief. Acta Philos. Fenn. **30**, 381–404 (1978)
17. Hadley, R.F.: The many uses of 'belief' in AI. Mind. Mach. **1**(1), 55–73 (1991)

18. Hansson, S.O.: Taking belief bases seriously. In: Prawitz, D., Westerståhl, D. (eds.) Logic and Philosophy of Science in Uppsala. Synthese Library (Studies in Epistemology, Logic, Methodology, and Philosophy of Science), vol. 236, pp. 13–28. Springer, Dordrecht (1994). https://doi.org/10.1007/978-94-015-8311-4_2

19. Hansson, S.O.: Belief change. In: Dubois, D., Prade, H. (eds.) Revision of Belief Sets and Belief Bases. Handbook of Defeasible Reasoning and Uncertainty Management Systems, vol. 3, pp. 17–75. Springer, Dordrecht (1998). https://doi.org/10.1007/978-94-011-5054-5_2

20. Hansson, S.O.: A Textbook of Belief Dynamics: Theory Change and Database Updating. Kluwer Academic Publishers, Dordrecht (1999)

21. Herzig, A., Rifi, O.: Propositional belief base update and minimal change. Artif. Intell. **115**(1), 107–138 (1999)

22. Hewitt, C., Woods, J. (eds.): Inconsistency Robustness. College Publications, London (2015)

23. van Hoeve, W.J., Katriel, I.: Global constraints. Found. AI **2**, 169–208 (2006)

24. Huber, F.: Formal representations of belief. In: Zalta, E.N. (ed.) The Stanford Encyclopedia of Philosophy. Stanford University, Palo Alto (2016)

25. Konieczny, S., Lang, J., Marquis, P.: DA^2 merging operators. Artif. Intell. **157**(1–2), 49–79 (2004)

26. Konieczny, S., Pérez, R.P.: Merging with integrity constraints. In: Hunter, A., Parsons, S. (eds.) ECSQARU 1999. LNCS (LNAI), vol. 1638, pp. 233–244. Springer, Heidelberg (1999). https://doi.org/10.1007/3-540-48747-6_22

27. Konieczny, S., Pino Pérez, R.: Merging information under constraints: a logical framework. J. Log. Comput. **12**(5), 773–808 (2002)

28. Lang, J.: Belief update revisited. In: Proceedings of the 20th IJCAI, pp. 2517–2522. Morgan Kaufmann (2007)

29. Liberatore, P.: The complexity of belief update. Artif. Intell. **119**(1), 141–190 (2000)

30. Małuszyński, J., Szałas, A.: Living with inconsistency and taming nonmonotonicity. In: de Moor, O., Gottlob, G., Furche, T., Sellers, A. (eds.) Datalog 2.0 2010. LNCS, vol. 6702, pp. 384–398. Springer, Heidelberg (2011). https://doi.org/10.1007/978-3-642-24206-9_22

31. Małuszyński, J., Szałas, A.: Partiality and inconsistency in agents' belief bases. In: Barbucha, D., et al. (eds.) Proceedings of the 7th KES AMSTA Conference, pp. 3–17. IOS Press (2013)

32. Marchi, J., Bittencourt, G., Perrussel, L.: A syntactical approach to belief update. In: Gelbukh, A., de Albornoz, Á., Terashima-Marín, H. (eds.) MICAI 2005. LNCS (LNAI), vol. 3789, pp. 142–151. Springer, Heidelberg (2005). https://doi.org/10.1007/11579427_15

33. Meseguer, P., Rossi, F., Schiex, T.: Soft constraints. In: Rossi, et al. [38], pp. 281–328

34. Meyer, J.J.C., van der Hoek, W.: Epistemic Logic for AI and Theoretical Computer Science. Cambridge University Press, Cambridge (1995)

35. Peppas, P.: Belief revision. In: van Harmelen, F., Lifschitz, V., Porter, B. (eds.) Handbook of KR, pp. 317–359. Elsevier, Amsterdam (2008)

36. Pigozzi, G.: Belief merging and judgment aggregation. In: Zalta, E. (ed.) The Stanford Encyclopedia of Philosophy. Stanford University, Palo Alto (2016)

37. Priest, G.: Paraconsistent belief revision. Theoria **67**(3), 214–228 (2001)

38. Rossi, F., van Beek, P., Walsh, T. (eds.): Handbook of Constraint Programming, Foundations of AI, vol. 2, Supplement C. Elsevier, Amsterdam (2006)

39. Santos, Y.D., Ribeiro, M.M., Wassermann, R.: Between belief bases and belief sets: Partial meet contraction. In: Proceedings of the 2015 International Conference on Defeasible and Ampliative Reasoning. DARe 2015, vol. 1423, pp. 50–56. CEUR-WS.org (2015)
40. Shepherdson, J.: Negation in logic programming. In: Minker, J. (ed.) Foundations of Deductive Databases and Logic Programming, pp. 19–88. Morgan Kaufmann, Burlington (1988)
41. Szałas, A.: How an agent might think. Log. J. IGPL **21**(3), 515–535 (2013)
42. Testa, R.R., Coniglio, M.E., Ribeiro, M.M.: Paraconsistent belief revision based on a formal consistency operator. CLE E-Prints **15**(8), 01–11 (2015)
43. Testa, R.R., Coniglio, M.E., Ribeiro, M.M.: AGM-like paraconsistent belief change. Log. J. IGPL **25**(4), 632–672 (2017)
44. Vitória, A., Małuszyński, J., Szałas, A.: Modeling and reasoning with paraconsistent rough sets. Fundam. Inform. **97**(4), 405–438 (2009)
45. Wooldridge, M.: Reasoning About Rational Agents. MIT Press, Cambridge (2000)

Empathic Autonomous Agents

Timotheus Kampik$^{(\boxtimes)}$ (ID), Juan Carlos Nieves (ID), and Helena Lindgren (ID)

Umeå University, 901 87 Umeå, Sweden
{tkampik,jcnieves,helena}@cs.umu.se

Abstract. Identifying and resolving conflicts of interests is a key challenge when designing autonomous agents. For example, such conflicts often occur when complex information systems interact persuasively with humans and are in the future likely to arise in non-human agent-to-agent interaction. We introduce a theoretical framework for an *empathic* autonomous agent that proactively identifies potential conflicts of interests in interactions with other agents (and humans) by considering their utility functions and comparing them with its own preferences using a system of shared values to find a solution all agents consider *acceptable*. To illustrate how empathic autonomous agents work, we provide running examples and a simple prototype implementation in a general-purpose programing language. To give a high-level overview of our work, we propose a reasoning-loop architecture for our empathic agent.

Keywords: Multi-agent systems · Utility theory · Conflicts of interests

1 Background and Problem Description

In modern information technologies, conflicts of interests between users and information systems that operate with a high degree of autonomy (*autonomous agents*) are of increasing prevalence. For example, complex web applications persuade end-users, possibly against the interests of the persuaded individuals[1]. Given the prevalence of autonomous systems will increase, conflicts between autonomous agents and humans (or between different autonomous agent instances and types) can be expected to occur more frequently in the future, e.g. in interactions with or among autonomous vehicles in scenarios that cannot be completely solved by applying static traffic rules. Consequently, one can argue for the need to develop *empathic* intelligent agents that consider the preferences or utility functions of others, as well as ethics rules and social norms when interacting with their environment to avoid severe conflicts of interests. As a simple example, take two vehicles (*A* and *B*) that are about to enter a bottleneck. Assume they cannot enter the bottleneck at the same time. A and B can either wait or drive. Considering only its own utility function, A might determine that *driving* is the best action to execute, given that B will likely stop and wait to avoid a crash. However, A should ideally assess both its own and B's utility

---

[1] E.g., research provides evidence that contextual advertisement influences how users process online news [25]; social network applications have effectively been employed for political persuasion (see for an example: [4]).

© Springer Nature Switzerland AG 2019
D. Weyns et al. (Eds.): EMAS 2018 Workshops, LNAI 11375, pp. 181–201, 2019.
https://doi.org/10.1007/978-3-030-25693-7_10

function and act accordingly. If B's utility for driving is considered higher than A's, A can then come to the conclusion that *waiting* is the best action. As A does not only consider its own goals, but also the ones of B, one can regard A as *empathic*, following Coplan's definition of empathy, as "a process through which an observer simulates another's situated psychological states, while maintaining clear self–other differentiation" [12]. While existing literature covers conflict resolution in multi-agent systems from a broad range of perspectives (see for a partial overview: [2]), devising a theoretical framework for autonomous agents that consider the utility functions (or preferences) of agents in their environment and use a combined utilitarian/rule-based approach to identify and resolve conflicts of interests can be considered a novel idea. However, existing multi-agent systems research can be leveraged to implement core components of such a framework, as is discussed later.

In this chapter, we provide the following research contributions:

1. We create a theoretical framework for an empathic agent that uses a combination of utility-based and rule-based concepts to compromise with other agents in its environment when deciding upon how to act.
2. We provide a set of running examples that illustrate how the empathic agent works and show how the examples can be implemented in a general-purpose programing language.
3. We propose a reasoning-loop architecture for a generic empathic agent.

The rest of this chapter is organized as follows: in Sect. 2, we present a theoretical framework for the problem in focus. Then, we illustrate the concepts with the help of different running examples and describe the example implementation in a general-purpose programing language in Sect. 3. Next, we outline a basic reasoning-loop architecture for the empathic agent in Sect. 4. In Sect. 5, we analyze how the architecture aligns with the belief-desire-intention approach and propose an implementation using the Jason multi-agent development framework. Finally, we discuss how our empathic agent concepts relate to existing work, propose potential use cases, highlight a set of limitations, and outline future work in Sect. 6, before we conclude the chapter in Sect. 7.

2   Empathic Agent Core Concepts

In this section, we describe the core concepts of the empathic agent. To allow for a precise description, we assume the following scenario[2]:

– The scenario describes the interaction between a set of empathic agents $\{A_0, ..., A_n\}$.
– Each interaction scenario takes place at one specific point in time, at which all agents execute their actions simultaneously.

---

[2] As we will explain later, the scenario and the resulting specification can be gradually extended to allow for better real-world applicability.

- At this point in time, each agent $A_i (0 \leq i \leq n)$ has a finite set of *possible* actions $Acts_i := \{Act_i^0, ..., Act_i^m\}$, resulting in an overall set of action sets $Acts := \{Acts_0, ..., Acts_n\}$. Each agent can execute an *action tuple* that contains one or multiple actions. In each interaction scenario, all agents execute their actions simultaneously and receive their utility as a numeric reward based on the actions that have been executed.
- The utility of an agent A_i is determined by a function u_i of the actions of all agents. The utility function returns a numerical value or $null$[3]:

$$u_i := Acts_0 \times ... \times Acts_n \rightarrow \{null, -\infty, \mathbb{R}, \infty\}$$

The goal of the empathic agent is to maximize its own utility as long as no conflicts with other agents arise. We define a conflict of interests between several agents as any interaction scenario in which there is no tuple of possible actions that maximizes the utility functions of all agents. I.e., we need to compare $\arg\max u_{A_0}, ..., \arg\max u_{A_n}$[4]. Note that $\arg\max u_{A_i}$ returns a *set of tuples* (that contains all action tuples that yield the maximal utility for agent A_i). For this, we create a boolean function c that the empathic agent uses to determine conflicts between itself and other agents, based on the utility functions of all agents:

$$c(u_{A_0}, ..., u_{A_n}) := \begin{cases} true, \; if : \\ \quad \arg\max u_{A_0} \cap ... \cap \arg\max u_{A_n} \neq \{\}; \\ false, \; otherwise. \end{cases}$$

Considering the incomparability property of the von Neumann-Morgenstern utility theorem [24], such a conflict can be solved only if a system of values exists that is shared between the agents and used to determine *comparable* individual utility values. Hence, we introduce such a shared value system. To provide a possible structure for this system, we deconstruct the utility functions into two parts:

- An actions-to-consequences mapping (a function $a2c_i$ that takes the actions the agents potentially decide to execute and returns a set of *consequences* (propositional atoms) $Consqs := \{Consq_i^0, ..., Consq_i^n\}$):

$$a2c_i := Acts_i \times ... \times Acts_n \rightarrow 2^{Consqs}$$

- A consequences-to-utility mapping (utility quantification function uq). Note that the actions-to-consequences mapping is agent-specific, while the utility quantification function is generically provided by the shared value system[5]:

$$uq := 2^{Consqs} \rightarrow \{null, -\infty, \mathbb{R}, \infty\}$$

---

[3] We allow for utility functions to return a $null$ value for action tuples that are considered impossible, e.g. in case some actions are mutually exclusive. While we concede that the elegance of this approach is up for debate, we opted for it because of its simplicity.

[4] The arg max operator takes the function it precedes and returns all argument tuples that maximize the function.

[5] I.e., for the same actions, an agent should only receive a different utility outcome than another agent if the impact on the two is distinguishable in its *consequences*. We again allow for $null$ values to be returned in case of impossible action tuples.

Then, agents can agree on the utility value of a given tuple of actions, as long as the *quality* of the consequence is observable to all agents in the same way. In addition, the value system can introduce generally applicable rules, e.g. to hard-code a prioritization of individual freedom into an agent. With help of the value system, we create a pragmatic definition of a conflict of interests as any situation, in which there is no tuple of actions that is regarded as *acceptable* by all agents when considering the shared set of values, given each agent executes the actions that maximize their individual utility function. To support the notion of *acceptability*, we introduce a set of agent-specific *acceptability functions* $accs := \{acc_{A_0}, ..., acc_{A_n}\}$. The acceptability functions are derived from the corresponding utility functions and the shared system of values and take a set of actions as their inputs. Acceptability functions are domain-specific and there is no generic logic to be described in this context:

$$acc_{A_i} := Acts_{A_0} \times ... \times Acts_{A_n} \rightarrow \{null, true, false\}$$

The notion of acceptability rules adds a *normative* aspect to the otherwise *consequentialist* empathic agent framework. Without this notion, our definition of a conflict of interests would cover many scenarios that most human societies regard as not conflict-worthy, e.g. when one agent would need to accept large utility losses to optimize its own actions towards improving another agents' utility. Considering the acceptability functions, we can now determine whether a conflict of interests in terms of the *pragmatic* definition approach exists for an agent A_i by using the following function cp that takes the utility function u_i of agent A_i and the acceptability functions $Accs := \{acc_{A_0}, ..., acc_{A_n}\}$ as input arguments:

$$cp(u_i, Accs) :=$$
$$\begin{cases} true, \ if : \\ \quad \nexists acts \in \arg\max u_i \wedge \forall_{acc \in Accs} : acc(acts) = true \\ false, \ otherwise. \end{cases}$$

We define an *empathic* agent A_i as an agent that, when determining the actions it executes, considers the utility functions of the agents it could potentially affect and maximizes its own utility only if doing so does not violate the acceptability function of any other agent; otherwise it acts to maximize the shared utility of all agents (while also considering the acceptability functions)[6]. Algorithm 1 specifies an initial, *naive* approach towards the empathic agent core algorithm. The empathic agent core algorithm of an agent A_i in its simplest form can be defined as a function that takes the utility functions $\{u_0, ..., u_n\}$ of the different

---

[6] As different aggregation approaches are possible (for example: *sum*, *product*) to determine the maximal shared utility, we introduce the not further specified aggregation function $aggregate(u_0, ..., u_n)$. In our running examples (see Sect. 3), we use the product of the individual utility function outcomes to introduce some notion of fairness; inequality should not be in the interest of the empathic agent. However, the design choice for this implementation detail can be discussed.

agents, the set of all acceptability functions $Accs := \{acc_0, ..., acc_l\}$, and all possible actions $Acts_i$ of agent A_i and returns the tuple of actions A_i should execute[7].

Algorithm 1. Naive empathic agent algorithm: D_A_N (*determine actions naive*)

1: **procedure** $D\_A\_N_i(\{u_0, ..., u_n\}, Accs, Acts_i)$ ▷ Utility & acceptability functions
   of all agents, actions of $A_i(0 \leq i \leq n)$
2:    **if** $\exists acts \in \arg\max u_i \wedge \forall_{acc \in Accs} : acc(acts) = true$ **then**
3:        $best\_acceptable\_acts \leftarrow \bigcup_{acts \in \arg\max u_i} : \forall_{acc \in Accs} acc(acts) = true$
4:        **return** $Acts_i \cap first(acts_k \in best\_acceptable\_acts)$
5:    **else**
6:        **return** $Acts_i \cap first(\arg\max(aggregate(u'_0, ..., u'_n))$
7:    **end if**
8: **end procedure**

Note that in the context of the empathic agent algorithms, the function $first(set)$ turns the provided *set of tuples* into a *sequence of tuples* by sorting the elements in decreasing alphanumerical order and then returns the first element of the sequence. This enables a deterministic action tuple selection. Moreover, we construct a set of new utility functions $\{u'_0, ..., u'_n\}$ that assign all not acceptable action tuples a utility of *null* (Algorithm 2)[8]:

Algorithm 2. Helper function: new utility function based on u_i; all not acceptable action tuples yield utility of *null*.

1: **procedure** $u'_i(u_i, \{acts_0, ..., acts_n\}, accs)$
2:    $is\_acceptable \leftarrow \forall acc \in accs : acc(acts_i) = true$
3:    **if** $is\_acceptable$ **then**
4:        **return** $u_i(acts_i, ..., acts_n)$
5:    **else**
6:        **return** *null*
7:    **end if**
8: **end procedure**

In Algorithm 1, we specify that the agent picks the first item in the sequence of determined action tuples if it finds multiple optimal tuples of actions. Alternatively, the agent could employ one of the following approaches to select between the optimal action tuples:

---

[7] To facilitate readability, we switch to a pseudo-code notation for the following algorithms.

[8] We already use *null* to denote *impossible* action tuples. This implies an acceptable action tuple should always exists. To achieve a distinction, a value of $-\infty$ could be assigned.

- **Random.** The agent picks a random action tuple from the list of the tuples it determined as optimal. This would require empathic agents to use an additional protocol to agree on the action tuple that should be executed.
- **Utilitarian.** Among the action tuples that were determined as optimal, the agent picks the one that provides maximal combined utility for all agents and falls back to a random or first-in-sequence selection between action tuples if several of such tuples exist.

Still, the algorithm is somewhat naive, as agents that implement it will decide to execute suboptimal activities if the following conditions apply:

- Multiple agents find that the actions that optimize their individual utility are inconsistent with the actions that are optimal for at least one of the other agents.
- Multiple agents find that executing these *conflicting* actions is considered *acceptable*.
- Executing these *acceptable* actions generates a lower utility for both agents than optimizing the shared utility would.

Hence, we extend the algorithm so that the agent selects the tuple of actions that maximizes its own utility, but falls back to maximize shared utility if the utility-maximizing action tuple is either not acceptable, or would lead to a lower utility outcome than maximizing the shared utility, considering the other agent follows the same approach (Algorithm 3):

Algorithm 3. Lazy empathic agent algorithm: D_A_L (*determine actions lazy*)

1: **procedure** $D\_A\_L_i(\{u_0, ..., u_n\}, Accs)$ ▷ Utility & acceptability functions of all agents, actions of all agents $\{A_0, ..., A_n\}$
2:     $\{acts\_max_0, ..., acts\_max_n\} \leftarrow DETERMINE\_ACT\_MAX(u_i, Accs)$
3:     $\{good\_acts\_max_0, ..., good\_acts\_max_n\} \leftarrow \{$
4:         $DETERMINE\_GOOD\_ACTS\_MAX(u_0, Accs, acts\_max_0),$
5:         ...,
6:         $DETERMINE\_GOOD\_ACTS\_MAX(u_n, Accs, acts\_max_n),$
7:     $\}$
8:     **if** $good\_acts\_max_0 \cap ... \cap good\_acts\_max_n \neq \{\}$ **then**
9:         **return** $Acts_i \cap first(good\_acts\_max)$
10:     **else**
11:         **return** $Acts_i \cap first(\arg\max(aggregate(u'_0, ..., u'_n)))$
12:     **end if**
13: **end procedure**

Algorithm 3 calls two helper functions. Algorithm 4 determines *acceptable* action tuples that maximize a provided utility function u_i:

Algorithm 4. Helper function: determine acceptable action tuples that maximize utility function u_i

1: **procedure** DETERMINE_ACT_MAX(u_i, $Accs$)
2:     **return** $\bigcup_{acts \in \text{arg max } u_i}$ $: \forall_{acc \in Accs} acc(acts) = true$
3: **end procedure**

Algorithm 5 determines all action tuples that would maximize an agent's (A_i's) utility if this agent could *dictate* the actions of all other agents, given the action tuples provide a better utility for this agent than the action tuples that maximize all agents' combined utility, given all agents execute an action tuple that maximizes their own utility if they could dictate the other agents' actions. Note that Algorithm 5 makes use of the previously introduced algorithm (Algorithm 1):

Algorithm 5. Helper function: determines all maximizing action tuples that would still yield a good utility result for agent $A_i(0 \leq i \leq n)$, given all other agents also pick an action tuple that would maximize their own utility, if all other agents "played along".

1: **procedure** DETERMINE_GOOD_ACTS_MAX(u_i, $Accs$)
2:     **return** $\bigcup_{acts \in \text{arg max } u_i}$ $: \forall_{acc \in Accs} : acc(acts) = true \wedge$
3:         $u_i(\bigcup_{k=0}^{n} D\_A\_N_k(\{u_0, ..., u_n\}, Accs, acts))$
4:         $\geq u_i(acts\_max)$
5: **end procedure**

However, this algorithm only considers two types of action tuples for execution: action tuples that provide the maximal individual utility for the agent and action tuples that provide the maximal combined utility for all agents. Action tuples that do not maximize the agent's individual utility, but are still preferable over the action tuples that maximize the combined utility, remain unconsidered. Consequently, we call an agent that implements such an algorithm a *lazy* empathic agent. We extend the algorithm to also consider all action tuples that could possibly be relevant. I.e., if an action tuple is not considered acceptable, or if the tuple is considered acceptable but the agent chooses to not execute it, the agent falls back to the tuple of actions that provides the next best individual utility. We construct a function ne that returns the *Nash equilibria* based on the updated utility functions $\{u'_0, ..., u'_n\}$, considering we have a strategic game $\langle N, (A_i) \succsim_i \rangle$, with $N := \{A_0, ...A_n\}$, $A_i := Acts_{A_i}$, and $acts \succsim_i acts' := u'_i(acts) \geq u'_i(acts')$[9]. Then, we create the *full* empathic agent core algorithm $D\_A\_F_i$ for an agent A_i that takes the updated utility functions $\{u'_0, ..., u'_n\}$ and all agents' possible

---

[9] See the Nash equilibrium definition provided by Osborne and Rubinstein [19, p. 11 et sqq.].

actions as inputs $\{Acts_0, ..., Acts_n\}$. The algorithm determines the (first of) the
Nash equilibria that provide the highest shared utility and, if no Nash equilibrium exists, chooses the first tuple of actions that maximizes shared utility:

Algorithm 6. Full empathic agent algorithm: D_A_F (*determine actions full*)

1: **procedure** $D\_A\_F_i(\{u_0', ..., u_n'\}, \{Acts_0, ..., Acts_n\})$
2:     $equilibria \leftarrow ne(\{u_0', ..., u_n'\}, \{Acts_0, ..., Acts_n\})$
3:     **if** $equilibria \neq \{\}$ **then**
4:         $shared\_max\_equilibria \leftarrow acts^* \in equilibria :$
5:             $\forall acts \in equilibria :$
6:                 $(u_0'(acts^*) \times ... \times u_n'(acts^*)) \geq (u_0'(acts) \times ... \times u_n'(acts))$
7:         **return** $Acts_i \cap first(shared\_max\_equilibria)$
8:     **else**
9:         **return** $Acts_i \cap first(\arg\max(aggregate(u_0, ..., u_n))$
10:
11:     **end if**
12: **end procedure**

Going back to the selection between several action tuples that might be determined as optimal, it is now clear that a *deterministic* approach for selecting a final action tuple is preferable for both *lazy* and *full* empathic agents, as it avoids agents deciding upon executing action tuples that are not aligned with one another and lead to an unnecessary low utility outcome. Hence, we propose using a *utilitarian* approach with a first-in-sequence selection if the utilitarian approach is inconclusive[10].

The proposed agent can be considered a *rational agent* following the definition by Russel and Norvig in that it "acts so as to achieve the best outcome or, when there is uncertainty, the best expected outcome" [22, pp. 4–5] and an *artificially socially intelligent agent* as defined by Dautenhahn as it instantiates "human-style social intelligence" in that it "manage[s] the individual's [its own] interests in relationship to the interests of the social system of the next higher level" [13].

3   Running Examples

In this section, we present two simple running examples of empathic agents and describe the implementation of the examples in a general-purpose programming language (JavaScript).

---

[10] As state above, we assume that the $first$ function sorts the action tuples in a deterministic order before returning the first element.

3.1 Example 1: Vehicles

We provide a running example for the "vehicle/bottleneck" scenario introduced above. Consequently, we have a two-agent scenario $\{A, B\}$. Each agent has a utility function $u_{A,B} := Acts_A \times Acts_B \rightarrow \{-\infty, \mathbb{R}, \infty\}$. $Acts_A$ and $Acts_B$ are the possible actions A and B, respectively, can execute. To fully specify the utility functions, we follow the approach outlined above and first construct the actions-to-consequences mappings $a2c_A$ and $a2c_B$ for both agents. The possible actions are $Acts_A = \{drive_A, wait_A\}$ and $Acts_B = \{drive_B, wait_B\}$. I.e., $Acts = \{drive_A, wait_A, drive_B, wait_B\}$. To assess the consequences that include *waiting*, we assume B is twice as fast as A (without waiting, A needs 20 time units to pass the bottleneck while B needs 10)[11]:

$$
a2c_A(acts) := \begin{cases}
crash, & if : acts = (drive_A, drive_B); \\
wait\ 0, & if : acts = (drive_A, wait_B); \\
wait\ \infty, & if : acts = (wait_A, wait_B); \\
wait\ 10, & if : acts = (wait_A, drive_B); \\
null, & otherwise.
\end{cases}
$$

$$
a2c_B(acts) := \begin{cases}
crash, & if : acts = (drive_A, drive_B); \\
wait\ 20, & if : acts = (drive_A, wait_B); \\
wait\ \infty, & if : acts = (wait_A, wait_B); \\
wait\ 0, & if : acts = (wait_A, drive_B); \\
null, & otherwise.
\end{cases}
$$

We construct the following utility quantification functions and subtract an amount proportional to the waiting time from the utility value 1 of $wait\ 0$:

$$
u2c_A(consqs) := \begin{cases}
-\infty, & if : consqs = \{crash\}; \\
0.9, & if : consqs = \{wait\ 20\}; \\
0 & if : consqs = \{wait\ \infty\}; \\
1, & if : consqs = \{wait\ 0\}, \\
null, & otherwise.
\end{cases}
$$

$$
u2c_B(consqs) := \begin{cases}
-\infty, & if : consqs = \{crash\}; \\
0.8, & if : consqs = \{wait\ 20\}; \\
0, & if : consqs = \{wait\ \infty\}; \\
1, & if : consqs = \{wait\ 0\}; \\
null, & otherwise.
\end{cases}
$$

---

[11] $drive_A \wedge wait_A$ and $drive_B \wedge wait_B$, respectively, are mutually exclusive ($\{drive_A \oplus wait_A, drive_B \oplus wait_B\}$, with $A \oplus B := (A \vee B) \wedge \neg(A \wedge B)$). I.e., the functions return *null* if $drive_A \wedge wait_A \vee drive_B \wedge wait_B$.

Actions-to-consequences mappings and utility quantification functions can then be combined to utility functions:

$$u_A(acts) = \begin{cases} 1, & if : acts = (drive_A, wait_B); \\ 0.9, & if : acts = (wait_A, drive_B); \\ 0, & if : acts = (wait_A, wait_B); \\ -\infty, & if : acts = (drive_A, drive_B); \\ null, & otherwise. \end{cases}$$

$$u_B(acts) = \begin{cases} 0.8, & if : acts = (drive_A, wait_B); \\ 1, & if : acts = (wait_A, drive_B); \\ 0, & if : acts = (wait_A, wait_B); \\ -\infty, & if : acts = (drive_A, drive_B); \\ null, & otherwise. \end{cases}$$

We assume scenarios where both agents are *driving* or both agents are *waiting* are not acceptable by either agents and introduce the corresponding acceptability rules:

$acc_{A,B}(acts) :=$
$$\begin{cases} false, & if : acts = (drive_A, drive_B) \vee (wait_A \wedge wait_B); \\ null, & if : (drive_A \in acts \wedge wait_A \in acts) \vee (drive_B \in acts \wedge wait_B \in acts); \\ true, & otherwise. \end{cases}$$

Based on the utility functions (u_A, u_B), we create new utility functions (u'_A, u'_B) that consider the acceptability rules:

$$u'_A(acts) := \begin{cases} \frac{1}{2}, & if : acts = (drive_A, wait_B); \\ \frac{1}{3}, & if : acts = (wait_A, drive_B); \\ null, & otherwise. \end{cases}$$

$$u'_B(acts) := \begin{cases} 1, & if : acts = (wait_A, drive_B); \\ \frac{1}{3}, & if : acts = (drive_A, wait_B); \\ null, & otherwise. \end{cases}$$

Finally, we apply the empathic agent algorithms to our scenario. Using the *naive* algorithm, the agents apply the acceptability rules, but do not consider the other agent's strategy. Hence, both agents decide to *drive*, (and consequently *crash*).

$$D\_A\_N_A(\{u'_A, u'_B, \}, \{acc_A, acc_B\}, Acts_A) = drive_A$$
$$D\_A\_N_B(\{u'_A, u'_B, \}, \{acc_A, acc_B\}, Acts_B) = drive_B$$

The resulting utility is $-\infty$ for both agents. None of the two other algorithms (*lazy*, *full*) allows any agent to decide to execute an action tuple that does not optimize shared utility. I.e., both algorithms yield the same result:

$$D\_A\_L_A(\{u'_A, u'_B, \}, \{acc_A, acc_B\}, Acts_A) = wait_A$$
$$D\_A\_L_B(\{u'_A, u'_B, \}, \{acc_A, acc_B\}, Acts_B) = drive_B$$
$$D\_A\_F_A(\{u'_A, u'_B, \}, \{acc_A, acc_B\}, Acts_A) = wait_A$$
$$D\_A\_F_B(\{u'_A, u'_B, \}, \{acc_A, acc_B\}, Acts_B) = drive_B$$

The resulting utility is 0.9 for agent A and 1 for agent B. As can be seen, the difference between agent types is not always relevant. The following scenario will provide a distinctive outcome for all three agent variants.

3.2 Example 2: Concert

As a second example, we introduce the following scenario[12]. Two empathic agents $\{A, B\}$ plan to attend a concert of music by either *Bach*, *Stravinsky*, or *Mozart* ($Acts := \{Bach_A, Stravinsky_A, Mozart_A, Bach_B, Stravinsky_B, Mozart_B\}$). A considers the Bach and Mozart concerts of much greater pleasure when attended in company of B (*utility* of 6, respectively 3) and not alone (either concert: 1). In contrast, the Stravinsky concert yields good utility, even if A attends it alone (4). Attending it in company of B merely gives a utility bonus of 1 (total: 5). B prefers concerts in company of A as well (2 for Stravinsky and 4 for Mozart), but gains little additional utility from attending a Bach concert with A (1.1 with A versus 1 alone) because they dislike listening to A's Bach appraisals. Attending any concert alone yields a utility of 1 for B. As the utility is in this scenario largely derived from the subjective musical taste and social preferences of the agents and to keep the example concise, we skip the actions-to-consequences mapping and construct the utility functions right away[13]:

$$
u_A(acts) = \begin{cases}
null, & if: length(acts) \neq 2 \vee \\
 & length(set(Bach_A, Stravinsky_A, Mozart_A) \cap set(acts)) \neq 1 \vee \\
 & length(set(Bach_B, Stravinsky_B, Mozart_B) \cap set(acts)) \neq 1; \\
6, & else\ if: acts = (Bach_A, Bach_B); \\
5, & else\ if: acts = (Stravinsky_A, Stravinsky_B); \\
4, & else\ if: Stravinsky_A \in acts \wedge Stravinsky_B \notin acts; \\
3, & else\ if: acts = (Mozart_A, Mozart_B); \\
1, & otherwise.
\end{cases}
$$

$$
u_B(acts) = \begin{cases}
null, & if: length(acts) \neq 2 \vee \\
 & length(set(Bach_A, Stravinsky_A, Mozart_A) \cap set(acts)) \neq 1 \vee \\
 & length(set(Bach_B, Stravinsky_B, Mozart_B) \cap set(acts)) \neq 1; \\
1.1, & else\ if: acts = (Bach_A, Bach_B); \\
2, & else\ if: acts = (Stravinsky_A, Stravinsky_B); \\
4, & else\ if: acts = (Mozart_A, Mozart_B); \\
1, & otherwise.
\end{cases}
$$

We introduce the following acceptability function that applies to both agents (although it is of primary importance for agent A). As agent A is banned from the venue that hosts the Stravinsky concert, the action $Stravinsky_A$ is not acceptable:

$$
acc_{A,B}(acts) := \begin{cases}
false, & if: acts = Stravinsky_A \in acts; \\
true, & otherwise.
\end{cases}
$$

---

[12] The scenario is an adjusted and extended version of the "Bach or Stravinsky? (BoS)" example presented by Osborne and Rubinstein [19, pp. 15–16].

[13] Note that the if-condition that triggers the return of a *null* value simply defines that $Bach_A$, $Stravinsky_A$, and $Mozart_A$ are mutually exclusive, as are $Bach_B$, $Stravinsky_B$, and $Mozart_B$.

Considering the acceptability function, we create the following updated utility functions:

$$
u'_A(acts) = \begin{cases} null, & if : length(acts) \neq 2 \vee \\ & length(set(Bach_A, Stravinsky_A, Mozart_A) \cap set(acts)) \neq 1 \vee \\ & length(set(Bach_B, Stravinsky_B, Mozart_B) \cap set(acts)) \neq 1 \vee \\ & Stravinsky_B \in acts; \\ 6, & else\ if : acts = (Bach_A, Bach_B); \\ 4, & else\ if : Stravinsky_A \in acts; \\ 3, & else\ if : acts = (Mozart_A, Mozart_B); \\ 1, & otherwise. \end{cases}
$$

$$
u'_B(acts) = \begin{cases} null, & if : length(acts) \neq 2 \vee \\ & length(set(Bach_A, Stravinsky_A, Mozart_A) \cap set(acts)) \neq 1 \vee \\ & length(set(Bach_B, Stravinsky_B, Mozart_B) \cap set(acts)) \neq 1 \vee \\ & Stravinsky_B \in acts; \\ 1.1, & else\ if : acts = (Bach_A, Bach_B); \\ 4, & else\ if : acts = (Mozart_A, Mozart_B); \\ 1, & otherwise. \end{cases}
$$

Now, we can run the empathic agent algorithms. The *naive* algorithm returns *Bach* for agent A and *Mozart* for agent B:

$$
D\_A\_N_A(\{u'_A, u'_B,\}, \{acc_A, acc_B\}, Acts_A) = Bach_A
$$
$$
D\_A\_N_B(\{u'_A, u'_B,\}, \{acc_A, acc_B\}, Acts_B) = Mozart_B
$$

The resulting utility is 1 for both agents. The *lazy* algorithm returns *Mozart* for both agents:

$$
D\_A\_L_A(\{u'_A, u'_B,\}, \{acc_A, acc_B\}, Acts_A) = Mozart_A
$$
$$
D\_A\_L_B(\{u'_A, u'_B,\}, \{acc_A, acc_B\}, Acts_B) = Mozart_B
$$

The resulting utility is 3 for agent A and 4 for agent B. The *full* algorithm returns *Bach* for both agents:

$$
D\_A\_F_A(\{u'_A, u'_B,\}, \{acc_A, acc_B\}, Acts_A) = Bach_A
$$
$$
D\_A\_F_B(\{u'_A, u'_B,\}, \{acc_A, acc_B\}, Acts_B) = Bach_B
$$

The resulting utility is 6 for agent A and 1.1 for agent B.

3.3 JavaScript Implementation

We implemented the running examples in JavaScript[14]. As a basis for the implementation, we created a simple framework that consists of the following components:

– **Web socket server: environment and communications manager.** The environment and communications interface is implemented by a web socket server that consists of the following components:

---

[14] The code, as well as documentation and tests, are available at http://s.cs.umu.se/qxgbfi.

- **Environment and communications manager.** The web server provides a generic environment and communications manager that relays messages between agents and provides the shared value system of acceptability rules.
  - **Environment specification.** The environment specification contains scenario-specific information and enables the server to determine and propagate the utility rewards to the agents.
- **Web socket clients: empathic agents.** The empathic agents are implemented as web socket clients that interact via the server described above. Each agent consists of the following two components:
  - **Generic empathic agent library.** The generic empathic agent library provides a function to create an empathic agent object with the properties *ID*, *utilityMappings*, *acceptabilityRules*, and *type* (*naive*, *lazy*, or *full*). The empathic agent object is then equipped with an action determination function that implements the empathic agent algorithm as described above.
  - **Agent specifications.** The agent specification consists of the scenario-specific information of all agents in the environment, as well as of the current agents' identifier and type (*naive*, *lazy*, or *full*) and is used to instantiate a specific empathic agent. Note that in the implementation, we construct the utility functions right away and do not use actions-to-consequences mappings.

The implementation assumes that the specifications provided to both agents agents and to the server is consistent. Figure 1 depicts the architecture of the empathic agent JavaScript implementation for the *vehicle* scenario. We chose JavaScript as the language for implementing the scenario to show how to implement basic empathic agents using a popular general-purpose programing language, but concede that a more powerful implementation in the context of MAS frameworks like Jason is of value.

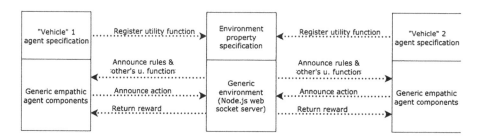

Fig. 1. Empathic intelligent: architecture

4   Reasoning-Loop Architecture

We create a reasoning-loop architecture for the empathic agent and again assume a two-agent scenario to simplify the description. The architecture consists of the following components:

- **Empathic agent (EA).** The empathic agent is the system's top-level component. It has three generic components (*observer*, *negotiator*, and *interactor*) and five dynamically generated functions/objects (*utility function* and *acceptability function* of both agents, as well as a formalized model of the *shared system of values*).
- **Target agent (TA).** In the simplest scenario, the empathic agent interacts with exactly one other agent (the *target agent*), which is modeled as a black box. Pre-existing knowledge about the target agent can be part of the models the empathic agent has of the target agent's utility and acceptability functions.
- **Shared system of values.** The shared system of values allows comparing the utility functions of the agents and creating their acceptability functions, as well as their actions-to-consequences mappings and utility quantification functions, from which the utility functions are derived.
- **Utility function.** Based on the actions-to-consequences mappings and utility quantification functions, each empathic agent maintains its own utility function, as well as models of the utility function of the agent it is interacting with.
- **Acceptability function.** Based on the shared system of values, the agent derives the acceptability functions (as described above) to then incorporate them into updated utility functions, which it feeds into the empathic agent algorithm to determine the best possible tuple of actions.
- **Observer.** The observer component scans the environment, registers other agents, *receives* their utility functions, and also keeps the agent's own functions updated. To construct and update the utility and acceptability functions without explicitly receiving them, the observer could make use of inverse reinforcement learning methods, as for example described by [10].
- **Negotiator.** The negotiator identifies and resolves conflicts of interests using the *acceptability function* models and instructs the interactor to engage with other agents if necessary, in particular, to propose a solution for a conflict of interest, or to resolve the conflict immediately (depending on the level of confidence that the solution is indeed acceptable). The negotiator could make use of argument-based negotiation (see e.g.: [3]).
- **Interactor.** The interactor component interacts with the agent's environment and in particular with the target agent to work towards the conflict resolution. The means of communication is domain-specific and not covered by the generic architecture.

Figure 2 presents a simple graphical model of the empathic agent's reasoning loop architecture.

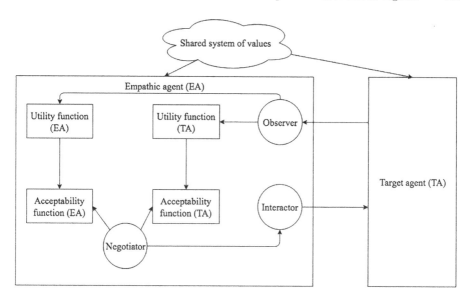

Fig. 2. Empathic intelligent: architecture

5 Alignment with BDI Architecture and Possible Implementation with Jason

Our architecture reflects the common belief-desire-intention (BDI) model as based on [7] to some extent:

- If a priori available to both agents in the forms of rules or norms, *beliefs*, and *belief sets* are part of the shared value system. Otherwise, they qualify the agents' utility and acceptability functions directly. In contrast, *desires* define the objective(s) towards which an agent's utility function is optimized and are–while depending on beliefs–not directly mutable through persuasive argumentation between the agents.
- Intentions are the tuples of actions the agents choose to execute.
- As it strives for simplicity, our architecture does for now not distinguish between desires and goals, and intentions and plans, respectively.

We expect to improve the alignment of our framework with the BDI architecture to facilitate the integration with existing BDI-based theories and implementation using BDI frameworks. The Jason platform for multi-agent system development [6] can serve as the basis for implementing the empathic agent. While simplified running examples of our architecture can be implemented with Jason, extending the platform to provide an empathic agent-specific abstraction layer would better support complex scenarios.

6   Discussion

In this section, we place our empathic agent concepts into the context of existing work, highlight potential applications, analyze limitations, and outline future work.

6.1   Similar Conflict Resolution Approaches

Our empathic agent can be considered a generic and basic agent model that can draw upon a large body of existing research on multi-agent learning and nego-tiation techniques for possible extensions. A survey of research on agents that model other agents is provided by Albrecht and Stone [1]. The idea of combining a utility-based approach with acceptability rules to emulate *empathic* behavior is to our knowledge novel. However, a somewhat similar concept is presented by Black and Atkinson, who propose an argumentation-based approach for an agent that can find agreement with one other agent on acceptable actions and can develop a model of the other agent's preferences over time [5]. While Black's and Atkinson's approach is similar in that it reflects Coplan's definition of empathy (it maintains "a process through which [it] simulates another's situated psycho-logical states, while maintaining clear self–other differentiation" [12]) to some extent we identify the following key differences:

– The approach is limited to a two-agent scenario.
– The agent model is preference-based and not utility-based. While this has the advantage that it does not require reducing complex preferences to a simple numeric value, it makes it harder to combine with existing learning concepts (see below).
– The agent has the ability to learn another agent's preferences over time. How-ever, the learning concept is–according to Black and Atkinson–"not intended to be complete" [5]. We suggest that while our empathic agent does not pro-vide learning capabilities by default, it has the advantage that its utility-based concept allows for integration with established inverse reinforcement learning algorithms (see: Subsect. 6.4).
– The agent Black and Atkinson introduce is not *empathic* in that it tries to compromise with the other agent, but rather uses its ability to model the agent's preferences to improve its persuasive capabilities by tailoring the arguments it provides to this agent.

6.2   Potential Real-World Use Cases

In this chapter, we exemplified the empathic agent with two simple scenarios, with the primary purpose of better explaining our agent's core concepts. These scenarios do not fully reflect real-world use cases. However, the core concepts of the agent can form the basis of solutions for real-world applications. Below, we provide a non-exhaustive list of use case types empathic agents could potentially address:

– **Handling aspects of traffic navigation scenarios that cannot be covered by static rules.** Besides adjusting the assertiveness levels to the preferences of their drivers, as suggested by Sikkenk and Terken [23], and Yusof et al. [26], autonomous vehicles could consider the driving style of other human- or agent-controlled vehicles to improve traffic flow, for example by adjusting speed or lane-changing behavior according to the (perceived) utility functions of all traffic participants or to resolve unexpected incidents (in particular emergencies).
– **Mitigating negative effects of large-scale web applications on their users.** Evidence exists that suggests the well-being of *passive* (mainly content-consuming) users of social media is frequently negatively impacted by technology, while the well-being of at least some users, who actively engage with others through the technology, improves [20]. To facilitate social media use that is positive for the users' well-being, an empathic agent could serve as a mediator between user needs (social inclusion) and the business goals of the technology provider (often: maximization of advertisement revenue).
– **Decreasing the negotiation overhead for agent-based manufacturing systems.** Autonomous agent-based manufacturing systems are an emerging alternative to traditional, hierarchically managed control architectures [16]. While agent-based systems are considered to increase the agility of manufacturing processes, one disadvantage of agent-based manufacturing systems is the need for negotiation between agents and the resulting overhead (see for example: Bruccoleri et al. [8]). Employing empathic agents in agent-based manufacturing scenarios can possibly help solve conflicts of interests efficiently.
– **Improving persuasive healthcare technology.** Persuasive technology– "computerized software or information system designed to reinforce, change or shape attitudes or behaviours or both without using coercion or deception" [18]–is frequently applied in healthcare scenarios [11], in particular, to facilitate behavior change. Persuasive functionality is typically implemented using recommender systems [14], which in general struggle to compromise between system provider and end-user needs [21]. This can be considered as a severe limitation in healthcare scenarios, where trade-offs between serving public health needs (optimizing for a low burden on the healthcare system) and empowering patients (allowing for a subjective assessment of health impact, as well as for unhealthy choices to support individual freedom) need to be made. Hence, employing the empathic agent concepts in this context can be considered a promising endeavor.

6.3   Limitations

The purpose of this chapter is to introduce *empathic agents* as a general concept. When working towards a practically applicable empathic agent, the following limitations of our work need to be taken into account:

– The agent is designed to act in a fully observable world, which is an unrealistic assumption for real-world use cases. For better applicability, the agent needs to support probabilistic models of the environment, the other agents, and the shared value system.

- Our formal empathic agent description is logic-based. Integrating it with Markov decision process-based inverse reinforcement learning approaches is a non-trivial endeavor, although certainly possible.
- In the example scenarios we provided, all agents are identically implemented empathic agents. An empathic agent that interacts with non-empathic agents will need to take into account further game-theoretic considerations and to have negotiation capabilities.
- The presented empathic agent concepts use a simple numeric value to represent the utility an agent receives as a consequence of the execution of an action tuple. While this approach is commonly employed when designing utility-based autonomous agents, it is an oversimplification that can potentially limit the applicability of the agent.
- Software engineering and technological aspects of empathic agents need to be further investigated. In particular, the implementation of an empathic agent library using a higher-level framework for multi-agent system development, as we discuss in Sect. 5 could provide a more powerful engineering framework for empathic agents.

6.4   Future Work

We suggest the following research to address the limitations presented in Subsect. 6.3:

- So far, we have chosen a logic-based approach to the problem in focus to allow for a minimalistic problem description with low complexity. Alternatively, the problem could be approached from a *reinforcement learning* perspective (see for an overview of multi-agent reinforcement learning: [9]). Using (partially observable) Markov decision processes, one can introduce a well-established temporal and probabilistic perspective[15]. A key capability our empathic agent needs to have is the ability to learn the utility function of other agents. A comprehensive body of research on enabling this ability by applying *inverse reinforcement learning* exists (for example: [10,17]). Hence, creating a Markovian perspective on the empathic agent to enable the application of reinforcement learning methods for the observational learning of the utility functions of other agents can be considered relevant future work.
- To better assess the applicability of the empathic agent algorithms, it is important to analyze its computational complexity in general, as well as to evaluate it in the context of specific use cases that might allow for performance-improving adjustments.
- To enable empathic agents to reach consensus in case of inconsistent beliefs argumentation-based negotiation approaches can be applied that consider uncertainty and subjectivity (e.g. [15]) for creating solvers for finding compromises between utility/acceptability functions. Similar approaches can be

---

[15] However, the same can be achieved with temporal and probabilistic logic.

used to enhance utility quantification capabilities by considering preferences and probabilistic beliefs.
– The design intention of the architectural framework we present in Sect. 4 is to form a high-level abstraction of an empathic agent that is to some extent agnostic of the concepts the different components implement. We are confident that the framework can be applied in combination with existing technologies to create a real-world applicable empathic agent framework, at least for use cases that allow making some assumptions regarding the interaction context and protocol.
– The ultimate goal of this research is to apply the concept in a real-world scenario and evaluate to what extent the application of empathic agents provides practically relevant benefits.

7   Conclusion

In this chapter, we introduced the concept of an *empathic agent* that proactively identifies potential conflicts of interests in interactions with other agents and uses a mixed utility-based/rule-based approach to find a mutually acceptable solution. The theoretical framework can serve as a general purpose model, from which advanced implementations can be derived to develop socially intelligent systems that consider other agents' (and ultimately humans') welfare when interacting with their environment. The example implementation, the reasoning-loop architecture we introduced for our empathic agent, and the discussion of how the agent can be implemented with a belief-desire-intention approach provide first insights into how a more generally capable empathic agent can be constructed. As the most important future research steps to advance the empathic agent, we regard the conceptualization and implementation of an empathic agent with learning capabilities, as well as the development of a first simple empathic agent that solves a particular real-world problem.

Acknowledgments. We thank the anonymous reviewers for their constructive critical feedback. This work was partially supported by the Wallenberg AI, Autonomous Systems and Software Program (WASP) funded by the Knut and Alice Wallenberg Foundation.

References

1. Albrecht, S.V., Stone, P.: Autonomous agents modelling other agents: a comprehensive survey and open problems. Artif. Intell. **258**, 66–95 (2018)
2. Alshabi, W., Ramaswamy, S., Itmi, M., Abdulrab, H.: Coordination, cooperation and conflict resolution in multi-agent systems. In: Sobh, T. (ed.) Innovations and Advanced Techniques in Computer and Information Sciences and Engineering, pp. 495–500. Springer, Dordrecht (2007). https://doi.org/10.1007/978-1-4020-6268-1_87

3. Amgoud, L., Dimopoulos, Y., Moraitis, P.: A unified and general framework for argumentation-based negotiation. In: Proceedings of the 6th International Joint Conference on Autonomous Agents and Multiagent Systems, AAMAS, pp. 158:1–158:8. ACM, New York (2007)
4. Berinsky, A.J.: Rumors and health care reform: experiments in political misinformation. Br. J. Polit. Sci. **47**(2), 241–262 (2017)
5. Black, E., Atkinson, K.: Choosing persuasive arguments for action. In: The 10th International Conference on Autonomous Agents and Multiagent Systems-Volume 3, pp. 905–912. International Foundation for Autonomous Agents and Multiagent Systems (2011)
6. Bordini, R.H., Hübner, J.F.: BDI agent programming in agentspeak using *jason*. In: Toni, F., Torroni, P. (eds.) CLIMA 2005. LNCS (LNAI), vol. 3900, pp. 143–164. Springer, Heidelberg (2006). https://doi.org/10.1007/11750734_9
7. Bratman, M.: Intention, Plans, and Practical Reason. Center for the Study of Language and Information, Stanford (1987)
8. Bruccoleri, M., Nigro, G.L., Perrone, G., Renna, P., Diega, S.N.L.: Production planning in reconfigurable enterprises and reconfigurable production systems. CIRP Ann. **54**(1), 433–436 (2005)
9. Busoniu, L., Babuska, R., De Schutter, B.: A comprehensive survey of multiagent reinforcement learning. IEEE Trans. Syst. Man Cybern. Part C **38**(2), 156–172 (2008)
10. Chajewska, U., Koller, D., Ormoneit, D.: Learning an agent's utility function by observing behavior. In: ICML, pp. 35–42 (2001)
11. Conroy, D.E., Yang, C.H., Maher, J.P.: Behavior change techniques in top-ranked mobile apps for physical activity. Am. J. Prev. Med. **46**(6), 649–652 (2014)
12. Coplan, A.: Will the real empathy please stand up? A case for a narrow conceptualization. South. J. Philos. **49**(s1), 40–65 (2011)
13. Dautenhahn, K.: The art of designing socially intelligent agents: science, fiction, and the human in the loop. Appl. Artif. Intell. **12**(7–8), 573–617 (1998)
14. Hors-Fraile, S., et al.: Analyzing recommender systems for health promotion using a multidisciplinary taxonomy: a scoping review. Int. J. Med. Inform. **114**, 143–155 (2018)
15. Marey, O., Bentahar, J., Khosrowshahi-Asl, E., Sultan, K., Dssouli, R.: Decision making under subjective uncertainty in argumentation-based agent negotiation. J. Ambient Intell. Humanized Comput. **6**(3), 307–323 (2015)
16. Monostori, L., Váncza, J., Kumara, S.: Agent-based systems for manufacturing. CIRP Ann. **55**(2), 697–720 (2006)
17. Ng, A.Y., Russell, S.J., et al.: Algorithms for inverse reinforcement learning. In: ICML, pp. 663–670 (2000)
18. Oinas-Kukkonen, H., Harjumaa, M.: Towards deeper understanding of persuasion in software and information systems. In: 2008 First International Conference on Advances in Computer-Human Interaction, pp. 200–205. IEEE (2008)
19. Osborne, M.J., Rubinstein, A.: A Course in Game Theory. MIT Press, Cambridge (1994)
20. Philippe, V., Oscar, Y., Maxime, R., John, J., Ethan, K.: Do social network sites enhance or undermine subjective well-being? A critical review. Soc. Issues Policy Rev. **11**(1), 274–302 (2017)
21. Ricci, F., Rokach, L., Shapira, B.: Recommender systems: introduction and challenges. In: Ricci, F., Rokach, L., Shapira, B. (eds.) Recommender Systems Handbook, pp. 1–34. Springer, Boston (2015). https://doi.org/10.1007/978-1-4899-7637-6_1

22. Russell, S.J., Norvig, P.: Artificial Intelligence: A Modern Approach. Pearson Education Limited, Malaysia (2016)
23. Sikkenk, M., Terken, J.: Rules of conduct for autonomous vehicles. In: Proceedings of the 7th International Conference on Automotive User Interfaces and Interactive Vehicular Applications, AutomotiveUI 2015, pp. 19–22. ACM, New York (2015)
24. Von Neumann, J., Morgenstern, O.: Theory of games and economic behavior. Bull. Amer. Math. Soc. **51**(7), 498–504 (1945)
25. Wojdynski, B.W., Bang, H.: Distraction effects of contextual advertising on online news processing: an eye-tracking study. Behav. Inf. Technol. **35**(8), 654–664 (2016)
26. Yusof, N.M., Karjanto, J., Terken, J., Delbressine, F., Hassan, M.Z., Rauterberg, M.: The exploration of autonomous vehicle driving styles: preferred longitudinal, lateral, and vertical accelerations. In: Proceedings of the 8th International Conference on Automotive User Interfaces and Interactive Vehicular Applications, AutomotiveUI 2016, pp. 245–252. ACM, New York (2016)

Dynamic Global Behaviour of Online Routing Games

László Z. Varga$^{(\boxtimes)}$ (iD)

Faculty of Informatics, ELTE Eötvös Loránd University, Budapest 1117, Hungary
lzvarga@inf.elte.hu
http://people.inf.elte.hu/lzvarga

Abstract. In order to ensure global behaviour of decentralized multi-agent systems, we have to have a clear understanding of the issue of equilibrium over time. Convergence to the static equilibrium is an important question in the evolutionary dynamics of multi-agent systems. The evolutionary dynamics is usually investigated in repeated games which capture the evolutionary dynamics between games. The evolutionary dynamics within a game is investigated in online routing games. It is not known if online routing games converge to the static equilibrium or not. The progress beyond the state-of-the-art is that we introduce the notion of intertemporal equilibrium in the study of the evolutionary dynamics of games, we define quantitative values to measure the intertemporal equilibrium, we use these quantitative values to evaluate a realistic scenario, and we give an insight into the influence of intertemporal expectations of the agents on the intertemporal equilibrium. An interesting result is that the prediction service, which is engineered into the environment of the multi-agent system as a novel type of coordination artifact, greatly influences the global behaviour of the multi-agent system. The main contribution of our work is a better understanding of the engineering process of the intertemporal behaviour of multi-agent systems.

Keywords: Agent-based and multi-agent systems ·
Agent theories and models · Coordination artifacts ·
Environment engineering

1 Introduction

Many information technology applications include several autonomous agents which make decentralised decisions. In order to be able to define and measure design criteria, designers need formal models. Currently the best model of multi-agent decision making is based on game theory [15]. The designers prefer multi-agent systems with an equilibrium, because none of the agents has an incentive to

This work was carried out in the project EFOP-3.6.3-VEKOP-16-2017-00001: Talent Management in Autonomous Vehicle Control Technologies – The Project is supported by the Hungarian Government and co-financed by the European Social Fund.

© Springer Nature Switzerland AG 2019
D. Weyns et al. (Eds.): EMAS 2018 Workshops, LNAI 11375, pp. 202–221, 2019.
https://doi.org/10.1007/978-3-030-25693-7_11

deviate from the equilibrium, therefore the equilibrium seems to be a stable and predictable state of the system. If the equilibrium meets the design criteria, then we can ensure global behaviour of the multi-agent system. Therefore ensuring the equilibrium is an important part of the engineering process of the multi-agent systems.

However the classic game theory models assume an idealistic situation: all the agents know what the equilibrium is, all the agents know what other agents do, and all the agents know what their role is in the equilibrium. In accordance with the basic theory of multi-agent systems [29], the agent behaviour goes in cycles: the agents perceive their environment (possibly communicating with other agents), decide what action to perform, and then perform the action. Can we be sure that multi-agent systems go to the equilibrium through these feedback cycles and stay in the equilibrium?

The classic game theory models describe static situations, while agent behaviour involves time. The time aspect is usually investigated in evolutionary game theory, where the (kind of static) game is repeated and the agents base their decisions on their experiences in the previous games. However many real world applications are *continuously evolving games*: agents join the game in a sequence, they influence the game for a while, and then they quit the game. In these games, the decisions of the agents are often *intertemporal choices*: the current decision of the agent may affect the utility of the agents in the future. The equilibrium of such evolving games is the *intertemporal equilibrium*. We want to use the concept of intertemporal equilibrium to characterise the global behaviour of decentralized, large-scale and open multi-agent systems.

Intertemporal equilibrium [9] has two interpretations in economic theory. One interpretation is related to the intertemporal aspect of the choice, e.g. is it better to spend now or is it better to save now and spend later. In this approach, the critical point is the expectations of the agents. The other interpretation is related to the temporal aspect of the equilibrium: at any given time, the economy is in disequilibrium, and the equilibrium can be interpreted only in the long term. In this chapter, we focus on the latter interpretation, and we take into account that agents have intertemporal expectations.

In order to study this complex behaviour, we take the large-scale and open multi-agent system of the road traffic application area, and in particular the *online routing problem*. The online routing problem is a network with traffic flows going from a source node to a destination node. The agents of the traffic flows continuously enter the network at the sources, they choose a full route to the destination of their trip, and quit the network at the destination. The subsequent agents of the same traffic flow may choose different routes, depending on the current status of the network. The traffic is routed in a congestion sensitive manner.

We contribute to the state-of-the-art with the following results: we introduce the notion of intertemporal equilibrium in online routing games, we define quantitative values to measure the intertemporal equilibrium, we use these quantitative values to investigate a realistic scenario, and we evaluate how the intertemporal expectations of the agents influence the intertemporal equilibrium. We point out that these aspects are important parts of the engineering process of large-scale multi-agent systems, namely they are part of the environment engineering process [14]. The implementation of the prediction service of the intention-aware online routing game model [18] can be a new type of coordination artifact that predicts the expected future state of the environment.

In Sect. 2, we shortly overview related work on convergence of games to the equilibrium. In Sect. 3, we shortly discuss the available multi-agent engineering concepts to implement the support for convergence to the equilibrium. In Sect. 4, we shortly describe two methods that can be built into the environment of the multi-agent system to handle the expectations of the agents in online routing games. In Sect. 5, we describe a realistic scenario for our investigations. In Sect. 6, we define the measurement of intertemporal equilibrium. In Sect. 7, we evaluate the realistic scenario. In Sect. 8, we present and analyse an artificial scenario to highlight the advantages and disadvantages of the two prediction methods for the global behaviour of the multi-agent system. Finally, we conclude the chapter in Sect. 9.

2   Related Work on Convergence to the Equilibrium

The *static equilibrium* is an important concept of game theory. Algorithmic game theory [13] investigated the routing problem where decentralised autonomous decision making is applied by the traffic flows. This game theory model is in line with the assumption of the traffic engineers, who assume that the traffic is always assigned in accordance with the static equilibrium [1,25]. The potential function is used to prove the existence of equilibria, and an upper limit on the price of anarchy is also proved [16]. In the routing game, the decisions are on the flow level, i.e. a flow is an agent.

The *evolutionary dynamics* of games is usually investigated in repeated games where the agents receive feedback by observing their own and other agents' actions and utility, and in the next game they change their own actions based on these observations. The potential function method is extended to prove that the repeated routing game, with the above mentioned feedback, converges to the static equilibrium [8,17]. Another type of feedback is used in *regret minimisation*, where agents compare their actually experienced utility with the best possible utility in retrospect. It is proved that if the agents of the routing game select actions to minimize their regret, then their behaviour converges to the static equilibrium [2]. The acyclicity concept is also important for proving the convergence to the static equilibrium in repeated finite games [7,12]. The repeated game approach captures the evolutionary dynamic between routing games, but not within the routing game.

The *deterministic queuing model* is an approximation to investigate how traffic flows evolve over time. In the queuing model, each edge consists of a queue followed by a link which has a constant delay and a maximum capacity. The cost of the edge is the waiting time in the queue plus the constant delay. The speed of the growth of the queue of the edge is proportional to the difference between the inflow to the edge and the maximum capacity of the edge. The Nash flows over time in non-atomic queuing networks is characterised and several bounds on the price of anarchy are proved in [11]. It is shown in [6] that single source fluid queuing networks reach a steady state in finite time if the inflow does not exceed the capacity of the network. It is shown in [10] that Nash equilibrium is not guaranteed in atomic queuing networks with FIFO policies. The queuing model does not have usage dependent cost of the edges if the queue is empty and the inflow is below the maximum capacity, because in this flow range the edge has a constant delay. The queuing model has a kind of usage dependent cost of the edges only when the inflow exceeds the maximum capacity of the edges. However, above the maximum-capacity flow, the queue grows to infinity over time at constant inflow. Therefore the queuing model is not a complete extension of the static routing game to the time dimension.

The appropriate extension of the static routing game to the time dimension is the online routing game model. The online routing game model has both the concept of the maximum capacity and the inflow dependent delays below the maximum capacity. Therefore, the online routing game describes the usage dependent cost of the edges in all flow ranges. The online routing game model may comprise other important aspects as well: intention-awareness and intention aware prediction. These are not investigated in the queuing model.

The evolutionary dynamic inside the routing game is captured by the *online routing game* model [19], where the traffic flow is made up of individual agents who follow each other, and the agents of the traffic flow decide individually on their actions based on the real-time situation. The reader is referred to the openly accessible article [18] for the formal description of the online routing game model. In short, the online routing game model is the sextuple $<t, T, G, c, r, k>$, where $t = \{1, 2, ...\}$ is a sequence of time steps, T time steps give one time unit (e.g. one minute), G is a directed multi-graph representing the road network, c is the cost function of G with $c_e : R^+ \to R^+$ for each edge e of G, r is a vector of flows, and $k = (k^1, k^2, ...)$ is a sequence of decision vectors $k^t = (k^t_1, k^t_2, ...)$ made in time step t. Edges have FIFO property, and there is a minimum following distance on the edges which corresponds to the maximum capacity.

In online routing games, the agents may have to make intertemporal decisions, because they may have to take into account what the expected traffic will be by the time they get to a given road. Selecting different routes involves different future points of time. The future traffic might be completely different from the currently observed real-time situation.

It is proved [19] that if the agents of the online routing game try to maximise their utility computed from the real-time situation (without taking into account any expectation), then equilibrium is not guaranteed, although a static equilibrium exists. "Single flow intensification" may also happen when agents subsequently entering the online routing game select alternative faster routes, and they catch up with the agents already on route, and this way they cause congestion. All-in-all, sometimes the online routing game may produce strange behaviour [20], and sometimes the agents may be worse off by exploiting real-time information than without exploiting real-time information.

In order to facilitate the agents to make predictions and include future conditions in their decisions, intention-aware prediction methods were proposed. In the intention-aware prediction methods, the agents communicate their intentions to a service. The service aggregates the data about the agent collective, and it sends a feedback to the agents [4]. The *intention-aware* [26] and the *intention propagation* [5] approaches are based on this scheme. The coordination mechanism provided by these schemes can scale with the complexity of real-world application domains.

The online routing game model was extended [18] to include intention-aware prediction. When an agent has made a decision on its planned route, then it sends its selected intention to the service. The service forecasts future traffic conditions. The prediction is based on the current situation and the intentions of the agents. The service provides the forecasts back to those agents who are still planning their action, and these agents use this information to make decision, and when they have made a decision, then they also communicate their intention to the service.

The navigation applications like Google Maps (http://maps.google.com/), Waze (http://waze.com), TomTom (http://www.tomtom.com), etc. know the intentions of the agents they serve, and they could use this information to make predictions. They could exactly tell what would happen in the near future if the agents that receive the routing plan from these applications exactly followed these plans.

It is proved [18] that there is no guarantee on the equilibrium, even if intention-aware prediction is applied, and in some networks and in some cases the agents may be worse off by exploiting real-time information and prediction than without. However, it is proved [21] that in a small but complex enough network of the Braess paradox [3], where there is only one source–destination pair, the agents might just slightly be worse off in the worst case with real-time data and prediction. It is also proved [23] that in the network of [21], the system converges to the static equilibrium within a relatively small threshold. The conjecture in [22] says that the system converges to the static equilibrium in bigger networks as well, if simultaneous decision making is prevented. This conjecture neither has been proved nor refuted analytically.

3   Multi-agent System Engineering Aspects

As the overview in the previous section says, the classic models assume that all the agents know of everything in the game, or at least they can observe every action and utility in the game. This is not realistic for large-scale and open multi-agent systems. In order to facilitate the coordination among many agents, the intention-aware online routing game model introduces the notion of a prediction service. We have to find the proper place in the multi-agent system engineering landscape for the implementation of such service.

The above models have in common that the goal of the agents is to maximise their expected utility according to the information available to them, so the key is the information sharing among the agents. Researchers discovered that the environment needs to be a first-order abstraction in the software engineering process in order to be able to use it as a robust shared memory, and as a medium for indirect coordination of agents [28]. The notion of artifact is introduced as an abstract building block for modelling and engineering environments. The artifacts are classified into three categories: resource, coordination and organisation artifacts. Coordination artifacts were used to control automatic guided vehicles [27]: the agents coordinate by putting marks in the environment, and by observing marks from other agents. The conclusion of [21] says that the intention-aware prediction service of online routing games establishes a kind of coordination among the agents, because the excessive swing of the system caused by the utilisation of real-time information is reduced. However, we cannot clearly say that the prediction service is a coordination artifact like the classical coordination artifacts, such as mutual exclusion and synchronisation operations.

The environmental artifact concept is further developed into the notion of environment programming of multi-agent systems [14] which means that the environment is part of the software system to be designed. This way the environment is used to design and program that part of the system which is functional to the agents' work, and the agents may adapt the environmental artifacts to better fit their needs. The main aspects of the model for environment programming are the action model (how the agents can change the state of the environment), the perception model (how the agents can perceive the environment), the environment computational model (how to program environment functionalities), the environment data model (the data interface between the agents and the environment), and the environment distribution model (how to handle the distributed structure of the environment).

The prediction service of online routing games is an extension of the perception model into the time dimension: it enables the agents to "perceive" the expected future state of the environment. The coordination is achieved through this extended perception capability. The online routing game involves intertemporal decisions, and the prediction service helps the coordination of the agents by computing the expected future state of the environment. Therefore the prediction service is a novel kind of coordination artifact, and it achieves coordination by enriching the perception model with intertemporal characteristics.

The work presented in this chapter focuses on environmental programming, and it helps to better understand how intertemporal perception models can influence the dynamic behaviour of multi-agent systems. We are not focusing on the implementation language, rather we focus on two prediction methods and their empirical evaluations.

4   Intention-Aware Prediction Methods

The formal description of the algorithms of two intention-aware prediction methods were presented at [24]: the detailed prediction method and the simple prediction method.

The *detailed prediction method* takes into account all the intentions already submitted to the service, then it computes what will happen in the future if the agents execute the plans assigned by these intentions, and then it computes for each route in the network the predicted travel time by taking into account the predicted future travel times for each road of the route. The prediction algorithm used in [26] is close to this detailed prediction method, but the main difference is that the prediction algorithm of [26] uses probabilistic values, while the detailed prediction method is deterministic.

The *simple prediction method* also takes into account all the intentions already submitted to the service, and then it computes what will happen in the future if the agents execute the plans assigned by these intentions. However when the simple prediction method computes for each route in the network the predicted travel time, then it takes into account only that travel time prediction for each road which was computed at the last intention submission. This way, the simple prediction method needs a little bit less computation. The simple prediction method is a kind of approximation and does not try to be an exact prediction of the future. As time goes by, if no new prediction is generated for a road, then the simple prediction method "evaporates" the last prediction for that road, like the bio-inspired technique of [5].

5   Experimental Set-up

In order to investigate empirically the intertemporal equilibrium, a region of Budapest (shown in Fig. 1) was modelled in the simulation software of [19]. The figure shows the route choices towards the destination *Rákóczi* bridge (E in the figure) as proposed by the navigation software. There are two sources: the suburban area (A in the figure) and the intercity road (B in the figure). Both trips ($A-E$ and $B-E$) have basically the same two choices between points C and D: the north (grey in the figure) and the south (blue in the figure) paths.

The road lengths are: $(A, C) = 1.4$ km, $(B, C) = 1.0$ km, $(C, D)_{north} = 4.0$ km, $(C, D)_{south} = 6.8$ km, and $(D, E) = 1.2$ km. Assuming that the cars can travel at speed 40 km/h on an empty road, the minimum travel time in minutes (fixed part of the cost function) for the roads is 1.5 times the distance. Information on the traffic flow going on these roads can be obtained from the web site[1] of the Hungarian Public Road Non-profit PLC. The variable part of the travel time is $roadlength * flow \div 10$, thus the cost functions of the roads are shown in Eq. 1, where the cost is in *minute* and the traffic flow is in $car \div minute$.

---

[1] http://internet.kozut.hu/Lapok/forgalomszamlalas.aspx.

$$c_{(A,C)}(flow) = 2.1 + 1.4 * flow \div 10$$
$$c_{(B,C)}(flow) = 1.5 + 1.0 * flow \div 10$$
$$c_{(C,D)_{north}}(flow) = 6.0 + 4.0 * flow \div 10 \qquad (1)$$
$$c_{(C,D)_{south}}(flow) = 10.2 + 6.8 * flow \div 10$$
$$c_{(D,E)}(flow) = 1.8 + 1.2 * flow \div 10$$

The experiment simulates a 90 min long rush hour period extended with a 17 min initial period to populate the roads to some extent. Several experiments were run at different incoming traffic flow values from 2.5 $car \div minute$ to 30 $car \div minute$ in steps of 2.5. The incoming traffic flow was constant during each experiment. The incoming flow values were the same at points A and B (in order to avoid too many combinations). Simultaneous decision making was excluded, so when an agent at one of the sources made a decision, then it submitted its intention, and the next agent made its decision only after that.

All the experiments were executed in three versions using three different routing strategies: (1) no prediction routing strategy, (2) detailed prediction routing strategy, and (3) simple prediction routing strategy. The no prediction routing strategy is the simple naive (SN) online routing game of [19], where the routing strategy selects the shortest travel time observable in the real-time status of the network (and not the shortest predicted travel time). The latter two strategies are intention-aware routing strategies where the routing strategy selects the shortest predicted travel time using the corresponding prediction method as described in Sect. 4.

The travel time of cars on trips $A-E$ and $B-E$ were measured during the whole experiment. The maximum value and the average of the travel times were computed.

Fig. 1. The Google Map extract showing the realistic scenario of the experiments (Color figure online)

6   Measure of Intertemporal Equilibrium

In order to explain how we quantify the intertemporal equilibrium, we measured and show the travel times of the trip $A-E$ with all three routing strategies in Fig. 2 at flow value 20 $car \div minute$. The horizontal axis is the elapsed time in the experiment in $minutes$. The vertical axis is the travel time of the agents of the trip $A-E$ when they arrive at point E. The vertical axis is in $minutes$ too. The time period of a bit more than 450 min was selected to show that the travel times do not seem to converge to a steady value. Because an analytical proof of convergence to a steady equilibrium value is not known, we do not know if the convergence would eventually happen or not. We formulate this in Requirement 1.

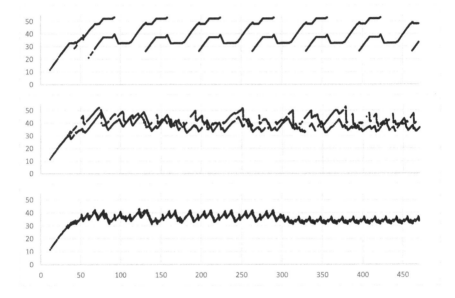

Fig. 2. Measured travel times of the trip $A-E$ for the no prediction (top part), detailed prediction (middle part), and simple prediction (bottom part) routing strategies in a longer period, at incoming flow value 20 $car \div minute$.

Requirement 1. *The measure of intertemporal equilibrium should be defined over a given period of time.*

We can also see in Fig. 2 that the travel time seems to remain within a limit from a kind of equilibrium value. Hopefully this limit is close to the value computed from the static equilibrium. The closer the better.

Requirement 2. *The measure of intertemporal equilibrium should contain the* worst case difference *(WD) from the static equilibrium.*

The worst case difference might be big, but if the system fluctuates around a kind of equilibrium, then we consider it as intertemporal equilibrium. Hopefully the medium of the fluctuation is close to the value computed from the static equilibrium. The closer the better.

Requirement 3. *The measure of intertemporal equilibrium should contain the* average difference *(AD) from the static equilibrium.*

We can see in Fig. 2 that sometimes there are big differences in the travel times of the agents that arrived at point E at almost the same elapsed time of the experiment. This means that there was an agent which arrived through a non congested route, and another agent arrived through a congested route almost at the same time. These differences are the biggest in the diagram of the no prediction strategy, because all the agents select the shortest reported route until they notice that the route becomes congested, and then they switch to the other route which becomes less congested by that time. When this switch happens, some of the agents go on a slow congested route, and some of the agents go on a fast uncongested route. The travel times are far from being equal, but the system is continuously swinging between these disequilibrium periods, so *this is a kind of equilibrium* which we call intertemporal equilibrium. The differences between the consecutive reported travel times are smaller in the diagrams of the detailed and the simple prediction strategies, which indicates that there are no so strong disequilibrium periods in the system. The smaller travel time differences seem to coincide with smaller swings in the system. The smaller swings are probably because the agents have almost equal intertemporal choices during the experiment, although the system is fluctuating all the time. We call this phenomenon "quasi equilibrium within the disequilibrium".

Requirement 4. *The measure of intertemporal equilibrium should contain an indicator of the scale of the* quasi equilibrium within the disequilibrium *(QE).*

Based on the above requirements, we define the quantitative measure of intertemporal equilibrium the following way:

Definition 1. *Let $ORG = <t, T, G, c, r, k>$ be an online routing game over the finite sequence of time steps t. Let $c_{r_i}(\tau)$ be the cost (i.e. total travel time) of the agent of trip $r_i \in r$ when it exits the game at the destination of trip r_i at time step $\tau \in t$. Let e_{r_i} be the static equilibrium travel time for trip r_i.*

The measure of intertemporal equilibrium *of ORG is $<WD, AD, QE>$ where*

- $WD = \max\limits_{r_i \in r}(\max\limits_{\tau \in t}((c_{r_i}(\tau) - e_{r_i}) \div e_{r_i}))$
- $AD = \mathrm{avg}_{r_i \in r}((\mathrm{avg}_{\tau \in t}(c_{r_i}(\tau) - e_{r_i})) \div e_{r_i})$
- $QE = \mathrm{avg}_{r_i \in r}(\mathrm{avg}_{\tau \in t}(|c_{r_i}(\tau) - c_{r_i}(\tau + 1)| \div e_{r_i}))$.

The intertemporal equilibrium of the multi-agent system is considered to be good, if the components of the measure of the intertemporal equilibrium are close to 0. The ideal equilibrium is when the system stays continuously in the static equilibrium, in which case the intertemporal equilibrium is $WD = 0$, $AD = 0$ and $QE = 0$. If $QE = 0$, then the system stays in a kind of equilibrium value, and the WD and AD values indicate how worse this equilibrium is than the static equilibrium.

Note that the QE is an important part of the intertemporal equilibrium, and it includes much more information than usual statistical values like for example the standard deviation of travel times. Two experiments may have the same standard deviation, but they may have different QE values.

7   Evaluation of the Experiments

Before the experiments, our expectation was that we could confirm the following hypotheses:

H1: The intention-aware routing strategies produce better intertemporal equilibrium values than the non predictive routing strategy.
H2: The detailed prediction routing strategy produces better intertemporal equilibrium values than the simple prediction routing strategy, because the simple prediction method does not try to be precise.

In order to evaluate the experimental measurements, we have to compute the static equilibrium values. We use the following notations for the flow rates on the routes of the experiment:

f_1 from point A to E through $(C, D)_{north}$
f_2 from point A to E through $(C, D)_{south}$
f_3 from point B to E through $(C, D)_{north}$
f_4 from point B to E through $(C, D)_{south}$

In the static equilibrium, the costs of the north and the south routes must be equal. The parameter of the experiments is a flow rate value $flow$ which is the incoming traffic flow rate value both at point A and point B. The flow rates cannot be negative. In order to get the static equilibrium cost values, we have to find a solution of Eq. 2 and compute the cost values of the routes (not detailed here).

$$f_1 + f_2 = f_3 + f_4 = flow$$
$$c_{(C,D)_{north}}(f_1 + f_3) = c_{(C,D)_{south}}(f_2 + f_4) \qquad (2)$$
$$f_1 \geq 0 \wedge f_2 \geq 0 \wedge f_3 \geq 0 \wedge f_4 \geq 0$$

The worst case difference values (WD) of the intertemporal equilibrium of the experiments were computed, and they are shown in Fig. 3. The horizontal axis is the traffic flow rate value $flow$ of each experiment, in $car \div minutes$. As we can see, the WD is zero at low traffic flows (e.g. 2.5). This is because at low traffic flows, all the traffic can go on the shortest route, and this is the static equilibrium as well. At higher traffic values, the WD increases, it even reaches 1 in the case of the no prediction routing strategy, which means that the travel time might be twice as much as the static equilibrium in the worst case. The WD of the detailed prediction routing is better than the WD of the no prediction routing in most of the experiments. The WD of the simple prediction routing is better than the WD of the detailed prediction routing. The WD values confirm hypothesis H1 in most of the experiments, but they refute hypothesis H2.

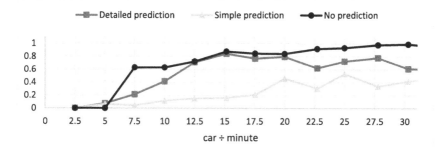

Fig. 3. The worst case difference values (WD) of the intertemporal equilibrium of the experiments

The average difference values (AD) of the intertemporal equilibrium of the experiments were computed, and they are shown in Fig. 4. As we can see, the AD is zero at low traffic flows, like in the case of the WD. At higher traffic values, the AD increases, but it is considerably less than the WD. The AD of the detailed prediction routing is better than the AD of the no prediction routing in most of the experiments. The AD of the simple prediction routing is better than the AD of the detailed prediction routing. The AD values confirm hypothesis H1 in most of the experiments, but they refute hypothesis H2.

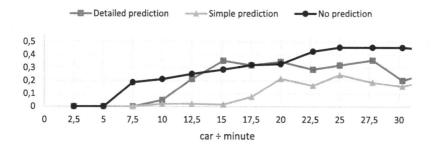

Fig. 4. The average difference values (AD) of the intertemporal equilibrium of the experiments

The quasi equilibrium values (QE) of the intertemporal equilibrium of the experiments were computed, and they are shown in Fig. 5. As we can see, the QE is zero at low traffic flows, like in the case of the WD and the AD. At higher traffic values, the QE increases, but they are much smaller for the detailed prediction routing and the simple prediction routing than for the no prediction routing. The QE of the simple prediction routing is better than the QE of the detailed prediction routing. The QE of the simple prediction routing is very close to zero, which means that the simple prediction brings about quasi equilibrium very well. The QE values confirm hypothesis H1, but they refute hypothesis H2.

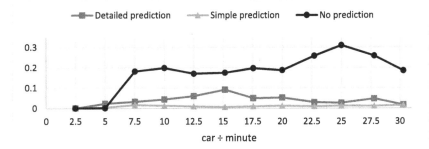

Fig. 5. The quasi equilibrium values (QE) of the intertemporal equilibrium of the experiments

8   An Artificial Scenario

In order to highlight how the different intention-aware prediction capabilities of the environment of the multi-agent system may influence the global behaviour of the multi-agent system, we present an artificial scenario shown in Fig. 6. The cost functions of the edges are shown in Eq. 3, where the cost is in $minute$ and the traffic flow is in $car \div minute$. There are two incoming traffic flows: r_1 from vertex v_0 to vertex v_4, and r_2 from v_1 to v_4. The incoming traffic flow r_2 has no other choice, but to go through the path $p_1 = (e_2, e_5)$. The incoming traffic flow r_1 may choose between the paths $p_2 = (e_1, e_4)$ and $p_3 = (e_1, e_3, e_5)$. If the incoming traffic flow r_1 chooses path p_3, then the only congestion sensitive edge e_5 is shared with r_2.

$$c_{e_1}(flow) = 2$$
$$c_{e_2}(flow) = 1$$
$$c_{e_3}(flow) = 8 \qquad\qquad (3)$$
$$c_{e_4}(flow) = 10$$
$$c_{e_5}(flow) = 1 + flow \div 20$$

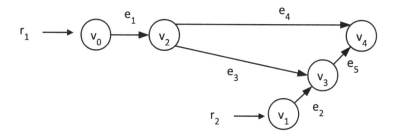

Fig. 6. The artificial scenario

If $r_1 + r_2 \leq 20$, then the rational choice in the static equilibrium for the agents of the incoming traffic flow r_1 is the path p_3, and their total travel time is $c_{p_3} = 11 + (r_1 + r_2) \div 20$. The total travel time for the agents of r_2 is $c_{p_1} = 2 + (r_1 + r_2) \div 20$.

If $r_1 + r_2 > 20$ and $r_2 < 20$, then part of the agents of r_1 (let us denote this flow r_{1_a}) chooses the path p_2 and another part of the agents of r_1 (let us denote this flow r_{1_b}) chooses the path p_3, so that $r_{1_b} + r_2 = 20$, and the total travel time for the agents of r_{1_a} is $c_{p_2} = 12$, for the agents of r_{1_b} is $c_{p_3} = 12$, and for the agents of r_2 is $c_{p_1} = 3$.

If $r_1 + r_2 > 20$ and $r_2 \geq 20$, then the rational choice for the agents of the incoming traffic flow r_1 is the path p_2, and their total travel time is $c_{p_2} = 12$. The total travel time for the agents of r_2 is $c_{p_1} = 2 + r_2 \div 20$.

8.1 Analysis

The scenario of Fig. 6 is invented to demonstrate an extreme case, where there may be big time shifts between the predictions for the different incoming traffic flows. If we take the case when $r_1 + r_2 < 160$, then we can be sure that the flow on e_5 is below 160, because the travel times on edges e_1, e_3 and e_2 are constant. An agent a_{2_t} of r_2 that starts at time t reaches vertex v_3 at time $t + 1$, and a_{2_t} exits the edge e_5 before time $t + 10$, because the flow on e_5 is below 160. An agent a_{1_t} of r_1 that starts at time t does not reach vertex v_3 before time $t + 10$, therefore none of the agents of r_2 that started at or before time t are on edge e_5 when a_{1_t} enters e_5, i.e. agents starting at the same time do not interfere on edge e_5. However the agents of r_2 that start later enough than t might interfere with agents of r_1 on edge e_5.

When the *detailed prediction* method makes a prediction at time t, then it simulates what happens if all the agents that entered the system up to time t execute their plan in accordance with their submitted intention. If $r_1 + r_2 < 160$, then the agents of the incoming flow r_1 believe that edge e_5 will be empty by the time they get to v_3, so they select path p_3. If $20 > r_1$, then after a while the agents of the incoming flow r_1 believe that their own flow r_1 starts to congest edge e_5, and the agents believe that the cost of edge e_5 reaches at least 2 by the time they get to v_3, so they select path p_2. However the actual travel time on edge e_5 reaches not only at least 2 but even at least $2 + r_2 \div 20$ because r_2 also goes on e_5. There is a difference between the beliefs of the agents of r_1 and the actually incurred travel time, because the detailed prediction simulates what happens after a given time t, but it does not take into account the agents entering the game after time t, because it does not yet know the intentions of those agents. If the agents of the incoming flow r_1 select path p_2, then the traffic on edge e_5 decreases, and after a while the agents of r_1 select path p_3 again. So the incoming flow r_1 alternates between paths p_2 and p_3, and the total travel time of r_1 alternates between $c_{p_2} = 12$ and $c_{p_3} > 12 + r_2 \div 20$. If, for example, the incoming traffic flows are in the ranges $20 < r_1 < 80$ and $20 < r_2 < 80$, then the total travel time of r_1 does not converge to the optimal value, because the incoming traffic flow r_1 sometimes selects path p_3 instead of the optimal p_2.

When the *simple prediction* method makes a prediction at time t, then it also simulates what happens if all the agents that entered the system up to time t execute their plan in accordance with their submitted intention. The simulation is updated at each intention submission, and the updated travel time becomes the prediction. If $r_1 + r_2 < 160$ and the incoming traffic flow r_1 is divided between paths p_2 and p_3 (r_{1_a} going on p_2 and r_{1_b} going on p_3), then after an agent of r_{1_b} submits its intention, the prediction for edge e_5 becomes $1 + r_{1_b} \div 20$, because the agents of the incoming flow r_1 believe that edge e_5 will be empty by the time they get to v_3. However, when an agent of the incoming traffic flow r_2 submits its intention, the prediction for edge e_5 becomes $1 + (r_{1_{b'}} + r_2) \div 20$, because the simulation shows that the agent of r_2 meets some agents of r_1 on edge e_5. If $20 > r_2$, then the agents of r_1 do not select path p_3 anymore, because the travel time prediction for e_5 is more than 2. In this case the simple prediction method performs better than the detailed prediction method. If $r_2 \leq 20$ and $1 + (r_{1_{b'}} + r_2) \div 20$ might become more than 2, then the simple prediction method warns the incoming flow r_1 in advance not to select path p_3, therefore the simple prediction method performs better than the detailed prediction method in this case as well.

If there is *no prediction*, and the decision of the agents is based on the real-time situation, and the incoming traffic flow r_2 is above 20, then after a while the travel time on edge e_5 becomes more than 2, and the agents of the incoming traffic flow r_1 select path p_2, which is the optimal choice. Because the agents of r_1 realize with a delay that the travel time on edge e_5 becomes more than 2, they make suboptimal decision for a while. If $r_1 + r_2 \leq 20$, then the travel time on edge e_5 never becomes more than 2, and the agents of the incoming traffic flow r_1 select path p_3, which is the optimal choice.

The above analysis shows that there may be situations, where the detailed prediction method is a bit misleading, and it produces worse results than the no prediction method. However the simple prediction method might be better than the detailed prediction method.

8.2   Experiments

The above artificial scenario was simulated in an experiment with parameters similar to the experiment of the realistic scenario of Sect. 5. A 90 min long period was simulated extended with a 17 min initial period to populate the roads to some extent. Several experiments were run at incoming traffic flow values from $2.5 \ car \div minute$ to $30 \ car \div minute$ in steps of 2.5. The incoming traffic flow was constant during each experiment. The incoming flow values r_1 and r_2 were equal. Simultaneous decision making was excluded, so when an agent at one of the sources made a decision, then it submitted its intention, and the next agent made its decision only after that.

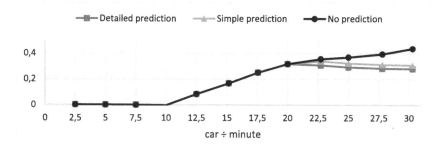

Fig. 7. The worst case difference values (WD) of the intertemporal equilibrium of the experiments with the artificial scenario

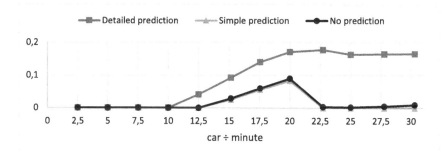

Fig. 8. The average difference values (AD) of the intertemporal equilibrium of the experiments with the artificial scenario

All the experiments were executed in three versions of the routing strategies: (1) no prediction routing strategy, (2) detailed prediction routing strategy, and (3) simple prediction routing strategy. The travel time of cars on paths p_1, p_2 and p_3 were measured during the whole experiment. The maximum value and the average of the travel times were computed. Figure 7 shows the WD values and Fig. 8 shows the AD values of the experiments.

In this extreme artificial scenario, the WD and AD values are smaller than in the realistic scenario, because in the artificial scenario the incoming traffic flow r_2 has no choice, and the incoming traffic flow r_1 may sometimes realise its optimal choice. The WD values are about the same for all routing strategies, except that the no prediction method performs worse than the others. This is in line with hypothesis H1. The AD value is the worst for the detailed prediction method, and the other two methods perform about equally. This is in line with the analysis in the previous subsection, however it confirms hypothesis H1 only for the simple prediction routing strategy, but not for the detailed routing strategy. In this extreme scenario, the detailed prediction method performs the worst in the AD values, but the WD values are more or less in line with the results of the realistic scenario.

9 Discussion

We have investigated in the routing problem how the prediction capabilities built into the environment of the multi-agent system can influence the global behaviour of the multi-agent system. In an idealistic situation, the global behaviour of the multi-agent system is characterised by a static equilibrium state. However, we cannot be sure that dynamically evolving large-scale and open multi-agent systems achieve a static equilibrium, and we may only hope that they converge to the equilibrium over time.

Convergence to the static equilibrium is an important question for the global behaviour of multi-agent systems. We have investigated the evolutionary dynamics inside games, in particular in online routing games. There is a conjecture that online routing games with specific properties converge to the static equilibrium.

In this chapter we took a different approach to the issue of convergence to the equilibrium. Instead of proving the convergence, we studied the nature of the kind of equilibrium that seems to appear in online routing games. Our major contribution is that we introduce the notion of intertemporal equilibrium in the study of the evolutionary dynamics of games, we define quantitative values to measure the intertemporal equilibrium, we use these quantitative values to evaluate a realistic scenario, and we give an insight into the influence of intertemporal expectations of the agents on the intertemporal equilibrium. With this work we contribute to the better understanding of the intertemporal behaviour of multi-agent systems.

One of the results is that exact convergence to the static equilibrium is unlikely in online routing games. The reason is that the static equilibrium does not take into account the waiting times at the entrance of the roads. Notably, if two agents arrive at the same road at the same time, then one of them has to wait a little bit until it can enter the road after the other one. This introduces delays, therefore the travel times in online routing games are often longer than in the classic routing game models. The WD and the AD values show how good the different routing strategies are in this respect.

Another result is that if the agents of the online routing game of the realistic scenario base their decisions only on the current situation, then the intertemporal equilibrium is worse than in the case when they have a prediction of the future. This is in line with our hypothesis H1 for the realistic scenario. However, in extreme situations the detailed prediction method may perform worse on average, than the no prediction method.

The third result is that making a more precise prediction of the future from all information known at the time of decision making does not lead to a better intertemporal equilibrium in the experiments. This is unexpected and it refutes our hypothesis H2. In our view, this is an important new result, because it demonstrates in a controllable experiment that the selfish adaptation of the individual agents to the expected future, which is computable from the intentions of the agents, may not lead to better global agent system behaviour in large scale and open multi-agent systems. Better knowledge of the currently expected future may not be better for the multi-agent system.

Finally, this work contributes to the engineering of multi-agent systems, and in particular to environment engineering. The contribution is the investigation of a novel type of coordination artifact to predict the future state of the environment. We have given better insight into the influence of the prediction capabilities of this kind of coordination artifact on the dynamic global behaviour of multi-agent systems. The prediction service of online routing games is an extension of the perception model of environment programming by allowing the agents to "perceive" the expected future state of the environment. The presented realistic experiments show that the better quasi equilibrium in the disequilibrium values correspond to better system behaviour. This result is a guidance for better environment engineering of multi-agent systems. In order to achieve a better global behaviour of a large-scale and open multi-agent system, it is recommended to engineer into the environment of the multi-agent system a predictive coordination atrifact, which can predict the expectable future equilibrium, and not just the expectable future.

An assumption of the online routing game is that the agents do not change their routes during their trips, which means that the agents apply blind commitment strategy. Investigating the engineering of the different commitment strategies and how the commitment strategies effect the convergence to the equilibrium is a future work.

References

1. Beckmann, M.J., McGuire, C.B., Winsten, C.B.: Studies in the Economics of Transportation. Yale University Press, New Haven (1956)
2. Blum, A., Even-Dar, E., Ligett, K.: Routing without regret: on convergence to nash equilibria of regret-minimizing algorithms in routing games. In: Proceedings of the Twenty-Fifth Annual ACM Symposium on Principles of Distributed Computing, PODC 2006, pp. 45–52. ACM, New York (2006). https://doi.org/10.1145/1146381.1146392

3. Braess, D.: Über ein paradoxon der verkehrsplanung. Unternehmensforschung **12**, 258–268 (1968). https://doi.org/10.1007/BF01918335. http://vcp.med.harvard.edu/braess-paradox.html (Alternatively an easily readable English description is in the link)
4. Claes, R., Holvoet, T.: Traffic coordination using aggregation-based traffic predictions. IEEE Intell. Syst. **29**(4), 96–100 (2014). https://doi.org/10.1109/MIS.2014.73
5. Claes, R., Holvoet, T., Weyns, D.: A decentralized approach for anticipatory vehicle routing using delegate multi-agent systems. IEEE Trans. Intell. Transp. Syst. **12**(2), 364–373 (2011). https://doi.org/10.1109/TITS.2011.2105867
6. Cominetti, R., Correa, J., Olver, N.: Long term behavior of dynamic equilibria in fluid queuing networks. In: Eisenbrand, F., Koenemann, J. (eds.) IPCO 2017. LNCS, vol. 10328, pp. 161–172. Springer, Cham (2017). https://doi.org/10.1007/978-3-319-59250-3_14
7. Engelberg, R., Schapira, M.: Weakly-acyclic (internet) routing games. Theor. Comput. Syst. **54**(3), 431–452 (2014). https://doi.org/10.1007/s00224-013-9474-z
8. Fischer, S., Vöcking, B.: On the evolution of selfish routing. In: Albers, S., Radzik, T. (eds.) ESA 2004. LNCS, vol. 3221, pp. 323–334. Springer, Heidelberg (2004). https://doi.org/10.1007/978-3-540-30140-0_30
9. Hicks, J.R.: Value and Capital: An Inquiry into Some Fundamental Principles of Economic Theory, 2nd edn. Oxford University Press, Oxford (1975)
10. Hoefer, M., Mirrokni, V.S., Röglin, H., Teng, S.H.: Competitive routing over time. Theor. Comput. Sci. **412**(39), 5420–5432 (2011). https://doi.org/10.1016/j.tcs.2011.05.055
11. Koch, R., Skutella, M.: Nash equilibria and the price of anarchy for flows over time. Theor. Comput. Sci. **49**(1), 71–97 (2011). https://doi.org/10.1007/s00224-010-9299-y
12. Meir, R., Polukarov, M., Rosenschein, J.S., Jennings, N.R.: Iterative voting and acyclic games. Artif. Intell. **252**, 100–122 (2017). https://doi.org/10.1016/j.artint.2017.08.002
13. Nisan, N., Roughgarden, T., Tardos, E., Vazirani, V.V.: Algorithmic Game Theory. Cambridge University Press, New York (2007). https://doi.org/10.1017/CBO9780511800481
14. Ricci, A., Piunti, M., Viroli, M.: Environment programming in multi-agent systems - an artifact-based perspective. Auton. Agents Multi-Agent Syst. **23**(2), 158–192 (2011). https://doi.org/10.1007/s10458-010-9140-7. Special Issue: Multi-Agent Programming
15. Rosenschein, J.S.: Multiagent systems, and the search for appropriate foundations. In: Proceedings of the 12th International Conference on Autonomous Agents and Multiagent Systems (AAMAS 2013), pp. 5–6. International Foundation for Autonomous Agents and Multiagent Systems (2013). www.ifaamas.org. http://www.ifaamas.org/Proceedings/aamas2013/docs/p5.pdf
16. Roughgarden, T.: Routing games. In: Nisan, N., Roughgarden, T., Tardos, É., Vazirani, V.V. (eds.) Algorithmic Game Theory, pp. 461–486. Cambridge University Press, Cambridge (2007)
17. Sandholm, W.H.: Potential games with continuous player sets. J. Econ. Theor. **97**(1), 81–108 (2001). https://doi.org/10.1006/jeth.2000.2696. http://www.sciencedirect.com/science/article/pii/S0022053100926966
18. Varga, L.: On intention-propagation-based prediction in autonomously self-adapting navigation. Scalable Comput. Pract. Exp. **16**(3), 221–232 (2015). http://www.scpe.org/index.php/scpe/article/view/1098

19. Varga, L.Z.: Online routing games and the benefit of online data. In: Klügl, F., Vizzari, G., Vokřínek, J. (eds.) ATT 2014 8th International Workshop on Agents in Traffic and Transportation, Held at the 13th International Conference on Autonomous Agents and Multiagent Systems (AAMAS 2014), Paris, France, 5–6 May 2014, pp. 88–95 (2014). http://www.ia.urjc.es/ATT/documents/ATT2014proceedings.pdf

20. Varga, L.Z.: Paradox phenomena in autonomously self-adapting navigation. Cybern. Inf. Technol. **15**(5), 78–87 (2015). https://doi.org/10.1515/cait-2015-0018

21. Varga, L.Z.: Benefit of online real-time data in the Braess paradox with anticipatory routing. In: Kounev, S., Giese, H., Liu, J. (eds.) 2016 IEEE International Conference on Autonomic Computing, ICAC 2016, Würzburg, Germany, 17–22 July 2016, pp. 245–250. IEEE Computer Society (2016). https://doi.org/10.1109/ICAC.2016.68

22. Varga, L.Z.: How good is predictive routing in the online version of the Braess paradox? In: Kaminka, G.A., et al. (eds.) ECAI 2016–22nd European Conference on Artificial Intelligence, The Hague, The Netherlands, 29 August–2 September 2016. Frontiers in Artificial Intelligence and Applications, vol. 285, pp. 1696–1697. IOS Press (2016). https://doi.org/10.3233/978-1-61499-672-9-1696

23. Varga, L.Z.: Equilibrium with predictive routeing in the online version of the Braess paradox. IET Softw. **11**(4), 165–170 (2017)

24. Varga, L.Z.: Two prediction methods for intention-aware online routing games. In: Belardinelli, F., Argente, E. (eds.) EUMAS/AT - 2017. LNCS (LNAI), vol. 10767, pp. 431–445. Springer, Cham (2018). https://doi.org/10.1007/978-3-030-01713-2_30

25. Wardrop, J.G.: Some theoretical aspects of road traffic research. Proc. Inst. Civ. Eng. Part II **1**(36), 352–378 (1952)

26. de Weerdt, M.M., Stein, S., Gerding, E.H., Robu, V., Jennings, N.R.: Intention-aware routing of electric vehicles. IEEE Trans. Intell. Transp. Syst. **17**(5), 1472–1482 (2016). https://doi.org/10.1109/TITS.2015.2506900

27. Weyns, D., Holvoet, T., Schelfthout, K., Wielemans, J.: Decentralized control of automatic guided vehicles: Applying multi-agent systems in practice. In: Companion to the 23rd ACM SIGPLAN Conference on Object-oriented Programming Systems Languages and Applications, OOPSLA Companion 2008, pp. 663–674. ACM, New York (2008). https://doi.org/10.1145/1449814.1449819

28. Weyns, D., Schumacher, M., Ricci, A., Viroli, M., Holvoet, T.: Environments in multiagent systems. Knowl. Eng. Rev. **20**(2), 127–141 (2005). https://doi.org/10.1017/S0269888905000457

29. Wooldridge, M.: An Introduction to MultiAgent Systems, 2nd edn. Wiley, Chichester (2009)

Modeling and Simulations

Gavel: A Sanctioning Enforcement Framework

Igor Conrado Alves de Lima[1,3(✉)], Luis Gustavo Nardin[2],
and Jaime Simão Sichman[3]

[1] Inst. de Matemática e Estatística, Universidade de São Paulo, São Paulo, SP, Brazil
igorcadelima@usp.br
[2] Department of Informatics, Brandenburg University of Technology,
Cottbus, Germany
nardin@b-tu.de
[3] LTI, Escola Politécnica, Universidade de São Paulo, São Paulo, SP, Brazil
jaime.sichman@poli.usp.br

Abstract. Sanctioning is one of the most adopted enforcement mechanisms in the governance of multiagent systems. Current enforcement frameworks, however, restrict agents to reason about and make sanctioning decisions. We developed the Gavel framework, an adaptive sanctioning enforcement framework that enables agents to decide for the most appropriate sanction to apply depending on various decision factors. The potential benefits and use of the framework are shown using a Public Goods Game in which agents are endowed with different strategies combining material and reputational sanctions.

Keywords: Enforcement system · Normative Multiagent Systems · Software engineering

1 Introduction

Norm enforcement is one of the central puzzles in social order and social control theories. It refers to the process in which an entity monitors and encourages others to comply with norms. Sanctioning is one of the most adopted and largely recognised norm enforcement mechanisms used to promote appropriate behavioural standards, in particular norm compliance [26]. Norm enforcement, specially sanctioning, has been addressed in a broad range of perspectives and disciplines, such as philosophy [3], law [16], economics [4], sociology [17] and social psychology [9]. These disciplines recognise that different sanction types (e.g., emotional, informational, reputational, and material [28]) are used by individuals and institutions to enforce and promote norms compliance.

In Normative Multiagent Systems (NMASs), norm enforcement enables reaction to norms violation (i.e., punishment) or compliance (i.e., reward) henceforth

---

Igor Conrado Alves de Lima was fully supported by CNPq, Brazil, grant number 131120/2016-6.

D. Weyns et al. (Eds.): EMAS 2018 Workshops, LNAI 11375, pp. 225–241, 2019.
https://doi.org/10.1007/978-3-030-25693-7_12

identified as *sanction*. The degree to which a norm is enforced plays a crucial role in NMAS dynamics and conveys a great deal of norm-relevant information that affects other normative processes.

There are two traditional approaches to norm enforcement in NMAS[1]: *regimentation* and *regulation*. The former assumes that agents can be controlled and non-compliant actions prevented. The latter allows violations, yet sanctions may be applied to the violator whenever a violation is detected.

Both approaches can be arranged in a centralised or distributed mode. The regimentation approach operates mostly in a centralised mode through normative institution frameworks, such as Electronic Institutions [13,25] and Organisation Models [12,14]. These frameworks provide a reference normative system to which agents have to abide and infrastructure entities enforce the compliance of agents' actions and interactions with the norms. The regulation approach, conversely, operates mostly in a distributed mode and requires that agents' architectures, such as BOID [7], NoA [18], and EMIL-A [1], are endowed with mechanisms that enable agents to enforce norms.

Cardoso and Oliveira [8] proposed a centralised norm enforcement mechanism for contractual commitments. Their mechanism pre-define sanctions that are applied by enforcer agents without taking into account any individual or contextual information. Centeno et al. [10] extended this approach to adapt sanctions based on contextual information. Modgil et al. [23] proposed a general distributed architecture for norm-governed systems that relies on distributed infrastructure agents to monitor and apply pre-defined sanctions. In line with López and Luck [20], Criado et al. [11] relaxed some of the constraints imposed on the infrastructural enforcer agents allowing them to punish or reward due to, respectively, norms violation or compliance. In this mechanism, each norm is associated with specific punishment or reward sanctions, thus limiting the agents' decision autonomy. To overcome this limitation, Villatoro et al. [30] proposed a technique that allows enforcers to adapt the strength of the sanction based on the number of defectors. Mahmoud et al. [21] proposed the use of the violation characteristics to adapt the magnitude or frequency of the sanction. Moreover, Mahmoud et al. [22] introduced the use of reputation as a means for enforcers to adapt the strength of the sanctions.

Although Pasquier et al. [27] identified the importance and need to have different sanction types and endow agents with sanction reasoning and decision capabilities, Nardin et al. [24] showed that the available norm enforcement frameworks lack full support to four main requirements to render these features possible:

R1 *Support for multiple categories of sanctions* (e.g., legal sanctions, ostracism, reputation spreading);
R2 *Potential association of multiple sanctions with a norm violation or compliance* (e.g., provide a set of sanction options instead of pre-establishing a fixed set to a norm);

---

[1] See [2] for an extended taxonomy of norm enforcement mechanisms.

R3 *Reasoning about the most adequate sanction to apply depending on different factors* (e.g., one might consider the sanctionee's history to determine an appropriate sanction to apply, if any); and
R4 *Adaption of the sanction content depending on context* (e.g., a norm violation of high magnitude might incur a more severe negative sanction).

Nardin et al. [24] propose a conceptual sanctioning process model that overcomes these drawbacks. However, they have not designed or implemented an adaptive sanctioning enforcement framework based on this conceptual model. This is precisely what we present in this chapter: the development of the Gavel framework, based on this previous conceptual model. Moreover, we show the potential benefits and use of this framework through a Public Goods Game (PGG) [19], in which agents are endowed with different strategies combining material and reputational sanctions.

2   Gavel Framework

Gavel is an adaptive sanctioning enforcement framework based on the conceptual sanctioning process model presented by Nardin et al. [24]. It enables agents to decide for the most appropriate sanctions to apply, depending on their current context assessed by a set of sanctioning decision factors.

The conceptual sanctioning process model specifies the features and components of our sanctioning enforcement framework. Both norm violation and compliance are considered in the process, respecting the general notion of sanction as a negative or positive reaction to normative behaviours. The entire sanctioning process is realised by agents endowed with special capabilities (i.e., Detector, Evaluator, Executor, Controller, and Legislator) supported by specialised data repositories (*De Jure* and *De Facto*). Next, we define the components of our norm enforcement framework.

2.1   NMAS

Definition 1 (NMAS). *A NMAS is a system composed of a set of autonomous and heterogeneous agents situated in a shared environment, whose actions and interactions are ruled by norms and sanctions. A NMAS, either open or closed, is defined as*

$$\text{NMAS} = \langle \mathcal{E}nv, \mathcal{A}g, \mathcal{R}, \mathcal{A}c, \mathcal{N}, \mathcal{S}, \mathcal{L} \rangle,$$

where

- *$\mathcal{E}nv$ is the environment that may assume any of a finite set of discrete states;*
- *$\mathcal{A}g = \{ag_i : i \leq |\mathcal{A}g|\}$ is the set of agents that can act on the environment or interact among themselves;*
- *$\mathcal{R} = \{r_i : i \leq |\mathcal{R}|\}$ is the set of roles that agents can play;*
- *$\mathcal{A}c = \{\alpha_i : i \leq |\mathcal{A}c|\}$ is the set of actions that agents can perform;*
- *$\mathcal{N} = \{n_i : i \leq |\mathcal{N}|\}$ is the set of norms prescribing the agents' behaviours;*
- *$\mathcal{S} = \{s_i : i \leq |\mathcal{S}|\}$ is the set of sanctions prescribing possible reactions to norm violation or compliance;*
- *$\mathcal{L} = \mathcal{N} \times \mathcal{S}$ is the set of links between norms and sanctions.*

2.2   Norms, Sanctions and Links

Definition 2 (Norm). *A norm* $n_i \in \mathcal{N}$ *is a guide of conduct prescribing how agents ought to behave in a given situation. A norm is defined as*

$$n_i = \langle \text{status, activation, issuer, target, deactivation, deadline, content} \rangle,$$

where

- status $\in$ {enabled, disabled} *indicates whether* n_i *is in force;*
- activation *is the set of contextual conditions that renders the norm applicable;*
- issuer $\in \mathcal{A}g$ *identifies the entity that originally issued the norm;*
- target $\in \mathcal{A}g$ *identifies the agent to which the norm is addressed;*
- deactivation *is the set of contextual conditions that renders the norm no longer applicable once active;*
- deadline *is the set of contextual and temporal conditions which determine the deadline to comply with the norm;*
- content *is the criteria prescribing the agents' behaviours.*

Definition 3 (Norm Instance). *A norm instance* n_i' *is the result of applying a ground substitution to a norm* n_i. *A norm instance is defined as*

$$n_i' = \langle \text{status}', \text{activation}', \text{issuer}', \text{target}', \text{deactivation}', \text{deadline}', \text{content}' \rangle,$$

where each term of n_i' *unifies with its corresponding in* n_i.

Definition 4 (Sanction). *A sanction* $s_i \in \mathcal{S}$ *is a reaction to a norm compliance or violation. A sanction is defined as*

$$s_i = \langle \text{status, activation, category, content} \rangle,$$

where

- status $\in$ {enabled, disabled} *indicates whether* s_i *is in force;*
- activation *is the set of contextual conditions that renders the sanction applicable;*
- category *is the sanction classification according to the sanction typology detailed in [24], defined as*

$$\text{category} = \langle \text{purpose, issuer, locus, mode, polarity, discernability} \rangle,$$

  where
    - purpose $\in$ {Punishment, Reward, Enablement, Guidance, Incapacitation},
    - issuer $\in$ {Formal, Informal},
    - locus $\in$ {Self-Directed, Other-Directed},
    - mode $\in$ {Direct, Indirect},
    - polarity $\in$ {Positive, Negative},
    - discernability $\in$ {Noticeable, Unnoticeable};
- content *is the specification of the set of actions representing the sanction.*

Definition 5 (Sanction Instance). *A sanction instance* s_i' *is the result of applying a ground substitution to a sanction* s_i. *A sanction instance is defined as*

$$s_i' = \langle \text{status}', \text{activation}', \text{category}', \text{content}' \rangle,$$

where each term of s_i' *unifies with its corresponding in* s_i.

Definition 6 (Link). *A link* $l_i \in \mathcal{L}$ *is an association between a norm and a subset of sanctions. A link is defined as*

$$l_i = \langle n_i, \mathcal{SL}_{n_i} \rangle,$$

where

- $n_i \in \mathcal{N}$ *is the norm being linked;*
- $\mathcal{SL}_{n_i} = \{ sl_j \mid sl_j = \langle \text{status}, s_j \rangle \}$ *is the set of sanction links to* n_i, *where*
  - status $\in \{$enabled, disabled$\}$ *indicates whether* sl_j *is in force and*
  - $s_j \in \mathcal{S}$ *is the sanction being linked.*

An enabled link states that an agent may consider a sanction s_j *as a possible reaction to the compliance or violation of the norm* n_i.

2.3 Repositories

We define two types of data repositories: *De Jure* and *De Facto*.

Definition 7 (De Jure). *De Jure* $(\mathcal{DJ})$ *is a repository which stores specifications of norms and sanctions and their associations. It is defined as*

$$\mathcal{DJ} = \langle \mathcal{N}^{\mathcal{DJ}}, \mathcal{S}^{\mathcal{DJ}}, \mathcal{L}^{\mathcal{DJ}} \rangle,$$

where

- $\mathcal{N}^{\mathcal{DJ}} \subseteq \mathcal{N}$ *is the set of all norms stored in* $\mathcal{DJ}$;
- $\mathcal{S}^{\mathcal{DJ}} \subseteq \mathcal{S}$ *is the set of all sanctions stored in* $\mathcal{DJ}$;
- $\mathcal{L}^{\mathcal{DJ}} \subseteq \mathcal{L}$ *is the set of all links between norms and sanctions stored in* $\mathcal{DJ}$.

Definition 8 (De Facto). *De Facto* $(\mathcal{DF})$ *is a repository of historical information about sanction decisions, applications, and outcomes. It is defined as*

$$\mathcal{DF} = \langle \mathcal{SD}^{\mathcal{DF}}, \mathcal{SA}^{\mathcal{DF}}, \mathcal{SO}^{\mathcal{DF}} \rangle,$$

where

- $\mathcal{SD}^{\mathcal{DF}}$ *(Sanction Decision Set) represents the set of sanction decisions made by Evaluators and stored in* $\mathcal{DF}$. *Each sanction decision* $sd_i \in \mathcal{SD}^{\mathcal{DF}}$ *is defined as*

$$sd_i = \langle \text{time}_d, \text{detector}, \text{evaluator}, \text{target}, n_j', s_k', \text{cause} \rangle,$$

where

- $time_d$ *indicates the global time at which the sanction was decided;*
- detector $\in \mathcal{A}g$ *identifies the agent that reported the norm compliance or violation;*
- evaluator $\in \mathcal{A}g$ *identifies the agent that decided the sanction;*
- target $\in \mathcal{A}g$ *identifies the agent to which the sanction is directed;*
- n_j' *is the norm instance which was evaluated by the* evaluator;
- s_k' *is the sanction decided by* evaluator *for* target *in response to* n_j';
- cause $\in \{$compliance, violation$\}$ *indicates what led* evaluator *to decide for the sanction* s_k'.

- $\mathcal{SA}^{\mathcal{DI}}$ *(Sanction Application Set) represents the set of sanction applications executed by* **Executors***. Each sanction application* $sa_i \in \mathcal{SA}^{\mathcal{DI}}$ *is defined as*

$$sa_i = \langle time_a, decision_j, executor \rangle,$$

where

- $time_a$ *indicates the global time at which the sanction was applied;*
- $decision_j \in \mathcal{SD}^{\mathcal{DI}}$ *is the sanction decision to which* sa_i *is related;*
- executor $\in \mathcal{A}g$ *identifies the agent that applied the sanction.*

- $\mathcal{SO}^{\mathcal{DI}}$ *(Sanction Outcome Set) represents the set of sanction outcomes observed by a* **Controller***. Each sanction outcome* $so_i \in \mathcal{SO}^{\mathcal{DI}}$ *is defined as*

$$so_i = \langle time_o, application_j, controller, efficacy \rangle,$$

where

- $time_o$ *indicates the global time at which the efficacy of the sanction was assessed;*
- $application_j \in \mathcal{SA}^{\mathcal{DI}}$ *is the observed sanction application;*
- controller $\in \mathcal{A}g$ *identifies the agent that observed the outcome;*
- efficacy *indicates how effective the sanction was in promoting norm compliance. It can use discrete (e.g.,* effective *and* ineffective*) or continuous (e.g.,* $[-1, 1]$*) values.*

2.4   Capabilities

The Gavel framework defines five capabilities: Detector, Evaluator, Executor, Controller, and Legislator. Agents having these capabilities perform tasks in different stages of the sanctioning process.

Definition 9 (Detector). *The* **Detector** *perceives the environment and detects a norm violation or compliance. It* watches *for normative events, creates norm instances, and* reports *compliances and violations to an* **Evaluator***. The* watch *function is defined as*

$$\text{watch} : e \times \mathcal{KB} \times n_{enabled} \rightarrow n', \tag{1}$$

where

- e *is the event to be analysed;*
- $\mathcal{KB}$ *is the* **Detector***'s knowledge base;*
- $\mathcal{N}_{\text{enabled}} = \{n_i \mid n_i \in \mathcal{N} \wedge n_i.\text{status} = \text{enabled}\}$ *is the set of enabled norms known by the agent;*
- $\mathcal{N}' = \{n_i' \mid n_i \in \mathcal{N}_{\text{enabled}} \text{ and } e \wedge \mathcal{KB} \models n_i'.\text{activation}\}$ *is the set of norm instances whose activation condition holds given* e *and* $\mathcal{KB}$.

Each norm instance obtained from watch *is assessed as complied, violated, or deactivated. If complied or violated, then the* **Detector** *reports such fact to an* **Evaluator***.*

Definition 10 (Evaluator). *The* **Evaluator** *receives from the* **Detector** *the report of a violation or compliance of a norm instance* n_i'. *It then obtains from the* De Jure *repository all the applicable sanctions associated with* n_i' *by enabled links to decide for the sanctions it judges appropriate to apply, if any. This task is performed by the* evaluate *function, which is defined as*

$$\text{evaluate} : n_i' \times \mathcal{KB} \times \mathcal{SL}_{n_i',\text{enabled}} \to \mathcal{SD}_{n_i'}^{\mathcal{DJ}}, \tag{2}$$

where

- n_i' *is the norm instance to be evaluated;*
- $\mathcal{KB}$ *is the knowledge base from which the agent extracted contextual factors to be considered in the evaluation;*
- $\mathcal{SL}_{n_i',\text{enabled}}$ *is the set of enabled sanction links associated with* n_i';
- $\mathcal{SD}_{n_i'}^{\mathcal{DJ}}$ *is the set of sanction decisions for* n_i'.

Definition 11 (Executor). *The* **Executor** *agent* ag_i *receives from the* **Evaluator** *a sanction decision* $sd_j \in \mathcal{SD}$ *and decides whether or not to* execute *it. The decision for not executing a sanction could result either from lack of resources to operate or personal interests. In a real-world setting, for example,* **Evaluators** *and* **Executors** *would be comparable to judges and police officers, respectively. The* execute *function maps a sanction decision to actions in the environment:*

$$\text{execute} : sd_j \to \mathcal{Ac}. \tag{3}$$

If the actions defined in sd_j *are successfully executed, then the* **Executor** *records the sanction application* $sa_k = \langle time_a, sd_j, ag_i \rangle$ *in the* $\mathcal{SA}^{\mathcal{DF}}$.

Definition 12 (Controller). *The* **Controller** ag_i *monitors the outcomes of a sanction application* sa_k *to determine its efficacy and records its judgement as a sanction outcome* $so_j = \langle time_o, sa_k, ag_i, \text{efficacy} \rangle$ *in* $\mathcal{SO}^{\mathcal{DF}}$.

Definition 13 (Legislator). *The* **Legislator** *creates, removes, and updates norms, sanctions, and their associations in* De Jure *based on the assessment of the* De Jure *and* De Facto *repositories along with its knowledge base.*

$$\text{legislate} : \mathcal{DJ} \times \mathcal{DF} \times \mathcal{KB} \to \mathcal{DJ} \tag{4}$$

3 Implementation

The Gavel framework[2] has been implemented in Java and is mainly divided into three packages (see Fig. 1):

gavel.api provides interfaces for all the elements of the model;
gavel.base provides abstract classes which can be used as basis for customisation of some elements of the model;
gavel.impl contains generic concrete implementations of the model elements (e.g., norms, sanctions, norm-sanction links, and data repositories) according to contracts prescribed by interfaces defined in *gavel.api* and provides utility classes with factory, parsing, and other supporting methods.

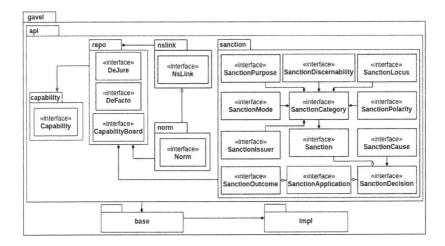

Fig. 1. *Gavel*'s architecture.

The framework includes generic *in-memory* data storage implementations for three data repositories:

– DeJure stores and provides operations to manage norms, sanctions, and norm-sanction links. Initial norms, sanctions and norm-sanction links may be loaded into DeJure by means of a *regulative specification* file. At runtime, these elements can be created, retrieved, updated, or deleted;
– DeFacto stores sanction decisions, applications, and outcomes at runtime;
– CapabilityBoard stores capability assignment rules and the capabilities possessed by agents. If an agent has a certain capability and the repository is informed, then such information will be available for the entire system. Also, initial capability assignment rules may be loaded into CapabilityBoard via a *capability assignment specification* file.

---

[2] Source code available at https://github.com/gavelproject/gavel/.

It is often desirable to specify norms, sanctions, norm-sanction links, and capability assignment rules before the system starts running. Thus, system designers can provide two XML (eXtensible Markup Language) specification files:

- *Regulative specification* defines norms, sanctions, and norm-sanction links specifications that will be initially stored in `DeJure`;
- *Capability assignment specification* defines rules specifying which agents will be allowed to possess which of the capabilities defined in the model.

Notice that Gavel does not provide execution plans for each capability as these are dependent on the multiagent system platform.

In addition to the standard Java implementation, we have designed and implemented *Gavel for JaCaMo*[3], a reusable framework which integrates Gavel with JaCaMo [5]. The benefit of such integration is twofold: (i) Gavel repositories are provided as CArtAgO [29] artefacts that may be used by agents; and (ii) agents may acquire plans at runtime from `CapabilityBoard` to learn how to perform tasks inherent to any of the sanctioning capabilities (Detector, Evaluator, Executor, Controller, Legislator), since Jason supports meta-programming [6]. We have used this implementation in our case study, presented next.

4 Case Study

We have used the *Gavel for JaCaMo* framework to implement a version of the Public Goods Game (PGG) partially inspired by Giardini et al. [15].

4.1 Public Goods Game Model

Broadly used in experimental economics, agents in the PGG have private tokens and secretly choose whether to contribute to a public pool. The tokens in this pool are multiplied by a benefit factor and evenly divided among players.

In our PGG model, agents are endowed with a number of tokens and play the game for a number of rounds (see Algorithm 1) or until they are in deficit of tokens. In each round, agents are randomly grouped (line 3) and they decide whether to free-ride or contribute a fixed amount to the public pool (line 4). The sum of the contributions in each group is multiplied by a benefit factor and evenly divided among the group agents regardless of their contribution (line 5). Next, the agents' decisions are disclosed to all other agents in their group (line 6) and agents decide whether or not to apply sanctions to other agents in their group (line 7). Once sanctions are applied (line 8), agents with less than zero tokens are eliminated from the game (line 9–13).

Agents may have one of four types of contribution strategies:

- *Cooperator* (C) who always contributes to the pubic pool and does not sanction other agents;

---

[3] Source code available at https://github.com/gavelproject/gavel-jacamo/.

Algorithm 1. Public Goods Game main cycle

1: Initialise agents
2: **for** number of rounds **do**
3:     Random group formation
4:     Agents make their contribution decision
5:     Gather and distribution of contributions in each group
6:     Disclose contribution decisions in the group
7:     Agents make their sanction decisions
8:     Apply sanctions
9:     **for** each agent **do**
10:        **if** Agent's tokens < 0 **then**
11:            Agent is culled from the game
12:        **end if**
13:    **end for**
14: **end for**

- *Free-Rider* (FR) who never contributes to the public pool and does not sanction other agents;
- *Nice* (N) who always contributes to the public pool and may apply sanctions if the percentage of detected free-riders in its group exceeds a threshold;
- *Mean* (M) who decides to free-ride and may apply sanctions if the percentage of detected free-riders in its group exceeds a threshold; otherwise, it contributes and does not sanction.

An agent ag_i identifies an agent ag_j as free-rider if the reputation that ag_i has about ag_j is below a certain threshold. Agents keep an individual record of all other agents in the game. Each agent ag_i calculates the reputation of ag_j by taking the weighted average of its direct experience and the reputation received from others about ag_j, which is defined as

$$R_{ij} = W \times \Delta E + (1 - W) \times \Delta I, \tag{5}$$

where $R_{ij} \in [0, 1]$ is the reputation the agent ag_i has about the agent ag_j, where 0 means the worst and 1 means the best reputation. ΔE is the proportion of good personal experiences ag_i had with ag_j, ΔI is the average reputation received about ag_j by ag_i, and W is the weight given to the personal experiences.

Nice and Mean agents also use features of the Gavel model to guide their sanction choice towards free-riders. The sanction strategies available are:

- *Random* (R): Agents decide randomly between gossiping about or punishing free-riders;
- *Threshold* (T): Agents decide whether to gossip or punish by comparing the reputation of the free-rider with a randomly picked number from a uniform distribution between 0 and 1. If the free-rider's reputation is less than the random number, the agent punishes the free-rider, otherwise it gossips.

There are some constraints to apply either type of sanction. Each agent has a limit on the number of reputation transmissions in each round. If this limit is reached, reputation transmission is not possible. The punishment inflicted on free-riders has a cost to the agent inflicting it, thus an agent can only sanction if it can afford. This cost, called *enforcement cost*, could be seen as the effort required to apply a sanction. It is worth noticing that agents do not lie in this model, thus only truthful information is transmitted and only defectors are punished.

4.2 Agents Interaction

Figure 2a depicts a fully norm-compliant round of the game. Once the manager opens the round, players start contributing to the pool. When all contributions are made, the manager applies the benefit factor, gathers the resulting amount, distributes each agent's portion, discloses contributions, and closes the round.

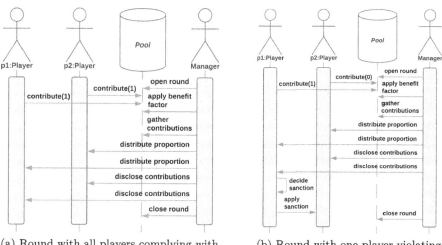

(a) Round with all players complying with the norm.

(b) Round with one player violating the norm.

Fig. 2. Sequence diagrams of a norm-compliant and a non-norm-compliant round.

Figure 2b illustrates a round in which a sanctioning occurs. After the manager discloses the contributions, the player *p1* notices that *p2* did not contribute. Then, player *p1* decides for a sanction and applies it to the player *p2*.

4.3 Implementation

For the simulation of our PGG[4], we have implemented two types of agents: game *manager* and *player*. The manager is responsible for (1) creating rounds; (2) defining groups; (3) gathering contributions; (4) multiplying the total contribution by a benefit factor; (5) dividing the result evenly among players; and

---

[4] Source code available at https://github.com/gavelproject/pgg/.

(6) disclosing the contribution of each player. Conversely, players are limited to (1) contributing to the pool; and (2) sanctioning other players based on the content of DeJure. The pools to which players cooperate are controlled by the manager and implemented as domain artefacts using CArtAgO.

All players are endowed with the Detector, Evaluator, Executor, and Controller capabilities, but for the sake of simplicity, no Legislator was included.

Only one norm regulates the players' behaviours in our PGG. As shown below, this norm, identified as positive_contribution, states that every player is obliged to contribute with 1 token to every pool it participates. If an agent does not comply with the norm before the pool finishes, then the norm is violated.

```
norm(
  id(positive_contribution),
  status(enabled),
  activation(pool_member(Player)),
  issuer(manager),
  target(Player),
  deactivation(false),
  deadline(pool_status("FINISHED")),
  content(obligation(contribution(Player,1)))
)
```

The following two links state that the positive_contribution norm is linked to two sanctions, punishment and gossip:

```
ns_link(
  nid(positive_contribution),
  sanction_links(sanction_link(status(enabled),sid(punishment)),
                 sanction_link(status(enabled),sid(gossip))
  )
)
```

The punishment sanction is only applicable if the player evaluating the violation is not the target and can afford the sanction. As shown below, this negative informal sanction counts as applied when the Executor directly punishes the target inflicting a pre-established cost.

```
sanction(
  id(punishment),
  status(enabled),
  activation(not .my_name(Target) & cost_to_punish(Cost) & tokens(Tokens) & Cost <= Tokens ),
  category(purpose(punishment), issuer(informal), locus(other_directed), mode(direct),
           polarity(negative), discernability(noticeable)),
  content(punish(Target))
)
```

Conversely, the gossip sanction is only applicable if the player evaluating the violation is not the target and has not reached the limit of reputation transmissions in that round, there is a player in another group, and the target is considered a free-rider. As shown below, this is a negative informal sanction that counts as applied when the Executor transmits reputation about the target to another agent from another group.

```
sanction(
  id(gossip),
  status(enabled),
  activation(not .my_name(Target) & not transmissions_credit(0) &
            not players_in_other_groups([]) &
            reputation(Target,Reputation) &
            min_reputation_cooperator(MinRepCoop) &
            Reputation < MinRepCoop),
  category(purpose(punishment), issuer(informal), locus(other_directed), mode(indirect),
          polarity(negative), discernability(unnoticeable)),
  content(gossip(Target,Reputation))
)
```

4.4   Evaluation Scenarios

We ran 2 evaluation scenarios to analyse how Gavel enables agents to reason about sanctions. These scenarios vary by just one feature, the type of sanctioning strategy (i.e., Random or Threshold) employed by all agents. For each scenario the agents population was formed by 400 agents, 100 of each contribution strategy (i.e., Cooperators, Free-riders, Nice, and Mean). The contribution to the public pool was set to 1 token, and the benefit factor was set to 3. Each agent was endowed with an initial amount of 50 tokens to be used to contribute to the public pool or to sanction others. Nice and Mean agents consider sanctioning other agents if they detect more than 20% of free-riders in their group. An agent is considered a free-rider if its reputation is below a threshold set to 0.6. A punishment involves a cost to the punisher (i.e., enforcement cost) and a cost to the punished agent (i.e., punishment cost). A gossip does not have a cost, although its use is limited by a maximum number of transmissions per round.

We ran the model for 100 rounds in each scenario, repeating 10 times with different random seeds for each combination of parameter values from Table 1.

Table 1. Simulation parameters.

Parameter	Values	
Enforcement cost	0.2	1
Punishment cost	2	5
Group size	5	
Number of transmissions	10	

In our scenarios we aimed at showing the potential benefits and use of Gavel to implement a simple (i.e., Random) and a more elaborated (i.e., Threshold) sanctioning strategies. We evaluated these scenarios by checking the average proportion of cooperation per group measured as the total number of agents contributing to the pool divided by the total number of agents per round. Four combinations of enforcement and punishment costs were identified: LcLp (low cost, low punishment), LcHp (low cost, high punishment), HcLp (high cost, low punishment), and HcHp (high cost, high punishment).

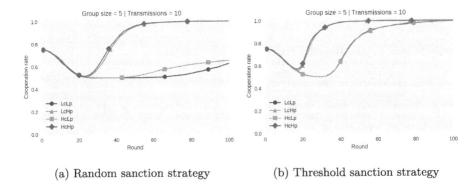

(a) Random sanction strategy   (b) Threshold sanction strategy

Fig. 3. Cooperation rates when agents employ different sanction strategies.

We started by evaluating the scenario in which agents employ the Random strategy. As shown in Fig. 3a, the agents were not able to achieve more than 70% of cooperation when the punishment cost was low. Starting approximately from the 70th round, however, both LcHp and HcHp allowed cooperation to reach 100% as a result from the death of free-riders.

Figure 3b shows that higher levels of cooperation were achieved when agents employed the Threshold strategy. Due to an informed heuristic used in this approach, agents were able to achieve 100% of cooperation for every combination of parameters. For the LcHp and HcHp combinations, 100% could even be achieved earlier when compared to Random.

Our results show that the sanction reasoning capability provided by Gavel allows agents to adapt to their current context improving the effectiveness of their actions and, specifically to PGG, it helps to improve the cooperation rate.

5   Conclusions and Future Work

In this chapter, we have designed and implemented an adaptive sanctioning enforcement framework, called Gavel, based on the conceptual model proposed by Nardin et al. [24]. We implemented *Gavel for JaCaMo*, an integration of Gavel with JaCaMo, and used it to implement a version of the Public Goods Game (PGG), in which agents can decide which type of sanction to apply at each stage of the game. Our results show that the Threshold sanction strategy, a simple sanctioning decision heuristic that uses reputation, improves the cooperation rate in the game compared to the Random sanction strategy, a sanctioning strategy that does not make any informed decision for sanctioning.

The main advantages for using Gavel are its flexibility and adaptability. Gavel can be treated as a component which can be connected to or implemented within any agent. By using it, agents are free to choose the sanctions and intensity they deem the best to sanction a violator or compiler agent. They may also update the legislation, or *De Jure*, to obtain higher levels of norm compliance. As these decisions are all dependent on the current context and historical facts, Gavel can, therefore, assure high level of flexibility and adaptability for norm enforcement in NMAS.

Conversely, Gavel's main disadvantages are limited control and predictability of final results. These are actually direct consequences of the flexibility it provides. As the sanctioning mechanism depends on the system's history and evolution, this influences how agents will learn and apply sanctions.

Our next main step is to further explore the adaptability Gavel provides. We intend to use reinforcement learning to allow Evaluators making better sanction decisions and Legislators updating De Jure based on De Facto. Furthermore, we plan to conduct experiments using different parameter values (e.g., group sizes) and dissociating cooperation from sanctioning strategy.

References

1. Andrighetto, G., Villatoro, D.: Beyond the carrot and stick approach to enforcement: an agent-based model. In: Kokinov, B., Karmiloff-Smith, A., Nersessian, N.J. (eds.) European Perspectives on Cognitive Science, pp. 1–6. New Bulgarian University Press, Sofia (2011)
2. Balke, T.: A taxonomy for ensuring institutional compliance in utility computing. In: Boella, G., Noriega, P., Pigozzi, G., Verhagen, H. (eds.) Normative Multi-Agent Systems. Dagstuhl Seminar Proceedings, vol. 09121, pp. 1–17. Schloss Dagstuhl - Leibniz-Zentrum fuer Informatik, Dagstuhl, Germany (2009)
3. Beccaria, M., Ingraham, E.D.: An essay on crimes and punishments, Chesnut St., no. 175. Philip H. Nicklin, Philadelphia (1819)
4. Becker, G.S.: Crime and punishment: an economic approach. J. Polit. Econ. **76**(2), 169–217 (1968)
5. Boissier, O., Hübner, J.F., Ricci, A.: The JaCaMo framework. In: Aldewereld, H., Boissier, O., Dignum, V., Noriega, P., Padget, J. (eds.) Social Coordination Frameworks for Social Technical Systems, pp. 125–151. Springer, Cham (2016). https://doi.org/10.1007/978-3-319-33570-4_7
6. Bordini, R.H., Hübner, J.F., Wooldridge, M.J.: Programming Multi-agent Systems in AgentSpeak Using Jason. Wiley Series in Agent Technology. Wiley, Chichester (2007)
7. Broersen, J., Dastani, M., Hulstijn, J., Huang, Z., van der Torre, L.: The BOID architecture: conflicts between beliefs, obligations, intentions and desires. In: Proceedings of the 5th International Conference on Autonomous Agents, pp. 9–16. ACM Press, New York (2001)
8. Cardoso, H.L., Oliveira, E.: Adaptive deterrence sanctions in a normative framework. In: Proceedings of the 2009 IEEE/WIC/ACM International Joint Conference on Web Intelligence and Intelligent Agent Technology, pp. 36–43. IEEE Computer Society, Washington, D.C. (2009)
9. Carlsmith, K.M., Darley, J.M., Robinson, P.H.: Why do we punish?: deterrence and just deserts as motives for punishment. J. Pers. Soc. Psychol. **83**(2), 284–299 (2002)
10. Centeno, R., Billhardt, H., Hermoso, R.: An adaptive sanctioning mechanism for open multi-agent systems regulated by norms. In: Proceedings of the IEEE 23rd International Conference on Tools with Artificial Intelligence, pp. 523–530. IEEE Computer Society, Washington, D.C. (2011)

11. Criado, N., Argente, E., Noriega, P., Botti, V.: MaNEA: a distributed architecture for enforcing norms in open MAS. Eng. Appl. Artif. Intell. **26**(1), 76–95 (2013)
12. Dignum, V.: A model for organizational interaction: based on agents, founded in logic. Ph.D. thesis, Utrecht University (2004)
13. Esteva, M., Rodríguez-Aguilar, J.A., Arcos, J.L., Sierra, C., Garcia, P.: Institutionalizing open multi-agent systems. In: Proceedings of the 4th International Conference on Multi-Agent Systems, pp. 381–382. IEEE Computer Society, Boston (2000)
14. Gâteau, B., Boissier, O., Khadraoui, D., Dubois, E.: MOISE^{Inst}: an organizational model for specifying rights and duties of autonomous agents. In: Gleizes, M.P., Kaminka, G.A., Nowé, A., Ossowski, S., Tuyls, K., Verbeeck, K. (eds.) Proceedings of the 3rd European Workshop on Multi-Agent Systems, pp. 484–485. Koninklijke Vlaamse Academie van Belie voor Wetenschappen en Kunsten, Brussels (2005)
15. Giardini, F., Paolucci, M., Villatoro, D., Conte, R.: Punishment and gossip: sustaining cooperation in a public goods game. In: Kamiński, B., Koloch, G. (eds.) Advances in Social Simulation. AISC, vol. 229, pp. 107–118. Springer, Heidelberg (2014). https://doi.org/10.1007/978-3-642-39829-2_10
16. Hart, H.L.A.: Punishment and Responsibility. Clarendon Press, Oxford (1968)
17. Horne, C.: The Rewards of Punishment: A Relational Theory of Norm Enforcement. Stanford University Press, Palo Alto, CA, US (2009)
18. Kollingbaum, M.J., Norman, T.J.: NoA - a normative agent architecture. In: Gottlob, G., Walsh, T. (eds.) Proceedings of the 18th International Conference on Artificial Intelligence, pp. 1465–1466. Morgan Kaufmann, San Francisco (2003)
19. Ledyard, J.: Public goods: a survey of experimental research. In: Kagel, J.H., Roth, A.E. (eds.) The Handbook of Experimental Economics, pp. 111–194. Princeton University Press, Princeton (1995)
20. López, F.L.y., Luck, M.: Modelling norms for autonomous agents. In: Chávez, E., Favela, J., Mejía, M., Oliart, A. (eds.) Proceedings of the 4th Mexican International Conference on Computer Science, pp. 238–245. IEEE Computer Society, Washington, D.C. (2003)
21. Mahmoud, S., Griffiths, N., Keppens, J., Luck, M.: Efficient norm emergence through experiential dynamic punishment. In: Raedt, L., et al. (eds.) Proceedings of the 20th European Conference on Artificial Intelligence - Including Prestigious Applications of Artificial Intelligence System Demonstrations Track. Frontiers in Artificial Intelligence and Applications, vol. 242, pp. 576–581. IOS Press, Monpellier (2012)
22. Mahmoud, S., Villatoro, D., Keppens, J., Luck, M.: Optimised reputation-based adaptive punishment for limited observability. In: Proceedings of the 6th IEEE International Conference on Self-Adaptive and Self-Organizing Systems, pp. 129–138. IEEE Computer Society, Washington, DC (2012)
23. Modgil, S., Faci, N., Meneguzzi, F., Oren, N., Miles, S., Luck, M.: A framework for monitoring agent-based normative systems. In: Proceedings of the 8th International Conference on Autonomous Agents and Multiagent Systems, pp. 153–160. IFAAMAS, Richland (2009)
24. Nardin, L.G., Balke, T., Ajmeri, N., Kalia, A.A., Sichman, J.S., Singh, M.P.: Classifying sanctions and designing a conceptual sanctioning process model for sociotechnical systems. Knowl. Eng. Rev. **31**(2), 142–166 (2016)
25. Noriega, P.: Agent mediated auctions: the fishmarket metaphor. Ph.D. thesis, Universitat Autònoma de Barcelona (1997)
26. Ostrom, E., Walker, J., Gardner, R.: Covenants with and without a sword: self-governance is possible. Am. Polit. Sci. Rev. **86**, 404–417 (1992)

27. Pasquier, P., Flores, R.A., Chaib-draa, B.: Modelling flexible social commitments and their enforcement. In: Gleizes, M.-P., Omicini, A., Zambonelli, F. (eds.) ESAW 2004. LNCS (LNAI), vol. 3451, pp. 139–151. Springer, Heidelberg (2005). https://doi.org/10.1007/11423355_10
28. Posner, R.A., Rasmusen, E.B.: Creating and enforcing norms, with special reference to sanctions. Int. Rev. Law Econ. **19**(3), 369–382 (1999)
29. Ricci, A., Piunti, M., Viroli, M., Omicini, A.: Environment programming in CArtAgO. In: El Fallah Seghrouchni, A., Dix, J., Dastani, M., Bordini, R. (eds.) Multi-Agent Programming: Languages, Tools and Applications, pp. 259–288. Springer, Boston (2009). https://doi.org/10.1007/978-0-387-89299-3_8
30. Villatoro, D., Andrighetto, G., Sabater-Mir, J., Conte, R.: Dynamic sanctioning for robust and cost-efficient norm compliance. In: Proceedings of the 22th International Joint Conference on Artificial Intelligence, pp. 414–419. AAAI Press, Menlo Park (2011)

Adding Organizational Reasoning to Agent-Based Simulations in GAMA

John Bruntse Larsen[✉]

DTU Compute, Technical University of Denmark, 2800 Kongens Lyngby, Denmark
jobla@dtu.dk

Abstract. The GAMA platform supports simulation with a bottom-up design from an agent perspective using a BDI framework. This chapter proposes a design for implementing the AORTA framework for organizational reasoning in the GAMA platform to support combining a bottom-up BDI model with a top-down organizational model. In doing so also we contribute towards maturing organizational reasoning for engineering multi-agent systems. The contribution is twofold: an operational semantics of the BDI framework in the GAMA platform, and an extension of it with operational semantics of AORTA.

1 Introduction

Social systems are systems that involve human interaction and decision making. Examples of social systems include private organizations, city regions and countries. Gaining insight into such systems is necessary for identifying workflows, bottlenecks and other important properties, but it is difficult because of the non-linearity of the systems. Agent-based simulation is an approach to gaining insight based on analysis of multiple runs of virtual simulation with agents that represent the real world actors in a social system. The advantage of the approach is that the designer of the simulation can focus on modeling the agents and have the system emerge as a result of their interaction, rather than having to model the system as an overall process. Agent-based simulation platforms, such as GAMA, provide general purpose tools to create environments and agents for any domain. In particular the BDI programming paradigm, which is also supported in GAMA, is a simple tool for modeling human reasoning in the agents. As argued in [1] however, the advances made in AI with frameworks and meta-models for agent environments and social systems could be further leveraged in agent-based simulation. In particular, the AORTA framework for adding organizational reasoning to agents can be useful for studying environments where humans enact roles and solve objectives of an organization. It enables BDI agents, modeled from a bottom-up perspective, to include organizational knowledge, modeled from a top-down perspective, in their reasoning and decision making. GAMA has useful features for setting up a simulation environment with geodata and supports BDI but does not support organizational reasoning. Contributing to the development of support for organizational reasoning in agent-based simulation could thus

© Springer Nature Switzerland AG 2019
D. Weyns et al. (Eds.): EMAS 2018 Workshops, LNAI 11375, pp. 242–262, 2019.
https://doi.org/10.1007/978-3-030-25693-7_13

benefit simulation of social systems. Doing so would also contribute towards maturing the concepts of organizational reasoning for engineering multi-agent systems. We contribute to the development in two parts: we provide an operational semantics of the GAMA BDI agents and extend it with concepts and rules based on the operational semantics of the AORTA framework. We show the design can be implemented with an example scenario and evaluate the extension by discussing the strengths and limitations of the implementation. We also discuss our contribution to engineering multi-agent systems.

2   Background

First we present some background on the GAMA platform and AORTA. GAMA is an agent-based simulation platform that is designed for simulation of spatial agents. It has rich features for visualizing simulations and is developed to be used by non-computer scientists. It uses a proprietary language call GAML which is originally designed for programming reflexive agents but supports multiple paradigms [2,3]. The style of GAML is a mixture of imperative statements and declarative statements, making it suitable for a wide range of models. In this chapter we focus on the parts of GAMA that are based on BDI, which is a paradigm for implementing human-like reasoning in agents. For more details on BDI as a paradigm for programming agents we refer to Shoham [4] and Woolridge and Jennings [5].

2.1   BDI Agents in GAMA

A simulation in GAMA is composed of two parts, a part that defines how agents behave and look like, and a part that defines how the simulation is shown and what experiments to execute. An agent is not coded individually but rather instantiated as a member of a larger class of agents referred to in GAMA as a *species* and defined with the keyword `species`. The species defines what properties an agent of the species have, and what actions an agent of the species can do. The typical way of coding a species is by defining `reflex` statements, which are functions that, provided their guard condition is fulfilled, are executed in every step of the simulation. Having a reference to some other agent, an agent can perform an `ask` operation to make the referenced actions change its state. A species can be annotated to use the `simple-bdi` module, which then extends agents of that species with BDI-based behavior. The module is developed with efficiency and easy-of-use for simulation creators in mind. Core concepts of BDI agents in GAMA:

- Simulation environment - The agents are spatially situated in a simulation environment that controls time and synchronizes agent execution.
- Belief base - A set of predicates that define the agent's internal knowledge about the world or its own state.
- Desires - A set of predicates that define the things that the agent wants.

- Intentions - A set of predicates that define the things that the agent is actively trying to achieve.
- Perception statements - Statements that the agent uses to observe changes in the world and update its knowledge base accordingly.
- Rule statements - Statements that the agent uses to infer new knowledge.
- Plan statements - Statements that the agent uses to perform actions toward achieving specific intentions.
- Agent properties - An agent has properties similar to that of an object in OOP. An agent can update and check both its own properties and properties of other agents.

In each step of the simulation, every agent (i) perceives the environment and updates beliefs, (ii) continues its current plan if it is not finished, or (iii) selects a new plan and possibly new intention and executes that plan. Figure 1 shows a simplified diagram of the agent behavior, which is our outset for the operational semantics we present in Sect. 3. We refer to [2] for the full diagram.

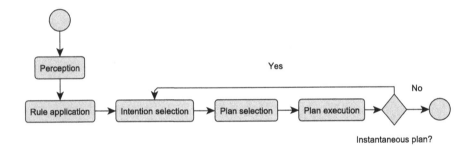

Fig. 1. Flowchart of agent behavior in GAMA.

2.2   AORTA

AORTA extends BDI agents with organizational reasoning capabilities according to the OperA meta-model [6], which gives a way of including a top-down model in a multi-agent system. The advantage of using AORTA is that it provides a complete operational semantics that only depends on the agents using BDI. The agents maintain organizational beliefs and options in knowledge bases separately from their internal beliefs and intentions. The organization defines what *roles* agents can enact, what *objectives* that agents enacting those roles should achieve, what *sub-objectives* should be achieved before achieving an objective, what *dependencies* there are between roles, and if there are additional objectives that should be achieved be others under certain *conditions*. We highlight the parts of the operational semantics of AORTA that we extend GAMA agents with and refer to [7] for the full definitions.

Agent Configuration. The mental state of an agent is based on four knowledge bases $\mathrm{MS}_{AORTA} = \langle \Sigma_a, \Gamma_a, \Sigma_o, \Gamma_o \rangle$ where Σ_a and Γ_a are its beliefs and intentions, Σ_o is its organizational state and Γ_o are its organizational options. The mental state thus ensures that an agent separates organizational and personal knowledge, and it is possible for agents to have different beliefs about an organization.

An agent configuration is defined as $A = \langle \alpha, \mathrm{MS}_{AORTA}, AR, F, C, \mu \rangle$ where α is the name of the agent, MS_{AORTA} is its mental state, AR are its reasoning rules, F is a set of transition functions, C are the capabilities of the agent, and $\mu = \langle \mu_{in}, \mu_{out} \rangle$ is its mailbox. Intuitively the agent configuration defines the state of the agent.

Transition System. The semantics of AORTA is defined in terms of a transition system that transforms the agent configuration in a sequence of phases. In the obligation check phase, the agent adds activated obligations or obligation violations to Σ_o, and retracts satisfied obligations from Σ_o. The phase is defined as the execution of the following rules, also giving rise to the name *obligation execution*.

$$\text{Obl-Activated} : \frac{\mathrm{rea}(\alpha, R) \in \Sigma_o \quad MS \models \mathrm{org}(\mathrm{cond}(R, p, \sigma, c)) \wedge \mathrm{bel}(c) \wedge \neg\mathrm{bel}(p)}{\Sigma_o \rightarrow \Sigma_o \cup \{\mathrm{obl}(\alpha, R, p, \delta)\}}$$

$$\text{Obl-Satisfied} : \frac{\mathrm{obl}(\alpha, R, p, \delta) \in \Sigma_o \quad MS \models \mathrm{bel}(p)}{\Sigma_o \rightarrow \Sigma_o \setminus \{\mathrm{obl}(\alpha, R, p, \delta)\}}$$

$$\text{Obl-Violated} : \frac{\mathrm{obl}(\alpha, R, p, \delta) \in \Sigma_o \quad MS \models \neg\mathrm{bel}(p) \wedge \mathrm{bel}(\delta)}{\Sigma_o \rightarrow \Sigma_o \cup \{\mathrm{viol}(\alpha, R, p)\}}$$

$$\text{Obl} ::= \text{Obl-Activated}^*; \text{Obl-Violated}^*; \text{Obl-Satisfied}^*$$

In the option generation phase, the agent generates organizational options and adds them to Γ_o. It can enact or deact a role, perform an objective, delegate objectives to other agents it depends on or inform others that depend on it about an objective. The execution of rules for this phase is named *option execution*.

$$\text{Enact} : \frac{\mathrm{role}(R, Os) \in \Sigma_o \quad \mathrm{rea}(\alpha, R) \notin \Sigma_o \quad \mathrm{cap}(\alpha) \cap Os \neq \emptyset}{\Gamma_o \rightarrow \Gamma_o \cup \{\mathrm{role}(R)\}}$$

$$\text{Deact} : \frac{\mathrm{role}(R, Os) \in \Sigma_o \quad \mathrm{rea}(\alpha, R) \in \Sigma_o \quad Os \subseteq \Sigma_a}{\Gamma_o \rightarrow \Gamma_o \cup \{\neg\mathrm{role}(R)\}}$$

$$\text{Objective} : \frac{\mathrm{obl}(\alpha, R, p, \delta) \in \Sigma_o \quad \mathrm{obj}(p, SubObj) \in \Sigma_o}{\Gamma_o \rightarrow \Gamma_o \cup \{\mathrm{obj}(p)\}}$$

$$\text{Delegate} : \frac{\{\mathrm{dep}(R_1, R_2, o), \mathrm{rea}(\alpha, R_1)\} \subseteq \Sigma_o \quad \mathrm{obj}(o) \in \Gamma_o}{\Gamma_o \rightarrow \Gamma_o \cup \{\mathrm{send}(R_2, achieve, o)\}}$$

$$\text{Inform} : \frac{\{\mathrm{dep}(R_1, R_2, o), \mathrm{rea}(\alpha, R_2)\} \subseteq \Sigma_o \quad MS \models o}{\Gamma_o \rightarrow \Gamma_o \cup \{\mathrm{send}(R_1, tell, o)\}}$$

$$\text{Opt} ::= \text{Enact}^*; \text{Deact}^*; \text{Objective}^*; \text{Delegate}^*; \text{Inform}^*$$

In the action execution phase, the agent considers its options, decides on a matching action reasoning rule to execute, and then executes the associated action. The outcome of the action is determined by the action transition function $\mathscr{A}$, which updates Σ_o and Γ_o. We refer to [7] for the definition of $\mathscr{A}$.

$$\text{Act-Exec} : \frac{(o : ctx \rightarrow a) \in R_A \quad o \in \Gamma_o \quad MS \models ctx \quad \mathscr{A}(a, MS) = MS'}{MS \rightarrow MS'}$$

$$\text{Act-Send} : \frac{(o : ctx \rightarrow \text{send}(rcp, msg)) \in R_A \quad o \in \Gamma_o \quad MS \models ctx}{\mu_{out} \rightarrow \mu_{out} \cup \{\text{msg}(rcp, msg)\}}$$

$$\text{Act} ::= (\text{Act-Exec}|\text{Act-Send}|\text{No-Op})$$

External changes are handled in the Ext rule, and incoming messages are handled in the Check rule.

$$\text{Ext} : \frac{}{\text{MS}_{AORTA} \rightarrow \text{MS}'_{AORTA}}$$

$$\text{Check} : \frac{\text{msg}(sender, msg) \in \mu_{in} \quad \mathscr{M}(sender, msg, \text{MS}_{AORTA}) = \text{MS}'_{AORTA}}{\mu_{in} \rightarrow \mu_{in} \setminus \{\text{msg}(sender, msg)\} \quad \text{MS}_{AORTA} \rightarrow \text{MS}'_{AORTA}}$$

Bringing it all together, the organizational cycle execution is defined as follows.

$$\text{Org} ::= \text{Check}^*; \text{Ext}; \text{Obl}; \text{Opt}; \text{Act}$$

3   Operational Semantics for AORTA Agents in GAMA

In order to extend GAMA BDI with AORTA we first design the extension as an operational semantics. As there is no existing formal semantics for GAMA BDI, we make one and then show how we extend that with AORTA semantics. The extended operational semantics comprises a design for implementing the extension.

3.1   GAMA BDI Operational Semantics

The operational semantics are based on the concepts for GAMA BDI agents that we highlighted and the diagram in Fig. 1.

We define an agent as $Agent = \langle P, \text{MS}_{GAMA}, Q, R, \Pi \rangle$ where P is a set of properties, $\text{MS}_{GAMA} = \langle B, D, I \rangle$ (with B, D and I being sets of predicates), Q is a set of **Perception** statements, R is a set of **Rule** statements and Π is a set of **Plan** statements of the form $t : c \rightarrow S$, where t is a trigger intention, c is a condition that must be *true* for the plan to be applicable, and S is a sequence of action statements. In any of the statements in Q, R and Π an agent can read meta-data from the simulation environment such as the step counter or time between steps. For the purpose of extending with AORTA semantics however, we simplify the simulation environment Env to be the set of all agents in the simulation $Env : Agent\ set$.

Given the above definition of an agent and the environment, we can define the BDI reasoning in GAMA in terms of functions on its mental state, applying statements relevant to that step. Perception and Rule application include the simulation environment and agent properties as an agent can perceive not only other agents in the environment but also its own properties.

$$\text{Perception} ::= Q, Env, \text{MS}_{GAMA}, P \to \text{MS}'_{GAMA}$$
$$\text{Rule application} ::= R, Env, \text{MS}_{GAMA}, P \to \text{MS}'_{GAMA}$$
$$\text{Intention selection} ::= \text{MS}_{GAMA}, I_{cur} \to I'_{cur}$$
$$\text{Plan selection} ::= \Pi, I_{cur}, \text{MS}_{GAMA} \to \Pi_{sel}$$

Having selected a plan to execute, the agent executes it which yields a new environment (and hence updated agents).

$$\text{Plan execution} ::= \Pi_{sel}, Env \to Env'$$

Given the above definitions, the activity semantics of a GAMA agent can be defined as the following sequence. If the selected plan is instantaneous, the agent may execute multiple plans for multiple intentions within one step.

$$\text{Act} ::= \text{Perception}; \text{Rule application};$$
$$(\text{Intention selection}; \text{Plan selection}; \text{Plan execution})^*$$

3.2 Extending with **AORTA** Semantics

Having defined an operational semantics of GAMA BDI agents, we proceed by defining the AORTA agent semantics in terms of the GAMA BDI semantics. Doing so comprises a design for how the semantics can be implemented in GAMA.

First we define the mental state and the agent configuration. We use a naming scheme to separate organizational beliefs and goals from regular beliefs and intentions.

$$(\Sigma_a) : \frac{b \in B \quad \textit{prefix}(pred(b)) \neq \mathbf{O}_-}{b \in \Sigma_a} \qquad (\Gamma_a) : \frac{i \in I \quad \textit{prefix}(pred(i)) \neq \mathbf{O}_-}{i \in \Gamma_a}$$

$$(\Sigma_o) : \frac{b \in B \quad \textit{prefix}(pred(b)) = \mathbf{O}_-}{b \in \Sigma_o} \qquad (\Gamma_o) : \frac{i \in I \quad \textit{prefix}(pred(i)) = \mathbf{O}_-}{i \in \Gamma_a}$$

Next we define the name of an agent as simply the **name** property of the agents.

$$\alpha = \mathbf{name}$$

The action reasoning rules AR are used in the Act phase to select an option, among those found in the Opt phase, and execute the action associated with that option. For example if the action is enact(ρ), the agent adds rea(α, ρ) to Σ_o, and adds send($\top, tell, rea(\alpha, \rho)$) to Γ_o. We define the reasoning rules in GAMA as a subset of instantaneous **Plan** statements that add intentions to Γ_a matching

the action reasoning rules. We also use instantaneous **Plan** statements to define
the set of transition functions of AORTA.

$$AR \subseteq \Pi \qquad\qquad F \subseteq \Pi$$

The capabilities of an agent are defined as the triggers of the plans in its plan
library Π. Note that this is only a subset of the beliefs that the agent can make
true, as carrying out a plan typically has side effects, but for simplicity we do
not include beliefs from side effects in Π.

$$(C) : \frac{t : c \to S \in \Pi}{t \in C}$$

As with the mental state, the mailbox is defined using a naming scheme that
separates mailbox beliefs from regular beliefs.

$$(\mu_{in}) : \frac{b \in B \quad prefix(pred(b)) = \mathbf{muIn\_}}{b \in \mu_{in}}$$

$$(\mu_{out}) : \frac{b \in B \quad prefix(pred(b)) = \mathbf{muOut\_}}{b \in \mu_{out}}$$

Next we extend with the AORTA transition system.

Obligation Execution. We integrate obligation execution in the rule application
step in GAMA, using the above definition of Σ_o and α. For simplicity, we only
make **Rule** statements with grounded predicates, meaning that we need a statement for each grounded premises for both (Obl-Activated), (Obl-Satisfied) and
(Obl-violated).

Option Execution. We also integrate option execution in the rule application
step, with **Rule** statements that add new predicates to Γ_o.

Action Execution. We integrate action execution in the looping part of the activity semantics as instantaneous **Plan** statements. By making them instantaneous,
the agent can perform an organizational action, such as enacting a role, updating
its mental state and possibly sending a message to other agents, and still carry
out an action as usual.

Ext and Check. Same as in AORTA, with the mental state as defined above.
    As a result we have defined AORTA semantics in terms of GAMA BDI opera-
tional semantics, which comprises a design for implementing AORTA in GAMA.

4   Implementation

Having an operational semantics for GAMA BDI agents extended with AORTA,
we make an implementation based on the operational semantics. In doing the
implementation we make details concrete that are left out of the more abstract

operational semantics, and the purpose of doing the implementation is to both
discuss these details and the operational semantics. As GAMA is a platform in
development with ongoing changes, the implementation we show here may be
improved upon by using features that are introduced in later versions.

In the following, the listed code is part of GAMA BDI agent species named
aortaAgent. We describe the parts of the code that is general and domain independent, and show an example of concrete version in a given domain in the next
section.

4.1 Agent Configuration

We define four functions to test if a predicate is in Σ_a, Σ_o, Γ_a or Γ_o. The
functions use the naming scheme we defined in the previous section, and can
be called with or without a list of arguments. The helper functions **isPrefix**,
believes and **intends** are not part of the standard library but functions we
define to make the code more comprehensible.

```
bool sigma_a(string pred, map args <- nil){
    if (isPrefix(pred, "O_")) {
        return false;
    }
    return believes(pred, args);
}

bool sigma_o(string pred, map args <- nil){
    if (!isPrefix(pred, "O_")) {
        return false;
    }
    return believes(pred, args);
}

bool gamma_a(string pred, map args <- nil){
    if (isPrefix(pred, "O_")) {
        return false;
    }
    return intends(pred, args);
}

bool gamma_o(string pred, map args <- nil){
    if (!isPrefix(pred, "O_")) {
        return false;
    }
    return intends(pred, args);
}
```

4.2   AORTA Predicates

Next we define functions that produce the predicates that are used in the
AORTA reasoning rules. Since these predicates, apart from the mailbox messages, reside only in Σ_o and Γ_o they all have O_ in their prefix. Note that the
functions role_pred and obj_pred can produce either a predicate with one argument, which in the AORTA semantics corresponds to an option, or a predicate
with two arguments, which correspond to an organizational meta-model definition. While we could make different predicate names to distinguish between the
1- and 2-argument versions, we stick with the original formulation from AORTA.
The mailbox messages are similarly produced by the two functions muIn_pred
and muOut_pred.

```
predicate role_pred(string r, list<predicate> objs){
  if (objs = nil) {
    return new_predicate("O_role",
      ["r"::r]);
  }
  return new_predicate("O_role",
    ["r" :: r, "objs"::objs]);
}

predicate obj_pred(predicate obj, list<predicate> objs){
  if (objs = nil) {
    return new_predicate("O_obj",
      ["obj" :: obj]);
  }
  return new_predicate("O_obj",
    ["obj" :: obj, "objs"::objs]);
}

predicate dep_pred(string r1, string r2, predicate obj){
  return new_predicate("O_dep",
    ["r1" :: r1, "r2" :: r2, "obj"::obj]);
}

predicate cond_pred(string r, predicate obj,
  predicate dl, predicate trig){
  return new_predicate("O_cond",
    ["r" :: r, "obj" :: obj, "dl"::dl, "trig"::trig]);
}

predicate rea_pred(string r, string ag){
  return new_predicate("O_rea",
    ["r" :: r, "ag" :: ag]);
}
```

```
predicate obl_pred(string ag, string r, predicate p,
   predicate delta){
   return new_predicate("O_obl",
     ["ag" :: ag, "r" :: r, "p" :: p, "delta" :: delta]);
}

predicate viol_pred(string ag, string r, predicate p) {
   return new_predicate("O_viol",
     ["ag" :: ag, "r" :: r, "p" :: p]);
}

predicate send_pred(string r, string ilf, predicate phi){
   return new_predicate("O_send",
     ["r"::r, "ilf"::ilf, "phi"::phi]);
}

predicate muIn_pred(string rcp, predicate msg){
   return new_predicate("muIn_msg",
     ["rcp"::rcp, "msg"::msg]);
}

predicate muOut_pred(string rcp, predicate msg){
   return new_predicate("muOut_msg",
     ["rcp"::rcp, "msg"::msg]);
}
```

4.3 AORTA Rules

Having functions for checking the knowledge bases of the agent configuration and functions that produce the AORTA predicates, we are now ready to implement the rules that enable organizational reasoning in the agents using the AORTA semantics. As specified in the extended operational semantics we defined in the previous section, we implement obligation execution, option execution using **Rule** statements and action execution using **Plan** statements.

For any of the **Rule** statements in obligation execution and option execution, its definition consists of three parts, building on the semantics of a GAMA rule:

1. A *trigger* predicate.
2. A *side-condition* for the activation of the rule.
3. A predicate to be *added* or *removed*.

The rules in the operational semantics of AORTA have a similar structure, so we make use of that in implementing them as **Rule** statements. As GAMA does not implement unification the statements use ground predicates and instead of entailment we define helper functions to look up ground predicates in the knowledge bases. For example for the obligation execution we define the following helper functions, which we use in the **Rule** statements.

```
bool obl_activated (string ag, string r, predicate p){
  return sigma_o (" O_rea ",[" r "::r ," ag "::ag ]) and
    !sigma_o (p.name,p.values );
}

bool obl_viol (string ag, string r, predicate p,
    predicate delta) {
  return isObliged (ag,r,p,delta) and
    !sigma_o (p.name,p.values );
}

bool isObliged (string ag, string r, predicate p,
    predicate delta) {
  return sigma_o (" O_obl ",[" ag "::ag, "r "::r, "p "::p,
    " delta "::delta ]);
}
```

The implementation of the AORTA rules as **Rule** statements is not straightforward so we describe each of them in turn. We start with the rules of obligation execution.

The obligation-activated rule in the AORTA semantics consists of three parts: two conditions and a consequence. The first condition is that the agent is enacting a certain role, and the second condition is that there is a conditional obligation for this role for which the precondition has been fulfilled and the objective has not been achieved. Expressed as a **Rule** statement, the precondition is the trigger of the statement, the objective to achieve and the enactment of the role are side-conditions, and the consequence of adding an obligation the predicate to be added. Expressed as a **Rule** statement it looks like below where c, p and `delta` are ground predicates and r is a constant string.

```
// obligation −satisfied
rule belief:c when:obl_activated (name,r,p)
  new_belief:obl_pred (name,r,p,delta );
```

We implement the obligation-violated and obligation-satisfied rules following a similar pattern. For obligation-violation, the achievement of the deadline objective is the trigger of the statement, the presence of the obligation and the unachieved objective are conditions and the consequence of adding a violation the predicate to be added. For obligation-satisfied, the achievement of the objective is the trigger, the presence of the obligation the condition and the consequence of removing the obligation the predicate to be removed. Expressed as **Rule** statements they look like below where p and `delta` are ground predicates and r is a constant string.

```
// obligation −violated
rule belief:delta when:obl_viol (name,r,p,delta )
  new_belief:viol_pred (name,r,p );
```

```
// obligation-satisfied
rule belief:p when:isObliged(name,r,p,delta)
  remove_belief:obl_pred(name,r,p,delta);
```

Next we consider the rules of option execution. The enact rule has four parts: three conditions and a consequence. The first condition is that the organizational knowledge base contains a definition of the role, the second condition is that the agent is not enacting the role and the third condition is that the capabilities of the agent intersect with the objectives of the role. Expressed as a **Rule** statement, the first condition is the trigger, the two other conditions the side-condition, and the consequence the desire to be added. The deact rule similarly has three conditions and a consequence but here we instead use the third condition as the trigger, and the first and second conditions as side-conditions. Here `objs` is a list of predicates and `r` is a constant string.

```
// enact options
rule belief:role_pred(r,objs) when:canEnact(name,r,objs)
  new_desire:role_pred(r,nil);
```

```
// deact options
rule beliefs:objs when:canDeact(name,r,objs)
  new_desire:role_pred(r,nil);
```

The obligation rule has two conditions and a consequence. The first condition is that the agent is obliged to achieve an objective before a deadline, and the second condition is that the agent knows what subobjectives the objective might have. The consequence is that the agent adds the objective to Γ_o. Expressed as a **Rule** statement, the first condition is the trigger, the second condition the side-condition and the consequence the desire to be added. Here `subObj` is a list of predicates, `delta` and `p` are predicates and `r` is a constant string.

```
// objective options
rule belief:obl_pred(name,r,p,delta)
  when:hasObj(p,subObj) new_desire:obj_pred(p,nil);
```

The delegate and inform rules both have two conditions and a consequence. For the delegate rule the first condition is that the agent enacts a role that depends on another role for achieving an objective, and the second condition is that objective is in Γ_o. Reversely for the inform rule, the first condition is that the agent enacts a role that another role depends on for achieving an objective, and the second condition is that the objective has been achieved. Expressed as **Rule** statements, the second condition is the trigger, the first condition the side-condition and the conclusion the desire to be added. Here `r1` and `r2` are constant strings and `o` is a predicate.

```
// delegate options
rule desire:obj_pred(o,nil) when:shouldDel(name,r1,r2,o)
  new_desire:send_pred(r2," achieve",o);
```

```
// inform options
rule belief:o when:shouldInform(name,r1,r2,o)
  new_desire:send_pred(r1," tell ",o);
```

4.4 Transition Functions

It remains to define the action execution and check rules. As specified in the previous section, we implement these using **Plan** statements. Before we do that though we implement the action transition function and a message transition function, which will be used in the **Plan** statements.

The action transition function alters the mental state accordingly to the action performed, and adds a desire to inform other agents about the action. It is defined for each of the four possible actions in AORTA: enact, deact, commit and drop. We define it as four different GAMA functions that each perform the updates as specified in the AORTA semantics.

```
action enact(string alpha, string r, string informRole){
  do add_belief(rea_pred(r,alpha));
  do add_desire(send_pred(informRole," tell ",
    rea_pred(r,alpha)));
}

action deact(string alpha, string r, string informRole){
  do remove_belief(rea_pred(r,alpha));
  do add_desire(send_pred(informRole," tell ",
    rea_pred(r,alpha)));
}

action commit(predicate phi, string informRole){
  do add_desire(phi);
  do add_desire(send_pred(informRole," tell ",
    obj_pred(phi,nil)));
}

action drop(predicate phi, string informRole){
  do remove_desire(phi);
  do add_desire(send_pred(informRole," tell ",
    obj_pred(phi,nil)));
}
```

The message transition function alters the mental state accordingly to messages in the inbox. Unlike the action transition function, the message transition function does not have a fixed definition but can be specified accordingly to how the simulation creator wants agents to handle messages.

4.5   Check and Action Execution

The check rule defines how to process inbox messages, applying the message transition function and then removing the message. We implement this using a combination of a **Rule** and a **Plan** statement. The first statement is for detecting new messages in the inbox in need of processing, which then adds a desire to process the inbox messages.

```
rule  belief:new_predicate("muIn_msg")
   remove_belief:new_predicate("muIn_empty")
   new_desire:new_predicate("muIn_empty");
```

The second statement is for processing the messages in the inbox. It is a **Plan** statement that is triggered by the aforementioned **Rule**. The plan body applies the message transition function to each message. The plan is instantaneous since it only involves changing the mental state of the agent.

```
plan  check  intention:new_predicate("muIn_empty")
   instantaneous:true{
   list<predicate> msgs <-
      get_beliefs_with_name("muIn_msg");
   loop msg over:msgs {
      do M(msg.values["rcp"], msg.values["msg"]);
      do remove_belief(msg);
   }
   do add_belief(new_predicate("muIn_empty"));
}
```

The action execution rule takes an applicable action reasoning rule and applies it using the action transition function. We implement this using **Plan** statements that are triggered by organizational options and have a plan body that applies the action transition function. The statement thus encodes the action execution rule for a given action reasoning rule. Below shows template code for such a statement, where AR1 is the name of the action reasoning rule, o is the trigger predicate, ctx is an optional condition for the statement to be applicable, and a is call to the action transition function. Like message processing, action execution only changes the mental state so the plan is instantaneous. The agent can then subsequently apply a non-instantaneous plan according to the updated Σ_o.

```
plan  AR1  intention:o  when:ctx
   instantaneous:true{
   do a;
   do add_belief(o);
}
```

5   Evaluation

We demonstrate the operational semantics and evaluate the implementation by creating an example simulation with a concrete scenario. For the example we use an organization meta-model based on the one in [8] (see Table 1), which defines a simplified organizational meta-model for patient treatment in a hospital emergency room. Patient treatment in hospital emergency rooms is a highly dynamic process where the staff continuously try to predict what the outcome of decisions are in order to ensure the safety for the patients. Simulation can provide a forecast of what the outcome of the staff's decisions is going to be given an expected mix of incoming patients. Organizational agent models are ideal for the scenario since the doctors and nurses have roles and objectives that they are expected to do, but they can choose to break these if they think the situation requires it. The simulation model we describe here only covers a small part of the scenario but we discuss the work necessary to extend the model to more of the scenario.

The simulation consists of two agents, a patient p and a nurse n who initially have the following mental states:

- Σ_o (for both agents): as specified in Table 1, plus the following predicates: "**O_rea(patient, p)**" and "**O_rea(nurse, n)**". The condition in Σ_o states that the nurse should perform triage before a patient is treated.
- Σ_a (for both agents): contains "**patient(p)**".
- Γ_o, Γ_a (for both agents): empty.

We implement the agents as members of an agent species that contains all of the statements we described in the previous section, with scenario specific versions of constants and action execution rules. We explain what constants and rules we need, and show what happens in the simulation.

Table 1. Initially Σ_o for all agents contains these predicates.

role(*patient*, {*treatment*(*Patient*)})
role(*nurse*, {*triage*(*Patient*)})
obj(*triage*(*Patient*), {})
dep(*patient*, *nurse*, *triage*(*Patient*))
cond(*nurse*, *triage*(*Patient*), *treatment*(*Patient*), *patient*(*Patient*))

In the agent species we define the following constants. We have constant strings for the name of the patient, the name of the nurse, the patient role and the nurse role. We use these to define grounded predicates that denote facts about the patient. When we define the meta-model, we also need predicates for the predicates with variables. Since GAMA does not allow us to define predicates with open variables, we define these as constants that, at a model level, represent meta-model variables.

```
string  patient_name <- "p";
string  nurse_name <- "n";

string  patient_role <- "patient";
string  nurse_role <- "nurse";

predicate  patient_p <- new_predicate("patient",
  ["var1"::patient_name]);
predicate  triage_p <- new_predicate("triage",
  ["var1"::patient_name]);
predicate  treatment_p <- new_predicate("treatment",
  ["var1"::patient_name]);

predicate  patient <- new_predicate("patient",
  ["var1"::"Patient"]);
predicate  triage <- new_predicate("triage",
  ["var1"::"Patient"]);
predicate  treatment <- new_predicate("treatment",
  ["var1"::"Patient"]);
```

We include the functions in Sects. 4.1 and 4.2 as they are shown. With these in place we can define an organizational meta-model. We initialize Σ_o as specified above using the following code.

```
init {
  do  add_belief(role_pred(patient_role ,[treatment]));
  do  add_belief(role_pred(nurse_role ,[treatment]));
  do  add_belief(obj_pred(triage ,[]));
  do  add_belief(dep_pred(patient_role ,
    nurse_role , triage ));
  do  add_belief(cond_pred(nurse_role , triage ,
    treatment , patient ));

  do  add_belief(rea_pred(patient_role , patient_name ));
  do  add_belief(rea_pred(nurse_role , nurse_name ));
}
```

We also include **Rule** and **Plan** statements as described in Sect. 4.3. For these statements we use the constants defined above. For example we make a **Rule** statement for the obligation-satisfied rule matching the cond-predicate in the meta-model.

```
rule  belief:patient_p
  when:obl_activated(name,nurse_role , triage_p )
  new_belief:obl_pred(name,nurse_role , triage_p ,
    treatment_p );
```

For action reasoning rules we include a **Plan** statement saying that if an agent has the option to perform triage, then the agent should commit to it.

```
plan commitTo intention:obj_pred(triage_p,nil)
  instantaneous:true{
  do commit(triage_p,patient_role);
  do add_belief(obj_pred(triage_p,nil));
}
```

Finally we create two agents for the simulation named n and p, who are of the `aortaAgent` species.

```
global{
  init{
    create species:aortaAgent number:1 with:(name:"n");
    create species:aortaAgent number:1 with:(name:"p");
  }
}
```

In the following we describe what happens in the first loop of the simulation, focusing on the changes to the mental state in agent n.

Perception. None of the agents perform any **Perception** statements.

Rule Application. Both obligation execution and option execution takes place in this step. The **Rule** statements concerning obligation execution adds the predicate "O_obl(n, nurse, triage(p), treatment(p))" to Σ_o. The **Rule** statements concerning option execution then adds "O_obj(triage(p))" to Γ_o.

Intention Selection. Having "O_obj(triage(p))" in Γ_o, and thus in I, it is selected as the current intention.

Plan Selection and Execution. Having a **Plan** statement with the trigger intention "O_obj(triage(p))", agent n then commits to triage(p), adding it to Γ_a. As the plans for the action reasoning rules and the action transition function are instantaneous, agent n can then select a plan with "triage(p)" as trigger intention and begin execution of that plan.

6   Discussion

In this section we first discuss the advantages and limitations of the implementation with respect to social simulation in GAMA, and then we discuss the contribution of our work to engineering multi-agent systems.

6.1   AORTA in GAMA

The example shows how a nurse agent can use a clearly defined organizational meta-model made from a top-down perspective to decide its course of action in patient treatment. To get similar behavior using only the existing BDI framework in GAMA, it would be necessary to design agents with a bottom-up method, which would make the organization less clear. By adjusting the action reasoning rules, we can also adjust how a nurse agent handles organizational obligations separately from how it handles its own intentions.

However the implementation have some limitations. The biggest limitation is not being able to use variables in **Rule** and **Plan** statements. In the example we have shown, we only created one of each of the obligation execution and action execution rules, but in a simulation with more roles and objectives, we would have to define the rules for each rule and objective. A possible solution to this limitation is to extend GAMA with unification so that open variables in a predicate are instantiated with values according to the beliefs, desires and intentions of the agent. Another significant limitation of the implementation is that the AORTA extension takes up a big part of the agent species code. The functions and operational semantics should be defined separately so that the agent species only defines action execution rules. Finally the implementation also shows that negated predicates are not handled properly. The Deact rule for example states that $\neg role(R)$ should be added to Γ_o but this is not reflected in the implementation. GAMA supports a primitive way of handling negated predicates which has not been accounted for in the design.

6.2   Engineering Multi-Agent Systems

While GAMA is dedicated to agent-based simulation and uses a proprietary agent programming language, we can also discuss our work in relation to use of AORTA and organizational reasoning for engineering multi-agent systems. While multi-agent programming platforms such as Jason to an increasing extent support generalized organization frameworks, there is a need in the community to find some consensus about which frameworks to use [9]. With AORTA we can extend existing BDI-based multi-agent systems with organizational reasoning. As we discussed above though, there are more important points to consider:

Open variables. The obligation and action execution rules involves checking if the beliefs in the knowledge bases satisfy certain side-conditions. However doing so is not trivial when the agent programming platform does not offer entailment with open variables that can bound by unification. For such platforms it is necessary to introduce elaborate code that circumvents this lack, possibly by implementing many versions of each rule for different combinations of rules and objectives.

Reuse of code. One of the strengths of AORTA is that it provides an operational semantics that can be implemented as an extension of a BDI-based agent framework. We have shown a collection of helper functions in order to make the implementation of the operational semantics comprehensible. However if we want multiple kinds of agents we would have to copy the code for each kind of agent. When engineering a multi-agent system, it is often convenient to create multiple kinds of agents with different specific sub-functions and action execution rules. In this case it would be better to have the operational semantics code in a module that all agents can access.

7   Related Work

We compare this work with other models and frameworks for social simulation. Network-oriented modeling has been applied for social system simulation to study the effects of various social parameters for the agent behavior on the outcome of the system [10–12]. The advantage of the network model is that one can tune the input parameters in the model to model different kind of behaviors in the agent and see the result. For example in an evacuation scenario, a parameter that controls how likely an agent is to mimic their peers can be increased to see if this behavior changes how quickly the agents evacuate a building. In comparison, AORTA is based on the BDI paradigm and logic. The behavior of our agents is determined by logical reasoning rather than tuning of parameters. To create a mimicking behavior the agents must be able to reason that it lets them solve their goals. MOISE+ is an organization meta-model which has been implemented in the Jason agent programming platform [13,14]. In contrast we use AORTA, which has also been implemented in Jason [15], and GAMA, which is an agent-based simulation platform. The advantage of using GAMA is that it is a simulation platform intended to also be used by people who are not computer scientists. The topic of AORTA vs MOISE is interesting as there is still a lack of consensus on a simple set of concepts for social aspects [9]. There are also other methods to include normative reasoning in agents which do not incorporate an organization meta-model [16–18]. Social practice theory in particular provides a model for social simulation which takes the view of activities that agents know of rather than the agents themselves. An activity is known by agents and some agents act out an activity as a habit given that they have the competences for it and the affordances for the activity are present. Through mimicking behavior, agents learn new activities and successful habits. In earlier work we have applied social practice theory to the emergency health care scenario but it was not used for simulation [19]. With version 1.8, GAMA also features a framework for normative reasoning which shows the growing interest in frameworks for social simulation. Finally there are also social simulation systems that are not based on agents. Business process models have been used to make flow-prediction in systems where it is clear what model the system follows. As it was discussed at the Operational Research Society's Simulation Workshop 2010 [20] and in the work of Liu et al. [21] however such models tend to grow unwieldy, especially in complex systems with humans decision making where goals can conflict. For this reason agent-based approaches seem promising as a way to break down complex systems in smaller comprehensible parts.

8   Conclusion

We have given an operational semantics for BDI agents in the GAMA platform for agent-based simulation, and extended them with concepts and rules that add organizational reasoning according to the AORTA framework. The extended semantics comprises a design for implementing AORTA in the GAMA platform.

We have also shown how the design can be implemented with a small example. It shows that we can add organizational reasoning to BDI-based simulation agents, thus providing generalized support for social simulation of organizations. We have also identified points we found important to consider when using AORTA and thus contributed to implementing organizational reasoning for multi-agent systems. If a multi-agent system is based on BDI, we can extend it with the operational semantics of AORTA to add organizational reasoning to the agents. We can do so even if the programming language does not offer unification with open variables although it then requires us to introduce elaborate code to circumvent the lack of it. In addition, the operational semantics should be implemented in a way so that multiple kinds of agents can use it without having to each have their own copy of the code. Future work includes more details in the semantics and improving upon the limitations of the implementation in order to use it for more complex social simulations.

Acknowledgements. This work is part of the Industrial PhD project *Hospital Staff Planning with Multi-Agent Goals* between PDC A/S and Technical University of Denmark. We would also like to thank Jørgen Villadsen for comments.

References

1. Larsen, J.B.: Agent programming languages and logics in agent-based simulation. In: Sieminski, A., Kozierkiewicz, A., Nunez, M., Ha, Q.T. (eds.) Modern Approaches for Intelligent Information and Database Systems. SCI, vol. 769, pp. 517–526. Springer, Cham (2018). https://doi.org/10.1007/978-3-319-76081-0_44
2. Taillandier, P., Bourgais, M., Caillou, P., Adam, C., Gaudou, B.: A BDI agent architecture for the GAMA modeling and simulation platform. In: Nardin, L.G., Antunes, L. (eds.) MABS 2016. LNCS (LNAI), vol. 10399, pp. 3–23. Springer, Cham (2017). https://doi.org/10.1007/978-3-319-67477-3_1
3. Caillou, P., Gaudou, B., Grignard, A., Truong, C.Q., Taillandier, P.: A simple-to-use BDI architecture for agent-based modeling and simulation. Adv. Intell. Syst. Comput. **528**, 15–28 (2017)
4. Shoham, Y.: Agent-oriented programming. Artif. Intell. **60**(1), 51–92 (1993)
5. Wooldridge, M., Jennings, N.R.: Intelligent agents - theory and practice. Knowl. Eng. Rev. **10**(2), 115–152 (1995)
6. Dignum, V.: A model for organizational interaction: based on agents, founded in logic. Ph.D. thesis, Utrecht University (2004). SIKS Dissertation Series 2004-1
7. Jensen, A.S., Dignum, V., Villadsen, J.: A framework for organization-aware agents. Auton. Agents Multi-Agent Syst. **31**(3), 387–422 (2017)
8. Larsen, J.B., Villadsen, J.: An approach for hospital planning with multi-agent organizations. In: Polkowski, L., et al. (eds.) IJCRS 2017. LNCS (LNAI), vol. 10314, pp. 454–465. Springer, Cham (2017). https://doi.org/10.1007/978-3-319-60840-2_33
9. Mascardi, V., Weyns, D., Ricci, A.: Engineering multi-agent systems: State of affairs and the road ahead. SIGSOFT Softw. Eng. Notes **44**(1), 18–28 (2019)
10. Treur, J.: Network-Oriented Modeling. Addressing Complexity of Cognitive, Affective and Social Interactions. Springer, Cham (2016). https://doi.org/10.1007/978-3-319-45213-5

11. van der Wal, C.N., Formolo, D., Robinson, M.A., Minkov, M., Bosse, T.: Simulating crowd evacuation with socio-cultural, cognitive, and emotional elements. In: Mercik, J. (ed.) Transactions on Computational Collective Intelligence XXVII. LNCS, vol. 10480, pp. 139–177. Springer, Cham (2017). https://doi.org/10.1007/978-3-319-70647-4_11

12. Formolo, D., Van Ments, L., Treur, J.: A computational model to simulate development and recovery of traumatised patients. Biologically Inspired Cogn. Architectures **21**, 26–36 (2017)

13. Hübner, J.F., Sichman, J.S., Boissier, O.: Developing organised multiagent systems using the MOISE+ model: programming issues at the system and agent levels. Int. J. Agent-Oriented Softw. Eng. **1**(3/4), 370–395 (2007)

14. Hübner, J.F., Boissier, O., Kitio, R., Ricci, A.: Instrumenting multi-agent organisations with organisational artifacts and agents: giving the organisational power back to the agents. Auton. Agents Multi-Agent Syst. **20**(3), 369–400 (2010)

15. Jensen, A.S., Dignum, V., Villadsen, J.: The AORTA architecture: integrating organizational reasoning in *Jason*. In: Dalpiaz, F., Dix, J., van Riemsdijk, M.B. (eds.) EMAS 2014. LNCS (LNAI), vol. 8758, pp. 127–145. Springer, Cham (2014). https://doi.org/10.1007/978-3-319-14484-9_7

16. Deljoo, A., van Engers, T., van Doesburg, R., Gommans, L., de Laat, C.: A normative agent-based model for sharing data in secure trustworthy digital market places. In: Proceedings of the 10th International Conference on Agents and Artificial Intelligence ICAART, vol. 1, pp. 290–296. SciTePress (2018)

17. Jager, W., Janssen, M.: An updated conceptual framework for integrated modeling of human decision making: the Consumat II. In: European Conference of Complex Systems (2012)

18. Ghorbani, A., Bots, P., Dignum, V., Dijkema, G.: MAIA: a framework for developing agent-based social simulations. J. Artif. Soc. Soc. Simul. **16**(2), 1–15 (2013)

19. Larsen, J.B., Dignum, V., Villadsen, J., Dignum, F.: Querying social practices in hospital context. In: Proceedings of the 10th International Conference on Agents and Artificial Intelligence ICAART, vol. 2, pp. 405–412. SciTePress (2018)

20. Siebers, P.O., Macal, C.M., Garnett, J., Buxton, D., Pidd, M.: Discrete-event simulation is dead, long live agent-based simulation! J. Simul. **4**(3), 204–210 (2010)

21. Liu, Z., Rexachs, D., Luque, E., Epelde, F., Cabrera, E.: Simulating the micro-level behavior of emergency department for macro-level features prediction. In: Winter Simulation Conference 2015, pp. 171–182. IEEE Press (2016)

Analyzing Radicalism Spread Using Agent-Based Social Simulation

Tasio Méndez[1], J. Fernando Sánchez-Rada[1], Carlos A. Iglesias[1(⊠)], and Paul Cummings[2]

[1] Intelligent Systems Group, Universidad Politécnica de Madrid, Madrid, Spain
{tasio.mendez,jf.sanchez,carlosangel.iglesias}@upm.es
[2] Krasnow Institute, GMU Computational Social, Fairfax, VA, USA
pcummin2@gmu.edu
http://www.gsi.dit.upm.es

Abstract. This work presents an agent-based model of radicalization growth based on social theories. The model aims at improving the understanding of the influence of social links on radicalism spread. The model consists of two main entities, a Network Model and an Agent Model. The Network Model updates the agent relationships based on proximity and homophily; it simulates information diffusion and updates the agents' beliefs. The model has been evaluated and implemented in Python with the agent-based social simulator Soil. In addition, it has been evaluated through sensitivity analysis.

Keywords: Radicalization · Terrorism ·
Agent-based social simulation

1 Introduction

Research works on political terrorism began in the early 1970s. These works were focused on collecting empirical data and analyzing it for public policy purposes. Terrorist activity was usually attributed to personality disorders or "irrational" thinking [4]. However, further research paints a richer picture and suggest that many additional factors need to be considered.

Many scholars, government analysts, and politicians point out that since the mid-1990s terrorism has changed. This "new" form of terrorism is often motivated by religious beliefs, and it is more fanatical, deadly, and pervasive. It also differs in terms of goals, methods, and organization [4,31]. However, the drivers of modern terrorism involve not only political or religious interests but also include fanaticism. Consequently, terrorism is the result of a complex process of radicalization. i.e., a progressive adoption of extreme political, social or religious ideals.

Nevertheless, this process does not always lead to violent acts such as terrorism [13]. It is of vital importance to understand the properties of radicalization in order to anticipate said violence. The primary challenge of understanding how

D. Weyns et al. (Eds.): EMAS 2018 Workshops, LNAI 11375, pp. 263–282, 2019.
https://doi.org/10.1007/978-3-030-25693-7_14

these organizations work is that information is not always available and, when it is available, it is often incomplete or inaccurate.

One common approach to face terrorism is trying to understand its roots, motivation, and practices. In particular, it is of vital importance nowadays to understand how terrorist organizations recruit new members and isolate them. Moreover, terrorist organizations have effectively used social media and social networks to expand their networks through real-time information exchange.

As society and new forms of communications evolve, terrorists are developing new forms of organization for their purposes. Organizations can thus flatten out their pyramid of authority and control. The resulting structure can take different forms, from a dense network to a group of more or less autonomous, dispersed entities, linked by communications and perhaps nothing more than a common purpose [32]. Thus, terrorist organizations can be modeled as Social Networks (SNs) where vertices represent members of the organization and links represent communication between members.

Regardless of their structure, terrorist organizations are by definition SNs and can be modeled as such. Hence, research based on Agent-based Social Simulation (ABSS) could be a good starting point for understanding the information flow within the network.

This chapter proposes an agent-based model of a terrorist organization growth which has been implemented in Soil [29], an agent-based social simulator designed for modeling social networks.

This remainder of the chapter is structured as follows. Section 2 introduces the ABSS Soil[1], paying particular attention to its modeling approach as well as specific features developed for modeling problems with a geographical component, as it happens in the radicalization process. Section 3 introduces the agent-based model of radicalization[2]. Section 4 describes the implementation of the model using Soil and provides an overview of the simulation results, including a sensitivity analysis of the simulation results to evaluate the developed model. Finally, some conclusions and insights are presented in Sect. 5.

2   Agent-Based Social Simulator Soil

Soil [29] is a modern ABSS for modeling and simulation of SNs. It has been applied to many scenarios, ranging from rumor propagation to emotion propagation and information diffusion. Each simulation consists of a set of agents, which typically represent humans, and a network that represents social links between agents.

Agents are characterized by their state and the behaviors they can carry out in every simulation step, usually depending on user state. Each behavior defines the actions carried out and how agent state evolves, depending on external factors or social factors. Those external or social factors are controlled by environment agents, which are not assigned to any network node.

---

[1] https://github.com/gsi-upm/soil.
[2] https://github.com/gsi-upm/soil/tree/master/examples/terrorism.

The main reason for using this simulator is that it is one of the few ABSS platforms that support social network analysis [29]. Two other alternatives were considered: Hashkat and Krowdix. Table 1 summarizes these platforms and the reviewed aspects.

Table 1. Review of ABSS platforms [29]

Name	Domain	Language	SNs	SNA	OS
HashKat	Social networks	C++	✓	✓	✓
Krowdix	Social networks	Java	✓	✓	✗
Soil	Social networks	Python	✓	✓	✓

HashKat [27] is a C++ ABSS platform specifically designed for the study and simulation of social networks. It includes facilities for network growth and information diffusion, based on a kinetic Monte Carlo model. It exports information to be processed by machine learning libraries such as NetworkX [14] or R's iGraph [5] and network visualization with Gephi [1]. The simulator is highly performant but has two significant drawbacks. Firstly, simulations are expressed in a descriptive language. Agents are created by specifying a set of highly configurable parameters. As a result, adding behaviors beyond those already included in the platform involves adding new capabilities to the framework. Secondly, and most importantly, modifications to these behaviors are very tied to the architecture of the platform, rather than being isolated for every type of agent. This modifications make customization costly, especially for someone without a C++ background.

On the other hand, Krowdix [2] is built on Java ABSS. It uses JUNG [23] for network functions and JFreeChart [12] for visualization. The simulation model considers users, their relationships, user groups, and interchanged contents. However, its main drawback is that it is not open source.

Conversely, Soil is open source and built using Python and benefits from all the Python ecosystem. Regarding the alternatives, Krowdix project is no longer active, while Hashkat provides many facilities for modifying the settings of the provided agent models, but makes hard the integration of new models. In contrast, Soil has been conceived for experimenting and developing easily new simulation models in Python. This practice has the advantage of Python's increased popularity, its very gradual learning curve, readability, clear syntax and availability of libraries for network processing and machine learning. The network features of Soil are based on NetworkX, which is the defacto standard library for Social Network Analysis (SNA) of small to medium networks. NetworkX provides functionalities for manipulating and representing graph models, generators of classical and popular graph models, including generators for geometric graphs, and graph algorithms for analyzing graph properties. Likewise, NetworkX is interoperable with a high number of graph formats, including GEXF, GML, GraphML and JSON among others.

The main benefit of using Soil is its capability to model agent relationships as graphs. This approach is different from other environments (i.e., MESA, NetLogo Repast or Mason) which do not provide yet this. Thus, Soil can be used for any problem that can benefit from a graph representation. Up to now, Soil has been mainly used for modeling social network related problems, such as viral marketing, emotion propagation in social networks and online radicalization. Some other areas that could benefit from Soil are transportation problems since they are frequently modeled with both agents and network models.

Soil provides several levels of reusability. First, we propose a methodological approach for modeling agent systems at macro and micro levels. This workflow can be used in other agent-based simulation tools for modeling systems where it is needed to update both macro and micro levels during the simulation. The second level is the framework Soil that can be used for developing different models, running simulations and analyzing the simulation results. The integration of Soil with the Python ecosystem enables using standard tools for data analysis and visualization (e.g., pandas [19]) as well as machine learning algorithms (e.g., scikitlearn [24]). Finally, models can be extended through inheritance and agents from one model can be reused for other models in the same domain.

2.1   Architecture

As previously stated, simulations in Soil consist of agents and a network that represents social links between agents. Agents are characterized by their state (e.g., infected) and the behaviors they can carry out in every simulation step, which usually depend on the user state. Each behavior defines the actions carried out (e.g., tweeting or following a user) and how the agent state evolves depending on external factors (e.g., news about a topic) or social factors (e.g., opinion of their friends). The likelihood or frequency of each action is typically configurable by either globally or agent-level variables.

This simulation model has been implemented in the architecture shown in Fig. 1 and consists of four main components.

The *NetworkSimulation* class is in charge of the network simulator engine. It provides a forward-time simulation of events in a network based on nxsim[3] and Simpy [18]. Based on configuration parameters, a graph is generated with NetworkX, and an agent class is populated to each network node. The main parameters are the network type, number of nodes, the maximum simulation time, number of simulations and timeout between each simulation step.

The *BaseAgentBehaviour* class is the essential agent behavior that should be extended for each social network simulation model. It provides basic functionality for generation of a JSON file with the status of the agents for its analysis with machine libraries such as Scikit-Learn [24].

The *SoilSimulator* class is in charge of running the simulation pipeline defined in Sect. 2.2, which consists of running the simulation and generating a visualiza-

---

[3] https://pypi.python.org/pypi/nxsim.

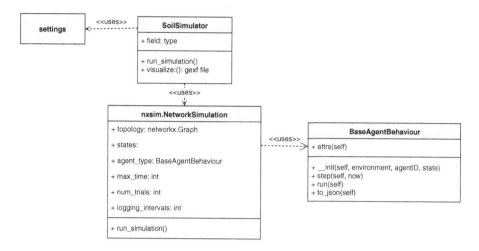

Fig. 1. Simulation components

tion file in Graph Exchange XML Format (GEXF) which can be visualized with Gephi. Besides, interactive analysis can be done with IPython web interface.

Settings groups the general settings for simulations and the settings of the different models available in Soil's simulation model library.

2.2   Simulation Workflow

An overview of the system's flow is shown in Fig. 2. The simulation workflow consists of three steps: configuration, simulation, and visualization.

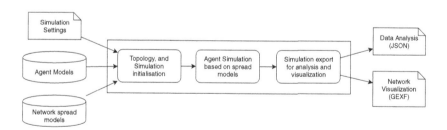

Fig. 2. Social simulator's workflow

In the first step, the main parameters of the simulation are configured in the JSON or YAML settings file. The main parameters are network graph type, number of agents, agent types and weights, maximum time of simulation and time step length. In addition, the parameters of the behavior model should be configured (e.g., initial states or probability of an agent action). Agent behaviors should be selected from the provided library or developed extending the *BaseAgentBehaviour* class.

Once the simulation is configured, the next step is the simulation, that can be done step by step or many steps. The class *BaseAgentBehaviour* stores the status of every agent in every simulation step into a JSON file to be exported once the simulation is finished. This feature allows us to automatize the process of generating the .gexf file. Finally, users can carry out a further analysis with the JSON file as well as visualize the evolution of the simulation with the generated .gexf.

2.3   Good Practices

Soil has been used both by developers and researchers. Based on this experience of developing models with Soil, some good practices can be recommended. Hopefully, this should help other researchers to implement their models. The first one relates to the use of the two types of agents within Soil: Network Agents and Environment Agents. Using these types correctly results in simpler models that are easier to understand, debug and extend.

Network agents are always attached to a node of the network and have connections with other network agents (i.e., friend of, follow to or influenced by). Hence, network agents should encapsulate individual behavior at the micro level. Conversely, environment agents are not assigned to a node in the network and should be used to model behavior at the macro level.

As of this writing, the type of the network agent is static through the simulation. Hence, behavior that does not change (e.g., content consumer vs. content producer) are better encoded as different subclasses of a base agent, whereas changes in behavior based on thresholds are better encoded as states within the same agent type.

For example, let us consider a model for radicalization in a nation, which takes into account inter-personal relations and the effect of social media. In this scenario, each citizen would be modeled as a network agent.

Each network agent would have a state, which encapsulates information such as the member's radicalization level, and it would be connected to other citizens in the social graph. Network agents also have behavior, which depends on agent state and social relations. In every step of the simulation, network agents will execute their behavior and update their radicalization level.

An environment agent could be in charge of updating the radicalization level of each citizen, based on the latest content in the media.

2.4   Load Test

Soil was subjected to a load test in which 200 simulations were executed with the same parameters but varying the number of agents in each one as shown in Fig. 3. The model used to accomplish this is the Counter Model which counts the number of nodes in the network and neighbors in each step and adds it to its state.

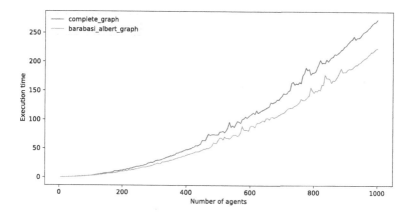

Fig. 3. Results of the load test

Two different algorithms were used for generating random scale-free networks. The first one is the Complete Graph Generator which returns the complete graph on n nodes. The other one used, is the Barabási-Albert Graph which returns a random graph according to the Barabási-Albert preferential attachment model. For this second algorithm, in addition to the totality of nodes, the number of edges to join of a new node to the existing nodes has been indicated, being this half of the number of nodes of the network.

3   Radical Simulation Model

3.1   Problem

As previously discussed, in the last years, the way people communicate has changed, becoming more relevant social networks, where everyone can exchange messages, images, and videos. Terrorist organizations have also moved forward by setting up radio stations, TV channels or Internet websites. These activities allow them to increase their strength, their funds, and better recruit new people.

Since terrorist organizations can be modeled as social networks, we can study how information is shared and how people become members of groups or even new relationships. Within the proposed model (Sect. 3.2), terrorist groups will be represented as graphs where vertices represent members and edges represent communication between those members.

However, radicalism is not only sustained by flow information. Multiple causes, rather than a single cause should be considered, including social and spatial relations which evolve over time. Estimating their evolution is essential for management, command and control structures, as well as for intelligence analysis research purposes. By knowing future social and spatial distributions, analysts can identify emergent leaders, hot spots, and organizational vulnerabilities [21].

In order to approach to the radicalism spread, spatial distribution is used based on Geometric Graph Generators [25], which provides geographical positions to agents, being able to manage real environments.

The physical space aims to produce more insightful results when considering the spread of terrorism [7]. Properties of space and place are vital components of terrorist training, planning, and activities.

Besides, based on the principle of homophily, as a contact between similar people occurs at a higher rate than among dissimilar people, it is more likely to have contact with those who are closer to us in geographic location than those who are distant [20]. It is theorized that, in general, proximity in geographic space strongly influences closeness in social space [7].

As it was discussed above, the proposed model will try to approach to the fact of the rise of radicalism within a specified geographic area considering real geographical connections between members.

3.2 Model Development

Three levels of analysis are widely accepted for the radicalization process [8]: *micro-level* (i.e. the individual level involving feelings of grievance, marginalization, etc.), *meso-level* (i.e. the social environment surrounding radicals and the population and lead to the formation of radical groups), and *macro-level* (i.e. impact of government policies, religion, media, including radicalization of the public opinion and political parties).

The model here proposed is focused on analyzing the macro-level and meso-level, including several aspects of the micro-level (such as the vulnerability level).

Several aspects have been considered for modeling the radicalism growth at the meso-level. First, the model considers the impact of *havens* [17] and *training areas* [9]. Havens, also known as sanctuaries, provide radical groups the possibility to obtain long term funding and serve the purposed of solidifying group cohesion. Terrorist training camps aim at providing indoctrination and teaching for terrorism and are distributed around the world. They foster group identity formation and group cohesion, and require geographical isolation and easy access to weapons.

The modeling of the radicalism spread involves population and places as it was discussed above. People can play two roles: (1) population as the people that can be radicalized and (2) terrorist that spread their message to locals and try to recruit civilians to join the terrorist network.

Based on a previous model proposed by Cummings [7], terrorists have little opportunities for effective training, planning, and other logistic necessities. Those areas are modeled by (1) training environments, which increase the influence on the nodes that are attached to them, and (2) havens where people are safe. The nodes that are joined to havens get less influenced if the havens are not radicalized, but it could get radicalized, and its behavior will change.

For implementing the environment described, we will use four different models that interact with each other.

- Spread model in charge of the information flow which determines the state of the population. Each node contains a threshold where once reached, the node is marked as informed, and it will pass from a civilian state to a radical state.
- Network model in charge of controlling spatial and social relations between population.
- Havens model which will modify nodes vulnerability depending on haven state, as explained below.
- Training areas model which will decrease neighboring nodes vulnerability.

The network consists of N nodes that have two coordinates, as since Geometric Graph Generators [25] are used, that position each node on a map. The edge between two nodes indicates direct bidirectional communication between both of them.

All agents are assumed to have similar parameters but are heterogeneous in their representation. Within the spread model, each node develops its own belief about whether the information is valid by calculating weighted mean belief B_i from its neighbors and combining that with its initial belief B_0, which is normalized between 0 and 1 [6]. In addition, in every step, two agents will exchange information given a probability of interaction.

The mean belief is calculated given its vulnerability and the neighbors' influence as well as the information spread intensity (α) which is also normalized and consider how much information is exchanged in every step of the simulation.

$$B_e = \sum_{i=0}^{n} \frac{B_i \, D_i}{\sum_{j=0}^{n} D_j} \tag{1}$$

The node influence D_i parameter has been included in Eq. 1 – where n is the number of neighbors of the node – as the change in behavior that one person causes in another as a result of an interaction [26] measured as degree centrality that is defined as the number of adjacencies upon a node, which is the sum of each row in the adjacency matrix representing the network. It can be interpreted within social networks as a measure of immediate influence – the ability to infect others directly or in one period [3]. This SNA function returns values that are normalized by dividing by the maximum possible degree in a simple graph $N-1$ where N is the number of nodes in G.

$$B_n = B_e \, \alpha + B_0 \, (1 - \alpha); \qquad 0 \leq \alpha \leq 1 \tag{2}$$

As it was explained above, in Eq. 2 the parameter to indicate the information spread intensity is included. When its value is 0%, no information is exchanged, and when it increases, the knowledge diffusion grows.

$$B_i = B_n \, N_v + B_0 \, (1 - N_v); \qquad 0 \leq N_v \leq 1 \tag{3}$$

The node vulnerability (N_v) parameter is included in Eq. 3 as the extent to which individuals conform or adopt variable attributes such as opinions from their attached nodes. In other words, if $N_v = 1$, the node will be entirely influenced by their connected nodes, where a value of $N_v = 0$, would mean it would not be influenced, so no change in the network is expected. Thus, individuals who are merely sympathetic may be influenced by more extreme opinions from their friends after they join the terrorist network.

Once the mean belief developed by the agent reaches the threshold, it is marked as informed, and it will change its state from civilian to radical. Every agent in the radical state will be only influenced by radical agents since the radical experience no restraining influence from non-radicals [10]. Furthermore, once an agent is in the radical state, the information spread intensity will begin to value 100%, as once an individual is radical the most information it gets from other radical agents.

With the purpose of determining the most relevant nodes within the terrorist network, they are marked as *leaders* based on the SNA function: betweenness centrality [6], that is defined of a node v as the sum of the fraction of all-pairs shortest paths that pass through v.

As (N_v) was explained above, training areas and havens will modify this attribute depending on their status. Training areas will decrease the parameter from its neighbors, where a value of 1 for training area influence will make all its neighbors entirely vulnerable. However, a value of 1 for haven influence will make invulnerable all its neighbors when the state of the haven is not radical. Nevertheless, once the haven is marked as radical, its behavior will be similar to training areas.

Finally, the network model in charge of controlling spatial and social relations takes into account that agents have the opportunity to interact with other agents. They select an agent to interact with according to a probability of interaction – different from the one mentioned above – based on two parameters: (1) social distance and (2) spatial proximity.

On one side, (SD) take into account the fact that if two agents must cross many social links, then the probability should be low and vice versa. It computes it by finding the shortest path between to agents and then dividing one by the number of links in that path.

$$SD_{i,j} = \frac{1}{|A\ A_{i,j}|} \tag{4}$$

where $|A\ A_{i,j}|$ is the shortest path from i to j. When computing the social distance, each agent can only reach all those nodes that are within its sphere of influence parameter. An agent can recognize and distinguish the closeness of other agents within the sphere of influence, but it cannot differentiate the closeness when the interacting agent is outside the perimeter.

On the other side, (SP) takes into account that two agents at the same location are more likely to talk than being in different locations. Some might argue that SP is not significant in the Internet age. However, in the terrorism domain, attending the same training area or the same location is a critical interaction indicator [21].

Table 2. Simulation input parameters

Model	Name	Implication
Terrorist spread	information_spread_intensity	The amount of information exchanged in every step of the simulation
	terrorist_additional_influence	Additional influence added to agents whom status is radical
	min_vulnerability	The minimum vulnerability that an agent could have (*default 0*)
	max_vulnerability	The maximum vulnerability that an agent could have. The allocation of this parameter follows a continuous uniform distribution. The maximum value that this parameter can take is the unit
	prob_interaction	The probability of two agents exchanging information in one step
Training area	training_influence	The influence of a training area over its neighbors
Haven	haven_influence	The influence of a haven over its neighbors
Terrorist network	sphere_influence	The maximum number of social links that an agent can cross for a new interaction
	vision_range	The range on the spatial-route network specifying the maximum distance an agent can move for a new interaction
	weight_social_distance	The weight of (SD) to calculate the interaction probability
	weight_link_distance	The weight of (SP) to calculate the interaction probability

As Geometric Graph Generators returns coordinates normalized between 0 and 1, the probability of being at the same location will be computed as the inverse of the distance between two agents.

$$SP_{i,j} = (1 - |d_{i,j}|) \tag{5}$$

where $|d_{i,j}|$ is the distance between the nodes. Like in the SD the probability is bounded by a sphere of influence parameter, in SP the probability will be bounded by a vision range parameter. All agents outside this perimeter will be unreachable by the current agent.

Once both parameters have been defined, we can compute the probability of interaction that will be calculated as follows.

$$P_{i,j}^{Interaction} = \omega_1 \, SD_{i,j} + \omega_2 \, SP_{i,j} \tag{6}$$

where ω_1 and ω_2 are the weights of SD and SP respectively with the purpose of customizing the environment.

None of the parameters will limit the probability of interaction. Thus, the candidate agents will be the sum of all the agents that are inside the perimeter of the sphere of influence or the vision range.

Thereby, an agent can establish a new way of communicating with its candidate agents, so the probability of interaction is calculated between each agent and its candidate agents.

As it was explained, the aim of the model is trying to approach to the fact of the radicalism spread within a specified geographic area. For that reason, in Table 2 all parameters of the simulation are detailed for representing a scenario as real as possible. Aside from all the parameters explained, the network can be modeled using one of the random network generation methods from NetworkX. It is also possible to control the ratio of each type of agent.

3.3 Workflow of the Simulation

In order to present a broad perspective of the general workflow of the simulation, Fig. 4 displays the simulation cycle of an agent. Each agent will follow this cycle in every step of the simulation for updating its properties and interacting with its neighbors.

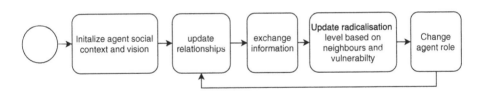

Fig. 4. General workflow of the simulation

At first, every agent is initialized taking into account several factors which have been described in the previous section, such as the stance on radicalism which is normalized between 0 and 1, where 0 represents pacifist, and 1 represents radical. Other factors that define an agent are its level of influence and vulnerability.

Once each agent has been initialized, it will update its relationships based on its position on the graph. Relationships are controlled by the Network Model regarding spatial and social relations. For computing the probability of interaction between two agents, two parameters are considered: (I) social distance and (II) spatial proximity. While the social distance is bounded by the sphere of influence of an agent, the spatial proximity is bounded by the vision range. Thus, the candidate agents to establish a new link of communications are all those who are inside the sphere of influence or the vision range.

After updating its relationships, each agent will exchange information with its neighbors. This step is controlled by the Spread Model as it was explained in the previous section. Each agent calculates a weighted main radicalism from its neighbors regarding the information spread intensity as how much information is exchanged between any two agents.

Once the agent has exchanged information with its neighbors, it will update its radicalism level which is computed combining mean radicalism and its initial level of radicalization. When computing the radicalism level, its vulnerability and neighbors' influence are considered.

Finally, at the end of the simulation cycle and once the own radicalism level developed by the agent reaches a threshold, its state will change from civilian to radical. Besides, as it was explained in the previous section, those whose betweenness centrality is the highest will be marked as leaders.

4   Experimental Results

The model has been implemented using the Soil Simulator as it was discussed above. The scenario represents a specified geographic area that can be customized with the purpose of approaching a real scenario.

Every agent exchange information several times during the simulation, and every portion of time is known as a *step*. On the one hand, an agent belonging to the Network Model will update its relationships based on the input parameters

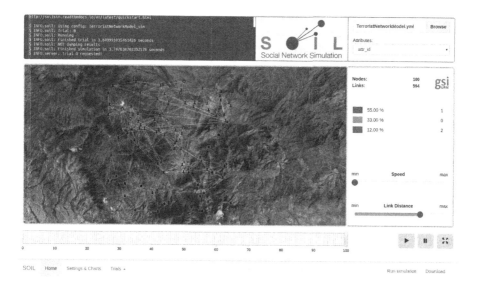

Fig. 5. Visualization of the simulation

in every step. After this action, the control is passed to the Spread Model that will be in charge of how the information will flow in that step. The current agent will be influenced by its neighbors depending on their internal parameters values.

On the other hand, if the current agent is a haven or a training area, the step will consist of modifying the internal parameters of their neighbors as it was explained in the previous section.

With the purpose of making the simulations more interactive, a web application has been developed using a client-server architecture. The server side has been implemented using Python while the client side uses D3.js [33] for visualizing the results. Server and client sides are divided into different modules that have dependencies between each other.

The modular server is in charge of handling the template which holds the visualization and the HTTP requests while the simulator will receive data from the server for running simulations. The client side is the one in charge of the visualization. It processes the information received from the server and the user configuration with the aim of representing the simulation in the browser.

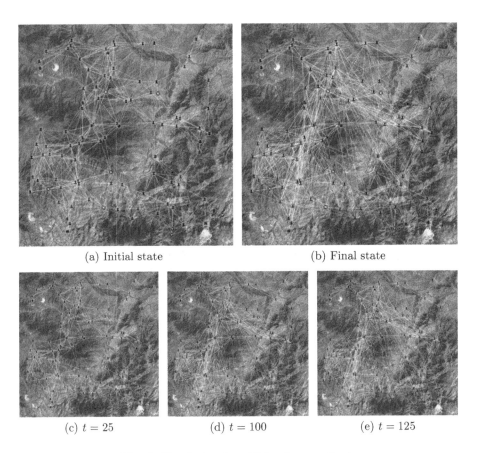

(a) Initial state   (b) Final state

(c) $t = 25$ (d) $t = 100$ (e) $t = 125$

Fig. 6. Simulation flow (Color figure online)

As we can notice in Fig. 5 the simulation returns a graph that is presented in the central area of the web application. The graph can be positioned in a map, and it could be represented depending on the step, being able to see it evolve. Furthermore, the interface allows users to filter the results or to change the simulation parameters.

The application not only allows the user to visualize the results, but it also provides statistics and the option of running more simulations changing the input parameters.

The web application also allows users to export the results of the simulation in different formats such as GEXF [11] or JSONGraph[4] to be analyzed with any other tool.

In order to present a simulation flow, in Fig. 6 an example is presented using the input values shown in Table 3 for a total of 100 nodes and a simulation time of 150 steps. Figure 6a and b present the initial and final state of the simulation respectively. The green nodes in the pictures represent the neutral agents while the red ones represent the radicalized ones. Places such as training areas and havens are represented with different shapes. The remaining figures represent the state of the simulation in different moments.

The network topology used is a random clustered network where nodes are connected when two of them are within 0.2 of distance. The distribution of agents has been made considering 80% of civilian agents, 10% of terrorist agents and 10% of heavens and training areas distributed equally.

Table 3. Simulation input values

Parameter	Initial value	Bounds
Information spread intensity	0.70	0.0−1.0
Terrorist additional influence	0.035	0.0−1.0
Maximum vulnerability	0.70	0.0−1.0
Probability of interaction	0.50	0.0−1.0
Training area influence	0.20	0.0−1.0
Heaven influence	0.20	0.0−1.0
Vision range	0.30	0.0−1.0
Sphere of influence	2.0	$1-N$
Weight of social distance	0.035	0.0−1.0
Weight of link distance	0.035	0.0−1.0

The model has been evaluated using two different sensitivity analysis methods. Sensitivity analysis allows studying how the uncertainty in the output of a model can be apportioned to different sources of uncertainty in the model

---

[4] http://netflix.github.io/falcor/documentation/jsongraph.html.

278   T. Méndez et al.

input [28]. The first one is a local approach known as One-at-Time (OAT) approach, that studies small input perturbations on the model output. 1.000 simulations have been launched to bring about this method with different input values and have been analyzed using the Seaborn [30] library available for Python for exploring and understanding the results.

The other method applied is the Morris method [22] that is referred to as "global sensitivity analysis" that in contrast to local sensitivity analysis, it considers the whole variation range of the inputs [16]. This method is computed using the SALib [15] library for Python.

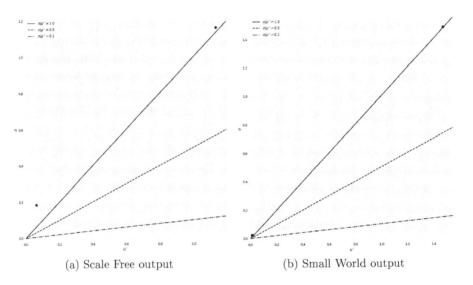

(a) Scale Free output   (b) Small World output

Fig. 7. Morris method results representation for radical population output for 200 trajectories

The primary model outputs of interest in the sensitivity analysis are: (1) the radicalism diffusion computed as the percentage of agents that have been radicalized during the simulation from those who were not radical at the beginning and (2) the mean radicalism within the network computed as the average radicalism of all the agents.

Both outputs will be measured taking into account different types of simulations. On one side, the network model will be studied assuming that the spread model inherits the another. On the other side, three different topologies (small world, scale free and random clustered) will be analyzed.

In Table 4 the Morris indices are detailed for the network model and mean radicalism output ordered by μ^*. A total of 200 trajectories were built for the model which results in 1.800 samples. Figure 8 plots result on the graph (μ^*, σ) and identify the probability of interaction, the maximum vulnerability and the information spread intensity as the most substantial influence on the mean radicalism within the network.

Table 4. Morris indices for network model and mean radicalism output.

Parameter	μ	μ^*	σ
prob_interaction	0.320631	0.367384	0.51795
max_vulnerability	0.243827	0.349831	0.413981
information_spread_intensity	0.252602	0.324202	0.379572
terrorist_additional_influence	0.036039	0.128335	0.206991
weight_social_distance	−0.004388	0.110129	0.186007
vision_range	0.019502	0.10909	0.18097
sphere_influence	0.006756	0.107522	0.173183
weight_link_distance	0.007996	0.101815	0.17993

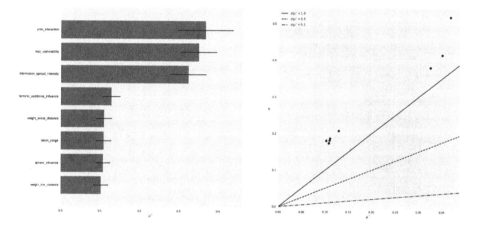

Fig. 8. Morris method results representation for network model and mean radicalism output for 200 trajectories

The analysis has been made using a random clustered topology that is created based on proximity between nodes for 100 nodes, and with the same number of radical agents at the beginning. However, taking into account the population radicalized in a simulation as we can notice in Table 5 and Fig. 9 are similar, but the maximum vulnerability and the information spread intensity is in this case more influential than the probability of interaction.

Morris indices for the three different topologies have similarities as the weight of the radical agents for the distribution through the network is the most influential parameter for both outputs as it can be noticed in Fig. 7 for Scale Free and Small World topologies. In addition, the model output linearly depends on the weight of the agents. Nevertheless, the size of the network does not influence the two model outputs.

The methods presented, attempt to validate certain factors such as types of network connections and the presence of certain kinds of meeting sites which facilitate radicalization while other plausible factors such as community size

Table 5. Morris indices for network model and radicalized population output.

Parameter	μ	μ^*	σ
max_vulnerability	0.466355	0.484857	0.596371
information_spread_intensity	0.392325	0.402566	0.541922
prob_interaction	0.268707	0.331403	0.568499
terrorist_additional_influence	0.092038	0.186473	0.415794
weight_link_distance	−0.012333	0.181102	0.401011
vision_range	−0.001680	0.176981	0.380602
sphere_influence	0.005437	0.169812	0.358775
weight_social_distance	0.003899	0.165475	0.375792

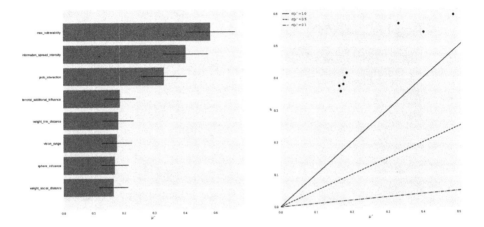

Fig. 9. Morris method results representation for network model and radicalized population output for 200 trajectories

have little effect. Network types can play an essential part in understanding how radicalism spreads and can be equally important when trying to destabilize or destroy a network.

5   Conclusions and Future Work

Understanding radicalization roots is a first step for being able to define and apply suitable counter-terrorism measures. There are many challenges for analyzing terrorist networks, given the lack of public datasets and the sensibility of this information. Nonetheless, the application of agent-based social simulation is a useful technique for modeling nonlinear adaptive systems, and they enable analyzing and validating social theories of the radicalization process.

In this work, we present a model and a tool for agent-based modeling of radical terrorist networks. We have proposed building the agent-based model around two main concepts, the Network Model and the Agent Model. While the first is in charge of managing agent relationships, the second defines the specific behavior of every agent. This approach has been applied to modeling terrorist growth. The proposed model is focused on analyzing the impact of the information exchange and environmental radicalization in the radicalization process. The evaluation and analysis of the simulation results provides insight regarding the importance of the simulation parameters, including the network characteristics.

Future work should include a broader and deeper perspective of absolute and relative deprivation and how each can influence the spread of radicalism.

Acknowledgments. This work is supported by the Spanish Ministry of Economy and Competitiveness under the R&D projects SEMOLA (TEC2015-68284-R), by the Regional Government of Madrid through the project MOSI-AGIL-CM (grant P2013/ICE-3019, co-funded by EU Structural Funds FSE and FEDER); by the European Union through the project Trivalent (Grant Agreement no: 740934) and by the Ministry of Education, Culture and Sport through the mobility research stay grant PRX17/00417.

References

1. Bastian, M., Heymann, S., Jacomy, M., et al.: Gephi: an open source software for exploring and manipulating networks. ICWSM **8**, 361–362 (2009)
2. Blanco-Moreno, D., Fuentes-Fernández, R., Pavón, J.: Simulation of online social networks with Krowdix. In: 2011 International Conference on Computational Aspects of Social Networks (CASoN), pp. 13–18. IEEE (2011)
3. Borgatti, S.P.: Centrality and network flow. Soc. Netw. **27**(1), 55–71 (2005)
4. Crenshaw, M.: The psychology of terrorism: an agenda for the 21st century. Polit. Psychol. **21**(2), 405–420 (2000)
5. Csardi, G., Nepusz, T.: The iGraph software package for complex network research. InterJ. Complex Syst. **1695**(5), 1–9 (2006)
6. Cummings, P.: Modeling the characteristics of radical ideological growth using an agent based model methodology. Master thesis, George Mason University (2017)
7. Cummings, P., Weerasinghe, C.: Modeling the characteristics of radical ideological growth using an agent based model methodology. In: MODSIM World (2017)
8. Dzhekova, R., Stoynova, N., Kojouharov, A., Mancheva, M., Anagnostou, D., Tsenkov, E.: Understanding radicalisation. Review of literature. Center for the Study of Democracy, Sofia (2016)
9. Forest, J.J.: Terrorist training centers around the world: a brief review. In: The Making of a Terrorist: Recruitment, Training and Root Causes, vol. 2. Praeger (2005)
10. Genkin, M., Gutfraind, A.: How do terrorist cells self-assemble: insights from an agent-based model of radicalization. Technical report, SSRN, July 2011
11. GEXF Working Group and others: GEXF file format (2015)
12. Gilbert, D.: The jFreeChart class library. Developer Guide. Object Refinery, vol. 7 (2002)
13. Gruebner, O., Sykora, M., Lowe, S.R., Shankardass, K., Trinquart, L., Jackson, T., Subramanian, S., Galea, S.: Mental health surveillance after the terrorist attacks in Paris. Lancet **387**(10034), 2195–2196 (2016)

14. Hagberg, A., Swart, P., S Chult, D.: Exploring network structure, dynamics, and function using NetworkX. Technical report, Los Alamos National Laboratory (LANL), Los Alamos, NM, USA (2008)
15. Herman, J., Usher, W.: SALib: an open-source Python library for sensitivity analysis. J. Open Source Softw. **2**(9) (2017). https://doi.org/10.21105/joss.00097
16. Iooss, B., Lemaître, P.: A review on global sensitivity analysis methods. In: Dellino, G., Meloni, C. (eds.) Uncertainty Management in Simulation-Optimization of Complex Systems, pp. 101–122. Springer, Boston (2015). https://doi.org/10.1007/978-1-4899-7547-8_5
17. Jean-Baptiste, A.: Terrorist safe havens: towards an understanding of what they accomplish for terrorist organizations. Ph.D. thesis, University of Kansas (2010)
18. Matloff, N.: Introduction to discrete-event simulation and the simPy language. Department of Computer Science, University of California at Davis, Davis, CA (2008). Accessed 2 Aug 2009
19. McKinney, W.: Python for Data Analysis: Data Wrangling with Pandas, NumPy, and IPython. O'Reilly Media, Inc., Sebastopol (2012)
20. McPherson, M., Smith-Lovin, L., Cook, J.M.: Birds of a feather: homophily in social networks. Annu. Rev. Sociol. **27**(1), 415–444 (2001)
21. Moon, I.C., Carley, K.M.: Modeling and simulating terrorist networks in social and geospatial dimensions. IEEE Intell. Syst. **22**(5), 40–49 (2007)
22. Morris, M.D.: Factorial sampling plans for preliminary computational experiments. Technometrics **33**(2), 161–174 (1991)
23. O'Madadhain, J., Fisher, D., Smyth, P., White, S., Boey, Y.B.: Analysis and visualization of network data using JUNG. J. Stat. Softw. **10**(2), 1–35 (2005)
24. Pedregosa, F., et al.: Scikit-learn: machine learning in Python. J. Mach. Learn. Res. **12**, 2825–2830 (2011)
25. Penrose, M.: Random Geometric Graphs. Oxford University Press, Oxford (2003)
26. Rashotte, L.: Social influence. In: Ritzer, G. (ed.) The Blackwell Encyclopedia of Sociology. Blackwell (2007)
27. Ryczko, K., Domurad, A., Buhagiar, N., Tamblyn, I.: Hashkat: large-scale simulations of online social networks. Soc. Netw. Anal. Min. **7**(1), 4 (2017)
28. Saltelli, A., Ratto, M., Andres, T., Campolongo, F., Cariboni, J., Gatelli, D., Saisana, M., Tarantola, S.: Global Sensitivity Analysis: The Primer. Wiley, Chichester (2008)
29. Sánchez, J.M., Iglesias, C.A., Sánchez-Rada, J.F.: Soil: an agent-based social simulator in Python for modelling and simulation of social networks. In: Demazeau, Y., Davidsson, P., Bajo, J., Vale, Z. (eds.) PAAMS 2017. LNCS (LNAI), vol. 10349, pp. 234–245. Springer, Cham (2017). https://doi.org/10.1007/978-3-319-59930-4_19 https://link.springer.com/chapter/10.1007/978-3-319-59930-4_19
30. Sheppard, K.: Introduction to Python for econometrics, statistics and data analysis. Self-published, University of Oxford, version 2 (2012)
31. Spencer, A.: Questioning the concept of 'new terrorism'. In: Peace, Conflict and Development, pp. 1–33 (2006)
32. Tucker, D.: What is new about the new terrorism and how dangerous is it? Terror. Polit. Violence **13**(3), 1–14 (2001)
33. Zhu, N.Q.: Data Visualization with D3.js Cookbook. Packt Publishing Ltd., Birmingham (2013)

Frameworks and Application Domains

Engineering World-Wide Multi-Agent Systems with Hypermedia

Andrei Ciortea[1](✉), Olivier Boissier[1], and Alessandro Ricci[2]

[1] Univ. Lyon, MINES Saint-Étienne, CNRS Lab Hubert Curien UMR 5516,
42023 Saint-Étienne, France
{andrei.ciortea,olivier.boissier}@emse.fr
[2] University of Bologna, Cesena, Italy
a.ricci@unibo.it

Abstract. A well studied problem in the engineering of open MASs is to enable uniform interaction among heterogeneous agents. However, AOSE as a field has grown to recognize that a MAS consists of more than only agents and thus should be designed on multiple dimensions (including the environment, organization etc.). The problem of enabling interaction among heterogeneous entities across dimensions is either not considered, or it is addressed in an *ad hoc* and non-uniform manner. In this chapter, we introduce a novel approach to use hypermedia as a general mechanism to support uniform interaction in MASs. The core idea is that agents use hypermedia to discover at runtime (i) other entities in a MAS (e.g., other agents, tools, organizations) and (ii) the means to interact with those entities (e.g., interaction protocols, APIs). This reduces coupling and enhances the scalability and evolvability of the MAS. We present a demonstrator that supports these claims. We believe that a hypermedia-based mechanism for uniform interaction in MASs could provide a foundation for engineering world-wide MASs.

Keywords: Multi-agent systems · Hypermedia systems · Interaction

1 Introduction

The vision of world-wide multi-agent systems (MASs) has been around for some time. In 2001, the Agentcities initiative was aiming to create a world-wide open network of heterogeneous agents to which any organization or individual researcher could connect their agents [38]. The same year, the seminal paper on the Semantic Web was published [1], which promoted the vision of a Web for both people and autonomous agents. Since then, we have witnessed significant progress both in MASs and Semantic Web research, but we have yet to witness the deployment of world-wide and long-lived MASs.

The Web, on the other hand, has had remarkable success as a world-wide and long-lived system *of people*. One way to look at the Web is that it provides people with a *distributed hypermedia environment* (composed of interrelated Web

© Springer Nature Switzerland AG 2019
D. Weyns et al. (Eds.): EMAS 2018 Workshops, LNAI 11375, pp. 285–301, 2019.
https://doi.org/10.1007/978-3-030-25693-7_15

pages) that they can navigate and use in pursuit of their goals. This hypermedia environment was specifically designed to be open, Internet-scale, and to allow people to use it in new and unanticipated ways [2,14]. All these properties were designed into the Web architecture, and its central distinctive feature is the use of hypermedia as an engine for uniform interaction between components [14]. We believe that we can apply the same design rationale as an effective means to engineer open, scalable, and evolvable MASs – which implies significantly more than just implementing MASs using Web services.

Our hypothesis is that we can use hypermedia to create a general mechanism for uniform interaction in MASs. Given such a mechanism, heterogeneous agents would then be able to interact in a uniform manner with other agents as well as other heterogeneous entities (tools, knowledge repositories, organizations, datasets etc.) that could help them achieve their goals. Engineers in different parts of the world could then develop and deploy agents and other entities independently from one another, and old and new implementations could co-exist in one system.

A mechanism for uniform interaction in MASs such as the one described above is currently lacking. Perhaps the closest solution can be found in the FIPA standards[1], but it only addresses interaction among agents. Interaction between agents and other entities in a MAS is not addressed.

In this chapter, we introduce an approach to use hypermedia for uniform interaction in MASs. In a *hypermedia MAS*, agents are situated in a distributed hypermedia environment (composed of interrelated resources) that they can navigate and use in pursuit of their goals. Agents use the hypermedia environment to discover and interact with heterogeneous entities in the MAS. To support our approach, we implemented a demonstrator in which BDI agents are able to discover and interact with artifacts in a hypermedia environment distributed across multiple nodes. Hypermedia allows the environment to be seamlessly distributed from the agents' viewpoint, and allows agents to discover and exploit new functionalities added to artifacts at runtime. This demonstrator confirms key elements of our hypothesis and suggests it could provide a foundation for engineering world-wide MASs.

We discuss background and related work in Sect. 2. In Sect. 3, we propose a set of design principles and a model for hypermedia MASs. We report on our implementation and experience in Sect. 4, and then conclude in Sect. 5.

2   Background and Related Work

In the following, we first discuss the role of hypermedia in the Web architecture, and then current approaches to engineer Web-based and world-wide MASs.

2.1   Hypermedia and HATEOAS

A central feature of REST, the architectural style of the Web, is that it uses hypermedia to drive interaction between components, a principle known as

---

[1] http://www.fipa.org/repository/standardspecs.html, accessed: 05.11.2018.

hypermedia as the engine of application state (HATEOAS) – see [14] for details. To illustrate this principle, an HTML page typically provides the user with a number of affordances, such as to navigate to a different page by clicking a hyperlink or to submit an order by filling out and submitting an HTML form. Performing any such action transitions the application to a new state, which provides the user with a new set of affordances. In each state, the user's browser retrieves an HTML representation of the current state from a server, but also a selection of next possible states and the information required to construct the HTTP requests to transition to those states. Retrieving all this information through hypermedia allows the application to evolve without impacting the browser, and allows the browser to transition seamlessly across servers. The use of hypermedia and HATEOAS is central to reducing coupling among Web components, and allowed the Web to evolve into an open, world-wide, and long-lived system.

In contrast to the above example, when using a non-hypermedia Web service (e.g., an implementation of CRUD operations over HTTP), developers have to hard-code into clients all the knowledge required to interact with the service. This approach is simple and intuitive for developers, but the trade-off is that clients are then tightly coupled to the services they use (hence the need for API versioning). In recent years, hypermedia has started to receive more attention in Web service design (e.g., [27]), in particular in the context of the Web of Things (WoT) [25] – where it is important for devices to be able to interact with one another in a loosely coupled manner rather than having developers in the loop to constantly update integrations as devices (and their exposed Web APIs) evolve.

2.2 Web-Based Multi-Agent Systems

There has been extensive research on using the Web as an infrastructure for distributed MASs. Early work was influenced by service-oriented architectures (SOA) based on the WS-* standards (SOAP, WSDL, UDDI etc.) [19,23,24,35]. However, Web service design has evolved drastically over the past decade. It is now well recognized that WS-* services use the Web merely as a transport layer [30]. Based on similar ideas, FIPA proposed a specification for using HTTP as a transport protocol for messages exchanged among agents [17], which was implemented by several FIPA-compliant platforms (e.g., [10,12,21]). The problem with systems that use the Web merely for transport is that they are misaligned with the Web architecture (see Section 6.5.3 in [15] for a detailed discussion). Consequently, such systems make limited use of the existing Web infrastructure and its future extensions, and – more importantly for our purposes – do not inherit the architectural properties that turned the Web into an open, world-wide, and long-lived system (e.g., scalability, loose coupling).

More recent approaches for engineering Web-based MASs have turned to resource-oriented architectures (ROA) based on REST-like, non-hypermedia services (e.g., [20,29]). In contrast to the WS-* services, which are typically designed in terms of operations, these services are designed in terms of resources. Clients then interact with the services using a small set of generic operations with well defined semantics, such as the ones defined by the HTTP protocol [13] (e.g., GET, PUT, POST, DELETE). These services use the Web as an application layer and are better aligned with the Web architecture, but they generally do not use hypermedia or HATEOAS, which leads to tight coupling (see the discussion in the previous section). To the best of our knowledge, the engineering of Web-based MASs using hypermedia services is not yet thoroughly investigated.

2.3 World-Wide Multi-Agent Systems

There have been considerable efforts to support the engineering of open, worldwide, and long-lived MASs – among the most prominent, the FIPA standards, Agentcities [38], DARPA CoABS GRID [26], and the Semantic Web [1]. These efforts have generally focused on enabling uniform interaction among heterogeneous agents (e.g., see [16,18]), but a general mechanism for uniform interaction with *any* entity in an open MAS is lacking. From an architectural perspective, most previous efforts to engineer large-scale MASs generally relied on RPC-like architectures.[2] When it comes to engineering world-wide systems, RPC-like architectures have shortcomings as compared to REST-style, resource-oriented architectures. For instance, they cannot (or make it very difficult to) use intermediary layers that can process requests almost as well as their intended recipients (see Section 6.5.2 in [15]). Intermediaries have proven very useful in world-wide systems such as the Web. Furthermore, in a REST-style architecture, hypermedia enables the serendipitous use of resources, a property promoted in recent years by the *linked data* initiative [3]. Support for new and unanticipated applications is an important property for sustaining long-lived systems.

3   Hypermedia Multi-Agent Systems

We consider that a sensible path towards the engineering of open, world-wide, and long-lived MASs is to use hypermedia as a uniform interaction engine in MASs. In a *hypermedia MAS*, agents are situated in a *distributed hypermedia environment* that they can navigate and use in pursuit of their goals. The environment is a first-class abstraction in the system and on the surface it provides agents with all typical functionalities of endogenous environments (see [32,37]), such as interaction with services, tools, and the external world, or mediating interaction and coordination with other agents. However, in contrast to typical endogenous environments, a *hypermedia environment* uses hypermedia to *drive interaction* in the MAS: agents navigate the hypermedia environment to discover other entities in the MAS, as well as the means to interact with those entities. This reduces coupling and enhances the scalability and evolvability of the systems. We introduce a set of design principles for hypermedia MASs in Sect. 3.1, and then present a concrete model in Sect. 3.2.

---

[2] This includes approaches that use Web services to tunnel RPC-like method invocations through HTTP (e.g., using SOAP).

3.1 Design Principles for Hypermedia Multi-Agent Systems

As discussed in Sect. 2.2, the mere use of any Web service design is not sufficient to create a hypermedia MAS. We introduce three key design principles meant to ensure the proper use of hypermedia as a general mechanism for uniform interaction in MASs. These principles are based on the design rationale behind the Web architecture [14]. As it is generally the case with software design principles, the proposed principles impose constraints on the design of MASs. Engineers can choose to ignore one or more of these principles, but then the MASs would most likely make limited use of hypermedia and would not achieve uniform interaction.

Principle 1 (Uniform resource space). *All entities in a hypermedia MAS and relations among them should be represented in the hypermedia environment in a uniform, resource-oriented manner.*

In a hypermedia system, and in particular in REST-style systems, a *resource* is the key abstraction of information [14]. The core idea behind this first principle is to project the entire observable state of the MAS into the distributed hypermedia environment in a uniform, resource-oriented manner (e.g., as an *RDF graph* [9]) such that agents can interpret, reason upon, and interact with the MAS by consuming and producing hypermedia. For instance, one agent could send a message to another by writing an RDF representation of the message in the hypermedia (e.g., using an OWL ontology for describing messages).[3] To receive messages, an agent could observe a resource that represents its mailbox in the hypermedia. To turn on a light bulb, an agent could manipulate the state of a resource that represents the light bulb in the hypermedia. Interactions between agents and resources in their hypermedia environment should conform to the REST constraints. In what follows, we discuss only three key aspects of applying REST to hypermedia MASs (and refer readers to [14] for more details about REST): *uniform identification* of entities, *uniform representation* of entities, and the use of *relations* among entities to enable discoverability.

Uniform identification (e.g., via IRIs [11]) allows entities in a hypermedia MAS to be referenced globally. Agents can then use hypermedia to interact with the entities regardless of their location. For instance, if an agent or a light bulb in its environment are identified via IRIs, then they can be referenced without the need for additional contextual information – such as how to interpret platform-specific identifiers, or low-level network information (e.g., IP addresses of hosts). In non-hypermedia MASs, this is not generally the case. FIPA defined its own standard uniform identifier for agents (see Section 3 in [18]), but uniform identification of other entities in a MAS is not addressed. Furthermore, the use of FIPA-specific identifiers requires custom infrastructure for managing entity identifiers and descriptions – as opposed to using IRIs and the existing Web infrastructure. Platforms that support distributed endogenous environments, such as

---

[3] Note that FIPA already proposed an RDF-based content language for FIPA messages: http://www.fipa.org/specs/fipa00011/XC00011B.html, accessed: 05.11.2018.

CArtAgO [32], either require agents to manage the low-level network information when joining remote nodes, or use additional infrastructure to manage this information (e.g., [28]).

Uniform representation of the externally observable state of entities in hypermedia MASs[4] allows to hide any implementation-specific details behind standardized knowledge models. For instance, the state of a light bulb could be represented in the hypermedia environment using RDF and some standard ontology. An agent could then interact with the light bulb by interpreting and manipulating its semantic representation either directly or via some intermediary tool (e.g., to translate it in a different knowledge representation language, or to use the light bulb via an artifact). A similar approach was taken by FIPA to define a standard format for ACL messages exchanged between agents [16], and to describe agents and the services they provide [18]. However, the uniform modeling of any other entities in a MAS is not addressed.[5]

In a hypermedia MAS, *relations* among entities (e.g., agents, tools, documents, organizations, datasets) can be represented explicitly in the hypermedia. The relations can then be crawled to discover entities of interest in the MAS. Agents could do the crawling themselves, or they could use search engines (i.e., external services) that do the crawling for them. This approach to discoverability has proven very practical for open, large-scale and decentralized systems, such as the Web [5]. In non-hypermedia MASs, discoverability is typically based on the registration of agents (and their services) to centralized directories, such as the *Directory Facilitator (DF)* standardized by FIPA [18]. Multiple DFs can then be federated to support decentralized searches, where requests are propagated between DFs up to a maximum depth level. However, this approach to discoverability is biased towards the locality of agents, which may prove inefficient in a Web-scale MASs. In contrast, crawling-based DFs could avoid the locality bias by exploiting relations in the distributed hypermedia environment. Furthermore, having typed relations among federated DFs could help propagate search requests in an informed manner.

The uniform resource space principle provides the underpinning for scalable and evolvable hypermedia MASs: it enables the seamless distribution of the hypermedia environment, and it allows agents to interact with other entities in the MAS in a uniform manner through hypermedia. The implied trade-off is interoperability vs. innovation: translating an implementation-specific model to a uniform representation promotes interoperability, but may loose implementation-specific features.

Principle 2 (Single entry point). *Given a single entry point into the environment of a hypermedia MAS, an agent should be able to discover the knowledge required to participate in the system by navigating the hypermedia.*

---

[4] We are not interested here in the entities' internal state.

[5] Note that while any entity in a MAS could be encapsulated behind an agent (and then described using existing FIPA standards), this approach would simply obscure large parts of the MAS. The literature on engineering MASs already provides arguments for considering MASs as composed of more than just agents (e.g., see [4,37]).

The core idea behind this second principle is to maximize the usage of hypermedia in order to minimize coupling in the MAS. As mentioned for Principle 1, hypermedia can help reduce coupling by enabling system-wide discoverability – agents can crawl the hypermedia to discover what other agents, tools, or entities in the system can help them achieve their goals (hard-coding any such relations into the agents would increase coupling). Equally important, however, agents can also discover in the hypermedia how to interact with entities: the affordances of resources in their environment (e.g., operations exposed by a light bulb and how to perform them), specifications of agent interaction protocols in a given language (e.g., BSPL [34]), specifications of organizations in a given language (e.g., MOISE [22]), polices created by policy engineers (e.g., the terms of service of a hypermedia search engine), or norms created by other agents (e.g., norms that emerged in a given society) etc. The single entry point principle implies that any knowledge required to participate in the system that can be represented in the hypermedia should be represented in the hypermedia.

In other words, given an entry point into the environment of a hypermedia MAS, agents should require minimal a priori knowledge to interact with entities in the system besides the general knowledge required to consume and produce hypermedia. Any a priori knowledge and assumptions required to participate in the system should be standardized at the system-level (i.e., shared by everyone in the system). All other knowledge required to participate in the system should be discovered in the hypermedia. Furthermore, if an agent has to interact with one or more entities to achieve its goals and those entities are present in the system, the hypermedia environment should allow their eventual discovery via crawling. Violating any of these two constraints (i.e., hard-coding *ad hoc* knowledge into agents instead of placing it in the hypermedia, not enabling navigability) would violate the single entry point principle.

To illustrate the above point with an example, say an agent in a hypermedia MAS has to turn on a light bulb. A priori knowledge required by the agent to achieve its goal could include the HTTP protocol, RDF standards, a general model of its environment, and an OWL ontology describing light bulbs and the operations they expose (e.g., turn on), which could all be standardized at the system-level. Knowledge that should be discovered in the hypermedia would include the uniform identifier of a light bulb and the specification of an HTTP request that turns on the light bulb. Hard-coding into the agent the light bulb's identifier or, for instance, the knowledge required to use the Philips Hue HTTP API[6] (e.g., the Philips Hue data model) would couple the agent to the light bulb, and similar knowledge would have to be hard-coded in order to use light bulbs from other manufacturers.

The single entry point principle is central to designing evolvable and long-lived hypermedia MASs. The main trade-off is that relying on knowledge discovered in the hypermedia can increase the complexity of programming the MAS, but this can be mitigated through the use of appropriate middleware (as we show in Sect. 4).

---

[6] https://developers.meethue.com/documentation/getting-started, accessed: 05.11.2018.

Principle 3 (Observability). *In a hypermedia MAS, any resource in the hypermedia environment that could be of interest to agents should be observable.*

The first two principles ensure the dynamic discovery of a hypermedia MAS via crawling. However, constantly crawling large hypermedia MASs to keep track of their evolution would be inefficient. Instead, this third principle promotes the use of mechanisms that allow agents to selectively observe entities of interest in the MAS via the entities' representation in the hypermedia environment, which could include the entities' states, affordances, relations to other entities etc. This principle improves the scalability of hypermedia MASs: agents can handle larger environments, and at the same time the load on the hypermedia infrastructure is decreased (and thus it can serve more agents). The trade-off is the extra complexity added by observability mechanisms, but this can be mitigated through the use of appropriate middleware and intermediary components (see Sect. 4).

3.2   A Model for Hypermedia Multi-Agent Systems

We applied the proposed design principles to define a model for hypermedia MASs. This model is intended to provide an extensible conceptual foundation and thus only defines the core abstractions required to design and program hypermedia MASs.[7] The model (see Fig. 1a) is based on the *Agents and Artifacts (A&A)* meta-model [32] and our previous research on *socio-technical networks* (e.g., see [6,8]). We present the model in what follows, and then introduce a Web ontology that formalizes this model and discuss its usage.

Cognitive Agents in Artifact-Based Hypermedia Environments. Following the A&A meta-model, we *design* and *program* hypermedia MASs in terms of *agents* and *artifacts*. In A&A, *artifacts* are first-class programming abstractions (and not just design abstractions): they are as much a programmable part of the MAS as are agents. We use artifacts to program the *application environment* (cf. Fig. 1a) such that it provides agents with a *uniform, general interface* defined in terms of *observable properties*, *observable events*, and *operations* (see [32] for more details on artifacts). Artifacts thus help reduce the coupling between agents and their environment.

As depicted in Fig. 1a, all entities (e.g., agents, their services, artifacts, workspaces), the relations among them, and the affordances of artifacts are projected into a uniform RDF abstraction layer – cf. Principle 1 (uniform resource space). This layer effectively decouples agents from the application environment and enables system-wide discoverability via crawling. From an agent's viewpoint, the set of all affordances of its environment is determined by the artifacts discovered in the hypermedia, where the affordances of a given artifact are also discovered in the hypermedia – see Principle 2 (single entry point). To avoid dealing with low-level manipulation of hypermedia, agents could use hypermedia controllers (similar to Web browsers) in order to interact seamlessly with artifacts through the hypermedia layer (see implementation in Sect. 4.2).

---

[7] We leave a more complete treatment of MASs as future work (see Sect. 5).

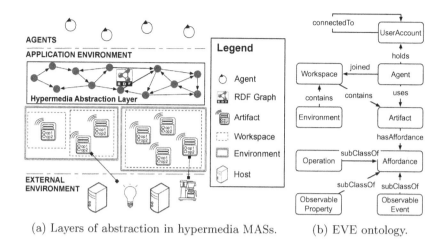

(a) Layers of abstraction in hypermedia MASs.   (b) EVE ontology.

Fig. 1. The core concepts used to model hypermedia MASs.

The *environment* and *workspace* abstractions (cf. Fig. 1a) are containers that allow agents to prune their crawling in the hypermedia environment, as well as focus their observations on those parts of the environment that are of interest – cf. Principle 3 (observability). When observing an artifact, the artifact's observable properties and events constitute percepts. In BDI architectures, such percepts can be modeled inside agents as beliefs about the state of their environment. Agents can use artifacts to observe other agents in the system regardless of their location.

Hypermedia Networks of Agents and Artifacts. We formalized the proposed model in an OWL 2 ontology, which we call the *Agent Environment (EVE)* ontology (see Fig. 1b). Engineers can use the ontology to create uniform representations of hypermedia MASs based on the proposed core model. The ontology can then be extended with modules for other dimensions of MASs, or with domain- and application-specific modules. A benefit of choosing Web standards is that engineers of hypermedia MASs can then benefit from all the results and resources provided by the Semantic Web community (ontologies, tooling etc.).

To enforce Principle 2 (single entry point), it is important to consider the navigability of hypermedia MASs. Representing explicitly in the environment all `eve:joined` and `eve:contains` properties guarantees that all agents and artifacts in the system are discoverable. Agents are represented in the system via *user accounts*, which can be used (among others) to interact with other agents and observe their relations. Representing explicitly the agents' relations (e.g., via `eve:connectedTo`) can help enhance navigability. The affordances of artifacts should also be described explicitly. The EVE ontology defines concepts and properties for this purpose (cf. Fig. 1b). However, it is outside the scope of this ontology to describe implementations of affordances. Other existing ontologies can be used in conjunction with the EVE ontology for this purpose (e.g., [25]).

4   Implementation and Experience

To demonstrate our approach, we developed a prototype platform for hypermedia MASs and used it to deploy a distributed hypermedia environment. We present the demonstrator scenario in Sect. 4.1, and an overview of the deployed system in Sect. 4.2. We discuss what has been achieved through this demonstrator and what are the limitations in Sect. 4.3. The software used in our demonstrator is available on GitHub.[8],[9]

4.1   Demonstrator Scenario

We implemented a demonstrator in which a BDI agent has to notify a human whenever an event occurs. The agent is situated in a hypermedia environment that contains one workspace with two artifacts: an artifact that generates two types of observable events (i.e., `positive` and `negative`), and a light bulb artifact that can be used to send visual notifications to humans. The hypermedia environment is distributed. The agent is given an entry IRI in the hypermedia environment and has to discover the rest of the system at runtime.

In the beginning of our demonstration, the environment contains only the event generator artifact (henceforth the `event-gen` artifact). The agent discovers the `event-gen` artifact and starts observing the generated events, but at this point the agent has no means to notify humans. The `light-bulb` artifact is added to the environment. The agent discovers the `light-bulb` artifact and its affordances, and can now send visual notifications to humans by flicking the light bulb. At this point, however, the visual notifications do not differentiate between `positive` or `negative` events – the light bulb is simply turned on and off.

While the system is running, a developer extends the `light-bulb` artifact with a new operation for setting the color of the light. The agent discovers the newly added operation and can now send visual notifications with different color codes (i.e., green light for `positive` events, blue light for `negative` events).

4.2   System Overview and Deployment

We deployed the hypermedia environment in our demonstrator scenario using a prototype platform for hypermedia MASs, named Yggdrasil[10]. The environment was distributed across two Yggdrasil nodes: one node hosted the `event-gen` artifact and was deployed on a virtual machine in the cloud, and the other node hosted the `light-bulb` artifact and was deployed on a Raspberry Pi in our local network. We used a Philips Hue light bulb that is accessed via the HTTP API exposed by a Philips Hue bridge in the local network. The BDI agent in our scenario was implemented in a separate JaCaMo [4] application that was deployed on a MacBook Air machine in the local network.

---

[8] https://github.com/andreiciortea/emas2018-yggdrasil, accessed: 05.11.2018.
[9] https://github.com/andreiciortea/emas2018-jacamo, accessed: 05.11.2018.
[10] Yggdrasil is a mythical tree that interconnects the nine worlds in Norse mythology.

In what follows, we first present the deployed hypermedia environment, and then discuss our implementation considerations for Yggdrasil and the JaCaMo application.

Hypermedia Environment. We constructed the hypermedia environment in our scenario using the EVE ontology. Dereferencing the environment's IRI retrieves the RDF representation shown in Listing 1.1. This representation points to one contained workspace (line 4), which allows agents to continue their crawling. Dereferencing the workspace IRI returns a similar representation (presented later in Listing 1.3) that points to the artifacts available in that workspace.

Listing 1.1. A Turtle [31] representation of the deployed environment created with the EVE ontology.

```
1  @prefix eve: <http://w3id.org/eve#> .
2
3  <http://yggdrasil.andreiciortea.ro/environments/env1> a eve:Environment ;
4    eve:contains <http://yggdrasil.andreiciortea.ro/workspaces/wksp1> .
```

Dereferencing the IRI of the `light-bulb` artifact retrieves the representation shown in Listing 1.2. In addition to the EVE ontology, this representation uses the W3C Web of Things (WoT) Thing Description (TD) ontology (currently being standardized [25]) and is based on a WoT TD used at the latest plugfest of the W3C WoT Working Group. The WoT TD ontology was designed to describe interactions with *things* in the WoT. Even though the *thing* and *artifact* abstractions have been developed independently in two different communities (and for different purposes), the abstractions define a similar interface composed of *observable properties*, *observable events*, and *actions* (or *operations*, respectively). This makes the WoT TD ontology a good candidate standard for describing interfaces of artifacts in hypermedia environments. Here, we use the WoT TD to describe the HTTP API of the Philips Hue light bulb in our deployment.

Listing 1.2 shows the description of an artifact operation for setting the color of a Philips Hue light bulb. In our demonstrator, this operation is added in the hypermedia by a developer while the system is running. We have created similar operation descriptions for turning the light bulb on and off.

Listing 1.2. This listing shows an excerpt from the RDF representation used for the `light-bulb` artifact in our deployment. The operation shown here allows an agent to set the color of a given Philips Hue light bulb. The description includes a full specification of the HTTP request that implements the operation.

```
1   @prefix td: <http://www.w3.org/ns/td#> .
2   @prefix xsd: <http://www.w3.org/2001/XMLSchema#> .
3   @prefix iot: <http://iotschema.org/> .
4   @prefix http: <http://iotschema.org/protocol/http> .
5
6   <http://85.204.10.233:8080/artifacts/hue1>
7     a eve:Artifact , td:Thing, iot:Light , iot:BinarySwitch ;
8     eve:hasName "Lamp"^^xsd:string ;
9     td:base "http://192.168.0.101/"^^xsd:anyURI ;
10    td:interaction [
11      a eve:Operation , td:Action , iot:SetColor ;
```

```
12    td:name "Set Color"^^xsd:string ;
13    td:form [
14      http:methodName "PUT"^^xsd:string ;
15      td:href "/api/YqqaHVH8QF-...-UQc/lights/3/state"^^xsd:anyURI ;
16      td:mediaType "application/json"^^xsd:string ;
17      td:rel "invokeAction"^^xsd:string
18    ] ;
19    td:inputSchema [
20      td:schemaType td:Object ;
21      td:field [
22        td:name "on"^^xsd:string ;
23        td:schema [ td:schemaType td:Boolean; td:const true ]
24      ] ;
25      td:field [
26        td:name "xy"^^xsd:string ;
27        td:schema [
28          td:schemaType td:Array ;
29          td:items [ a iot:CIExData; td:schemaType td:Number ],
30            [ a iot:CIEyData; td:schemaType td:Number ]
31    ] ] ] ],
32  (...)
```

Yggdrasil. The hypermedia environment deployed in our demonstrator was hosted on Yggdrasil. While still under early development, Yggdrasil provides two core functionalities required by our demonstrator: (i) it serves as a repository for hypermedia environments that conform to the model in Sect. 3.2, and (ii) it acts as a hub that (partially) implements the W3C WebSub recommendation[11]; agents (or any software clients) can use this functionality to observe resources in the environment. The Yggdrasil version used in our demonstrator is available on GitHub.[12]

Yggdrasil implements an event-driven non-blocking architecture using $Vert.x$[13], a framework that is both powerful enough to support high-throughput Web servers[14], and lightweight enough to perform well on small devices, such as the Raspberry Pi[15]. The platform exposes a REST HTTP API for creating, updating, and deleting RDF representations of *environment*, *workspace*, and *artifact* abstractions. For instance, Listing 1.3 shows an HTTP request that retrieves a Turtle [31] representation of the workspace used in our deployment. Lines 12–14 point to the artifacts contained in this workspace (and make them discoverable).

Listing 1.3. A sample HTTP request (and the corresponding response) for retrieving the representation of a workspace from Yggdrasil.

```
1 GET /workspaces/wksp1 HTTP/1.1
2 Host: yggdrasil.andreiciortea.ro
3
4 HTTP/1.1 200 OK
5 Content-Type: text/turtle
6 Link: <http://yggdrasil.andreiciortea.ro/hub>; rel="hub"
7 Link: <http://yggdrasil.andreiciortea.ro/workspaces/wksp1>; rel="self"
```

[11] https://www.w3.org/TR/2018/REC-websub-20180123/, accessed: 05.11.2018.
[12] https://github.com/andreiciortea/emas2018-yggdrasil, accessed: 05.11.2018.
[13] http://www.vertx.io/, accessed: 05.11.2018.
[14] According to independent benchmarks for Web frameworks: https://www.techempower.com/benchmarks/, accessed: 05.11.2018.
[15] http://vertx.io/blog/vert-x3-web-easy-as-pi/, accessed: 05.11.2018.

```
 8
 9  <http://yggdrasil.andreiciortea.ro/workspaces/wksp1>
10      a <http://w3id.org/eve#Workspace> ;
11      <http://w3id.org/eve#hasName> "wksp1" ;
12      <http://w3id.org/eve#contains>
13          <http://85.204.10.233:8080/artifacts/hue1> ,
14          <http://yggdrasil.andreiciortea.ro/artifacts/event-gen> .
```

The response shown in Listing 1.3 contains two `Link` headers that conform to the W3C WebSub recommendation. Agents can thus *discover and use* these headers to subscribe for notifications whenever the workspace evolves (e.g., an artifact is added or removed, the workspace is deleted). All resources hosted on Yggdrasil support WebSub by default.

JaCaMo Application. To facilitate access to the hypermedia environment, our JaCaMo application[16] provides agents with "middleware" they can use. Given the IRI of a hypermedia environment (e.g., see Listing 1.1), the middleware automatically reflects into the local CArtAgO environment all the workspaces discovered in the hypermedia and the artifacts they contain. Agents are notified whenever a workspace or an artifact has been reflected. The middleware also provides agents with a CArtAgO artifact that serves as a hypermedia controller (i.e., a facade) for hypermedia artifacts with WoT TDs (e.g., see Listing 1.2). A controller is instantiated for each such artifact discovered in the hypermedia. Using these controllers, agents can then interact with hypermedia artifacts as they would typically interact with local CArtAgO artifacts. The main difference is that each controller instance exposes metadata via observable properties, such as what are the operations supported by the hypermedia artifact. To perform an operation, such as the one of changing the light color in Listing 1.2, agents use a generic `act` operation provided by the controller, as shown in Listing 1.4. This generic operation takes as arguments the IRI of the actual intended operation and its parameters, which can also carry semantics via IRIs. The IRIs could denote terms defined by an ontology.

Listing 1.4. The Jason plan used to send visual notifications via colored light.
```
1  +!thing_colored_light_notification(ArtifactName, CIEx, CIEy) : true <-
2      act("http://iotschema.org/SetColor", [
3              ["http://iotschema.org/CIExData", CIEx],
4              ["http://iotschema.org/CIEyData", CIEy]
5          ])[artifact_name(ArtifactName)];
6      .wait(2000);
7      act("http://iotschema.org/SwitchOff", [])[artifact_name(ArtifactName)].
```

In addition to hypermedia controllers, the middleware can also instantiate regular CArtAgO artifacts based on semantic descriptions discovered in the hypermedia, such as the one in Listing 1.5 for the `event-gen` artifact in our demonstrator. This allows offloading the execution of artifacts on the client-side – if the artifact code can be retrieved at runtime (e.g., via JavaScript, OSGi).

---

[16] https://github.com/andreiciortea/emas2018-jacamo, accessed: 05.11.2018.

Listing 1.5. RDF description of the `event-gen` artifact, which includes the canonical name of the Java class of the corresponding CArtAgO artifact. Initialization parameters could also be specified in the description.

```
1  <http://yggdrasil.andreiciortea.ro/artifacts/event-gen> a eve:Artifact ;
2      eve:hasName "event-gen" ;
3      eve:hasCartagoArtifact "emas.EventGeneratorArtifact" .
```

4.3 Discussion

Our demonstrator proves key elements of our hypothesis. In what follows, we analyze what has been demonstrated for the scalability and evolvability of hypermedia MASs, and then discuss the limitations of our demonstrator.

Scalability. Our demonstrator shows that agents can perceive and act upon a distributed hypermedia environment while being agnostic to the underlying infrastructure. The environment in our demonstrator is distributed across loosely coupled origin servers, and agents observe the environment using WebSub hubs discovered at runtime. All entities in our demo use the same WebSub hub, but each entity could use any number of hubs (e.g., to distribute the load). Other publish/subscribe mechanisms for Web resources can also be used, such as the one built into CoAP [33]. In principle, any mechanisms that have proved useful for managing the growth of the Web (e.g., load balancers, intermediaries for enforcing security or encapsulating legacy systems) could be applied to manage the growth of the hypermedia environment infrastructure.

Evolvability. Our demonstrator shows that hypermedia-driven interaction allows agents and their environments to be deployed and to evolve independently from one another. Agents can discover the distributed hypermedia environment at runtime starting from a single entry point, and they can observe the environment as it evolves – for instance, as workspaces and artifacts are added to the environment. Artifacts themselves can also evolve at runtime without disrupting the behavior of agents. This allows engineers to enrich the MAS with features that were not anticipated when the system was initially deployed. Furthermore, both engineers and agents could further exploit the hypermedia to enrich the system over time, for instance by writing new resources for agents to discover and use (e.g., shared knowledge) or by rewiring relations among resources (e.g., to create mash-ups of artifacts). The Web has already shown that a resource-oriented, evolvable environment can support new and unanticipated applications, which is essential for sustaining long-lived MASs.

Limitations. In our demonstrator, agents are able to use artifacts as they evolve at runtime, but the behaviors that use the artifacts are pre-programmed (e.g., see Listing 1.4). However, this is a limitation of our demonstrator and not an intrinsic limitation of our approach. One way to avoid this limitation would be to advertise in the hypermedia *artifact manuals* (e.g., [7,36]) that would allow agents to infer how to achieve their goals using the discovered artifacts.

As mentioned, Yggdrasil is in an early stage of development. As such, it does not yet implement an engine for actually running the artifacts, such as CArtAgO [32]. The logic of the `event-gen` artifact was simulated for the purpose of this demonstrator by sending the generated events via HTTP to Yggdrasil, which then dispatches the events to subscribers. The "middleware" developed in our JaCaMo application is an *ad hoc* solution meant to demonstrate that the additional programming complexity that comes with hypermedia environments can be mitigated through tooling. A proper extension would require a deeper integration into CArtAgO.

5 Conclusions

This chapter presents an approach to enable uniform interaction among heterogeneous entities in an open MAS such that the entities can be developed, deployed and can evolve independently from one another. The core idea is to use hypermedia to drive the interaction between agents and their environment. Our demonstrator proves that this approach: (i) can effectively decouple agents from their environment, and (ii) allows a seamless distribution of the environment. Even though in this chapter we focus on the agent ↔ environment interaction, the environment can also mediate interaction with other dimensions of a MAS: it can be used to discover and interact with other agents (e.g., as we have shown in [6,8]), with organizations (e.g., by means of organizational artifacts [4]) etc. In principle, any abstract entity in a MAS that is relevant to agents can be reified in the hypermedia environment – either as a passive resource that agents can discover and consume (e.g., to learn a new interaction protocol), or as an active resource (e.g., a tool) that agents can interact with. The results presented in this chapter suggest that using hypermedia as a general mechanism to support uniform interaction in MASs enhances the systems' scalability and evolvability – and could potentially enable the deployment of world-wide and long-lived MASs.

References

1. Berners-Lee, T., Hendler, J., Lassila, O.: The semantic web. Sci. Am. **284**(5), 34–43 (2001)
2. Berners-Lee, T., Fischetti, M.: Weaving the Web: The Original Design and Ultimate Destiny of the World Wide Web by Its Inventor. DIANE Publishing Company, Darby (2001)
3. Bizer, C., Heath, T., Berners-Lee, T.: Linked data - the story so far. Int. J. Semantic Web Inf. Syst. (IJSWIS) **5**(3), 1–22 (2009)
4. Boissier, O., Bordini, R.H., Hübner, J.F., Ricci, A., Santi, A.: Multi-agent oriented programming with JaCaMo. Sci. Comput. Program. **78**(6), 747–761 (2013)
5. Brin, S., Page, L.: The anatomy of a large-scale hypertextual web search engine. Comput. Netw. ISDN Syst. **30**(1), 107–117 (1998). Proceedings of the Seventh International World Wide Web Conference

6. Ciortea, A., Boissier, O., Zimmermann, A., Florea, A.M.: Give agents some REST: a resource-oriented abstraction layer for internet-scale agent environments. In: Proceedings of the 16th Conference on Autonomous Agents and MultiAgent Systems, AAMAS 2017, Richland, SC, pp. 1502–1504. International Foundation for Autonomous Agents and Multiagent Systems (2017)
7. Ciortea, A., Mayer, S., Michahelles, F.: Repurposing manufacturing lines on-the-fly with multi-agent systems for the web of things. In: Proceedings of the 17th Conference on Autonomous Agents and MultiAgent Systems, pp. 813–822 (2018)
8. Ciortea, A., Zimmermann, A., Boissier, O., Florea, A.M.: Hypermedia-driven socio-technical networks for goal-driven discovery in the web of things. In: Proceedings of the 7th International Workshop on the Web of Things (WoT). ACM (2016)
9. Cyganiak, R., Wood, D., Lanthaler, M.: RDF 1.1 concepts and abstract syntax, W3C recommendation. W3C Recommendation, World Wide Web Consortium (W3C), 25 February 2014
10. Dikenelli, O.: SEAGENT MAS platform development environment. In: Proceedings of the 7th International Joint Conference on Autonomous Agents and Multiagent Systems: Demo Papers, pp. 1671–1672. International Foundation for Autonomous Agents and Multiagent Systems (2008)
11. Duerst, M., Suignard, M.: Internationalized Resource Identifiers (IRIs). RFC 3987 (Proposed Standard), January 2005
12. Exposito, J., Ametller, J., Robles, S.: Configuring the JADE HTTP MTP (2010). http://jade.tilab.com/documentation/tutorials-guides/configuring-the-jade-http-mtp/. Accessed 15 Nov 2016
13. Fielding, R., Reschke, J.: Hypertext Transfer Protocol (HTTP/1.1): Semantics and Content. RFC 7231 (Proposed Standard), June 2014
14. Fielding, R.T., Taylor, R.N.: Principled design of the modern web architecture. ACM Trans. Internet Technol. 2(2), 115–150 (2002)
15. Fielding, R.T.: Architectural styles and the design of network-based software architectures. Ph.D. thesis, University of California, Irvine (2000)
16. Foundation for Intelligent Physical Agents. FIPA ACL Message Structure Specification (2002). http://www.fipa.org/specs/fipa00061/SC00061G.html. Document number: SC00061G
17. Foundation for Intelligent Physical Agents. FIPA Agent Message Transport Protocol for HTTP Specification (2002). http://www.fipa.org/specs/fipa00084/SC00084F.html. Document number: SC00084F
18. Foundation for Intelligent Physical Agents. FIPA Agent Management Specification (2004). http://www.fipa.org/specs/fipa00023/SC00023K.html. Document number: SC00023K
19. Gibbins, N., Harris, S., Shadbolt, N.: Agent-based semantic web services. Web Semant.: Sci. Serv. Agents World Wide Web 1(2), 141–154 (2004)
20. Gouaïch, A., Bergeret, M.: REST-A: an agent virtual machine based on REST framework. In: Demazeau, Y., Dignum, F., Corchado, J.M., Pérez, J.B. (eds.) Advances in Practical Applications of Agents and Multiagent Systems, vol. 70, pp. 103–112. Springer, Heidelberg (2010). https://doi.org/10.1007/978-3-642-12384-9_13
21. Gregori, M.E., Cámara, J.P., Bada, G.A.: A jabber-based multi-agent system platform. In: Proceedings of the Fifth International Joint Conference on Autonomous Agents and Multiagent Systems, pp. 1282–1284. ACM (2006)
22. Hübner, J.F., Sichman, J.S., Boissier, O.: Developing organised multiagent systems using the MOISE+ Model: programming issues at the system and agent levels. Int. J. Agent-Oriented Softw. Eng. 1(3/4), 370–395 (2007)

23. Huhns, M.N.: Agents as web services. IEEE Internet Comput. **6**(4), 93 (2002)
24. Huhns, M.N., Singh, M.P.: Service-oriented computing: key concepts and principles. IEEE Internet Comput. **9**(1), 75–81 (2005)
25. Kaebisch, S., Kamiya, T.: Web of Things (WoT) Thing Description, W3C Working Draft 5 April 2018
26. Kahn, M.L., Cicalese, C.D.T.: Coabs grid scalability experiments. Auton. Agent. Multi-Agent Syst. **7**(1), 171–178 (2003)
27. Lanthaler, M., Gütl, C.: Hydra: a vocabulary for hypermedia-driven web APIs. In: Proceedings of the WWW 2013 Workshop on Linked Data on the Web, vol. 996. CEUR WS (2013)
28. Limón, X., Guerra-Hernández, A., Ricci, A.: Distributed transparency in endogenous environments: the JaCaMo case. In: El Fallah-Seghrouchni, A., Ricci, A., Son, T.C. (eds.) EMAS 2017. LNCS (LNAI), vol. 10738, pp. 109–124. Springer, Cham (2018). https://doi.org/10.1007/978-3-319-91899-0_7
29. Mitrović, D., Ivanović, M., Budimac, Z., Vidaković, M.: Radigost: interoperable web-based multi-agent platform. J. Syst. Softw. **90**, 167–178 (2014)
30. Pautasso, C., Zimmermann, O., Leymann, F.: Restful web services vs. "big" web services: making the right architectural decision. In: Proceedings of the 17th International Conference on World Wide Web, WWW 2008, New York, NY, USA, pp. 805–814. ACM (2008)
31. Prud'hommeaux, E., Carothers, G.: RDF 1.1 Turtle - Terse RDF Triple Language. W3C Recommendation, World Wide Web Consortium (W3C), 25 February 2014
32. Ricci, A., Piunti, M., Viroli, M.: Environment programming in multi-agent systems: an artifact-based perspective. Auton. Agent. Multi-Agent Syst. **23**(2), 158–192 (2011)
33. Shelby, Z., Hartke, K., Bormann, C.: The Constrained Application Protocol (CoAP). RFC 7252 (Proposed Standard), June 2014
34. Singh, M.P.: Information-driven interaction-oriented programming: BSPL, the blindingly simple protocol language. In: The 10th International Conference on Autonomous Agents and Multiagent Systems - Volume 2, AAMAS 2011, Richland, SC, pp. 491–498. International Foundation for Autonomous Agents and Multiagent Systems (2011)
35. Singh, M.P., Huhns, M.N.: Service-Oriented Computing: Semantics, Processes, Agents. Wiley, Hoboken (2006)
36. Viroli, M., Ricci, A., Omicini, A.: Operating instructions for intelligent agent coordination. Knowl. Eng. Rev. **21**(1), 49–69 (2006)
37. Weyns, D., Omicini, A., Odell, J.: Environment as a first class abstraction in multiagent systems. Auton. Agent. Multi-Agent Syst. **14**(1), 5–30 (2007)
38. Willmott, S., Dale, J., Burg, B., Charlton, P., O'Brien, P.: Agentcities: a worldwide open agent network. Agentlink News, vol. 8 (2001)

Designing a Cognitive Agent Connector for Complex Environments: A Case Study with StarCraft

Vincent J. Koeman$^{(\boxtimes)}$, Harm J. Griffioen, Danny C. Plenge, and Koen V. Hindriks

Delft University of Technology, Delft, The Netherlands
{v.j.koeman,h.j.griffioen,p.c.plenge,k.v.hindriks}@tudelft.nl

Abstract. The evaluation of cognitive agent systems, which have been advocated as the next generation model for engineering complex, distributed systems, requires more benchmark environments that offer more features and involve controlling more units. One issue that needs to be addressed time and again is how to create a connector for interfacing cognitive agents with such richer environments. Cognitive agents use knowledge technologies for representing state, their actions and percepts, and for deciding what to do next. Issues such as choosing the right level of abstraction for percepts and action synchronization make it a challenge to design a cognitive agent connector for more complex environments. The leading principle for our design approach to connectors for cognitive agents is that each unit that can be controlled in an environment is mapped onto a single agent. We design a connector for the real-time strategy (RTS) game StarCraft and use it as a case study for establishing a design method for developing connectors for environments. StarCraft is particularly suitable to this end, as AI for an RTS game such as StarCraft requires the design of complicated strategies for coordinating hundreds of units that need to solve a range of challenges including handling both short-term as well as long-term goals. We draw several lessons from how our design evolved and from the use of our connector by over 500 students in two years. Our connector is the first implementation that provides full access for cognitive agents to StarCraft: Brood War.

1 Introduction

Multi-agent systems, consisting of multiple autonomous agents interacting with an external environment, have been promoted as the approach for handling problems that require multiple problem solving methods, multiple perspectives, and/or multiple problem solving entities [8]. In the past twenty years, the research community has combined multi-agent system (MAS) concepts and approaches into mature frameworks for agent-oriented programming (AOP) [2,15]. Current cognitive agent technology thus offers a viable and promising

---

An earlier version of this work was presented at the 2018 EMAS workshop [10].

D. Weyns et al. (Eds.): EMAS 2018 Workshops, LNAI 11375, pp. 302–319, 2019.
https://doi.org/10.1007/978-3-030-25693-7_16

alternative to other approaches for engineering complex distributed systems [6,14]. However, Hindriks [6] also concludes that "if [cognitive] agents are advocated as the next generation model for engineering complex, distributed systems, we should be able to demonstrate the added value of [multi] agent systems."

Designing a connector that can demonstrate this added value by connecting cognitive agents with an environment that puts strict real-time constraints on the responsiveness of agents, requires coordination at different levels (ranging from a few agents to large groups of agents), and requires complex reasoning about long-term goals under a high level of uncertainty is not a trivial task. The connectors that are currently available for use with cognitive agent systems have remained rather simple, and thus do not fully demonstrate the added value of cognitive agent technology.

In this chapter, we aim to establish a *design approach for developing connectors for complex environments*, aimed at facilitating the development of more connectors that can be used to demonstrate the ease of use of cognitive technologies for engineering large-scale complex distributed systems for challenging environments. We believe that RTS games that deploy large numbers of units provide an ideal case study to this end [4,17]. The basic idea is to control each unit with a cognitive agent. Based on this, and in accordance with Google (DeepMind) and many other AI researchers [13,16], we believe that StarCraft is the most suitable RTS game to target in our case study. Moreover, several popular competitions exist for StarCraft AI that can serve as a benchmark for implementations that use cognitive technologies [16]. By carefully designing and efficiently implementing a cognitive agent connector to StarCraft, and then testing this connector with large groups of students, we iteratively refine our approach for the development of agent-environment connectors.

Our focus in this work is on the case study of designing a connector that enables and facilitates the use of cognitive agent technology for engineering strategies for StarCraft (Brood War) based on a *one-to-one unit-agent mapping*, which is different from most existing StarCraft AI implementations. This unit-agent mapping introduces important challenges that need to be addressed:

1. The connector should facilitate a MAS that operates at a level of *abstraction* that is appropriate to cognitive agents.
2. The connector should be sufficiently *performant* in order to support a sufficient variety of viable MAS implementations using cognitive agents (i.e., both different approaches to implementing strategies as well as the use of different agent platforms).

In other words, the connector design should not force a cognitive MAS to operate at the same level of detail as bots written for StarCraft in C++ or Java, but also not promote the other extreme and abstract too much (e.g., clearly the extreme abstraction of providing a single action 'win' is not useful). To make optimal use of the reasoning typically employed by cognitive agents, the connector should leave low-level details to other control layers whilst still allowing agents sufficiently fine grained control.

The remainder of this chapter is organized as follows. In Sect. 2, we discuss the current state-of-the-art in environments available for cognitive agents. Next, in Sect. 3, we introduce StarCraft as a case study for connector design. In Sect. 4, we detail our design approach of a multi-agent connector by introducing general guidelines, applying them to our case study, and discussing the lessons learned from this. Finally, Sect. 5 concludes this chapter with recommendations for future work on both cognitive agent connectors as well as cognitive agent technologies in general.

2   Related Work

Connectors that support connecting cognitive agent technology to games have been made available for other games [3]. So far, however, most connectors have remained rather simple. The most complex cognitive multi-agent connectors that have been made available so far, are connectors for Unreal Tournament [7]. The design of such a connector involves similar issues related to the facilitated level of abstraction and the resulting performance as in this work. However, the resulting implementation as reported on by Hindriks [7] does not support running more than 10 agents, whereas for a StarCraft interface we need to connect hundreds of cognitive agents to control the hundreds of units in game. Moreover, corresponding agent systems for Unreal Tournament generally offer only a very restricted set of actions that agents can perform (i.e., mostly just a "go to" action because other middleware software is used to take care of path planning, shooting, etc.) or communication (i.e., mostly just informing others about enemy positions), limiting the complexity of decision making that is required. Relatively speaking, compared to StarCraft, the diversity in strategies or tactics that can be deployed is rather small. Another problem related to Unreal Tournament is that games cannot be sped up, complicating testing and debugging. It is therefore not feasible to derive a design approach for connectors to richer environments from this work.

RTS games are widely regarded as an ideal testbed for AI [13,17]. An RTS game like StarCraft involves long-term high-level planning and decision making, but also short term control and decision-making with individual units. This distinction between respectively strategical and tactical decision making is generally referred to as *macro* and *micro* respectively. These factors and their real-time constraints with hidden information make RTS games like StarCraft ideal for iterative advancement in addressing fundamental AI challenges [17]. Although machine learning solutions have been applied to some problems at the micro level, learning techniques have not been successfully applied to other aspects, mainly due to the vast state spaces involved [16]. The concepts of cognitive agents seem to be a good fit for addressing these challenges, allowing individual cognitive agents to reason about their tactical decision making whilst also inherently facilitating communication to make decisions at a joint strategical level. The reasoning typically applied by cognitive agents seems to lend itself for macro really well, but such systems can potentially employ learning techniques to perform specific sub-tasks (at the micro level) as well. A cognitive agent connector can also facilitate the use of MAS as an approach for allowing several individual AI techniques to work together.

The work of Weber et al. [19] recognizes the value of agent-oriented techniques for StarCraft AI. Their "EISBot" uses a reactive planner combined with external components like case-based reasoning and machine learning. Similar to multi-agent systems, the concepts of percepts and actions are used. However, there is only a single 'agent' that is compartmentalized into several specific managers. This approach is thus still based on a single-bot approach, whilst in this work, we instead aim to design a connector for multi-agent systems in which each in-game unit is connected to an individual cognitive agent. Moreover, it is not made clear which percepts and actions are provided, and what the gain in terms of abstraction level and the loss in terms of performance in this implementation is, as the focus is on the implementation of the StarCraft bot itself, instead of on the design of a (generic) connector as in this paper.

The prototypical RTS game is StarCraft [16], originally developed by Blizzard in 1998, but still immensely popular both in (professional) gaming and AI research. An API for StarCraft (Brood War) has been developed for several years: BWAPI [5]. BWAPI reveals the visible parts of the game state to AI implementations, facilitating the development of competitive (non-cheating) bots. Several dozens of such bots have been created with this API, mostly written in C++ or Java, aimed at participating in one of the tournaments that are being held for StarCraft AI implementations. However, this work does not directly facilitate cognitive agents that use knowledge technologies and realise a one-to-one unit-agent mapping.

A first attempt at creating a cognitive interface for StarCraft was performed by Jensen et al. [9]. In this work, a working proof-of-concept that ties in-game units to cognitive agents was introduced. However, it does not address the major challenges such an implementation faces concerning the level of abstraction and corresponding performance, as we do in this work. When using this connector, it is not possible to create viable (diversities of) strategies, as the range of strategies it supports is quite limited. This connector only offers a small subset of all possible actions associated with each unit in the game, and the percepts made available by the connector do not provide sufficient information for in game decision making either. In this work, we aim to allow virtually any strategy to be implemented with a sufficient level of performance using a cognitive agent connector based on the design approach we propose.

3   Case Study: StarCraft

In StarCraft, each of the three playable races have their own set of unit types, with roughly 15 types of air/ground units and 15 types of buildings per race. Although many races share similar types of buildings (e.g., depots to bring resources to), there are also substantial differences to take into account (e.g., one race requiring units to 'morph' into a different type of unit). For most types of units, there are usually multiple 'instances' (i.e., individual units) in a game, thus allowing anywhere from 5 up to 400 units representing one army in the game at a certain time. Depending on factors such as game length, the average number of units for an army in a typical game at any point in time is around 100, although many units will also die during the game (i.e., the total number of agents used is much higher). Performance is thus of vital importance, as a substantial performance impact caused by large amounts of percepts for example, will limit the amount of viable strategies.

Our cognitive agent connector to StarCraft was developed and refined in three iterations. We draw several general lessons from these iterations, which we have incorporated into our proposal for a connector design approach. Initially, a pilot was held with around 100 Computer Science master's students that worked in groups on creating a StarCraft bot using this connector. Shortly after, over 200 first year Computer Science bachelor's students did the same with an improved version of the connector, being the largest StarCraft AI project so far. We continued development of the connector after this project, and made several additional improvements, after which 300 first year Computer Science bachelor's students used the 'final version' of our connector.

4   Connector Design Approach

In this section, we discuss our design approach for a cognitive agent connector. The core of such a connector consists of three components: (i) the *entities* that are provided for agents to connect to (i.e., units in an RTS game), (ii) the outputs that are generated by each entity (and thus which *percepts* a corresponding agent receives), and (iii) the inputs that are available for each entity (and thus which *actions* an agent controlling the entity can perform). This structure is illustrated in Fig. 1. Each of these aspects will be discussed, starting with general guidelines, their application to our case study of StarCraft, and the refinements that were made after practical use of the StarCraft connector. Next, key steps for evaluating whether the connector design is fit for use in practice for developing cognitive MAS will be given and performed for our connector.

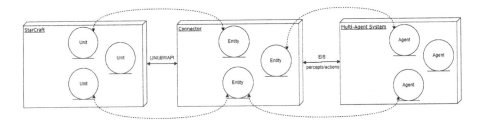

Fig. 1. An overview of the various components, with StarCraft on the left, our connector in the center, and a cognitive agent system playing the game on the right.

We make some basic assumptions about the architecture of a *cognitive agent*, as illustrated in Fig. 2. We assume such an agent pro-actively reasons about the *actions* that it should take based on (for example) its goals and beliefs in some

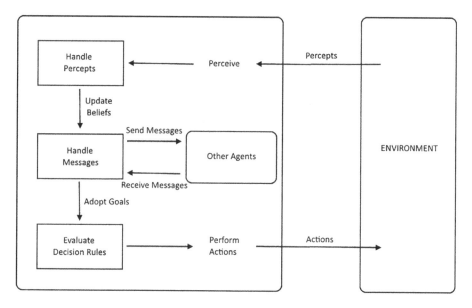

Fig. 2. The assumed structure of a cognitive agent in a multi-agent system (left) interacting with an external environment (right).

fixed *decision cycle* that is asynchronous from the environment in which it operates (for a certain *entity* in that environment), from which it receives information through *percepts*. Multiple agents can work together in one multi-agent system, which is not centrally controlled but does facilitate direct *messaging* between (groups of) agents. Our connector makes use of the Environment Interface Standard [1] in order to facilitate interacting with MAS platforms.

4.1 Micro and Macro Management

In complex environments such as StarCraft, a crucial distinction exists between top-down strategical decision making (macro) and bottom-up tactical decision making (micro). The basic assumption that we make is that a connector needs to provide support for a multi-agent approach based on a one-to-one unit-agent mapping, which inherently facilitates decision making from a bottom-up perspective. At the micro level, *every unit that is active in the environment should be mapped onto an entity* that a cognitive agent can connect to in order to control the behaviour of the unit. For StarCraft, this thus means that any moving or otherwise active unit such as a building will be controlled by a cognitive agent.

Although we initially assumed that the emergent behaviour from these agents would be sufficient to cover the strategical aspects, in practice this was hindered by the high dynamicity of an environment such as StarCraft, for example illustrated by the fact that any unit can be killed at any point in time. To facilitate macro management, we therefore have introduced a new, special kind of entities, so-called *managers*, which are made available by the connector. Managers do not match with unique in-game units, and as such they do not naturally have percepts or actions associated with them. However, as they still need to be informed about the state of the game in order to perform strategical decision making, they instead should have the ability to receive desired global information through percepts, as for example indicated by a developer in the initialization settings of a MAS.

Manager agents are especially useful to reason about groups of units. For example, without managing agents, all agents for resource gathering units in StarCraft (of which there are generally several dozen) would have to process information about the available resources and resource depots (i.e., subscribe to the relevant percepts and handle them), and then coordinate amongst each other about the division of tasks (i.e., implement some decentralized messaging protocol). Instead, a single manager agent can be the only one to have to deal with all the information about resources, and then use this information to assign a task to each resource gathering unit (i.e., through messaging), whilst in contrast the agents for those units would still handle defending themselves for example. This significantly reduces the total amount of percept processing and message sending that is required in such a situation. Moreover, in our case study we found that there is a need for dynamically adding or removing managers in order to for example temporarily centralize the reasoning for a group of attacking units, which is another frequently occurring situation in which using managers is beneficial for both performance and the effectiveness of the coordination between the relevant agents. The specific type and choice of managers that are made available by a connector and the resulting organizational structure is, however, not specified in our design approach so as to facilitate as many multi-agent system structures as possible. As there is information that is specific to certain units (and thus specific agents), and each unit has its own set of actions (which a single agent needs to call), it is not possible to completely centralize the reasoning.

Because our approach is to provide an entity (i.e., to which an agent can connect) for each unit, and the available actions for each unit are mainly defined by the (interface to) the environment itself, the main challenge when balancing the level of abstraction with the resulting performance is in determining the percepts that are available. As we assume cognitive agents here that explicitly represent their beliefs and goals, this essentially means we need to design an ontology that includes all relevant concepts for representing and reasoning about the environment at an appropriate level of abstraction.

4.2 Local and Global Information

The set of available percepts determines what information a specific entity 'sees' during the game, and thus what information its corresponding agent will receive. Percepts have a *name* to describe them and a set of *arguments* that contain the actual data. For example, a percept could be defined as map(Width, Height), and an agent could then receive map(96, 128) in a match. In order to determine the percepts that are created for each type of unit, our approach proposes several design guidelines. A key foundation of our approach to handling information from complex environments such as StarCraft is that there is a difference between 'local' information that is specific to a certain unit in the game (e.g., a unit's health) and '*global*' information that is potentially relevant to all units (e.g., the locations of enemy units). An agent should be able to *perceive all local information* that is specific to its corresponding unit's state, whilst a manager agent should be able to *perceive all global information* that is needed for its strategic (macro) reasoning. However, pieces of global information might also be needed in the agent for a specific unit (e.g., nearby enemy units in StarCraft).

To this end, we initially pushed all global information to all unit and manager entities, as a connector cannot determine which parts of this information a specific agent will need. However, our case study showed that this caused a significant performance impact with larger numbers of units. We have therefore found it useful to provide specific mechanisms to a developer to fine-tune the delivery of global percepts. Through the connector's initialization settings, a list of desired 'global information' (i.e., names of percepts) can be given ("subscribed to") for each unit type. For example, the (pseudocode) initialization rule `zergHatchery: [friendly, enemy]` will ensure that all agents for all *Zerg Hatchery* entities in a match will receive information about all friendly units and all visible enemy units. In this way, a developer can decide which information is relevant for certain agents, instead of such information being sent to agents at all times. This mechanism can also be used for specifying in more detail which global information a certain manager agent needs to be made aware of. Finally, we assume that when local information is needed for macro reasoning, this can be sent to the appropriate manager agent by the agent for a specific unit within the agent platform; it is thus not required to handle this within the connector (design) itself, as illustrated by the wave-shape in Fig. 3.

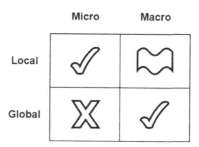

Fig. 3. Main design approach for organizing information into local and global percepts for micro (unit) or macro (manager) entities.

The ease of use of the percepts for an agent programmer should also be taken into consideration, i.e., by grouping related pieces of information together. The design guideline here is that one should *only group sets of parameters that naturally belong together*. Moreover, to avoid having to deal with different kinds of percepts for each type of unit, a design guideline is that *the percepts should be as generic as possible in order to facilitate re-use* between different agents. This guideline is aimed at reducing the number of different concepts introduced in our percept ontology, and thus aims for efficiency of design. An example of this is the `status` percept for each unit, as its structure (i.e., the set of parameters) is the same for each unit, even though not all information might be relevant for each unit (not all units use energy for example, but a unit's energy level is always provided in the percept). This also allows for specifying generic code for handling the `status` percept for all agents only once in the program, instead of having to specify this specifically (and nearly identically) for each unit type; special cases for certain types of units can then be programmed only where necessary.

Performance. One of the main challenges is how to deliver all percepts while guaranteeing sufficient performance levels. It is important to manage the percept load of individual agents, as creating the information needed for percepts (i.e., in the connector) and relaying that information to one or multiple agents who then have to make this information available for use in reasoning (i.e., by representing them in a Prolog base) is the most resource intensive task in a connector. In contrast to actions, of which usually at most one is selected per decision cycle, there are usually many percepts (all containing various amounts of information) sent to each agent per decision cycle. We therefore introduce a number of optimization guidelines which aim to either reduce the total number of percepts an agent will have (to store) or the amount of updates to this set of percepts that an agent will have to process.

Complex environments have a lot of static information to which all individual agents may need to have access, like what a certain unit costs to produce or what kinds of units a certain building can produce in StarCraft. Because such environments also introduce many units (and thus many agents), the initialization costs for such information for each of these agents can have a rather big impact on a connector's performance. To avoid this issue as much as possible, we introduce another design guideline to *only create percepts for information that changes in a single match or between matches*. Static information is better suited to be encoded in the agent system itself instead of being sent through percepts, as this will significantly reduce the performance when initializing an agent (which as aforementioned can happen many times during a game as large numbers of units come and go almost constantly). To this end, information that is fixed by the game itself can be coded as a separate part of the ontology that can and needs to be loaded only once at the start of the game. Agents will still need to be informed about changes between matches, e.g., map-specific information should not be included in the 'fixed part' of the ontology. Another guideline to keep the number of percepts low is to ensure that *no data is sent through percepts that can either be calculated based on other data* (e.g., the number of friendly units by counting the number of percepts about their status), *or retrieved from other agents* (e.g., the position of a friendly unit). Relaying information (like friendly unit positions) through messaging between the agents in a MAS is usually much more efficient, as an agent programmer can then selectively choose at which times and to which units to send specific pieces of information, as opposed to percepts always being sent to certain units even when they do not require them (at that time).

In order to improve the performance of the percepts that we do have to send, the Environment Interface Standard (EIS) [1], that we have used as a foundation for implementing our connector, differentiates between three types of percepts[1]:

- **Send once:** this type of percept is only sent once. Such percepts are generally used to send data about the (specific) match when an agent is created, such as information about the map on which the match is played.
- **Send on change:** a percept of this type will only be sent if the percept changes. Such percepts are generally used to update known information, such as a unit's health or the number of available resources.
- **Send always:** a percept of this type will be perceived every time the corresponding agent asks for percepts. Such percepts are generally used to indicate temporary information, such as seeing an enemy unit (which can die, after which the corresponding percept is no longer generated).

Send once percepts will be most performant, whilst send always percepts will be least performant. However, as indicated, some information cannot be represented in a 'more performant' type. It is thus important for to carefully consider which percept category certain (groups of) information would best fit in order to optimize the performance.

For StarCraft, combining the (finite set of) information that is available through the BWAPI interface with the guidelines as posed in this section lead to a set of about 25 percepts[2].

We have designed and optimized our algorithms to compute the difference between information states in order to generate new percepts as fast as possible. Most percepts are only generated if some change occurred. Our connector has been carefully designed so as to optimize the generation of percepts by first and only once generating the global percepts (i.e., that are not specific to units), such as the list of (visible) friendly and enemy units, followed by the generation of the percepts specific to each entity. This structure also ensures that agents receive their percepts immediately when they ask for them, i.e., they are not generated when requested (which would slow down the agent significantly) but only when information actually changes.

4.3   Asynchronous Actions

The actions available for a certain entity define the range of behaviour that is possible for a corresponding agent implementation. The basic design guideline here is that as a rule, *any action that a unit can do* (i.e., that is available in the environment) should be available to its corresponding entity (and thus agent).

---

[1] There are actually four percept types, but we do not consider *on-change-with-negation* as this type will be removed in future versions of EIS due to compatibility issues with knowledge representation languages other than Prolog.

[2] For the full set of percepts and actions that are available, we refer to the Star-Craft Connector Manual at https://github.com/eishub/Starcraft/blob/master/doc/Resources/StarCraftEnvironmentManual.pdf.

A unit in StarCraft can roughly choose from about 15 types of actions at any given time. Certain actions are only available to specific types of units (e.g., loading a unit into a loadable building). Some abstractions were used in order to better facilitate the usability of this set of actions for agent programmers. For example, instead of using pixel coordinates, StarCraft allows tile coordinates to be used, i.e., corresponding to a certain block of 32 by 32 pixels (buildings in StarCraft always have a size that is a multiple of 32 pixels in any dimension). This abstraction of pixels to tiles is also used in coordinates in percepts, thus not only ensuring easy compatibility with the actions but also allowing for percepts containing coordinates to be updated significantly fewer times when a unit is moving for example. We also note that BWAPI does not explicitly support grouping units (i.e., as a human player would do), and thus each unit needs to choose its own course of action. However, creating group behaviour in a multi-agent system is facilitated through inherent mechanisms such as messaging between agents. Manager agents thus do not need specific actions from a connector, as they can rely solely on the facilities in the agent platform.

However, as a MAS platform uses and runs agents in its own (set of) thread(s) that need to be connected to the environment, synchronisation issues arise that in particular for StarCraft pose a challenge, as StarCraft runs at a specific rate, updating the game logic at fixed millisecond intervals in so called '*match frames*'. In existing (C++/Java) BWAPI bots, the match frame function is used as the starting point (or even single function) for all decision making. In principle, this conflicts with a multi-agent approach in which all cognitive agents run in their own separate (autonomous) thread(s). As a solution, we use several synchronisation mechanisms. First, and most importantly, for each entity all requested actions are recorded (queued). On each match frame call, all queued actions (for all entities) are executed, i.e., 'forwarded' to the corresponding unit in StarCraft itself. Agents have to carefully rely on feedback from the environment (i.e., through percepts) to detect the effect of their actions, or when an action has failed (e.g., because some other action by another agent just used up some resources). A basic understanding of the synchronisation issues is thus needed when developing agents for highly dynamic environments such as StarCraft.

Debugging and Testing. For complex environments such as real-time strategy games and StarCraft in particular, it is also essential to provide a developer with environment-specific visualization tooling that provides easy access to information that will allow the developer to understand what is going on in this environment. Which (types of) tooling can be provided is specific to an environment and the access provided by the basic API made available by the environment.

In our case study, we have found that visualization tooling is most useful for providing insight into basic capabilities such as navigation, the status of units, and the progress of long-term actions such as a buildings producing a unit. For example, even though agents do not exercise low-level navigation control, agents do control the setting of target locations where units will move to. We therefore provide a developer with the option to enable visual cues about where a unit is moving to in order to be able to debug the agent code that sets these target locations. Another example of what our connector supports is visualizing when a unit is being produced by a building, removing the need to click on each building to see what it is producing (and how far along this production is) when trying to debug the production logic in a specific building agent. Visualizations like this can be implemented in StarCraft by using its debug drawing features that support drawing lines or writing text in the game window. Using these basic features, our connector allows for specific visualizations to be created by agents themselves (i.e., through calling specific actions), also facilitating drawing custom texts above in-game units. Examples of such 'debug visualizations' in StarCraft are shown in Fig. 4.

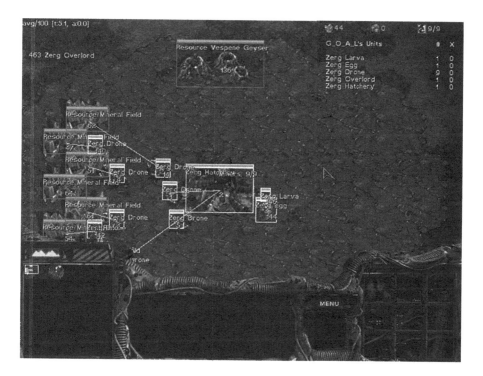

Fig. 4. A screenshot of StarCraft with a bot performing many debug draw actions.

More generally, to be able to debug and test multi-agent systems effectively and efficiently in an environment such as StarCraft where hundreds of agents are running simultaneously, requires a developer to have access to cheats that disclose or even modify gaming information that is not normally available to a player. StarCraft specifically offers useful development functionalities (through BWAPI calls) like removing the fog of war (i.e., making the whole map visible to the player), quickly gaining resources, or to making units invincible. We have integrated these functionalities in a separate development tool (that includes a button for gaining resources for example) and through initialization properties of the connector (e.g., making units invincible right from the start of a match) in order to make them easily accessible.

4.4 Evaluation

As high performance is critical for any cognitive approach that uses many agents to deal with the challenges of AI for RTS, it is important to verify the (CPU) performance of a connector. In addition, one should evaluate the requirement that a connector does not restrict the strategy space in any essential way by for example examining the success (i.e., in tasks in the environment) of a set of cognitive MAS implementations that make use of the connector. We do so by discussing the lessons we learned from the use of our connector by over 500 students in two years.

Performance. Complex real-time tasks, such as effectively attacking enemy units in StarCraft, potentially require a new decision to be made in each match frame (based on the new information such a frame generates). As our approach is based on an unit-agent mapping, there are at least as many agents as units in the game. To be performant, we need to show that all agents have the opportunity to receive new percepts and make a decision (i.e., perform an action) each match frame. AI tournaments run StarCraft at speeds of at least 50 match frames per second, which implies that in our case every agent should receive new information and be able to perform a new action at least 50 times per second as well, i.e., averaging[3] at most 20 ms for performing all cycles of the agents in a MAS. We assume here that no single agent should perform less than 50 decision cycles per second, even though many agents will not need that many decision cycles (e.g., most buildings would not as the decision making for production is not as time critical as for combat for instance). We aim to demonstrate that the minimum load required in the execution of the StarCraft connector leaves sufficient CPU time for adding the key decision logic in an agent program. We do so for our StarCraft connector by evaluating a simple multi-agent system that keeps producing simple units ('Zerglings') that continuously move to a random location on the map. In addition, all of these units are subscribed to all percepts (i.e., have to process them every decision cycle). A cheat was also enabled to ensure that these units cannot die. In this way, the maximum amount of units that a player can have (which is close to 400) can be reached without being influenced by the enemy in the game. Even though a player is very unlikely to reach this number of units in a game in practice, or to have all units subscribed to all percepts, we aim for our connector to provide sufficient CPU time for strategic reasoning even in this worst-case scenario.

---

[3] Most tournaments allow bots to take more time for a limited amount of frames during a single match, but we disregard that here.

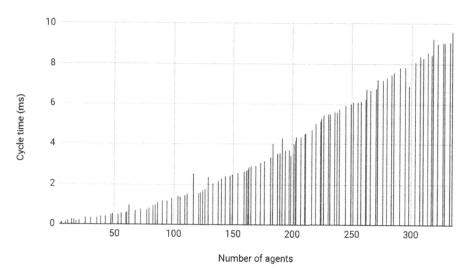

Fig. 5. The average speed of a decision cycle for all agents in the system under a growing number of agents.

The results of this evaluation for a minimum baseline are shown in Fig. 5. The evaluation was performed on a system with an Intel i7-6500U CPU and 8 GB RAM, with the StarCraft game speed set to the default tournament speed of 50 FPS. As each agent runs in its own thread(s), the average time any agent's cycle takes will increase when the number of agents increases due to limited system resources (e.g., the number of available CPU cores). However, even in this worst-case situation with up to 400 agents all processing all information available in the environment, the average cycle time per agent grows to about 10 ms at most. This thus leaves 10 ms for any additional reasoning to be implemented in the MAS in this extreme scenario. In practice, there will be fewer agents that are all subscribed to percepts more selectively. Therefore, in general, we see that around 18 ms (out of the possible 20 ms enforced by the tournaments themselves) will be available to a MAS that uses our connector.

We note that we have designed this baseline MAS such that all of the agents continuously execute decision cycles, whilst in practice, a decision is not required by each agent in every frame. This fact provides further support for our claim that sufficient processing power remains for implementing decision logic, as agents in a MAS with a more diverse set of agents should refrain from executing decision cycles (i.e., 'sleep') from time to time, thus freeing up CPU time for where it is needed most.

Success. As we cannot directly establish whether the full strategy space is made available by a connector, we aim to indirectly determine this by how well a cognitive MAS is able to perform relative to an environment measure that we would like to optimize. For a game like StarCraft, being successful at the game by winning (against other AI implementations) can provide such a measure.

Over the course of two years, groups of students created a varied range of full-fledged StarCraft AI implementations using (different versions of) our connector. After at most 8 weeks of work, nearly all of their implementations are able to defeat the game's built-in AI consistently. Some of the groups joined the Student StarCraft AI Tournament (SSCAIT) [20] with their implementations, successfully competing with the over 100 other active bots (which are mostly written in C++ or Java, frequently based on other well-established implementations, and have often been around for many years or developed by companies like Facebook). One of the students' StarCraft AI implementations that makes use of our connector is currently ranked at around the 50th place with a win-rate of roughly 60%. Altogether, this suggest that we have made the strategy space associated with StarCraft sufficiently available.

During the development and initial uses of the connector, we also gained valuable insights into the benefits and challenges of using current cognitive technologies for engineering complex distributed systems. One particularly challenging development issue that developers face when environments become more complex and the number of agents increases, is that every run of the system will produce different results. For this reason, it is very hard for a developer to test a specific scenario that s/he has in mind without additional tooling to provide a developer with control over the type of scenario that will evolve in the game. This makes testing very difficult and it thus is of the utmost importance to do whatever possible to provide a developer with tooling and capabilities to handle this. Testing against StarCraft's built-in AI, for example, will give different results on each run. More importantly, it can take quite a while before a scenario of interest occurs (if it does at all). In order to test specific (defined) scenarios, agent programmers should be allowed to *save the state of the game* at any given point, and then load that specific game again at a later stage, which is supported by StarCraft itself. Although our connector has been designed to support such state saving, in practice this will only provide support to some extent, and agent platforms should provide some way of storing and restoring the state of all agents at the same time.

4.5   Impact on Cognitive Technology

Even though the StarCraft connector has been optimized as far as possible when it comes to percept delivery, we found that there still are optimizations that can and should only be provided by the cognitive technology that is used, as we can only do so much; if the MAS platform itself is inefficient, it will not be possible to create an effective MAS approach for StarCraft with its strict real-time response requirements. One issue is for example that cognitive agents typically try to run as many decision cycles as possible. Considering the large number of agents that are typically employed in StarCraft, however, this is not ideal. In order to free up cycle time for e.g. agents that that have received new information to reason about. Therefore, we believe that functionalities that reduce the total load on the CPU, such as a '*sleep mode*' in which an agent that does not receive new percepts from the connector or new messages from other agents will not execute any reasoning, should be provided by agent platforms.

However, problems do arise in this mode when for example an agent is supposed to do something (e.g., move around) after it has not received new information for some time. Therefore, a *timing mechanism* should be introduced as well, facilitating the automatic generation of timer percepts upon a certain requested interval (thus waking up the agent after a set amount of time). A *sleep* action can be added as well, allowing a developer to manually sleep an agent for a certain amount of time, and thus free up performance for other agents if they do not need to do any reasoning for a while (even when new information comes in). An example of this is when a building agent starts producing a new unit, and is sure it will keep producing this unit (which takes a while). In addition, to allow developers to get more insight into the performance of their agents, specific logging messages can be added to agents that when enabled, after each decision cycle, show how many queries were performed and how many beliefs, goals, percepts and messages the agent has (received) in total. This can be useful for a developer to for example improve the ordering or nesting of rules in order to reduce the average amount of queries that are executed per cycle, or to keep tabs on the amount of messaging between agents (e.g., one agent might flood another agent with redundant messages due to some bug).

Another observation is that communication with large amounts of agents poses many challenges. In practice, with peer-to-peer based messaging, as is typically done in cognitive architectures, developers often use broadcasts to all agents in order to prevent having to use numerous bookkeepings of agents, which has an especially large performance impact in systems with many agents (such as those for StarCraft). We believe that this suggests that agent platforms should support a *publish-subscribe* messaging system to be effective, as this prevents agents that need to send messages to other agents from having to deal with continuously keeping track of which agents are relevant for its messages (i.e., interested in the information and still alive). Publish-subscribe messaging facilitates sending messages to a '*channel*'. Agents can subscribe to (and unsubscribe from) such channels, thus receiving messages sent to a certain channel only if they have explicitly indicated they want to do so. This allows for messaging based on content instead of specific targets. This is especially convenient for 'manager agents' to communicate with other (groups of) agents, as such an agent could for instance relay all required information about enemy units in a specific region to a certain channel, to which agents that need that information can then subscribe.

We believe that the application of cognitive agent technologies to complex environments such as StarCraft will yield more ideas for further development.

5   Conclusions and Future Work

We have presented a design approach for creating connectors for cognitive agent technology to (complex) environments, illustrated by a case study of such a connector that provides full access to StarCraft. A major challenge that was addressed during the development of this connector was to ensure corresponding cognitive agent systems can be programmed at a high level of abstraction whilst simultaneously allowing sufficient variety in strategies to be implemented by such systems. Based on this challenge, design guidelines for determining the set of available percepts and actions in agent-environment connectors were determined. The viability of our approach is demonstrated by multiple large-scale practical uses of the StarCraft connector, resulting in a varied set of competitive AIs. Based on the development of the connector and this initial use, we gained valuable insights such as the benefits of using publish-subscribe based messaging and the challenges of debugging large sets of agents.

Ensuring a sufficient level of performance of the connector was a significant challenge that had to be addressed in particular in order to demonstrate that a unit-agent mapping (MAS) approach is viable. In our evaluations, we determined the baseline performance of the connector in a worst-case scenario, which shows that on average there remains sufficient CPU time for strategic reasoning in a cognitive MAS. Even though the performance of such a MAS depends largely on the agent technology used itself, we believe that our connector can be effectively used in practice. Although our case study is focused on the 'Brood War' version of StarCraft, the new 'raw API' of StarCraft 2 is reported to be similar to BWPAI by Vinyals et al. [18], and tour work should therefore be relatively straightforwardly applicable and/or portable to StarCraft 2 (and possibly other RTS games) in future work.

Finally, through the development and use of our connector for StarCraft, a number of challenges to cognitive agent technologies were identified. One of those challenges is the fact that debugging (cf. Koeman et al. [12]) becomes increasingly difficult with increasing numbers of agents. As debugging concurrent programs is a hard problem in general, more work is required in this area; it could for example be useful to visualize the interaction between agents or the CPU time required by each agent. In addition, in order to better support automated testing, (cf. Koeman et al. [11]), it may be beneficial to develop a mechanism that automatically saves the state of a MAS when a save game is created in StarCraft. This can be used to immediately initialize a MAS to the desired state when executing a test with a specific save game (i.e., a scenario). Another observation is that communication with large amounts of agents poses many challenges, requiring more investigation in future work, for example into messaging architectures based on a publish-subscribe pattern. Finally, the performance of a MAS itself (i.e., all processing that takes place outside of a connector) is of critical importance in highly dynamic environments such as StarCraft. Functionalities that can reduce the CPU load of a MAS are thus important to explore as well.

References

1. Behrens, T.M., Hindriks, K.V., Dix, J.: Towards an environment interface standard for agent platforms. Ann. Math. Artif. Intell. **61**(4), 261–295 (2011)
2. Bordini, R.H., Dastani, M., Dix, J., El Fallah Seghrouchni, A. (eds.): Multi-Agent Programming: Languages, Tools and Applications. Springer, Boston (2009). https://doi.org/10.1007/978-0-387-89299-3

3. Dignum, F.: Agents for games and simulations. Auton. Agents Multi-Agent Syst. **24**(2), 217–220 (2012)

4. Dignum, F., Westra, J., van Doesburg, W.A., Harbers, M.: Games and agents: designing intelligent gameplay. Int. J. Comput. Games Technol. **2009**, Article ID 837095 (2009)

5. Heinermann, A.: Brood War API (2008). https://github.com/bwapi/bwapi. Accessed 12 May 2018

6. Hindriks, K.V.: The shaping of the agent-oriented mindset. In: Dalpiaz, F., Dix, J., van Riemsdijk, M.B. (eds.) EMAS 2014. LNCS (LNAI), vol. 8758, pp. 1–14. Springer, Cham (2014). https://doi.org/10.1007/978-3-319-14484-9_1

7. Hindriks, K.V.: UNREAL GOAL BOTS. In: Dignum, F. (ed.) AGS 2010. LNCS (LNAI), vol. 6525, pp. 1–18. Springer, Heidelberg (2011). https://doi.org/10.1007/978-3-642-18181-8_1

8. Jennings, N.R., Sycara, K., Wooldridge, M.: A roadmap of agent research and development. Auton. Agents Multi-Agent Syst. **1**(1), 7–38 (1998)

9. Jensen, A.S., Kaysø-Rørdam, C., Villadsen, J.: Interfacing agents to real-time strategy games. In: SCAI, pp. 68–77 (2015)

10. Koeman, V.J., Griffioen, H.J., Plenge, D.C., Hindriks, K.V.: Designing a cognitive agent connector for complex environments: a case study with starcraft. In: Proceedings of the 6th International Workshop on Engineering Multi-Agent Systems. EMAS 2018, July 2018

11. Koeman, V.J., Hindriks, K.V., Jonker, C.M.: Automating failure detection in cognitive agent programs. In: Proceedings of the 2016 International Conference on Autonomous Agents & Multiagent Systems, AAMAS 2016, pp. 1237–1246. International Foundation for Autonomous Agents and Multiagent Systems, Richland (2016)

12. Koeman, V.J., Hindriks, K.V., Jonker, C.M.: Designing a source-level debugger for cognitive agent programs. Auton. Agents Multi-Agent Syst. **31**(5), 941–970 (2017)

13. Lara-Cabrera, R., Cotta, C., Fernández-Leiva, A.: A review of computational intelligence in RTS games. In: 2013 IEEE Symposium on Foundations of Computational Intelligence (FOCI), pp. 114–121, April 2013

14. Logan, B.: A future for agent programming. In: Baldoni, M., Baresi, L., Dastani, M. (eds.) EMAS 2015. LNCS (LNAI), vol. 9318, pp. 3–17. Springer, Cham (2015). https://doi.org/10.1007/978-3-319-26184-3_1

15. Müller, J.P., Fischer, K.: Application impact of multi-agent systems and technologies: a survey. In: Shehory, O., Sturm, A. (eds.) Agent-Oriented Software Engineering, pp. 27–53. Springer, Heidelberg (2014). https://doi.org/10.1007/978-3-642-54432-3_3

16. Ontañón, S., Synnaeve, G., Uriarte, A., Richoux, F., Churchill, D., Preuss, M.: A survey of real-time strategy game AI research and competition in StarCraft. IEEE Trans. Comput. Intell. AI Games **5**(4), 293–311 (2013)

17. Robertson, G., Watson, I.: A review of real-time strategy game AI. AI Mag. **35**(4), 75–104 (2014)

18. Vinyals, O., et al.: StarCraft II: a new challenge for reinforcement learning. arXiv preprint arXiv:1708.04782, August 2017

19. Weber, B.G., Mateas, M., Jhala, A.: Building human-level AI for real-time strategy games. In: AAAI Fall Symposium: Advances in Cognitive Systems, vol. 11 (2011)

20. Čertický, M., et al.: Student StarCraft AI Tournament (2011). https://sscaitournament.com. Accessed 12 May 2018

Decision Process in Human-Agent Interaction: Extending Jason Reasoning Cycle

Antonio Chella, Francesco Lanza, and Valeria Seidita[✉]

Dipartimento di Ingegneria, Università degli Studi di Palermo, Palermo, Italy
{antonio.chella,francesco.lanza,valeria.seidita}@unipa.it

Abstract. The main characteristic of an agent is acting on behalf of humans. Then, agents are employed as modeling paradigms for complex systems and their implementation. Today we are witnessing a growing increase in systems complexity, mainly when the presence of human beings and their interactions with the system introduces a dynamic variable not easily manageable during design phases. Design and implementation of this type of systems highlight the problem of making the system able to decide in autonomy. In this work we propose an implementation, based on Jason, of a cognitive architecture whose modules allow structuring the decision-making process by the internal states of the agents, thus combining aspects of self-modeling and theory of the mind.

Keywords: Human-agent interaction · BDI agent · Jason

1 Introduction

Today we want software able to cooperate with us, to anticipate our needs and to coordinate its activities with us. We also wish to have software that can autonomously and intelligently intervene and act in dynamic and changing contexts, operating as humans would do. For example, an agent-human team has to cooperate to achieve a common goal in an environment not fully known. All the members of the team have to decompose the overall goal into a series of subgoals. They should then be able to understand or learn which actions are needed to reach the objective. Finally, they should match their skills with the correct steps to perform, and eventually, they should delegate some task to each other. This scenario concerns fully autonomous cooperative work that requires a complex software system with runtime adaptation to new situations that may lead to new requirements and constraints. Everything injected and evaluated at runtime cannot be defined during design phases, and therefore the system has to be handled as a self-adaptive system. In brief, a self-adaptive system must be aware of its objectives; it must be able to monitor the working environment and understand how far it is and if it is deviating from the objective. Moreover,

© Springer Nature Switzerland AG 2019
D. Weyns et al. (Eds.): EMAS 2018 Workshops, LNAI 11375, pp. 320–339, 2019.
https://doi.org/10.1007/978-3-030-25693-7_17

it must be able to adopt alternative plans and it must also be able to generate new plans when necessary.

Important challenges in this field concern knowledge representation and updating, the selection and creation of plans at runtime, the invention of techniques for purposefully and efficiently conveying the (runtime) decision process. These challenges lead to different solutions depending on whether we look at the architectural level or the system level. At the architectural level, it is necessary to identify a set of cognitive modules for modeling the cognitive process behind decisions in the before said scenario. At the system level, it is necessary to employ the right technological solution for coding and implementing a system working in changing conditions and in continuous interaction with the human.

In this chapter, we focus on the system level counterpart of the decision process that we achieve by employing BDI agents paradigm [15] and Jason as an agent language [5,6]. Decision processes elaborate data coming from external sources and the environment. In many domains, it would not be enough, or it would be hard to design and implement the decision process merely employing the monitoring, analyzing, planning, acting (MAPE) cycle [2]. In our view, the decision process should take as input all the internal states of agents involved in the environment, including human. Internal states then embody the changes occurring at runtime. The work we discuss aims at considering, as a crucial part of the decision process, the data coming from the capability of attributing mental states (beliefs, desires, emotions, knowledge, abilities) to itself and the other. In brief, we take into account self-modeling and theory of mind capabilities. Also, we briefly illustrate the architectural level in the form of the cognitive architecture we identified to include modules for knowledge representation and management, for internal states modeling and for the decision process.

Contribution and Outline of the Chapter. In this chapter, we illustrate the first steps of our ongoing work aiming at integrating self-modeling and the theory of mind in an architectural structure to implement an adaptive decision process at the architectural and the system level. The architectural part extends the MAPE cycle with modules allowing the perception of the external and the inner world in the form of internal states. The way we structured the architectural part and the rationale it underpins let us quickly fill the gap with the system level. We then present the core of this chapter, an extended version of the Jason reasoning cycle to map the architectural level into an agent framework.

The chapter is organized as follows. Section 2 discusses the features and challenges of human-agent interaction; in Sect. 3 we briefly describe the architectural level of the proposed work; in Sect. 4 we illustrate Jason features and its reasoning cycle and in Sect. 5 we show how we extend Jason reasoning to implement the cognitive architecture and its decision process modules at the system level. Finally, Sect. 6 draws some discussions and conclusions.

2   Human-Agent Interaction. Features and Challenges

Agent paradigm [27] has been used since decades as a solution, both from a theoretical and an implementation point of view, for systems providing aid to humans in their everyday life. An agent is thought and programmed to act on behalf of humans. Cases studied and implemented since now refer to automated systems emulating in some way the autonomous behavior of humans involved in complex tasks. However, automation is very different from autonomy; real autonomy also implies self-adaptation and self-organization abilities.

Autonomy intervenes in scenarios where agents have to intelligently interact with humans and with other agents to reach a common objective in an unknown or partially known environment. The environment may be not totally known at design time or may change during agents' working. A possible scenario is a human-agent team. Normally, teammates share the same objectives and the same knowledge on the environment. They know the goal and have a plan to reach it, collaborating and cooperating with the others. Collaboration and cooperation amount to knowing own abilities and others' ones, interacting each time something is unknown or is going wrong or each time a task has to be delegated to another or adopted by another. Also, collaboration and cooperation imply explaining why an action/task has failed or cannot be done. Moreover, the teammate may anticipate actions of another member as the result of continuously observing the other and the environment. Knowledge of the environment is continuously updated to let teammates re-plan or create new plans if necessary. Knowledge on the environment also includes the ability to develop a model of the self, the inner state of the teammate changes over time and influences, along with the general knowledge on the environment and on the goal to pursue, the decision-making process. We also consider that the result of anticipating actions, both on the inner and outer world, greatly affects the decision process of the action to perform.

Generalizing, features of human-agent team systems require to investigate and analyze *(i)* knowledge acquisition, representation and updating, including memory management, *(ii)* environment representation, inner and outer one, *(iii)* plans selection or creation *(iv)* learning, *(v)* introspection, for allowing team members to be aware of himself and his capabilities.

Human-agent interactions can be encoded from simple situations where everything may be identified and established at design time (environment, plans, actions and changing situations) to more complex ones where changes occur at any time and where the agent has to decide autonomously and self-adapt.

To better explain the case we are facing, let us consider the following three scenarios. In the first case, a team composed of agents and humans working together to carry out a task known to both. Let's suppose that the working environment is known in advance and during runtime, there are no changes other than those resulting from the actions of some pre-programmed agents. In this situation, agents may act in complete autonomy, and goals may be achieved performing actions in the repertoire. The collaboration is apparent in the sense the agents and humans do not need mutual help; the BDI logic [22] and its implementation using Jason [6] are perfectly efficient and usable.

In the second case, let us suppose the agent needs collaboration by a human for performing some part of the overall goal. For instance, the agent may realize to be not able to do an action for some physic limitations even though having the know-how for doing the action. This situation implies an intervention of the human under an explicit request of the agent. It is a collaborative work. This case requires some "soft" self-adaptation; the agent has to be endowed with the capability to understand when it cannot select/perform an action to achieve a goal. This case can also be handled with the use of the Jason interpreter by customizing methods of some of its predefined classes (see [6] for more details).

In the third case, the most complicated one, let us suppose that only part of the environment is known beforehand. The common goal, as well as a set of plans to achieve it, are identified at design time, but the ongoing interaction of the agent with the environment and with the human change conditions unpredictably. This fact happens when interactions bring out new terms of operability that must be worked out to decide what action to take. Generally, when a team is made up of only humans, they choose actions from their experience, the knowledge they have of the other team member, the trust they place in the other team, their emotional state or the anticipation of the actions of others.

For example, suppose that two people are caring for a disabled patient. Routine care includes the administration of medicines, cleaning, help during meals, etc. and each of the two has been assigned tasks. Suppose that during lunch the patient spills a glass of water. In this case, it is required picking up the glass from the ground and cleaning the patient, but none of the two actions have been assigned to a specific caregiver it may happen that if one takes the initiative and decides to clean the patient, then the other chooses to pick up the glass. Moreover, if there is no procedure to respond to an emergency, the two caregivers generally do not stay still, they decide what to do based on their experience and in general on their internal state. Besides, they will collaborate, even delegating to each other what to do. Our long-term work is to replicate this way of behaving in human-(multi) agent systems.

A human-agent team is a complex system [11], designing and developing different levels of cooperation and self-adaptation are the main challenges in this context. The system has to be equipped with the ability to select the best action to perform, to conduct the right decision-making process basing on goals, capabilities, mental state and so on not totally known at design time.

Actually, designers have not tools to analyze and identify all the possible elements that cause perturbation and change in the environment nor to implement an efficient system level (the running multi-agent system). They cannot determine the decision-making process to be implemented at the system level.

There not exist design approaches handling cooperative and self-adaptive systems where requirements and goals change at runtime, during systems working, and where systems configuration and features are the results of the interaction system, environment and humans; the system behavior emerges from interactions. Thus, a gap still exists between design and implementation level of such a kind of systems. We claim that this gap may be filled by employing theory coming from the cognitive process area: the *cognitivist* and the *emergent* system approaches [13, 16, 25]. The first approach relies on the common perceive-decide-act loop and on symbolic representations to physically instantiate code operations devoted to realize and implement cognitive agents behavior and decision process. The emergent system approach considers cognition as a dynamic emergent process implying self-organization. Many emergent approaches consider anticipative skills more important than knowledge acquisition and consider the physical instantiation of the cognitive model as an important factor. Issues related to the research area we are investigating may be faced using a cognitive architecture relying on the principles of an emergent approach. However, we believe that separating knowledge acquisition from anticipative skills is not the right direction. Thus, we are moving towards a hybrid model form that will be illustrated in the following section.

It is necessary to have means for analyzing how the mind builds a model of self and uses the theory of mind. Our proposal is to integrate self-modeling and theory of mind in the modules of a cognitive architecture to implement all the human-human team features handled by a multi-agent system. The work focuses both on theoretical aspects and on low-level ones. Indeed, we aim at identifying an abstract cognitive model (see Sect. 3) and the related implementation counterpart (see Sect. 5). In the literature, some promising approaches [3,4] propose to solve this problem by shifting the design time to runtime. Also, some architectures containing modules for learning and memory have been introduced to pass the decision-making process through the stored and processed sensing data [14,20,26]. However, these approaches do not take into account the use of mental states and cognitive processes, which are the primary element in our hypothesis to be able to create human-agent interaction systems behaving as human-human systems.

We focus on the multi-agent system managing interactions with humans in a human-like fashion. We employ the multi-agent systems paradigm for implementing our cognitive architecture; each *module* becomes an *agent* which interacts with all the others for achieving its objectives and at the same time the overall system objective. In particular, we pay attention to the *Belief-Desire-Intention model* (BDI) [22] for modeling the cognitive reasoning process of each agent.

3   The Architectural Level for the Decision Process

To realize an emergent cognitive approach and conceive a cognitive architecture useful for our purposes, we took inspiration from the standard model of the mind [19]. The standard model of the mind has been developed along three different levels, from the purely biological level of mind to the more complex deliberative one. Hence, from simple behavior to complex one. The standard model has been conceived in a way that allows extending modules in each level; the higher levels are constrained by the lower ones. The scenario we are studying lays at the higher level, the one ruling an intelligent and deliberative behavior.

The standard model is intended to be a reference model and a theoretical driving approach. It has been based on three well known cognitive architectures (ACT-R, SOAR and Sigma [1,18,20]) and presents a core composed of the cognitive cycle: perception, working memory and action. ACT-R decomposes the cognition process in five specialized modules and shows how to integrate the modules in order to create a complete cognitive process. SOAR is based on a cyclic process that includes the production process and the decision one. One decision cycle follows each production cycle. Sigma blends elements both from ACT-R and SOAR and provides just a single long-term memory. We also studied other cognitive architectures [12,14,17,24]. The result was, starting from the standard model in Fig. 1 and the influence of all the other architectures, the architecture shown in Fig. 2. The figure recalls the deliberative behavior of an agent that perceives, reasons and acts. This architecture may be implemented, at the system level, by using Jason agents and their reasoning cycles[1].

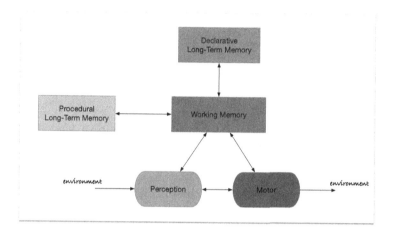

Fig. 1. The standard model of the mind - redrawn from [19]

Both this standard model and Jason, however, do not account the internal states, the fact that the environment may continually change in a not prescribed way and that the representation of the agents' environment also includes own inner world. To face this problem, we extended the higher level of the standard model, without modifying its core cycle.

Figure 2 shows an extended version of the perception-action cycle in which we added modules for handling decision process and memory in the most useful way for our purposes. It can be seen that a cognitive agent uses, for deciding which action to execute, inputs coming from the environment perception and from the memory. Agent decides actions to perform after a reasoning process and then it executes and continuously observes the results of its action on the environment.

This part is perfectly in line with existing cognitivist approaches. In order to integrate self-modeling and theory of mind abilities that, as already said, we guess to be fundamental for triggering the decision process in a way useful for

---

[1] Details about Jason reasoning cycle are given in Sect. 4.

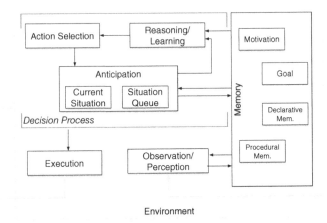

Environment

Fig. 2. The cognitive architecture model that includes self-modeling ability for the decision-process.

human-agent teaming interactions, we needed to shift to a kind of emergent approach and we added some elements in the decision and memory modules.

We decided to represent knowledge not only including all the objects in the environment but also including goals to be pursued and motivations for executing a specific action. This allows us to consider the new perspective on the environment we introduced before: the environment is seen as something composed of objects, cognitive agents and all that is inside each agent. This latter elements, such as for instance the awareness to be able to do something, constitutes agent's self-model and then trigger the decision process along with the whole available knowledge on the "static" environment.

Continuous observing and perceiving allow to constantly update and increase knowledge even during execution phase. In addition, in the ANTICIPATION module, we consider the possibility of creating an anticipation of an action result, some kind of post-condition on the state of affairs (the whole environment) at the end of each action. This part is fundamental for realizing human-like reasoning and decision process since it allows to anticipate also all other cognitive agents' behaviors and actions. In so doing, we may implement the elements of the theory of mind letting agents coordinating, cooperating and delegating actions at run-time and in a totally autonomous fashion. In the ANTICIPATION module we also included the elements for generating the CURRENT SITUATION and a QUEUE of possible situations, generated starting from the knowledge base and gained when the current situation is not applicable. The module, we simply named MOTI-VATION, includes all the elements related to a human-like mental state; these elements have to be considered during the decision process. Examples of some of these elements are the emotional state, the level of trust in the other and in itself. Motivations, along with knowledge on goals, environment, including the self and own capabilities lead to take purposeful decisions.

In summary, in our architecture, the design process has the same input of the standard model but it also has an intermediate part. Executing an action has effects on the environment and also on the internal state. The perception refers to the external and internal world and also to the working memory, in our case goals and motivations. The working memory, so as the reasoning/learning process and action selection, is affected by the ability to generate anticipation.

In the following, we explain how we extended the Jason reasoning cycle to implement this architecture.

4   The BDI Agent and Its Implementation by Using Jason

Due to its features, the BDI agent-oriented paradigm well fits our need to model and implement the modules of the cognitive architecture shown in the previous section. Indeed, *Belief-Desire-Intention model* has been recognized as the most useful paradigm to implement human-like agents. We can talk about computer programs as cognitive agents owning a *mental state*. So, an agent is characterized by beliefs, desires and intentions:

- beliefs - are information that the agent has about the surrounding area or the world in general.
- desires - are all the possible *states of affairs* that an agent perform. The desire is not a *must to do action* but it could be seen as a condition that influences other actions.
- intentions - are the *states of affairs* that an agent decides really to perform. The intentions can be normally intended as a particular operation that other can be delegated to the agent or agent's consideration. This latter definition comes from practical reasoning systems inside agent.

Moreover, the BDI paradigm has its natural equivalent in the agent programming language: Jason [6]. Jason is an implementation of AgentSpeak language [21] that somehow allows overcoming the old denotation of software. The software is no longer something that provides a service by an exact coding, and that depends heavily on the intervention of the user. In Jason's logic, a computer program is something that has the know-how and chooses actions to pursue a goal on behalf of the human and without his intervention. For this reason, a Jason program is called Agent. It does not yet have the characteristics to perfectly replicate how a human acts, but it can autonomously process the knowledge it possesses about how to do things. The basic idea behind Jason is to define what is called the program's know-how in the form of a set of plans. The Jason platform allows executing the deliberation process of a BDI agent that leads to choosing the intention to pursue within a set of possible states of affairs.

An agent can decide what to do, the set of actions in its repertoire to be undertaken starting from a set of data obtained through sensing and to modify the surrounding environment. In AgentSpeak, and therefore in Jason, deciding what to do means manipulating plans and the environment. Typically, a Jason agent has partial control over the environment in which it lives because it is also populated by other agents having control over their part of the environment. It can autonomously work because it is structurally defined to do this but cannot adapt itself in a dynamic environment; especially if the dynamicity of the environment derives from interactions with humans and other agents. The procedure for handling agent-agent interaction is standardized and mainly established at design time. Human-agent interactions have to be still explored, especially in the context of cooperation between humans and agents which presupposes delegation and/or selection of actions to be undertaken even by observing the human actions and skills. Jason is an optimum language to implement the standard model with the perception-action cycle. Figure 3 represents the Jason agent's reasoning cycle and its modules realizing the beforesaid cycle; however it lacks means for implementing the architecture in Fig. 2. The agent reasoning cycle consists of three main processes, (i) a knowledge updater, (ii) an event handler and (iii) a module to act.

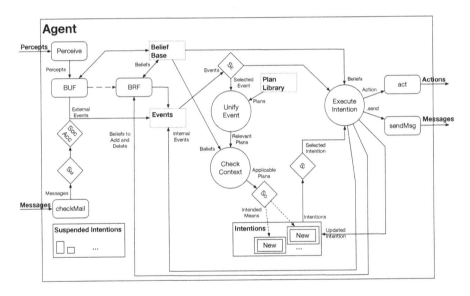

Fig. 3. The original reasoning cycle of Jason language - redrawn from [6].

According to [6], *rectangles* represent the principal components that determine the agent's state, such as belief base component and all the components that handle the set of events, plan library and intentions. *Diamonds, circles* and *rounded boxes* are used for describing the functions used in the reasoning cycle. In particular, *circles* model the application processes and *diamonds* represent the selection functions. Jason allows to modify and customize the functions represented by *round boxes* and *diamonds*.

In the following section, we give a detailed description of the Jason reasoning cycle and then in Sect. 5 we explain where and how we added new modules.

4.1   The Jason Reasoning Cycle

The main concepts in the Jason reasoning cycle are illustrated and described in the following table (Table 1). This subsection, Tables 1 and 2 are loosely based on Chap. 4 in the book by Bordini et al. [6].

Table 1. A complete summary of Jason's components and elements.

Agent	An agent is an entity with several capabilities. An agent is able to perceive and act in environment, communicate with others and reason about possible events. Agents have several skills and offer services
Belief	Beliefs are information about the world
Belief Base	A Belief Base is the structure where all beliefs are organized
Plan	A Plan is composed by three parts: the triggering event, the context, and the body. The body contains other plans or actions
Plan Library	A Plan Library is where all plans are stored and lets agent choosing which plan is more applicable or not to reach the goal
Event	An event is a couple where the first component denotes the change that are taking place, and the second is the associated intention. It may be internal or external, the first is related to the goal the second is related to environment's changes
Intention	Intentions are the states of affairs that the agent has decided to commit
Percepts	Percepts are referred to state of affairs in the surrounding world.
Context	As mentioned in [7] a context is the place where agents take into account others and/or where the others act to realize tasks

In an AgentSpeak program, we define an agent type where we can set the initial state of beliefs, the events and the set of the plans that an agent could execute during its life-cycle.

The first thing that an agent does at the beginning of each reasoning cycle is perceiving the environment through its senses. This operation involves the belief base and the related function[2]. Beliefs are represented by using a symbolic form, the architecture has an internal *Literal* component that converts perceptions into a list of Literals; each of these is a single *percept* and this is a symbolic representation of a specific property perceived from the environment. This *percept* is detected by *perceive method* that implements the process. Once the agent has perceived the environment, it *updates* its internal belief base to reflect changes in the environment. The method able to do this is the *belief update function*, also known as *buf*. The Jason's *buf* presumes that every perceptible thing could be included into the list of percepts generated by the perceive module.

---

[2] During the description of the reasoning cycle, we refer to Fig. 4 for the sequence of agent's activities and Fig. 5 for the related implemented classes. In Fig. 5 both classes of the original cycle and those of the extended one (in green) are represented.

Generally, the *buf method* updates the belief base in a simple way; this method consists of two points: (i) each literal l in p not currently in b is added to b; (ii) each literal l in b no longer in p is deleted from b; where the symbol p is the set of current percepts and b is the set of literals in the belief base that the agent obtained from the last sensing process.

An *event* in Jason is considered as a couple, where the first component is the change occurred and the second is the associated intention. Furthermore, the event could be divided mainly into two categories, *internal* and *external events*. Each change produced by *buf method* invokes an *external event*. This kind of event is created when the source of belief is related to the percept. In this case, the associated couple contains as the first member the change produced and as the second member an *empty intention* denoted by a ⊤.

Another important module is the communication system. Inside the cycle, an agent could retrieve information about the environment or other agents through others in the same system. At this point, the cycle checks for new messages that might have been sent from others. This distribution system is just integrated into Jason and it works such a mailbox for each agent.

The method within the reasoning cycle is called *checkMail* that simply checks for received messages and makes them available at the level of AgentSpeak interpreter to be handled by agents.

The *message selection function*, denoted by $\mathcal{S_M}$ in Fig. 3, selects the first message in the list in the default implementation. By security reason a *social acceptance function* is defined into the system, the aim is ignoring potential malicious attack that others could do or bypass wrong messages that could spoil the reasoning loop, the default implementation accepts all messages from all agents.

A relevant role is taken by events since they represent the effective changes in the environment or agent's own goal. The principal cognitive skill of the BDI Jason Agent is handling events, this happens only managing them one at time; for instance in a hypothetic cooperative scenario, the agent could have the necessity to evaluate other events before the first in the set of events; to solve this problem Jason lets the user customize a specific function called *event selection function* denoted with $\mathcal{S_\varepsilon}$ in Fig. 3. The default implementation selects the first event in the list of events; it works like a FIFO structure if not customized.

Once relevant event has been selected, the agent needs to select a set of reliable plans from a collection called *Plan Library* that will permit to react to a specific event with a designed action. The agent searches into the *library* all necessary plans for each event. After selecting the relevant plans, a unification process helps the reasoning cycle to catch a set of relevant plans on which a check context process will be applied. The output of the latter process lets deleting all plans that do not match with the current context and only a subset of all relevant plans will be marked as *applicable plans*.

Given the set of applicable plans and all the knowledge acquired by agent through perception and communication skills, converted into a set of literals represented as beliefs, the agent is able to choose one of the selected applicable plans

Table 2. Description of functions for the Jason reasoning cycle.

Function	Description
perceive	The perceive method lets agents sense the environment and retrieve from it information about things. It implements the perceive function in Fig. 3
socAcc	Social Acceptance Function establishes the reliability of other agents, it implements the *socAcc* function in Fig. 3
selectEvent	Selects the events that will be handled in the reasoning cycle; it implements the $S_{\mathcal{E}}$ function in Fig. 3
selectIntention	Selects an Intention to be further executed in the reasoning cycle; it implements the $S_{\mathcal{I}}$ function in Fig. 3. The default implementation executes intentions with a *round robin* scheduling process
selectOption	This method is used to select one among several options (an applicable plan and an unification) to handle an event. It implements the $S_{\mathcal{O}}$ function in Fig. 3
selectMessage	Selects the message that will be handled in the current reasoning cycle; it implements the $S_{\mathcal{M}}$ function in Fig. 3
buf	Updates the belief base with the given percepts and adds all changes that were actually carried out as new events in the set of events
brf	Revises the belief base with a literal to be added (if any), a literal to be deleted (if any), and the Intention structure that required the belief change
act	Act function lets agents execute action in the environment

through an internal method: *Option Selection Function* denoted with the symbol $S_{\mathcal{O}}$ in the Fig. 3. The output of $S_{\mathcal{O}}$ produces what is called *intended means* and this name is associated to the mean that the agent intends to execute to handle the related event. It is worth to remind that each plan in the set of applicable plans represents an alternative to reach the goal. The default implementation of this function considers as applicable plan the first in order of appearance in the plan library; the position of each plan is defined in the agent definition file written in AgentSpeak. Thus in the default implementation, the agent attempts to choose the applicable plan according to the agent's developer.

To select which intention to be computed during the cycle, a *intention selection function* denoted with the symbol $S_{\mathcal{I}}$ is used. $S_{\mathcal{I}}$ has a default implementation like a *round-robin scheduler*. Moreover every times an intention is extracted, it is removed from the list of intention after the execution and when this will be inserted back into the list, this will be added at the end of the list. In this way every intention have the same portion of agent's attention.

The last stage of the reasoning cycle performs an action in the agent environment or produces a message to communicate with other agents. Generally, the action that an agent performs are (i) *environment action*, (ii) *achievement action*, (iii) *test goal*, (iv) *mental notes*, (v) *internal actions* or (vi) *expressions*.

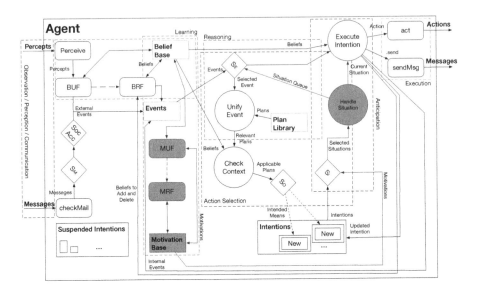

Fig. 4. The extended reasoning cycle for Jason's agents

Table 3. Definitions new elements integrated in Jason.

Component	Description
Motivation	A Motivation is a form of belief for self-awareness modeling. Motivations are information that the agent has about itself. Motivation contains knowledge about the consciousness of the agent
Motivation Base	A Motivation Base is where all motivations are organized
Situation	A Situation is an extension of *Intention*. It represents the future state of affairs after the execution of agent's action

5   The Jason Reasoning Cycle Extension

The reasoning cycle proposed in Fig. 3 as said before develops three general processes: the knowledge update process, the handle event and the acting module.

The elements: motivation, goal, anticipation (current situation and queue) are not handled by the traditional Jason reasoning cycle. In some way, goals are implicitly treated in the plan and the plan library plus the context and the intention. However, it is not enough for our objectives. We need a structure to match goals with the anticipated results of single actions. This provides a cornerstone for realizing self-modeling.

Motivation serves for modeling all that is related to the internal state, the inner world. It is a kind of belief (the state of the environment) but they differ from a conceptual point of view. In fact, beliefs are data about the environment,

Table 4. Description of functions for the extended Jason reasoning cycle.

Function	Description
perceive	The perceive method lets agents sense the environment and retrieve from it information; in our approach, the function gets information about itself through sensing the status of internal parts and the status of the mind. It implements the perceive function in Fig. 4
selectEvent	Our implementation takes in input a queue of events and motivations to select the plan that accomplish agent's desires (see Algorithm 2)
selectIntention	Selects an Intention to be further executed in the current reasoning cycle; it implements the $\mathcal{S}_\mathcal{I}$ function in Fig. 4. Our implementation uses an intelligent scheduling that selects the right intention considering not only the queue of intentions but also a queue of situations that helps the algorithm to choice the better situation to compute in the handle situation. This function looks in future scenario to accomplish the desires and respects the agent's motivation (see Algorithm 4)
muf	*Motivation update function* updates the motivation base with given perception
mrf	*Motivation revision function* revises the motivation base with a literal to be added (if any), a literal to be deleted (if any)
buf, brf, $\mathcal{S}_\mathcal{M}$, socAcc, $\mathcal{S}_\mathcal{O}$	These functions are not modified. For a description read the Table 2

are values providing pre-conditions for a plan to be activated or selected. Motivation is, in some senses, a superstructure of beliefs including the agent's mental state.

Anticipation, in the two forms, current situation and situation queue, is used for generating a sort of simulation of the scene, the state of the world, if everything would go well. During the reasoning cycle, the agent decides which action to commit also after having evaluated the anticipation against the first component of the event, thus reinforcing the decision process.

In Tables 3 and 4 a summary of definition of concepts used in the extended cycle (Fig. 4) is reported.

Jason reasoning cycle does not allow to implement these elements, above all the anticipation so, in order to add them, we created two new functions MUF and MRF with their related methods muf and mrf in the agent class (Fig. 5), one other principal component, the "Motivation Base" and one new application process, the "Handle Situation". We also modified some selection functions as will be illustrated later in this section. Through motivations, it is possible to solve other complex plans and to force to select an intention to accomplish agent's desires. The deliberative process of actions is not limited to simple execution of a plan assigned to agents at design time and stored into the Plan Library, but the extension provides a valid alternative built on the motivation base. With this knowledge, the agent tries to define new alternative *applicable plans* that should be successful plans cause these are generated by checking the status of the agent internal state and the context.

Anticipation, as said before, has the aim to produce a *queue of situations* where the head of the queue is the situation (alias intention) that the cycle is scheduling to handle for acting. The tail of the queue contains all possible future situations in according to the inner state of the agent including its motivation. The mechanism of the anticipation module recalls the perception loop described in [23]. Another important module that we add to the reasoning cycle is motivation.

The reasoning process starts with a *perceive method*. In Fig. 4 percept is handled by a *perceive function*, this latter handles two kinds of percept, the first is external perception or better, percepts that come from the environment and the second is the internal perception. In this last, the agent sense itself looking for features such as for instance execution time, stress-level, emotive state and other motivational features. This is the first significant difference with the original cycle. Inner perceptions are not defined as normal beliefs (*Literal*) but once agent perceives the feature this is converted into motivation. Each motivation is organized in a MotivationBase that is an extension of the BeliefBase (see in Fig. 5). In the same UML diagram, it is possible to find some changes that we did to implement the cycle. As described we extended the *AgArch class* by creating another derived class called *AgArchMotivated* that implements the handling of internal perceptions. Knowledge is updated by means of *belief update function* and *motivation update function*. As said for the *buf method* in the original Jason reasoning cycle, the operating mechanism is not modified but we added a new branch to handle the inner state.

Initially every perception acquired is a belief with some operations the belief update function and the belief revision function convert internal perceptions in motivations and using the *motivation update function*, the system saves internal perceptions (aka motivations) in the *MotivationBase*. Processing motivations involves also motivation revision function to revise the MotivationBase. These functions are implemented in *AgentMotivated* class, this class extend the Jason *Agent* class. Information about the state of affairs of the environment is also perceived by the communication module. The reasoning contains methods to communicate with other agents.

For this purpose, Jason has two important functions to handle the communication between agents. The *checkMail method* is the first function that the agent does as shown in Fig. 4 and it gets external messages sent by agents and organizes them into a mailbox assigned to the agent. Here, the function remains the same of the original cycle (*AgArch* class in Fig. 5). The *social acceptance function*(aka *socAcc*) and its associated method are modified for our purposes and their functionalities are described in Table 2. After beliefs and motivations are updated, new events are generated. At this point, in the original cycle the *selectEvent* function, given as parameter a queue of events, returns the related *poll function*. Algorithm 1 shows as the original *selectEvent* function works. Algorithm 2 shows how we modified the *selectEvent* function in order to consider the situation.

Algorithm 1. The *selectEvent* algorithmn implemented in Jason.

```
1: procedure 𝒮_ℰ (Queue<Event> events)
2:     queue← events
3:     return queue.poll()
4: end procedure
```

Algorithm 2. The *selectEvent* algorithmn implemented in the extended Jason reasoning cycle.

```
1: procedure 𝒮_ℰ (Queue<Event> events, Queue<Situation> situations)
2:     Queue<Event> eventsQueue ← events
3:     Queue<Situation> situationsQueue ← situations
4:     Queue<Event> queue := generateEventsQueue(eventsQueue, eventsSituations)
5:     Event selectedEvent := queue.poll()
6:     return selectedEvent
7: end procedure
```

So $\mathcal{S}_\mathcal{E}$ function implements an algorithm that, given as parameters the event queue and the situation queue generated at the previous cycle, executes a *generateEventsQueue function* to obtain a queue of events that are reformulated considering the queue of possible future scenarios carried by the queue of situations (if any). Once the algorithm has generated the *Selected Event* as shown in Fig. 4, such a result of the *diamond* $\mathcal{S}_\mathcal{E}$ function, a *unification process* is fired. It unifies events evaluating the previous results and a list of plans generated by a *plan library* module. This process is exactly the one described in the previous Sect. 4. The result of this process is a list of relevant plans. Once plans are selected another process is started.

The following process *check context* (Fig. 4) is the same of the original cycle. This process is not influenced by the *motivation module* or *anticipation module* because the relative check context for our scope is included in the *select event function* with the *generateEventQueue* function as you can see in Algorithm 2. After the context is verified, the process generates *applicable plans* that are given as input to the function *applicable plan selection function* denoted as $\mathcal{S}_\mathcal{O}$ in Fig. 4. The output of this function is called *intended means* that is the chosen applicable plan because the actions executed by that plan is the means that the agent intends to execute to handle the chosen event. The intended means is converted into intentions and will be handled by the *intention select function*. The list of intentions, this is given as argument for the *intention select function* and through a handle situation process our reasoning cycle extracts from this latter process the current situation, that is shown in the UML diagram a derived class of Intention. The original *intention selection function* $\mathcal{S}_\mathcal{I}$ implements a poll function as argument as described in Algorithm 3. Our implementation, instead, involves two functions (Algorithm 4). The first creates a simulation process that implements a structure similar to the one described in [23] and the second verify the queue of situations generated at the step before. In Algorithm 4, it is proposed our pseudo-code for the reasoning cycle.

Algorithm 3. The *selectIntention* algorithm implemented in Jason.

1: **procedure** $\mathcal{S}_{\mathcal{I}}$(Queue<Intention> *intentions*)
2:     queue← intentions
3:     **return** queue.poll()
4: **end procedure**

Algorithm 4. The *selectIntention* algorithm implemented in the extended Jason reasoning cycle.

1: **procedure** $\mathcal{S}_{\mathcal{I}}$(Queue<Intention> *intentions*, Queue<Motivation> *motivations*)
2:     intentionsQueue ← intentions
3:     motivationsQueue ← motivations
4:     Queue<Situation> situations := simulate(intentionsQueue, motivationsQueue)
5:     Queue<Situation> selectedSituations := verify(situations)
6:     **return** selectedSituations
7: **end procedure**

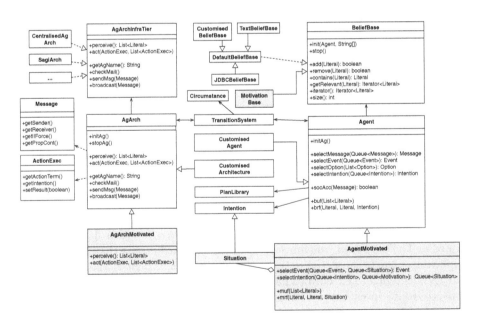

Fig. 5. Agent and agent architecture class diagram and the related extensions for implementing the new reasoning cycle. (Color figure online)

Regarding code, the situation queue is internal to the agent so the code structure is not changed because a poll function is always called on the result of the previous function. So the execute intention process has as input a situation that is an intention as evidenced in the UML diagram in Fig. 5. This process tries to perform all actions included in the current situation and the agent is able to produce the *act* function, after which the reasoning cycle could be restart.

6   Discussion and Conclusions

The work presented in this chapter deals with systems (such as human-agent interaction systems) working in not completely known operational conditions. This research area lacks techniques and tools for modeling and implementing all that regards the decision-process activities of systems intrinsically self-adaptive and autonomous.

We present the implementation of agent's decision making process in a dynamic context. Our proposal is based on the fact that agent's decision-making-process is determined by processing data coming from observation of the external environment and also by the knowledge the agent has about itself and other agents acting around. The implementation of such a system is a hard task because its features can be seen only at runtime, during the interaction with the whole environment. Therefore, the system must be treated and implemented with self-adaptive characteristics.

We have exploited the power of BDI agents and the Jason language, which natively allow creating agents that perform a deliberation and means-ends reasoning process. We modified the Jason reasoning cycle to include modules to manage events, plans, and intentions selection in order to take into account what we call motivations in addition to traditional beliefs. To complete the infrastructure, even at the agent coding level, we modified classes of the Jason component called *user-defined*. In particular, we added the classes needed to implement the part of the new reasoning cycle by adding the methods necessary for the agent to be able to choose the plan to pursue; in this way agents use a cognitive process based on what we called motivations that embody the mental states of the agent.

In order to model and implement motivations, we could have extended the belief concept instead of creating a new element. We decided to separate the two for two reasons: first, we want to resemble the human mind where these two aspects are considered separately, indeed the observation of the state of the environment brings to computation on data whereas elaboration on mental state gives an agent the attitude to make propositions such as believing, hating, loving and so on. The second reason, the most important for us, is that the continuation of this work will regard the modification of the Jason interpreter. We think that it will be more efficient t work in a modular fashion and adding elements to the interpreter instead of extending the existing one so to maintain a high degree of modularity and a low coupling.

It is worth to note that the proposed cycle extension does not alter the original Jason agent reasoning at a high level, but extends its capabilities, allowing the development of agents able to manage at the same time the sense of self and the theory of the mind together with the usual decision-making process. This work is the initial part of a larger project for the implementation of complex adaptive systems including knowledge update, selection and creation of new plans at runtime. The approach we are suggesting has given some good results in the validation phase during a series of experiments conducted in the robotics laboratory of the University of Palermo [8–10]. In the future, we think to definitively formalize the approach with the addition of all the design aspects to experiment with a complex case study.

Acknowledgment. This material is based upon work supported by the Air Force Office of Scientific Research under award number FA9550-17-1-0232.

References

1. Anderson, J.R., Matessa, M., Lebiere, C.: ACT-R: a theory of higher level cognition and its relation to visual attention. Hum. Comput. Interact. **12**(4), 439–462 (1997)
2. Andersson, J., et al.: Software engineering processes for self-adaptive systems. In: de Lemos, R., Giese, H., Müller, H.A., Shaw, M. (eds.) Software Engineering for Self-Adaptive Systems II. LNCS, vol. 7475, pp. 51–75. Springer, Heidelberg (2013). https://doi.org/10.1007/978-3-642-35813-5_3
3. Baresi, L., Ghezzi, C.: The disappearing boundary between development-time and run-time. In: Proceedings of the FSE/SDP Workshop on Future of Software Engineering Research, pp. 17–22. ACM (2010)
4. Blair, G., Bencomo, N., France, R.B.: Models@ run.time. Computer **42**(10), 22–27 (2009). https://doi.org/10.1109/MC.2009.326
5. Boissier, O., Bordini, R.H., Hübner, J.F., Ricci, A., Santi, A.: Multi-agent oriented programming with JaCaMo. Sci. Comput. Program. **78**(6), 747–761 (2013)
6. Bordini, R.H., Hübner, J.F., Wooldridge, M.: Programming Multi-agent Systems in AgentSpeak Using Jason, vol. 8. Wiley, Chichester (2007)
7. Castelfranchi, C., Falcone, R.: Trust Theory: A Socio-Cognitive and Computational Model, vol. 18. Wiley, Chichester (2010)
8. Chella, A., Lanza, F., Pipitone, A., Seidita, V.: Knowledge acquisition through introspection in human-robot cooperation. Biol. Inspired Cogn. Arch. **25**, 1–7 (2018). https://doi.org/10.1016/j.bica.2018.07.016
9. Chella, A., Lanza, F., Seidita, V.: A cognitive architecture for human-robot teaming interaction. In: Proceedings of the 6th International Workshop on Artificial Intelligence and Cognition, Palermo, 2–4 July 2018 (2018)
10. Chella, A., Lanza, F., Seidita, V.: Representing and developing knowledge using Jason, CArtAgO and OWL. In: Proceedings of the 19th Workshop "From Objects to Agents", Palermo, Italy, 28–29 June 2018, pp. 147–152 (2018)
11. Cheng, B.H.C., et al.: Software engineering for self-adaptive systems: a research roadmap. In: Cheng, B.H.C., de Lemos, R., Giese, H., Inverardi, P., Magee, J. (eds.) Software Engineering for Self-Adaptive Systems. LNCS, vol. 5525, pp. 1–26. Springer, Heidelberg (2009). https://doi.org/10.1007/978-3-642-02161-9_1

12. Christensen, W.D., Hooker, C.A., et al.: Representation and the meaning of life. In: Clapin, H. (ed.) Representation in Mind: New Approaches to Mental Representation, pp. 41–69. Elsevier, Amsterdam (2004)
13. Clark, A.: Mindware: An Introduction to the Philosophy of Cognitive Science. Oxford University Press, Oxford (2000)
14. Franklin, S., Madl, T., D'Mello, S., Snaider, J.: LIDA: a systems-level architecture for cognition, emotion, and learning. IEEE Trans. Auton. Ment. Dev. 6(1), 19–41 (2014)
15. Georgeff, M., Rao, A.: Rational software agents: from theory to practice. In: Jennings, N.R., Wooldridge, M.J. (eds.) Agent Technology, pp. 139–160. Springer, Heidelberg (1998). https://doi.org/10.1007/978-3-662-03678-5_8
16. Kelso, J.S.: Dynamic Patterns: The Self-organization of Brain and Behavior. MIT Press, Cambridge (1997)
17. Kieras, D.E., Meyer, D.E.: An overview of the epic architecture for cognition and performance with application to human-computer interaction. Hum. Comput. Interact. 12(4), 391–438 (1997)
18. Koller, D., Friedman, N., Bach, F.: Probabilistic Graphical Models: Principles and Techniques. MIT Press, Cambridge (2009)
19. Laird, J.E., Lebiere, C., Rosenbloom, P.S.: A standard model of the mind: toward a common computational framework across artificial intelligence, cognitive science, neuroscience, and robotics. AI Mag. 38(4) (2017)
20. Laird, J.E., Newell, A., Rosenbloom, P.S.: SOAR: an architecture for general intelligence. Artif. Intell. 33(1), 1–64 (1987)
21. Rao, A.S.: AgentSpeak(L): BDI agents speak out in a logical computable language. In: Van de Velde, W., Perram, J.W. (eds.) MAAMAW 1996. LNCS, vol. 1038, pp. 42–55. Springer, Heidelberg (1996). https://doi.org/10.1007/BFb0031845
22. Rao, A.S., Georgeff, M.P., et al.: BDI agents: from theory to practice. In: ICMAS 1995, pp. 312–319 (1995)
23. Seidita, V., Cossentino, M.: From modeling to implementing the perception loop in self-conscious systems. Int. J. Mach. Conscious. 2(02), 289–306 (2010)
24. Shanahan, M., Baars, B.: Applying global workspace theory to the frame problem. Cognition 98(2), 157–176 (2005)
25. Stillings, N.A., Chase, C.H., Feinstein, M.H.: Cognitive Science: An Introduction. MIT Press, Cambridge (1995)
26. Sun, R.: The importance of cognitive architectures: an analysis based on clarion. J. Exp. Theor. Artif. Intell. 19(2), 159–193 (2007)
27. Wooldridge, M., Jennings, N.R.: Intelligent agents: theory and practice. Knowl. Eng. Rev. 10(2), 115–152 (1995)

Exposing Agents as Web Services
in JADE

Arthur Casals[1,2]([✉]), Amal El Fallah Seghrouchni[1], Orso Negroni[1],
and Anthony Othmani[1]

[1] Sorbonne Université, LIP6-CNRS UMR 7606, 4 place Jussieu, 75005 Paris, France
{arthur.casals,amal.elfallah}@lip6.fr,
orso.negroni@etu.upmc.fr, anthony.othmani@gmail.com
[2] IPSA (Institut Polytechnique des Sciences Avancées),
63 Boulevard de Brandebourg, 94200 Ivry-sur-Seine, France

Abstract. The objective of this chapter is to revisit and explore how
intelligent agents can be used in conjunction with modern Web technologies. We use JADE and BDI4JADE to expose cognitive agents using a
BDI architecture as web services that can be integrated with different
modern cloud-based services, such as Amazon AWS services and Google
Home.

Keywords: Multi-agents systems · Web service agents · JADE/WSIG

1 Introduction

Agents can be described as relatively independent and autonomous entities that
can be used to solve problems of different complexity degrees [16]. These entities
can be organized in communities and work together using different interaction
mechanisms in order to solve complex problems. Such communities are also
known as multiagent system (MAS): a system composed of multiple agents that
interact among themselves in a single environment [36].

Due to their autonomous and interactive capabilities, agents can be seen as
a paradigm for software engineering. In fact, since software architectures may
contain many different components, each one with its own thread of control and
attributions, agents can be used as a paradigm when designing such systems
[41]. Moreover, such paradigm can be adopted within complex systems, since
interaction is one of the most important characteristics of complexity in software.

Using agents and MAS in conjunction with web services has been explored
for a long time, from simple interactions between web services and agents [3,15,
17,23,27] to using existing software engineering methodologies such as model-
driven development (MDD) [7,32,42] to support the development of web-based
MAS [29,37,38].

Using agents exposed as web services to design systems for the Semantic
Web [5] was also studied [13,35]. Designing such systems involves not only creating systems with distributed capabilities, but also systems capable of using

© Springer Nature Switzerland AG 2019
D. Weyns et al. (Eds.): EMAS 2018 Workshops, LNAI 11375, pp. 340–350, 2019.
https://doi.org/10.1007/978-3-030-25693-7_18

existing communication protocols and mechanisms in order to share and reuse knowledge. This is so because the Semantic Web is an extension of the web by adding semantics to the current data format representation in order to turn web information understandable not only for humans but also for software entities [5].

However, despite the extensive research already done in this field, the advent of new paradigms such as the Web of Things (WoT) [18] has encouraged a revisitation on the use of agents in the Web as a viable approach for deploying autonomous systems [9]. This idea revolves around the fact that in the WoT, it is possible for web services to perceive the real world and act on it though the use of physical devices (sensors).

In this context, our research interests reside in the Agent-Oriented Software Engineering (AOSE) [24] domain, focused on agents capable of interacting with the Web and its services. We refer to such agents as *web-based agents*. Our objectives are (i) to review the existing software engineering techniques used in conjunction with web agents and (ii) to explore how web agents and MAS can be extensively used with different new Web-related paradigms. In particular, we would like to understand the difficulties involved in the use of multiagent technologies in real-world situations. This also involves studying the use of well-established multiagent platforms and concepts by developers and development teams already employed in the industry, which are not necessarily familiar with agents. Before exploring these topics, however, it is necessary to better understand the current state-of-the-practice on web-based agents and related frameworks. For that reason we established a process composed of three different steps: (i) reviewing existing work relating agents and the Web; (ii) evaluating existing multiagent frameworks and Web-related capabilities; and (iii) implementing web-capable agents (exposed as web services) to serve as an evolving proof-of-concept, to be used during the course of our work. This process is fundamental to our subsequent research, and it constitutes the basis of the present chapter.

With that in mind, we implemented a Smart Agenda MAS using one of the multiagent platforms of our interest (JADE). At the same time that we understand this platform is fairly mature, we would like to understand how difficult it would be for students recently introduced to multiagent theory to use and apply this platform in the process of solving a problem based in a real-world scenario. For this reason, an agent-based personal assistant was proposed as the evolving proof-of-concept.

This chapter is organized as follows: in Sect. 2, we provide some background on intelligent agents. Section 3 contains some of the existing work related to using agents in conjunction with Web-related technologies. In Sect. 4, we illustrate the implementation of the Smart Agenda system, using agents deployed as a web services. Finally, Sect. 5 presents some discussion and concludes this chapter with some perspectives for future work.

2   Background

In this section we present some concepts that will be used along this chapter. First we provide a brief description of web services, followed by an overview on intelligent agents (with emphasis on one particular architecture). After that we provide an overview on languages used by the agents to interact between themselves, referred to as *agent communication languages.*

2.1 Web Services

Web services can be generically described as "a software system designed to support inter-operable machine-to-machine interaction over a network, providing a standard means of inter-operating between different software applications, running on a variety of platforms and/or frameworks"[1]. It possesses an interface that allows other systems (or web services) to interact with it using structured messages [2].

In practical terms, a web service can be described as a mean to interact with existing applications using Web-related technologies. A web service can be *discoverable* if it is published in a registration or directory service, which acts as an yellow-pages equivalent. Its specification also includes a *Web Service description* defining all message formats, protocols, and data types used by the web service. From this description, valid messages can be formed and used to communicate with the web service in question. When a web service is published in a directory service, its description is also included.

From a distributed systems perspective, web services enable multiple applications to interact between themselves using Web technologies and protocols [1]. A web service can be used to remotely access a database, or to execute specific processes in a remote machine with a certain set of parameters. They embody the concepts of a service-oriented architecture (SOA)[2] [14]. This allows for different web services to be used together in order to obtain the functionalities of an equivalent larger system.

2.2 Intelligent Agents

An agent is a computer system with autonomous capabilities, which are able to take decisions on what is needed to do in order to satisfy their objectives [41]. While this definition is not consensual, it revolves around the concept of autonomy.

Agents are also capable of interacting with other agents, exchanging data and engaging in complex interactions such as cooperation, coordination, and negotiation. A multiagent system is a system composed of multiple agents that interact among themselves in a single environment [36]. The main purpose of a MAS is to autonomously solve complex problems that would otherwise be impossible (or very difficult) to solve by using a monolithic system.

Intelligent agents are capable of reason and decide which action to perform according to available information. This information usually is related to the conditions or consequences of the actions to be executed [41]. Taking advantage

---

[1] https://www.w3.org/TR/ws-arch/.
[2] http://www.opengroup.org/subjectareas/soa.

of the agents' inherent capabilities allow MAS to adapt to changes in the environment. Also, the use of multiple agents allow for cooperation mechanisms to take place in situations where solving the problem at hand is beyond the capabilities of any single agent. Applications of MAS include manufacturing control, production planning, logistics, transportation, among others [34].

BDI is one of the software architectures used to model and implement intelligent agents. It is based on the human practical reasoning model [6] and any BDI agent uses the concepts of belief, desire, and intention in its reasoning process. These concepts are used by agents in a means-ends reasoning process. In this sense, the agent's actions are organized in an execution plan built on top of what it believes to be true, and what it desires to achieve as a goal. This reasoning process is usually referred to as "planning" [26]. By using this separation between information, planning, and execution, the agent is capable of adapting to different conditions presented by the environment it is situated in.

3   Related Work

The idea of integrating agents and the web services has been proposed (and experimented on) since the late 1990s [3,15,17,23,27]. The main idea at that time was to use agents as assistants for web-based services, such as web stores [3], or even for web browsing [27].

In particular, the idea of using agents *as* web services and using the Semantic Web appeared in early 2000s [20,22]. Specifically, the use of BDI agents as web services was also proposed around that time by Dickinson and Wooldridge [13]. Their work was later referenced in different works using agent as web services, including collaborative testing [4] and e-learning [21].

Part of the subsequent work on agents as web services, however, was also related to web-based MAS [29,37,38] and agent architectures [33,39]. Software engineering methodologies related to this topic were also being developed and studied [19,25,44]. In 2007, a survey on existing agent methodologies based on the agent-oriented paradigm was published [8] with the aim of evaluating in what extent existing agent-oriented methodologies were also oriented to the development of services. From the AOSE perspective, the study served to demonstrate that all evaluated methodologies could be used to model service-oriented agents. At this point, the focus was on modeling agents as services, or generally using the concepts around services in order to facilitate the interaction between agents.

In 2010, however, Ricci *et al.* introduced a platform called CArtAgO-WS [35], intended to allow the development of service-oriented applications (SOA) populated by agents. This was a more embracing approach from the MAS perspective, since it took into account both the concepts of artifacts - "objects" or services that could be used by the agents - and the use of heterogeneous agent architectures (including BDI). This idea was further explored and used in conjunction with other agent frameworks, such as JaCaMo[3] (we will briefly introduce this

---

[3] http://jacamo.sourceforge.net/.

framework later in the text). More recently, another step in the same direction was proposed by Ciortea *et al.* [10]: they proposed that the World Wide Web (WWW), in its current state, could be suitable as a middleware for Internet-scale multiagent systems. This would be achieved through the use of a resource-oriented layer that would allow the application environment to be decoupled from its deployment context. In order to demonstrate this proposal, an agent environment was developed using JaCaMo. This environment was specifically aimed at the Internet of Things (IoT), emphasizing the separation between the application environment and the deployment context.

It is interesting to notice, however, that while different research has been performed in web-based MAS, most of this work perceives the Internet environment as a means of communication. Even larger proposals such as Agentcities [40] and distributed platforms for data processing [31] rely on web protocols and agent communication standards to establish and coordinate the communication processes, while the agents - although exposed as services and sharing resources - are reasoning blocks taking advantage of such structure. In addition, the lower-level communication mechanisms are still based in procedure calls, not taking advantage of newer mechanisms. There is very recent work on this field that aims at addressing such issues [9,10].

In the current state of the Web, using it as a middleware for MAS is certainly appealing. At the same time, modeling MAS while taking full advantage of the web environment (not only as a communication-enabled environment) is partially subject to the constant evolution of the Internet itself. From a higher-level perspective, it is possible to model web-based agents and MAS using existing AOSE methodologies (such as GAIA [43] and O-MASE [11,12]) while abstracting the Internet environment. From a lower-level perspective, however, different communication protocols, web-specific components and technologies can influence the way web-based agents and MAS can be build and deployed into the Internet environment.

Our motivation comes from this context. From the modeling perspective, we would like to explore how we could structure web-based agents that could take full advantage from the Internet environment. Also, from the implementation perspective, we would like to explore how the newest mechanisms and protocols could be used by agents and MAS when deployed into the Internet.

4   Smart Agenda

As part of our study process, we modeled a simple MAS that used agents deployed as web services. The objective of this step was to verify how this could be built and deployed using the current technologies and tools. As mentioned before, we chose JADE as the target framework. Part of the reason behind this choice was related to the framework's web-related functionalities previously described. While the modeled MAS is not complex, we intend to explore and evolve this implementation as our research advances.

Integrating Web Services and JADE agents has already been done in the past [28,30]. Nevertheless, we decided to design a simple MAS completely based in agents deployed as web services. For that purpose, we adopted a JADE add-on aimed at providing support for exposing agents as web services called WSIG[4]. This add-on acts as a relaying gateway, handling all requests coming from the Web and sending them to the MAS.

In order to be exposed as a web service, a JADE agent must possess an *Ontology* and a set of *Actions*. Ontologies are structures used to define the vocabulary and semantics used in the communication between JADE agents. The WSIG add-on also uses the ontologies to define which agent operations will be exposed as web services. Moreover, an action is an object corresponding to a request. Once a request is made from the Web, the resulting action object containing the request elements is sent to the JADE agent.

In this first phase of our project, our objective was to implement an MAS that would be able to handle all the tasks associated with an specific event. For this purpose, we modeled a Smart Agenda MAS, which is built to function as an agent-based personal assistant. For example, if the user updates his agenda with a meeting in Brussels and he is in Paris, the Smart Agenda system is supposed to detect that the user needs a train to go from Paris to Brussels, and use a text-to-speech service in order to ask Google Home to book a train ticket. The text-to-speech service is named AWS Polly[5].

4.1   Requirements and Architecture

The Smart Agenda possesses a web page used as an interface between the user and the MAS. After creating an account, the user can set personal preferences regarding transportation, hotel stars, and hours. The web page is used to schedule new events and to modify or view existing events. The system also allows the user to create events involving other users, or to join existing events created by other users. Events are classified either as "individual events" or "group events".

Individual events are scheduled solely according to the user's preferences. They possess two distinct properties, named "Automatic" and "Movable". An automatic event can be scheduled by the agent arbitrarily along the day, according to the preset user preferences. A movable event can be rescheduled without the user's confirmation if it's necessary. Thus, if an automatic event is created, the agent will try to find an available time slot in the agenda according to the user's preferences. If there is not a free slot long enough to accommodate it, the agent will try to reorganize other movable events to optimize the day.

Group events are events shared by two or more users. They are non-movable by default. When a user creates an event, he can assign it to an existing users group. Group events can be marked as "Optional", meaning that the attendance for all users is not mandatory. If at least two users within the group are available at the scheduled time, the event will be created and added to these users' agenda. In the case the event is not marked as "Optional", the attendance is considered

---

[4] http://jade.tilab.com/doc/tutorials/WSIG_Guide.pdf.
[5] https://aws.amazon.com/polly/.

mandatory for all participants - meaning that if at least one user is not available at the scheduled time the event will not be created.

The Smart Agenda MAS is composed by four different agents: Coordinator, Manager, Agenda, and Assistant. The Coordinator is responsible for handling all requests from the Web. When a new user account is created, the request is forwarded to an available Manager agent, which creates two new agents linked to this user: the Agenda agent, and the Assistant agent. In order to provide scalability to the system each Manager agent is responsible for a limited number of users. The Agenda agent is responsible for processing all future event operations for the new user, and the Assistant is the BDI agent responsible for processing complementary actions related to an event (such as booking a ticket) and generating the final sentence with the help of AWS Polly. Consequently, there are two agents (Assistant and Agenda) for each user registered in the system.

When a new event is created in the user's calendar, the Coordinator forwards it to the corresponding Manager, which then sends it to user's Agenda agent. This event is added to the agenda and, if this is an individual event, the Assistant agent creates its related Goals. A plan will be selected from an existing plan library according to the user's preferences and context-dependent feasibility. If it fails, the next one will be tried. If the event contains the keywords "rdv", "rendez vous" or "meeting", and "@SomeTown", the resulting plan will be a sentence containing all the event's elements: the date, the time, the starting and arrival towns. This sentence is then translated into audio (speech) through the use of the AWS Polly service, and finally played to Google Home with the help of speakers. This architecture is shown in Fig. 1, and its demonstration can be found at: http://bit.ly/Emas18Demo.

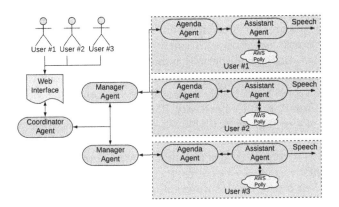

Fig. 1. Implementation architecture for the Smart Agenda agents

5   Discussion

In this chapter, we revisited some of the existing work on web-based agents and MAS. We also implemented a simple MAS using JADE and agents deployed as web services. Although not being complex, the idea behind the implementation was to create an MAS that could be further evolved and explored during the course of our research. Thus, the implemented system is meant to be an evolving proof-of-concept. We found a few difficulties related to the implementation (mostly related to WSIG), but the MAS architecture was simple enough to be modeled using a traditional BDI architecture. At the moment, the BDI model is limited to individual events and sequential goals (context dependency and AWS integration).

From the development process perspective, we found a few difficulties related to using the JADE platform. Most of these difficulties were related to the WSIG plugin, used to expose JADE agents as web services. Despite being a mature platform, we identified a few discrepancies in the framework documentation, and apparently the platform itself possesses some outdated dependencies (considering the state-of-the-art of web-related technologies and base frameworks, such as the http server and the graphical user interface). Also, the initial use of the platform raised questions related to its scalability, and how it could be used by a truly distributed system. Applying multiagent concepts to the proposed problem, however, was not difficult - most of the development effort was concentrated on learning and running the JADE platform according to the desired conditions.

This work is meant to be a stepping stone to our research interests in the AOSE domain. Our long-term objective is to study and explore web-based agents and MAS from both the modeling and the implementation perspective, considering AOSE methodologies and new Web-related paradigms. The next steps in this research topic involve (i) studying architectural patterns for web-based agents and related interaction protocols, as well as their relationship with existing agent modeling methods; and (ii) exploring new Web-related paradigms and studying how web-based agents could be used in conjunction with such paradigms. From the development perspective, we intend not only to evaluate existing multiagent frameworks and Web-related capabilities, but also to explore the existing platforms considering the current state-of-the-art scenario in terms of technologies and tools. In particular, we intend to address the problem of implementing distributed MAS using the available platforms, and which are the current limitations in this sense.

As for our initial proof-of-concept, we intend to evolve it by (i) implementing the same MAS in different frameworks, in order to establish a common baseline for future performance and scalability comparisons; and (ii) expanding the BDI model used in the implementation, increasing the complexity of the agents and their associated reasoning processes. The next steps reside in (i) expanding the BDI model (taking geographical constraints and group preferences into consideration), (ii) the original related research (architectural patterns for web-capable agents and related interaction protocols, as well as their relationship with existing agent modelling methods) and (iii) the implementation itself (comparing non-agent and agent-based approaches, automating the ticket booking process, improve shared events).

References

1. Alonso, G., Casati, F., Kuno, H., Machiraju, V.: Distributed information systems. Web Services: Concepts, Architectures and Applications, pp. 3–27. Springer, Heidelberg (2004). https://doi.org/10.1007/978-3-662-10876-5_1
2. Alonso, G., Casati, F., Kuno, H., Machiraju, V.: Web services. Web Services: Concepts, Architectures and Applications, pp. 123–149. Springer, Heidelberg (2004). https://doi.org/10.1007/978-3-662-10876-5_5
3. Ardissono, L., Barbero, C., Goy, A., Petrone, G.: An agent architecture for personalized web stores. In: Proceedings of the Third Annual Conference on Autonomous Agents, pp. 182–189. ACM (1999)
4. Bai, X., Dai, G., Xu, D., Tsai, W.T.: A multi-agent based framework for collaborative testing on web services. In: The Fourth IEEE Workshop on Software Technologies for Future Embedded and Ubiquitous Systems, 2006 and the 2006 Second International Workshop on Collaborative Computing, Integration, and Assurance, SEUS 2006/WCCIA 2006, 6 pp. IEEE (2006)
5. Berners-Lee, T., Hendler, J., Lassila, O.: The semantic web. Sci. Am. **284**(5), 34–43 (2001)
6. Bratman, M.: Intention, Plans, and Practical Reason. Cambridge University Press, Cambridge (1987)
7. Bresciani, P., Perini, A., Giorgini, P., Giunchiglia, F., Mylopoulos, J.: Tropos: an agent-oriented software development methodology. Auton. Agent. Multi Agent Syst. **8**(3), 203–236 (2004)
8. Cabri, G., Leonardi, L., Puviani, M.: Service-oriented agent methodologies. In: 16th IEEE International Workshops on Enabling Technologies: Infrastructure for Collaborative Enterprises, 2007, WETICE 2007, pp. 24–29. IEEE (2007)
9. Ciortea, A., Boissier, O., Ricci, A.: Beyond physical mashups: autonomous systems for the web of things. In: Proceedings of the Eighth International Workshop on the Web of Things, pp. 16–20. ACM (2017)
10. Ciortea, A., Boissier, O., Zimmermann, A., Florea, A.M.: Give agents some rest: a resource-oriented abstraction layer for internet-scale agent environments. In: Proceedings of the 16th Conference on Autonomous Agents and MultiAgent Systems, AAMAS 2017, pp. 1502–1504. International Foundation for Autonomous Agents and Multiagent Systems, Richland (2017). http://dl.acm.org/citation.cfm?id=3091125.3091342
11. DeLoach, S.A.: The MaSE methodology. In: Bergenti, F., Gleizes, M.P., Zambonelli, F. (eds.) Methodologies and Software Engineering for Agent Systems. Multiagent Systems, Artificial Societies, and Simulated Organizations (International Book Series), vol. 11, pp. 107–125. Springer, Boston (2004). https://doi.org/10.1007/1-4020-8058-1_8
12. DeLoach, S.A., Garcia-Ojeda, J.C.: The O-MASE Methodology. In: Cossentino, M., Hilaire, V., Molesini, A., Seidita, V. (eds.) Handbook on Agent-Oriented Design Processes, pp. 253–285. Springer, Heidelberg (2014). https://doi.org/10.1007/978-3-642-39975-6_9

13. Dickinson, I., Wooldridge, M.: Agents are not (just) web services: considering BDI agents and web services. In: Proceedings of the 2005 Workshop on Service-Oriented Computing and Agent-Based Engineering (SOCABE 2005), Utrecht, The Netherlands (2005)
14. Erl, T.: Service-Oriented Architecture - Concepts, Technology, and Design, 1st edn. Prentice Hall, Upper Saddle River (2005)
15. Etzioni, O.: Moving up the information food chain: deploying softbots on the world wide web. In: Proceedings of the National Conference on Artificial Intelligence, pp. 1322–1326 (1996)
16. Ferber, J.: Multi-agent Systems: An Introduction to Distributed Artificial Intelligence, vol. 1. Addison-Wesley, Reading (1999)
17. Greenwood, D., Calisti, M.: Engineering web service-agent integration. In: 2004 IEEE International Conference on Systems, Man and Cybernetics, vol. 2, pp. 1918–1925. IEEE (2004)
18. Guinard, D., Trifa, V., Wilde, E.: A resource oriented architecture for the web of things. In: Internet of Things (IOT), 2010, pp. 1–8. IEEE (2010)
19. Hahn, C., Jacobi, S., Raber, D.: Enhancing the interoperability between multiagent systems and service-oriented architectures through a model-driven approach. In: 2010 IEEE/WIC/ACM International Conference on Web Intelligence and Intelligent Agent Technology (WI-IAT), vol. 2, pp. 415–422. IEEE (2010)
20. Hendler, J.: Agents and the semantic web. IEEE Intell. Syst. 16(2), 30–37 (2001)
21. Hirsch, B., Ng, J.W.: Education beyond the cloud: anytime-anywhere learning in a smart campus environment. In: 2011 International Conference for Internet Technology and Secured Transactions (ICITST), pp. 718–723. IEEE (2011)
22. Huhns, M.N.: Agents as web services. IEEE Internet Comput. 6(4), 93–95 (2002)
23. Jennings, N.R., Sycara, K., Wooldridge, M.: A roadmap of agent research and development. Auton. Agent. Multi Agent Syst. 1(1), 7–38 (1998)
24. Jennings, N.R., Wooldridge, M.: Agent-oriented software engineering. In: Handbook of Agent Technology, vol. 18 (2001)
25. Kardas, G., Goknil, A., Dikenelli, O., Topaloglu, N.Y.: Model driven development of semantic web enabled multi-agent systems. Int. J. Coop. Inf. Syst. 18(02), 261–308 (2009)
26. Konolige, K., Nilsson, N.J.: Multiple-agent planning systems. In: AAAI 1980, pp. 138–142 (1980)
27. Lieberman, H., et al.: Letizia: an agent that assists web browsing. In: IJCAI 1995, vol. 1, pp. 924–929 (1995)
28. Liu, S., Küngas, P., Matskin, M.: Agent-based web service composition with JADE and JXTA. In: SWWS 2006, pp. 110–116 (2006)
29. Muldoon, C.: An agent framework for ubiquitous services. Ph.D. thesis, Citeseer (2007)
30. Nguyen, X.T., Kowalczyk, R.: WS2JADE: integrating web service with Jade agents. In: Huang, J., Kowalczyk, R., Maamar, Z., Martin, D., Müller, I., Stoutenburg, S., Sycara, K.P. (eds.) SOCASE 2007. LNCS, vol. 4504, pp. 147–159. Springer, Heidelberg (2007). https://doi.org/10.1007/978-3-540-72619-7_11
31. O'Reilly, R.D.: A distributed architecture for the monitoring and analysis of time series data (2015)
32. Padgham, L., Winikoff, M.: Prometheus: a methodology for developing intelligent agents. In: Giunchiglia, F., Odell, J., Weiß, G. (eds.) AOSE 2002. LNCS, vol. 2585, pp. 174–185. Springer, Heidelberg (2003). https://doi.org/10.1007/3-540-36540-0_14

33. Paletta, M.: A scouting-based multi-agent system model to deal with service collaboration in cloud computing. In: Systems and Software Development, Modeling, and Analysis: New Perspectives and Methodologies: New Perspectives and Methodologies, p. 282 (2014)
34. Pěchouček, M., Mařík, V.: Industrial deployment of multi-agent technologies: review and selected case studies. Auton. Agent. Multi Agent Syst. **17**(3), 397–431 (2008). https://doi.org/10.1007/s10458-008-9050-0
35. Ricci, A., Denti, E., Piunti, M.: A platform for developing SOA/WS applications as open and heterogeneous multi-agent systems. Multiagent Grid Syst. **6**(2), 105–132 (2010)
36. Russell, S.J., Norvig, P.: Artificial Intelligence: A Modern Approach, 2nd edn. Pearson Education, Upper Saddle River (2003)
37. Tapia, D.I., Rodríguez, S., Bajo, J., Corchado, J.M.: FUSION@, a SOA-based multi-agent architecture. In: Corchado, J.M., Rodríguez, S., Llinas, J., Molina, J.M. (eds.) DCAI 2008. ASC, vol. 50, pp. 99–107. Springer, Heidelberg (2009). https://doi.org/10.1007/978-3-540-85863-8_13
38. Thiele, A., Kaiser, S., Konnerth, T., Hirsch, B.: MAMS service framework. In: Kowalczyk, R., Vo, Q.B., Maamar, Z., Huhns, M. (eds.) SOCASE 2009. LNCS, vol. 5907, pp. 126–142. Springer, Heidelberg (2009). https://doi.org/10.1007/978-3-642-10739-9_10
39. Tolk, A., Uhrmacher, A.M.: Agents: agenthood, agent architectures, and agent taxonomies. In: Agent-Directed Simulation and Systems Engineering, pp. 75–109 (2009)
40. Willmott, S., Dale, J., Burg, B., Charlton, P., O'Brien, P.: Agentcities: a worldwide open agent network. Agentlink News 8(LIA-ARTICLE-2001-002) (2001)
41. Wooldridge, M.: An Introduction to Multiagent Systems. Wiley, London (2009)
42. Wooldridge, M., Jennings, N.R., Kinny, D.: The gaia methodology for agent-oriented analysis and design. Auton. Agent. Multi Agent Syst. **3**(3), 285–312 (2000)
43. Zambonelli, F., Jennings, N.R., Wooldridge, M.: Developing multiagent systems: The gaia methodology. ACM Transactions on Software Engineering and Methodology (TOSEM) **12**(3), 317–370 (2003)
44. Zinnikus, I., Hahn, C., Fischer, K.: A model-driven, agent-based approach for the integration of services into a collaborative business process. In: Proceedings of the 7th international joint conference on Autonomous agents and multiagent systems-Volume 1. pp. 241–248. International Foundation for Autonomous Agents and Multiagent Systems (2008)

Author Index

Printed in the United States
By Bookmasters